THE PSYCHOLOGY OF HOPE

THE PSYCHOLOGY OF
Hope

YOU *CAN* GET THERE FROM HERE

C.R. Snyder

THE FREE PRESS

NEW YORK   LONDON   TORONTO   SYDNEY   TOKYO   SINGAPORE

The Free Press
A Division of Simon & Schuster Inc.
866 Third Avenue, New York, N. Y. 10022

Printed in the United States of America

printing number
1   2   3   4   5   6   7   8   9   10

Library of Congress Cataloging-in-Publication Data

Snyder, C.R.
    The psychology of hope: you can get there from here/C.R. Snyder.
        p.   cm.
    Includes bibliographical references and index.
    ISBN 0–02–929715–X
    1. Optimism.   2. Hope.   I. Title.
BF698.35.O57S68   1994
155.2'32—dc20   94–17719
                                                          CIP

CREDITS

The author and publisher would like to acknowledge several sources for their permission to use selected materials.

Chapter 1: The items of the Hope Scale (pp. 26) are taken from "The Will and the Ways: Development and Validation of an Individual Differences Measure of Hope" by C. R. Snyder, Cheri Harris, John R. Anderson, Sharon A. Holleran, Lori M. Irving, Sandra T. Sigmon, Lauren Yoshinobu, June Gibb, Charyle Langelle, and Pat Hearney, *Journal of Personality and Social Psychology*, 1991, Vol. 60 (4), 570–585. Copyright © 1991 by the American Psychological Association. Adapted by permission of the publisher.

Chapter 4: The case of Cliff Evans (pp. 152–153) is taken from "Cipher in the Snow" by J. E. Mizer, *National Educational Association Journal*, 1964, Vol. 53 (8), 8–10. Reproduced through the permission of the National Educational Association.

Chapter 5: The opening quote (p. 163) is "Listen to the Mustn'ts," from *Where the Sidewalk Ends* by Shel Silverstein. Copyright © 1974 by Evil Eye Music, Inc.; reprinted by permission of HarperCollins Publishers and Edite Kroll Literary Agency. The therapist-child interaction (p. 170) is taken from *Principles of Psychotherapy with Children*, 2nd ed., by John M. Reisman and Sheila Ribordy, copyright © 1993 by Lexington Books, an imprint of Macmillan, Inc.; reproduced by permission.

TO REBECCA LEE

CONTENTS

PREFACE

What is this thing called hope? To give you an idea of my new definition of hope, I would like to retrace how I came to this perspective. This unfolding story of hope has special autobiographical significance for me, but more importantly, it forms the basis of a much larger human and scientific tale.

In 1987, I faced a paradoxically frightening year. I had been awarded a sabbatical from my regular faculty position in the psychology department at the University of Kansas. In contrast to my previous routine, I was to have lots of time to think and write about my own ideas. This freedom scared me.

I also had celebrated my forty-second birthday. In a life filled with doing, doing, and more doing, I was haunted by the question, "Where are you going?" Drifting professionally and personally, I had chosen a topic for my sabbatical that would serve as an antidote. That topic was hope. So, uncertainty in mind and briefcase in hand, I set out for the library. Sabbaticals, I reasoned, must start at the sacred place where all the books live. First stop, the reference desk.

"Where can I find something on hope?" I asked, naively expecting some magical guidance.

The aide, nearing laughter, shook her head. "What kind of hope are you looking for?"

"Maybe she knows something I don't!" I thought to myself. Not wanting to appear a total fool, I backed away and softly muttered, "I think I know where to look" (a classic male bluff that I learned in junior high).

"Can't hear you," she said, obviously unimpressed.

"Never mind, thanks," I countered, backing away from the desk.

I paced back and forth, feeling like a caged animal. I had to get out of there.

Spotting the exit, I attempted a quick escape. As I bolted through the front passageway, however, a loud buzzer went off. It was the alarm system, alerting everyone in earshot that an attempt was being made to get a book out of the library without properly checking it out. Caught in this modern-day ambush, I was called to the front desk for an inspection. My trial, held in front of everyone in the lobby, was presided over by a nineteen-year-old inquisitor. Leaning forward on her desk top, she asked sternly, "Sir, could I see the contents of your briefcase?" Opening it, all I had was some paper, a pen, and a necktie. Happily, I was judged innocent of the crime suggested by the accusing alarm. The onlookers, sensing the spectacle was over, returned to whatever they were doing.

My quest for hope did not begin in the bold image of Indiana Jones, but it did propel me to look for hope outside of the library. For this, I am grateful. Instead of the library, I began to observe people and ask them questions about hope. This is how hope theory was born. Even though I have been in and out of the library on numerous forages for hope since that time, it is through watching and interacting with people that I have learned the most important lessons about hope. Of course, I have been in the people business for years, and I tell about some of these people in the following pages.

Although this book is based on empirical studies of hope, I have filled the pages with case histories derived from several sources. First, I describe psychotherapy cases that I have had in either individual or group sessions conducted over the last twenty-five years. Second, in this same period, I have given workshops and classes for psychotherapists in training, as well as mental health professionals garnering continuing education. Several examples come from the lives of these students and practicing therapists, as well as descriptions they have given of their clients. Third, in the process of teaching undergraduate, graduate, and postdoctoral students over the years, I have heard countless personal stories. Fourth, as a seasoned people watcher, I have observed people in a variety of places over the years. The various names and specifics of these people have been changed to make the identification of any individuals impossible. Further, in some cases I have formed composites based on the lives of particular people. To these people, I owe a debt of gratitude for teaching me about hope. I also have borrowed selected cases from the descriptions provided by other therapists. Lastly, there are descriptions of a few people whom I identify by name. These are public figures whose words and deeds are a matter of record; others are people I have known personally and can be identified.

This book simply could not have happened were it not for the stimulation of a small army of undergraduate, graduate, and post-doctoral students, as well as my colleagues and family. Special thanks are due to John Anderson, David Barnum, Walter Bethay, Ty Borders, Bill Bowerman, Jennifer Brownlee, John Crouch, Carla Dykeman-Berkich, Lew Curry, David Cook, Grant Duwe, June Gibb, Elizabeth Ham, Patricia Harney, Cheri Breda Harris, Lori Highberger, Sharon Holleran, Lori Irving, Steve Laird, Charyle Langelle, Phil McKnight, Rocio Munoz-Dunbar, Terry O'Neil, Nate Regier, Eric Rieger, Sandy Sigmon, Susie Sympson, Mary Vance, Leanne Ware, Cindy Wiklund, Flo Ybasco, and Lauren Yoshinobu. All these people have at one time or another been part of my hope research group. To my Graduate Training Program in Clinical Psychology colleagues Rue Cromwell, B. Kent Houston, Ray Higgins, Michael Rapoff, Annette Stanton, and Beatrice Wright, I extend my thanks for their helpful input along the way. Special gratitude is extended to Ray Higgins, Michael Rapoff, Mary Vance, and Beatrice Wright, who provided suggestions about earlier drafts. Two other Kansans, Fritz Heider and Karl Menninger, provided encouraging input through our early discussions about the development of hope theory.

To my immediate and growing extended family, thanks for the time to complete this project. I know that I was not always there when you may have needed me.

My editor at Free Press, Susan Arellano, has been a source of hope in getting this book completed. Although she insists that she has only the normal level of hope, I think that she is a closet high-hoper.

The research contained herein was supported, in part, by National Institute of Mental Health Grant 5 T32 MH17071, with C. R. Snyder as principal investigator, as well as a 1993 General Research Fund Grant from the Graduate School at the University of Kansas.

The period in which I have written this book has been the most difficult one in my life. Ironically, I have experienced more physical pain and uncertainty than in all the other previous years put together. After three surgeries, many hospital stays, and so many medical tests and procedures that I have lost count, I have needed all the hope I could muster. When I would come out of one of these adventures, however, there usually was someone special looking at me. Her name is Rebecca Lee, my wife. This amazing person has taught me more about love, hope, and relationships than I can possibly tell. Without her, this book never would have happened.

C. R. Snyder
Lawrence, Kansas

THE PSYCHOLOGY OF HOPE

CHAPTER ONE

Discovering Hope

I learned this at least by my experiment; that if one advances
confidently in the direction of his dreams, and endeavors to live
that life which he has imagined, he will meet with success
unexpected in common hours. If you have built castles in the air,
your work need not be lost; that is where they should be.
Now put the foundations under them.

— Henry Thoreau, *Walden*

THROUGH A
LOOKING GLASS

Whenever I go to a hospital, I try to find the window where you can see the babies who have just been born. I don't know which I enjoy more, looking at the newborns or soaking up the joy of the relatives viewing their offspring. This day was different, however. I walked quickly past the baby-viewing window of the Kansas City hospital and headed to my daughter's room. There I met my granddaughter for the first time. As I held her, I wanted to give her a gift. Surely I could come up with something very special for my first grandchild. Not the usual stuffed animals and outfits, but something she could use for the rest of her life. She should get a lasting gift from her grandfather. It came to me that I'd like to give her hope. When the other gifts have long since worn out and lost their usefulness, she still would have hope. Of course, I cannot hand over a neatly wrapped package of hope to my granddaughter or to all of the other newborns behind the viewing mirror. But, I can try. This book is a start. The following pages tell the unfolding scientific story about this empowering way of thinking. I share the strides made in understanding hope, and how it can be measured and nurtured in children and adults alike. But already I am getting ahead of my story.

FOCUSING HOPE

Let's start with the most famous tale of hope. According to Greek mythology, Zeus became furious at the mortal Promethius for stealing fire from the gods. Seeking revenge, the gods created the astoundingly beautiful Pandora, who was sent earthward to entice Promethius' brother. She carried a dowry chest that the gods warned her never to open. Zeus, evidently practicing an early form of reverse psychology, knew Pandora could not resist the temptation to peek into the treasured box. Indeed, off came the lid at Pandora's hand, and a swarm of plagues spewed out to torment people forever. There was colic, gout, and rheumatism for the body, as well as spite, envy, and revenge for the mind. Hurrying to return the lid to the chest, Pandora found the only thing remaining inside was hope.[1] Did she really get the lid back on the box in time to contain hope? I think not. Why else would we be giving so much attention to hope if it hadn't been unleashed on the world?

Where does this story leave us? Aside from providing a clue about why a bride's dowry is called a *hope chest*, it is a puzzling tale.[2] Was hope to be something that prolonged the suffering generated by the ills loosed on the world, or was it to be the antidote?

The verdict on hope appears to turn on whether it is perceived as being realistic.[3] Questioning whether hope is built on anything substantial, many have viewed it as a curse. That is to say, hope is portrayed as an illusion, totally lacking a basis in reality. For these writers, hope is a structure whose foundation is unsound at best and nonexistent at worst. Consider the following quotes:

Vain hopes are often like the dreams of those who wake.

— Marcus Fabius Quintilianus, *De Institutione Oratoria*

When I consider life, 'tis all a cheat; Yet fool'd with hope, men favor deceit.

— John Dryden, *Aureng-Zebe*

It is natural for men to indulge in the illusion of hope.

— Patrick Henry, *Speech in Virginia Convention*

He that lives upon hope will die fasting.

— Benjamin Franklin, *Poor Richard's Almanac*

Hope is a good breakfast, but a bad supper.

— Francis Bacon, *Apothegums*

Hope lies to mortals, and most believe her.

— Edgar Watson Howe, *Country Town Sayings*

As you can see by these quotes, this type of hope can be particularly dangerous; it has enormous power to seduce us — but it is a harmful illusion. It supposedly captivates our thoughts, but doesn't deliver as promised. William Shakespeare evidently agreed, when he wrote in *The Rape of Lucrece*, "And so by hoping more they have but lesse."[4]

Historically speaking, hope is rather hopeless for those who assume it totally lacks a realistic basis. But suppose hope is tied to something realistic. As Samuel Coleridge, in his *Work Without Hope*, put it, "Hope without an object cannot live."[5] This simple idea — anchoring hope to a concrete goal — provided a starting point in my model of hope.[6] In this venture, I join recent social scientists who suggest that hope involves the perception that one's goals can be met.[7] It is how we think about reaching those goals that provides the key to understanding hope. My conclusion is that we have been bestowed a very favorable gift, as long as it is goal-directed hope that escaped from Pandora's box.[8]

The Inevitable Goal

If you watch people, almost invariably you notice they are not wandering about aimlessly. We say they are trying to get somewhere, that they have some goal in mind.[9] Now, as you are reading this, close your eyes and think of the future. What is the first image or thought that comes to your mind, and how long did it take you to see that something?[10] If you are like others I have engaged in this quick-trip exercise, it took only a few seconds to imagine something you want to happen. You may have big or small goals; your goals may be for the short run or the long haul. Although some goals may have a reality that we can touch (e.g., I really want a pizza), our minds must represent these physical realities before we can do anything to reach them. Advertisers know this exceedingly well. They sell us the images of commodities (products, experiences, political candidates, etc.). The real marketplaces for these imagined goals are not in shopping centers throughout our land; rather, they are in our minds.

We are inherently goal-oriented as we think about our futures.[11] In the words of the noted psychotherapist Alfred Adler, "We cannot think, feel, will, or act without the perception of a goal."[12] Indeed, goals capture our attention from the time we awaken in the morning until the time we go to sleep (where, should we dream, goals still appear in the theater of our minds). This conclusion holds whether you live in a Western or an Eastern culture, or any other for that matter. It is simply unthinkable not to think about goals.[13] Can you do it right now? Careful, because if you try not to entertain a goal, you have one.

Getting from Point A to Point B

At some point in our evolution we humans were able to generate mental representations of ourselves and the world around us. We also developed a linear sense of time in which, roughly speaking, there was a past, a present, and a future. We came to think of ourselves as travelers moving through time, going somewhere.[14]

We were not just going anywhere, however. We gave careful thought to where we wanted to go. These thoughts, of course, were about goals. Humanity's earliest goals were basic and centered, perhaps, on shelter or food. Whatever the goal, we began to think of ourselves as moving toward the achievement of those goals, and our species succeeded in the grand survival game.

Just as our ancestors did, today we think about getting from where we are now, let's call it Point A, to where we want to go, say Point B. In this context, Point B stands for any of the many goals we may envision ourselves wanting to pursue. In aiming at goals, we are constantly engaging in mental target practice. At the risk of appearing overly simplistic, I believe that life is made up of thousands and thousands of instances in which we think about and navigate from Point A to Point B.[15] This is the basic premise on which my model of hope is built. Indeed, it is the reason this book is subtitled *You* Can *Get There from Here.*

NEW HOPE: WHAT IS IT?

Hope is the sum of the mental willpower and waypower that you have for your goals.[16] To understand this definition, I break it down into three basic mental components—goals, willpower, and waypower—and give details for each.

Goals

Goals are any objects, experiences, or outcomes that we imagine and desire in our minds. Thus, a goal is something we want to obtain (such as an object) or attain (like an accomplishment). Earlier, I described these as the Point B's appearing as mental targets for our thoughts. They may vary from the exceedingly concrete, such as the desire for a new coat, to the truly vague, such as the search for happiness or meaning in life. We may set goals expecting to reach them fairly quickly, such as today I want to get that paper done; or, we may have goals taking a long time to reach, such as I'm going to lose weight.

We need only concern ourselves with goals of some magnitude or importance when it comes to hope.[17] It seems foolish, for example, to assert "I hope to put on my shoes."[18] Likewise, we do some things so automatically that we should not associate hope with them. Having said this, however, I hasten to note that seemingly small goals can be subgoals for the larger, more important goals that do befit hope.

Neither a goal you have no chance of obtaining nor one you are absolutely certain of meeting is part of hope as I am defining it. Why? If the probabilities of getting your desired goal are truly 0 percent or 100 percent, the outcomes are so overdetermined that hopeful thoughts are irrelevant. My conclusion, therefore, is that the goals involving hope fall somewhere between an impossibility and a sure thing.[19] Of course, there are a lot of goals in this range.

Before leaving these qualifying points, I remind you of a sign that, according to Dante, hangs over the entrance of hell. It reads "Leave every hope you who enter."[20] This advice seems appropriate. After all, we might as well jettison our hope if Dante's hell is truly a place where we have a 0 percent chance of achieving any of our goals.[21] If what I have suggested in the previous paragraph is true, however, shouldn't a sign with the same message hang outside the gates of heaven? Heaven, being the place where all of our goals have a 100 percent chance of being fulfilled, should leave no need for hope. Hope should be left behind for us mortals whose probabilities of goal attainment are in the vast middle.

Willpower

Willpower is the driving force in hopeful thinking. As shown in Figure 1.1, it is the sense of mental energy (as shown by the arrow) that over time helps to propel the person (at Point A) toward the goal (Point B).

A   B

Figure 1.1

Willpower, as I use this term, is a reservoir of determination and commitment that we can call on to help move us in the direction of the goal to which we are attending at any given moment. It is made up of thoughts such as I can, I'll try, I'm ready to do this, and I've got what it takes.[22] As such, willpower taps our perception that we can initiate and sustain actions directed at a desired goal. There is a vibrancy and strength in willful thinking. Consider, for example, the sign that dentist Ed Delavega painted on the outside of his burned-out office after the 1991 riots in Los Angeles: "YOU BURNED MY PLACE, BUT *NOT* MY SPIRITS."[23]

Although we can apply our determination to a wide range of goals, generally it is easier to activate willful thinking when we imagine important goals. People talk about getting psyched up for major goals such as hunting for a job, finding a mate, having children, or dealing with an illness. Indeed, it is advantageous to each of us individually, as well as to our species more generally, to become primed mentally to meet the big goals in life.

Willpower also should be ignited more easily when we can clearly understand and represent a goal in our minds. Vague goals, therefore, do not provide the mental spark to get us moving. In doing psychotherapy, for example, I sometimes encounter lethargic clients who cannot focus on what they want. Such people have never learned how to pinpoint their goals. (I discuss how to improve this skill for children in chapter 5 and for adults in chapter 6). Once people clarify their goals, they often are filled with active and empowering thoughts.

Willpower taps the sense of potential for action that we bring to situations in general and to given situations in particular. It reflects our thoughts about initiating and sustaining movement toward desired goals. Our ability to produce this mental willfulness is based, in part, on a previous history of successfully activating our mind and body in the pursuit of goals. It is important to highlight, however, that willpower is not acquired through a life of ease in which goal pursuits occur without any hindrances. On the contrary, it is based on our tacit knowledge that, even during stressful times when we run into blockages on the way to our goals, we have been able to generate the mental efforts required to overcome them. Indeed, the most willful people are the ones who have overcome previous difficulties.[24]

Consider the example of Tom, a thirty-eight-year-old participant in a graduate student support group I was running. Having worked in many jobs, including a ten-year stint in the army, Tom completed his undergraduate diploma. Now working on his Ph.D. in sociology, Tom was fervent in his desire to get this degree. In fact, he became the pep leader of the group. His enthusiasm and support for other group members in their pursuit of graduate degrees were remarkable. At one point in the group, he had the sophisticated and sedate graduate students chanting, "We can do it! We can do it!" This enlivening chant was followed with a good laugh by all. When group members were feeling particularly low, they would call on Tom for one of his pump-up cheers. In Tom, therefore, we see the prototype of willful thinking. In my experience, his level of high determination was unmatched.

Waypower

Waypower reflects the mental plans or road maps that guide hopeful thought.[25] As shown in Figure 1.2, it shows the route (the arrow) through which the person (at Point A) must travel over time toward the goal (Point B).

Figure 1.2

Waypower is a mental capacity we can call on to find one or more effective ways to reach our goals. That is to say, the perception that one can engage in planful thought is essential for waypower thinking.

The factors influencing our mental waypower are similar to those described previously for willpower. In particular, our waypower (planning) capabilities can be applied to many different goals; generally, it is easier to plan effectively when our goals are well defined. For example, it may be difficult to plan to become a better parent, but it is considerably easier to resolve to spend more time with one's children in the evenings.

It also is more likely that waypower thinking should occur for more as compared to less important goals. Important goals not only beckon our mental willpower, therefore, but these goals also elicit enhanced planfulness. This is true because in growing up we spend a good deal of time thinking about how to achieve our important goals. Indeed, we should have considerable practice planning for the recurring important goals in our lives.

Waypower capabilities are based, in part, on a previous history of successfully finding one or more avenues to one's goals. Relevant research suggests that our memory, in fact, is organized in goals and plans.[26] In other words, we mentally file information according to our goals and the associated pathways. Furthermore, our sense of being able to generate ways to our goals probably is enhanced by previous successes at coming up with new routes to goals when our original passageways have been blocked. As we know, life places barriers in our paths.[27] In such instances, waypower thinking also embodies the general motto, "If you can't do it one way, do it another way." This mental flexibility to find an alternative route to a desired goal is depicted in the arrows in Figure 1.3.

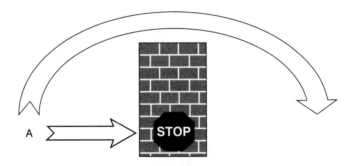

Figure 1.3

Here we see that the straight path from Point A to Point B, the one that we may have taken previously, is now impassable. So, we perform mental gymnastics in which we plot another path, an end run. Of course, people generating alternative paths may not stop at just one. Because persons with high waypower capabilities believe they can find several ways to reach goals, in any given situation they change this mental blueprint to fit the particular goal and barriers that must be faced. Not everyone perceives they can produce the new pathways, however; these people often find themselves feeling painfully stuck when encountering a goal blockage. As such, a mind low in planfulness is disadvantaged under normal circumstances, and especially problematic during difficult times.

The mind filled with waypower thoughts is exemplified by Joni, another participant in one of my graduate student support groups. Joni, a forty-six-year-old woman who came back to school after more than two decades, was going for a graduate degree in speech pathology. She had laid out her degree plans very carefully, and she often spoke of these in detail. Her approach to life goals was to make lengthy lists of the things she needed to do. Indeed, she had a list for each day. Being somewhat older than other group members, Joni was viewed as a wonderful source for ideas and planning. Admired for this capability to produce strategies for reaching goals, Mother Joni's advice was valued and solicited.

Hope = Mental Willpower + Waypower for Goals

Now that we have explored sufficiently the components of hope, we can put them together. Simply put, hope reflects a mental set in which we have the perceived willpower and the waypower to get to our destination. For my purposes, I like to slightly alter the saying, "Where there is a will, there is a way." People who have the personal sense of willpower typically should have the accompanying waypower thoughts (pathways) to their goals, but sometimes they may not. Indeed, our research consistently has supported this latter supposition in that persons with willpower thinking may not have waypower thoughts.[28] If the person does not have both the willpower and waypower for goals, there cannot be high hope. Put another way, neither willpower nor waypower alone is sufficient to produce high hope.

The following examples illustrate that willpower or waypower alone cannot yield high hope. First, consider an instance in which the person has lots of willpower to get somewhere, but lacks the perceived pathways. Remember Tom, the high-willpower member of my graduate student support group? Given the previous description of Tom as being full of energy to pursue his doctorate in sociology, you may wonder why he felt the need to attend the group. The answer is that for all his enthusiasm and determination, Tom could not think of ways to embark effectively on his dissertation project. In fact, he had repeatedly become bogged down in generating the necessary steps to reach his desired goals. This pattern of high willpower/low waypower thinking is not synonymous with high hope.

Opposite to Tom is Joni, whose pattern of thinking exemplified low willpower and high waypower. Mother Joni, despite all her capabilities at finding pathways to get to her degree, was at a standstill in the determination to carry out her good plans. Indeed, Joni described herself as immobilized and incapable of getting started. After enrolling and attending the first week of orientation, she was having trouble motivating herself to go to class and to do the readings. Joni, though admired for her planfulness, was low on willpower. This, of course, is not high hope. All the planfulness one can muster, if not backed up with mindful energy to drive it, leaves one painfully stuck.

A person who possesses both willpower and waypower for goals exemplifies high hopefulness. High-hope thinking provides a special advantage when things get tough. In many instances in life, our paths are impeded by something or someone. In such times, high-hope people begin to think of alternative routes to their goals and then apply themselves to the pathway that appears most likely to work.[29] In other words, high-hope people channel their energy to an effective alternative pathway.

Perhaps a more lengthy example of a high-hope person may bring this definition to life. Consider my Grandpa Gus and his mindset about fishing. We used to pile into his Chevy and bounce along the bumpy Iowa roads until we came to a lake. Sitting under the shade of a tree, or in an old rowboat, the lessons in fishing and life seemed to appear as gently as the summer breezes.

"You can," said Gus, "just about always catch fish." He wasn't exaggerating; he was a bit of a legend in our town because of his fishing exploits. If anyone caught fish, it was Gus. When he talked about fishing, people listened.

He would ask me what kind of fish we were going after — northern pike, walleyes, bass, crappie, or catfish. Now, you might ask, what difference can that make? Well, a lot. If you want to catch a bass, you go about it differently than if you are after some other kind of fish. Grandpa Gus was teaching me the importance of being clear about my goal.

Once we had decided what we were fishing for, Gus seemed to become even more certain we would succeed. He would tell me to think about how great it would be to catch a fat bass. In his mind's eye, he could see it happening. I could, too. When fishing with Grandpa Gus, there was a sense of excitement. Even on those rare occasions when he wasn't catching anything, he was constantly thinking and experiencing. Long hours would fly by and it was as if, in modern terms, we were in some altered state of consciousness. There was a flow to the whole experience.[30] Getting tired never was much of a problem because things were so interesting.

Gus tried many different ways to catch fish. Opening his battered aluminum tackle box, he looked over trays revealed every lure and bait imaginable. And he would use most of them. The menu of live baits included such delicacies as worms, leeches, grasshoppers, and minnows. We would fish in shallow water, in deep water, beside weed beds, near docks, in open water, on and on. We might anchor and still fish, cast, drift, or troll. He would teach me to move my rod tip in different ways. Sometimes we would fish in the morning, sometimes at night. Gus was an experimenter willing to try new things. He said that much of the fun and excitement came from changing how we fished.

Now here was a guy who saw fishing as a challenge, not as a failure waiting to happen. Gus was a model of hope. This lesson happened to be in the context of fishing, but the basic high-hope message was the same across situations: Set clear goals and then get energized about ways to reach those objectives.

In summary, I am suggesting the following formula: Hope = *mental* willpower + waypower for goals. Note that *mental* is italicized in this definition. It is worth highlighting again that hope is a process constantly involving what we think about ourselves in relation to our goals. Our thoughts, in turn, can influence our actual behaviors. At times, the external environment obviously has an enormous impact on us. Later, I discuss how external factors can influence hope profoundly at the level of the individual and groups more generally. Having acknowledged this point, however, I would emphasize that *how we think about and interpret our external environment is the key to understanding hope.*[31] By analogy, a person high in hope thinks of a glass as being half-full of water, while a low-hope individual thinks of this same glass as half-empty. Grandpa Gus must have been of this former mindset. My guess is that he thought of most lakes as being half-full of fish.

NEW HOPE: WHAT IT IS NOT

Discovery is one part finding out what something is and another part finding out what it isn't. In defining this new version of hope, therefore, it may be helpful to clarify what it is not. In this section, I introduce you to concepts seemingly related to hope in varying degrees.[32] Let's begin with the most obvious candidate — optimism. I give the most attention to the distinction between hope and optimism because on the surface they seem to have such similar meanings.

Not Pollyanna Optimism

What would you think if someone called you a Pollyanna? This probably would take the wind out of your psychological sails because the meaning is clear: You are being unrealistically optimistic about something you want to happen. This is the story behind the Pollyanna message: Eleanor Porter's novel, *Pollyanna*, was published in 1913.[33] The leading character, Pollyanna, was a little girl who lost her parents and was sent out West to live with her aunt. Before her father died, however, he taught Pollyanna to play the "glad game." The basic premise of this game is that you always can find a positive in something negative. When her father died, for example, Pollyanna played her first real version of the glad game and said it was good that her dad could go to heaven to be with her mother. In the rest of this best-selling little book, Pollyanna extols people to see the good side of whatever bad things happen to them.

Although Pollyanna undoubtedly meant well, her historic legacy backfired on the very optimism she promoted. Critics pounced on the unrealistic optimism attributed to Pollyanna. Her approach of telling people how they should feel and that things always would work out contributed to a skepticism about any optimism not clearly linked to some realistic planning for the future. For example, after the 1929 crash of Wall Street and the Great Depression, writers blamed Pollyannaish optimism for these events. They reasoned that Americans had overextended the economy without any forethought to the repercussions.[34] In this sense, optimism leads us on to expecting the best, but it does not necessarily provide any critical thinking about how we are going to arrive at this improved future. Indeed, this 1930s skepticism about optimism is similar to the historical views about hope I discussed earlier.

I do not want to continue the tradition of bashing optimism for recent research suggests it plays a positive role in the lives of people.[35] Furthermore, having been fed a steady diet of praise for optimism by social leaders such as Dale Carnegie and Henry Ford from industry, to Norman Vincent Peale and Robert H. Schuller from the pulpit, we have learned over the last several decades that optimism epitomizes the American spirit.[36] Even today, optimism probably has positive connotations for most people. But there is an edge, an uneasiness about our advocacy of optimism. My sense is that we collectively still embrace optimism, as long as it is not equated with the unrealistic optimism associated with Pollyanna.

The underlying concern is that optimism without plans may be a hollow promise; as such, it is not the same as hope as I am defining it. One common view among lay people and psychologists alike is that optimists believe positive things will happen to them. Optimists, however, do not necessarily have clear plans for getting where they want to go. If optimists encounter impediments, which life inevitably throws at people, they may be stuck or frustrated unless they seek solutions to problems. Hopeful persons, on the other hand, should become especially adaptive in stressful situations because they think of new pathways around such obstacles.

The 1992 presidential campaign of Bill Clinton exemplifies this distinction between optimism and hope. Attending to the shaky sense of optimism among the American electorate about where we were going as a country, Bill Clinton and his advisers apparently seized upon the important notion that planfulness needed to be emphasized. Indeed, the key word in the Democratic convention and throughout the campaign trail was *hope*. A Place Called Hope became a metaphor describing Bill Clinton's boyhood Arkansas home town. Its larger meaning also conveyed his advocacy for a way of thinking that engendered willfulness and planning. President Clinton was elected because this vision of hope with its emphasis on planning appealed to the voters wary of the previous hollow Pollyannaish optimism that had become the norm in the political arena.

Two additional case histories may sharpen the distinction be-

tween optimism and hope. Mara was a classic optimist. Her childhood, while not without the usual bumps and psychological bruises,
was a very happy one. She was generally successful at getting what
she wanted, including good grades and friends. Since age eight, she
had a special attachment and interest in children. As a child, she
would talk about what she called "the mother thing." This was
her catch phrase for all the joys, sorrows, and responsibilities that
come with having and raising children. In her twenties, Mara was
a grown-up version of her buoyant, outgoing child. She enjoyed
college and without much effort got B's in her journalism courses.
Her guiding belief, written under her picture in the college year-
book, was "Things will work out." Indeed, they always had. Mara
met Vince during the second semester of her junior year; after several weeks the topic of dating turned to marriage. Mara and Vince
were very much in love, and they planned to get married after graduation. As the wedding date neared, Mara's childhood interest in
the mother thing resurfaced. She and Vince wanted to have children as soon as possible, and this was the major item on their relationship agenda after the wedding. It was not to be, however; Mara
and Vince did not conceive a child. After three years of increasingly
intense attempts to bear a child, Mara's things-will-work-out attitude collapsed. She became angry, frustrated, and depressed with
her plight. Eventually divorced and living alone, Mara was disillu-
sioned. Her optimism, which had previously propelled her toward
her goals, had not worked for her.

The case of Rachel is similar to that of Mara except for one
important difference: Rachel also had learned to think of herself as a
flexible problem solver. When she encountered difficulties in getting what she wanted, she became especially adaptive. Although
Rachel previously had not been into what Mara would call the
mother thing, at age thirty-five she began to hear the tickings of her
biological clock. After years of practicing birth control, Rachel and
her husband decided to try to have a child. The months passed, and
Rachel did not conceive. This bothered her but she was determined
to succeed. An extensive series of medical tests on both Rachel and
her husband followed, with the conclusion that there was no readily
apparent medical reason for their inability to conceive. Rachel was
unbowed in her desire to have children, however; after another year
of unsuccessful attempts at conception, she initiated adoption

procedures. Given there were no available newborn infants, Rachel and her husband expanded their search to older children. Their search ended when they adopted Alex, a four-year-old mixed-race child. Later, they adopted an eight-year-old child with learning disabilities, and all the previous efforts at bearing biological off-spring ceased because, as Rachel put it, "We have our children." Throughout this process, Rachel had an unfaltering belief that, in one way or another, she would have children. Unlike Mara the optimist, Rachel pursued medical answers as to why she and her husband were not conceiving a child; moreover, Rachel stayed ener-gized for her goal and, even more importantly, came up with new ways to have a child when the original plan to conceive a child was not working. Overall, Rachel's hopeful thinking enabled her to find alternative ways to reach her goals.

Not Learned Optimism

The learned optimism approach suggests that optimists have a style of explaining events so they distance and circumscribe their failures. In other words, optimists make mental excuses to lessen the impact of current and potential failures. Conversely, pessimists chronically take total responsibility for setbacks, and because of this tendency they become depressed.

Learned optimism is a way of thinking about the things that happen to a person, especially the bad things. The optimist is said to think about bad outcomes on three critical dimensions: First, op-timists place the blame for a bad outcome on factors outside of themselves (an externalizing explanation, e.g., He was the cause of our problems), rather than concluding that the reason for a failure resides internally. Second, the optimist evaluates the failure by whether or not it will continue in the future. More specifically, the optimist concludes that a setback or problem is just a temporary thing (a variable explanation, e.g., I only screwed up this one time), rather than something that will continue in the future (a stable explanation). Third, the optimist concludes that the failure only happened in one performance arena (a specific explanation), instead of overgeneralizing that failures also would occur in several other unrelated arenas (a global explanation). Thus, an optimist would say, "Yeah, I'm a lousy swimmer, but you should see me play basketball or baseball." In summary, the optimist gives external, variable, and specific reasons for failures, whereas the pessimist makes internal, stable, and global attributions.[37]

A case history of national proportions reveals the essential ingredients of the explanatory style of learned optimism.[38] In the final months of 1986, former President Ronald Reagan had a problem. It appeared there had been an arms-for-hostages deal with Iran; to make matters worse, some of the money from this sale, after laundering, went to the Nicaraguan Contras. The Tower Commission had been appointed to find out what transpired and released its report in February of 1987. The report did not lift the blame from the president, however, and the crisis deepened. President Reagan's speech on March 4, 1987, was the epitome of learned optimism. At the beginning, the president offered a self-diagnosis as he stated, "I'm often accused of being an optimist, and it's true that I had to hunt pretty hard to find any good news in the board's report." He then offered several externalizing explanations for his part in the Iran arms scandal.

"Let's start with the part that is most controversial. A few months ago I told the American people I did not trade arms for hostages. My heart and best intentions still tell me that it is true, but the facts and evidence tell me that it is not." Here we are learning that it did not happen according to the internal factors of his heart and best intentions, and thus the cause must have been some other more external source.

The president continued by saying, "First, let me say that I take full responsibility for my own actions and for those in my administration. As angry as I may be about activities undertaken without my knowledge, I am still accountable for these activities." The operative externalizing phrase in this passage is "As angry as I may be about activities undertaken without my knowledge," as the president implicitly points a finger to his subordinates.

And yet another externalizing statement was, "As I told the Tower Board, I didn't know about the diversion of funds to the Contras. But as president, I cannot escape responsibility." Although the president could not distance himself totally from the diversion of funds as evidenced by the telling "I cannot escape responsibility," he invoked the externalizing explanation of "I didn't know."

In his closing comments, President Reagan also suggested it wouldn't happen again (i.e., an explanation of variability in that it would change in the future), and that it would not happen in other areas of his administration (i.e., a situation specific explanation): "You know, by the time you reach my age, you've made plenty of mistakes if you've lived your life properly. So you learn. You put things in perspective. You pull your energies together. You change. You go forward." President Reagan was suggesting in this soothing passage that we subsequently could expect a different and, by inference, better response from him in the same or different situations.

What we see in the words of President Reagan is the learned optimism approach of externalizing and delimiting the bad performance. Indeed, he was known as the Teflon president, which reflected the perception that bad things just had a way of sliding off him. This perspective of the optimist as an effective excuse maker has been useful as a means of understanding the adaptive coping styles of people. It is a normal coping mechanism used by most people to some degree.[39] There is a certain irony, however, in the fact that the learned optimism concept is built on an excuse-making explanatory style. This follows because most people have positive connotations for optimism and negative connotations for excuse making.

Hope differs fundamentally, however, from the learned optimism perspective. *Hope is more than distancing oneself from and delimiting the impact of failures; hope is the essential process of linking oneself to potential success.*[40] While it is true that higher-hope persons do not dwell on failures, this is basically because they are mentally invested and focused on accomplishing their goals. Accordingly, hope is a way of thinking that moves us toward good outcomes and thereby protects us from bad outcomes.

Not Type A Behavior Pattern

Another recent popular concept that may be compared to hope is the Type A behavior pattern. Type A persons, as measured through interviews and questionnaires, are characterized as hard-charging, time-urgent, and goal-oriented people.[41] Consider the case history of Jack, a former psychotherapy client. Jack was a twenty-nine-year-old man who sold cars for a living. His presenting problem was that his coworkers and girlfriend thought he was far too impatient and verbally hostile with people. Jack seemed edgy, almost as if he were ready to leap out of the chair. I imagined that he was listening to a voice in his head saying, "On your mark, get set . . ."

"Got to get my life together," he blurted out in voice that was urgent, almost sharp in tone. "I'm pushing thirty, and I haven't done much yet. Oh, well, I'm pretty successful and all that. I mean I sell more cars than the other guys, that's for sure. But, it seems like I have to work harder all the time. Time is money, as they say."

"You feel pressured?" I asked.

"Absolutely. There's so much I need to do."

"Like what?" I asked.

"Not sure, exactly, but I'm going full speed. I give it everything I can. Other people think I push too hard, but I'm not so sure. I think we all could stand to work harder. Everyone could get things done faster if they worked harder." Jack was looking around the room, his eyes darting from one thing to another.

"So, you get impatient with people?"

"Yeah, yeah, and I don't think that I get enough credit. I mean I'm a working machine. What time is it?" (I gave Jack the time.) "How long are we going to go on just talking?" Jack demanded.

Over time, I learned that underneath his high-performance front, Jack harbored thoughts that he was not good enough. Further, this not-good-enough hole could not be filled, even though he believed that the only way to do so was to work harder. He seemed to be propelled by vague negative thoughts that he was not doing enough. Even if he did accomplish something, Jack never got any satisfaction.

Jack illustrates many of the markers or characteristics of people with Type A behavior pattern. They are busy, in a hurry, and they let you know it. Their speech is explosive, and they frequently interrupt other people. This naturally causes interpersonal difficulties, but these individuals typically are so egocentric they do not attend to other people. Type A people are not team players, and their interactions often are characterized by an impatient, hostile style. They feel they constantly must win their competitions with others, but no amount of winning generates any true satisfaction. Demanding long hours of work from themselves, they may be quite successful in their careers, as long as they do not have professions in which they must interact extensively with other people. Although Type A persons may accomplish things, their goals are often ill-defined, and they are haunted by the perception that no matter what they do, they are just not quite good enough. Lastly, Type A people feel they are not appreciated by other people. Of course, what has made this concept especially noteworthy is that Type A persons have more heart attacks than their Type B counterparts.

High-hope persons, in contrast to people with Type A behavior pattern, generally are not hostile.[42] Quite the contrary, high-hope people tend to have excellent social relations and they enjoy a good laugh at their own expense. By laughing at themselves, high-hope people do not feel as stuck when they are up against a stiff obstacle; moreover, a good laugh can be energizing to one's mind and body. The credo of the high-hope person may well be, "If you don't laugh at yourself, you have missed the biggest joke of all." Another point in distinguishing these two constructs is that high-hope persons appear to be in good psychological health and are not so self-absorbed.[43] High-hope people also have concrete goals, unlike the vague goals of Type A persons. Another important difference is that high-hope people feel satisfied with themselves, and they are not preoccupied with the I'm-not-good-enough mindset of Type A persons.

Perhaps, the most noteworthy contrast to the demeanor of Type A persons involves the process by which high-hope people pursue their goals. As I discuss more fully in later chapters, high-hope people appear to enjoy thoroughly the moment-by-moment activities related to their goal pursuits. Rather than being driven by their goals, high-hope people gain satisfaction all along the journey. In the words of one high-hope individual, "All the steps involved in getting there are as much fun as actually finishing a project." Consistent with this sentiment, I have found that high-hope people are quite patient with experiencing the course of unfolding events.

Not Emotion and Self-Esteem

The hope model also offers a contrast to previous writers who have suggested that emotions are the wellsprings of human action. My view, based on hope theory, is that we can best understand emotion and self-esteem as a by-product of how effective we are in the pursuit of goals. That is to say, positive emotions and self-esteem, when carefully examined, actually reflect instances in which we perceive that we are reaching, or have reached, our desired goals. On the other hand, negative emotions reflect times when we sense that a goal is not being met.[44] This is a different take on emotions and self-esteem; while it does not suggest they are unimportant, hope theory emphasizes it is more parsimonious and useful to focus on thoughts of goal attainment to understand and help people.

The present emphasis on the importance of goal-directed thoughts as determinants of one's emotional reactions can be juxtaposed against the fascination we Americans have with the concept of self-esteem. Self-esteem is the craze; we are bombarded with the importance of this concept though the written and visual media. We read Gloria Steinem's *Revolution from Within: A Book of Self-Esteem*, and television programs from "*Oprah*" to "*Donahue*" suggest that we must cultivate this precious commodity.[45] The National Council on Self-Esteem puts out a bulletin, *Self-Esteem Today*. Indeed, our preoccupation with self-esteem is shown in the case of a Maryland man wanted for several rapes. Local inhabitants were warned by the police to be on the lookout for a man with a medium build in his thirties with "low self-esteem."[46]

Collectively we are encouraged to put reward stickers and stars on our children's work. California Assemblyman John Vasconcellos went so far as to establish a task force on self-esteem because he and others believed that the absence of it is the real cause of most of our social ills. In a California report entitled "Toward a State of Self-Esteem," the conclusion was "Self-esteem is the likeliest candidate for a *social vaccine*, something that empowers us to live responsibly and that inoculates us against the lures of crime, violence, substance abuse, teen pregnancy, child abuse, chronic welfare dependency and educational failure."[47]

There are several problems with this emphasis on self-esteem. Despite thousands of scientific studies on self-esteem, we still cannot settle on what it is. Similarly, there are approximately 200 tests of self-esteem, with a typical item being "I am satisfied with myself." Although the common meaning in these various tests appears to be an overall sense of self-worth, there is considerable debate about the exact definition. Whatever it is, however, we are encouraged to have more of it. I am uneasy about this search for self-esteem because it strikes me as a misplaced attempt to put a happy face on our lives without attending to the more important, underlying issue. Lillian Katz, president of the National Association for the Education of Young Children, echoed these concerns when she stated, "Schools have established award structures — the happy helper of the week, the reader of the week. Teachers think that if they don't do this stuff, the kids won't do the work, but that's ridiculous. We don't need all this flattery. No other country does this."[48]

My view is that the considerable amounts of money and effort spent in self-esteem programs would be better invested in teaching our children how to set and attain their goals (i.e., raising hope) and in having these achievements appreciated by their parents and teachers. Children have low self-esteem at home, in school and, most importantly, in their minds, because they are not able to reach their goals. In the future of our species, the bottom line is that we are going to have to think about and achieve some difficult individual and collective goals. Hope is the underlying cognitive mechanism for this process, and self-esteem is a natural, welcomed bonus when we succeed.

Perhaps this successful goal movement and self-esteem sequence is best illustrated in children. Young children almost automatically think positively of themselves (i.e., high self-esteem); as they grow older, however, some children have higher while others have lower self-esteem. What has happened? The answer, in part, is that the children have adjusted their levels of self-esteem to reflect their overall success at reaching goals. The higher hope, more successful child also has high self-esteem; more poignantly, the low-hope, unsuccessful child acquires low self-esteem. I pick up on this issue later in chapters on the development and demise of hope.

Not Intelligence or Previous Achievement

Does the underpinning of hope rest purely on genetic differences in intellectual abilities? The basis for this possibility is that the greater capabilities associated with high intelligence may help people to generate more pathways to their goals. Put in its strongest form, some argue that hope is nothing more than an index of intelligence. I think not. The correlation, for example, between the Hope Scale (a self-report index at the end of this chapter) and a measure of intelligence is negligible.[49] Of course, if one were to define intelligence as involving the ability to plan ways to reach one's goals, then intelligence and hope would by necessity share similar premises at least in regard to the waypower cognitive component.[50]

This example may illustrate that native intelligence is not the same as hope: When I started college, one of my friends was exceptionally intelligent by the usual standards. Beyond her superb intellectual capabilities, she had an almost photographic memory for the massive amounts of reading required. Certainly, she appeared to have the markings of a star student, except for one thing — she did not think she could do the work. She told me this in our first semester; by the end of the first year, she had been dismissed because of poor performance. My guess is that my friend was at the top of our entering class in raw intellectual talent and at the bottom of the class in hope.

Rather than being based on native intelligence, hope is a learned way of thinking about oneself in relation to goals. Hope is not a birthright, although a child may be born into an environment fostering hope. In chapter 3, we discuss factors in our early environments that teach us to think about our goals in more or less hopeful ways. Likewise, the discussion in Chapter 5 provides ways to instill and maintain hopeful thinking in children.

Another potential explanation for hope is that it is based solely on our record of achievement. You would certainly expect high-hope people to have a successful history of achievement. In fact, we have found that high-hope persons have done better in school. In all of our studies, however, we have found that even when the previous level of achievement is taken into account, hope still predicts performance on a variety of outcomes. In other words, it is possible through statistical procedures to take out that part of hope related to how well the student has performed previously in school. When these achievements are removed, hope still enables us to predict how well a person will perform on academically related activities such as learning and being tested on new information.[51] To put this another way, if you were placing a bet on what a person will do, you probably would win far more often if you wagered on the person's level of hope rather than previous record of achievement.

Our conclusion then is that hope is not merely synonymous with intellectual ability or with one's record of achievement. It is more. I believe that high hope may assure people of some success in reaching goals; high intelligence or a record of achievement only gives them a chance.

Not Useless

In an interview I did for National Public Radio, I was asked why it was important to study and measure hope. This question was disarming in its simplicity, and my mouth started answering before my mind was aware of what was being said. "To measure hope," I said, "would answer a long-standing debate about whether it could be measured." True enough, but hardly startling.

My next, more cogent answer was that once we could measure hope, we could find out whether it helps us understand how people cope. In other words, do persons higher in hope actually have better outcomes in their lives compared to those lower in hope? The answer is a resounding yes. In this sense, the research rebuts the common stereotype about useless hopes.

The advantages of higher hope are many. As research shows, as compared to lower-hope people high-hope persons have a greater number of goals, have more difficult goals, have more success at achieving their goals, have greater happiness and less distress, have superior coping skills, recover better from physical injury, and report less burnout at work.[52] Hope often predicts these positive outcomes even when one controls statistically for the effects of intelligence and other motives and emotions (e.g., optimism, positive and negative affect). This message, given in previous sections in this chapter, is worth repeating: Hope is not synonymous with intelligence, nor is it the same as optimism or emotion.

Another benefit of studying hope is that we can identify high-hope people and see how they achieve their advantages in living. Beyond the obvious fact that they have more mental energy and pathways for their goals, high-hope people can give us clues about how they do it. We have much to learn from high-hope people, and I examine their teachings in subsequent chapters.

The study of hope also provides some insights about questions involving sexism and racism in our country. Given the history of differential societal expectations and rewards in our society, one obvious guess would be that women and persons of color should be lower in reported hope than Caucasian men. I discuss these findings and their implications in the next chapter; for now I merely assert that the answers to these questions are surprising, perhaps disturbing, but never useless.

Lastly, I would submit that to know your level of hope is an important piece of self-knowledge. Toward this end, you can find out your level of hope in the next section.

Not Vague

I agree with those who have dismissed hope because of its seeming vagueness. Hope certainly will continue to be little more than an empty promise if we simply recycle the definitions espoused in the past. From my earliest days in thinking about hope, I have struggled with its clouded, rather vague definition. A new view of hope is needed as we enter the twenty-first century. My belief is that hope is a specific way of thinking about oneself rather than some nebulous, immeasurable philosophical notion.

The discernible mental markers of hope — goals, and our associated willpower and waypower — are understandable; furthermore, they can be seen in the context of our daily lives. Equally important, a valid index of this new hope is now available.[53] If you would like to take this test, the Hope Scale, turn to page 26 at this point.

After you have completed the Hope Scale, to calculate your overall hope score, add the numbers you wrote in the blanks before the items. Hope Scale scores can range from a low of 8 to a high of 32.

What is your score? Because we have administered the Hope Scale to thousands of people, I can give you some norms about your score. Scores around 24 approximate an average amount of hope. I would emphasize, however, that average in this context actually

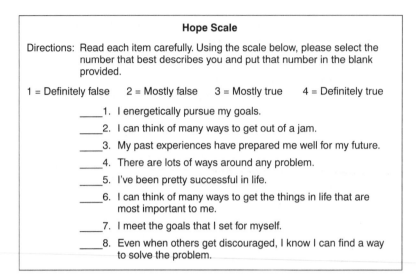

Hope Scale

Directions: Read each item carefully. Using the scale below, please select the number that best describes you and put that number in the blank provided.

1 = Definitely false   2 = Mostly false   3 = Mostly true   4 = Definitely true

_____1. I energetically pursue my goals.

_____2. I can think of many ways to get out of a jam.

_____3. My past experiences have prepared me well for my future.

_____4. There are lots of ways around any problem.

_____5. I've been pretty successful in life.

_____6. I can think of many ways to get the things in life that are most important to me.

_____7. I meet the goals that I set for myself.

_____8. Even when others get discouraged, I know I can find a way to solve the problem.

suggests a strong base of hope. This follows because a person with a score of 24 on the Hope Scale has indicated that all eight items measuring hopeful thoughts are mostly true of them (i.e., a response of 3 on the 4-point continuum).

A score of more than 24 indicates that you usually think in ways that are very hopeful. On the other hand, to the extent that your score was less than 24, you probably do not typically approach things with a hopeful mindset.

Your Hope Scale score reveals your thoughts about getting the things you want in life. Whether you have scored low, average, or high on the Hope Scale, various parts of this book may interest you. Not surprisingly, your childhood shaped the level of hope you have as an adult. Kid hope begets grownup hope. Therefore, you will see yourself in at least one of the childhoods described in the subsequent developmental chapter. Also, for those of you who are parents, the information on fostering hope in your children may be especially interesting. In the ensuing chapters, high-hope readers will see themselves in the characteristics of other high-hope people. Whether you are a low-, average-, or high-hope person, however, you can pick up tips for further enhancing hope in the subsequent pages.

At this point, you probably want to know more about your hope score, including your willpower and waypower subscale scores. We explore this issue further in the next chapter. Chapter 3 details the developmental processes that lay the foundation for hopeful thinking. You may find aspects of your childhood recounted in this chapter, and you can learn how your adult hope was influenced by the forces of childhood. This chapter also is relevant to parents. Chapter 4 explores how hope is destroyed in both children and adults. If you score low on the Hope Scale, you may recognize some of the factors that rob us of hope. For parents interested in nurturing hope in their children, chapter 5 explains how we can increase hopeful thinking in our offspring. Similarly, chapter 6 describes how hope can be kindled in adults; its tips are useful whatever your level of hope. Because hope is so important in our interactions with others, chapter 7 discusses how hope operates in relationships involving lovers, teachers and students, managers and employees, coaches and athletes, physicians and patients, and psychotherapists and clients. For anyone in such relationships, which means all of us, there are guidelines for promoting hopeful interactions.

The following pages tell the stories of people trying to get something done, trying to get somewhere. Many are successful, others are stuck. If such people sound familiar, they should, because they are our children, our friends, our coworkers, the people we love, the people we dislike, the people we know, and the people we would like to know. Most importantly, this book is about you and where you are going. To help you understand this journey, the following pages lead you inward into the workings of your mind. Hope serves as our guide. Welcome.

CHAPTER TWO

Measuring Hope

Always be ready to make your defense to anyone who demands
from you an accounting for the hope that is in you, yet do it with a
gentleness and reverence.

—*New Testament I Peter 3:15*

THE NEED FOR
ASSESSMENT

Imagine for a moment that all the measurement devices in our daily lives have vanished. Rulers, yardsticks, scales, thermometers, speedometers, odometers, clocks, and the other implements of measurement are nonexistent. Lacking a common language to describe the magnitude of various important aspects of our lives, we would be bewildered. Although we take such assessments for granted, they were not always available. Through the efforts of inventors and scientists, however, assessment principles have been developed so that we can make sense of our world. An essential starting point, whether you are a scientist testing a hypothesis or a person trying to understand yourself, is to perform an accurate analysis of the subject matter. Assessment is fundamental to understanding and especially in regard to your level of hope. In this chapter, I am not out to raise your hope; this important issue comes later in the book. Rather, at this point, I help you consider your hope in the context of what we have learned in measuring more than 10,000 people.

THE WILL AND WAYS:
THE CASE OF YOU

To derive your overall Hope Scale score in chapter 1, you summed the responses to the eight self-report items. At this point, you can break down your total Hope Scale into two component scores — willpower and waypower. To calculate your willpower subscale score, add your responses to the four odd-numbered items; to produce your waypower subscale score, add your responses to the four even-numbered items.

Your willpower subscale score, like your waypower subscale score, can range from a low of 4 to a high of 16. The average or normal amounts of willpower or waypower are each about 12.[1] If both your willpower and waypower subscale scores are close to 12, this normal pattern suggests a solid foundation of hope. In terms of willpower, in most situations you should find that you have sufficient determination to move you into action. As one woman with normal willpower described this, "I'm not superwoman or anything, but I do seem to keep at it. Even if I'm tired, I can tell myself to get going, and I generally do." Complementing this normal sense of willpower, most people also believe they can think of ways to get to their goals. This waypower or planfulness can be counted on to produce the routes to one's objectives.

Perhaps the most noteworthy characteristic of persons with normal willpower and waypower is that they maintain this way of thinking even when faced with impediments to goals. In other words, the good news is that people with normal amounts of willpower and waypower continue their quests for goals even when they encounter obstacles varying in magnitude from minor daily hassles (e.g., losing one's gloves) to major life traumas (e.g., losing one's job). Furthermore, the majority of people have average hope in which they produce this pattern of willpower and waypower.

Based on your willpower and waypower subscale scores, you can begin to have a clearer understanding of your overall hope. Although the most typical profile is one where the person has equal willpower and waypower subscale scores of 12, your subscale scores may differ. Each willpower/waypower profile tells its own story about hope. The next four subsections give you more information about particular profiles of hope. As you will see, the components of willpower and waypower come together in differing forms in these people. Your profile may be similar to one of the following.

LITTLE WILL, LITTLE WAYS

If your willpower and waypower subscale scores are both less than 9, you are decidedly low in hope. You evidently do not have very much willpower to reach your important goals, nor are you producing ideas about how to get where you want. This pattern is truly low hope, which is shown in the next two case histories.

Marty: Down and Out in Seattle

It was to be a fairly long flight from Dallas to Seattle. I was settling into a window seat as we taxied for takeoff, when I noticed that the man next to me was crying. My first thought was that he might be afraid of flying. "What's wrong?" I asked.

"Oh, my mother died, and I am going to her funeral. Sorry." He was trying to gain his composure, but his pain was obvious. For the next two hours, I listened to Marty talk. His life story poured out as we crossed the western skies.

His mother's death had left him feeling very alone. In truth, however, he always had been unable to connect with people. "I'm a loner," noted Marty. "In fact, in school they gave me the nickname Drainpipe."

"Why?" I asked, having missed his meaning.

"Well, you know, I'm kind of a downer, like a drainpipe." He didn't smile, the humor had long since gone from this clever, but cruel nicknaming. This thirty-five-year-old man obviously still was hurt by a nickname given him as a teenager.

Marty was unmarried but desperately wanted a long-term relationship. To hear him talk, he thought about this topic constantly.

"I'm sure you will find someone," I said, attempting some support.

"No, I don't think so. I can't imagine myself ever finding a woman. You know, it's awfully hard. I've basically given up."

This fairly handsome man, with a decent job as a computer systems analyst, seemed to have no zest for going after what he wanted most. I tried a little pep talk, but it went nowhere.

"Have you tried to meet women, I mean, really tried?" I inquired.

"Can't get anywhere. It's no use," replied Marty. "I've long since stopped believing it will ever happen. Don't get me wrong, it's the thing I want most, but how would I meet a woman at my age?"

I reeled off ideas from my long-outdated dating armamentarium (things that sort of were effective in the 1960s), and Marty listened patiently, shaking his head at each suggestion.

"Can't see any of those working," he said. "And even if they did, I couldn't try them. Or, let me put it this way. If I tried them, they would flop."

Marty was discouraged, make no mistake. He knew what he wanted more than anything in life, but his mind told him it wasn't going to happen. It was a done deal, he was stuck.

The plane landed, and we wished each other well. I think he had shared more with me than he had with anyone in years. Knowing you will never see someone again can release such disclosure. As I watched him disappear into the airport, I was sad. Sad for Marty. Sad for the relationship that likely would not happen. Surely he had some hope for his computer job, but in the arena in which he placed greatest importance — a loving relationship — his hope was dismal.

Isabel: From Breakup to Breakdown

Isabel was profoundly depressed and full of apprehension when she came to treatment. She dreaded waking up in the early morning. It meant another stretch of hours in which she was conscious of her pain and suffering. While many people believe each day offers at least the possibility of interesting activities, Isabel saw the minutes and hours of the clock as cruel reminders of her awful plight. There was no way she could go back to sleep because she was distraught about her breakup with her boyfriend some four months earlier. She reported that her depression had come on quickly, and it appeared to have a life of its own. An artist who was to have an exhibition of her paintings in three months, Isabel was completely unable to work. Unlike previous times, she could find no solace in her painting. In fact, she seemed paralyzed with a sense of worthlessness.

Her days were spent brooding, smoking cigarette after cigarette. Isabel's friends became increasingly concerned about her as she became more isolated and withdrawn. She also seemed to have lost any interest in any pleasurable experiences. She wasn't eating regularly and had lost weight. Additionally, her appearance had deteriorated — she was a mess. Although Isabel was just sad at first after the end of her relationship, she said the splitup was for the best. Her self-doubt and seeming inability to do anything, however, only deepened as the weeks passed. Eventually, she spent most of her days in bed, ruminating about her worthlessness.[2]

Low Hope Overview

These cases reveal two instances in which people have exceedingly low levels of willpower and waypower for their goals. Marty is focused on his goal of establishing a meaningful relationship with a woman, but he always has lacked any belief he could be successful in achieving this goal. In other words, his shortage of willpower and waypower thoughts were long-standing. Isabel, on the other hand, appears to have lost her willful and waypower-producing capabilities on the heels of breaking up with her boyfriend. As such, she does not have a chronic history of low hope. Unlike Marty, Isabel also has the problem of being without goals. Her ability to engage in goal-directed thinking is minimal. Because relationships are so important to Marty, any success he may experience in his computer job does not have much of an impact on his overall thinking. For Isabel, although the genesis of her problem appears to have been an interpersonal relationship, her low-hope pattern of thinking has spread to all facets of her life, including her painting. As such, low hope can envelop a person's life. Without a sense of action and planfulness, Isabel and Marty are caught in a cycle that may be labeled as depression. As noted in chapter 1, such depressive emotions often are fueled by people thinking they are incapable of attaining their goals. To make matters worse, such profoundly negative emotional states can be intensified when people lack clearly defined goals. I return to this notion of depression and its relationship to hopeful thinking in the subsequent chapters on the demise of hope (chapter 4) and the interventions to raise it in children (chapter 5) and adults (chapter 6).

BIG WILL, LITTLE WAYS

If you scored 12 or more on the willpower subscale, but your score on waypower was 9 or less, you may find yourself partly stuck in the pursuit of your goals. You have the necessary mental energy to get where you want, but somehow you do not think you can produce workable routes to your goals. Although you learned how to energize yourself to reach goals, the waypower may be lacking because you were not necessarily taught to think of ways to get to these goals. Or, even if you may have had some training and success in generating goals in the past, you do not think of yourself as being particularly adept at this process. See if either of the following case histories reflecting this profile strikes a familiar cord.

Mike: Wired for Radio

Mike was twenty-two years old and already had held three jobs — all as a disc jockey on local radio stations. When he came to see me for therapy, I was impressed with what a good story he told. He was a marvelous talker, one of those people with whom you can just sit back and allow the words to flow over you like waves on a beach. Mike's voice was deep, easy listening, so I could see how he had gravitated to radio.

"So, if everything is OK, why did you come to see me?" I asked, immediately wondering if I had been a bit too confrontational. I shouldn't have worried, for he took no offense.

"I'm a talker, I know it, but I can think of so many things that I want to happen. It's just that I may be all talk."

"How do you mean?" I asked.

"I think I can do all kinds of things, but I don't seem to be able to follow through. I can't come up with ways to get what I want.

Right now, for example, I don't want to be doing this disc jockey thing. What I want is to be a social worker."

"What's holding you back?" I inquired.

"Now don't laugh, but I can't see how I can do this. If I go back to school, how would I get enough money to live? I have to support my wife and child. Also, my grades aren't so hot. Even without all this stuff in my way, I don't have the first idea about how to go about it. I want it bad, but maybe I better keep doing this DJ thing."

Mike, looking out the window, continued his stream of consciousness.

"It's frustrating, because I know I could do it if I had a plan. I'd be a good social worker, but I'm not going to get there, or anywhere I want, if I can't get started."

"Maybe you don't want to change at all?" I was pushing, trying to get a sense of Mike's resolve.

Again, I found he wasn't offended. In fact, he seemed to have thought this through before. "Well, I know I can follow through with something if I know what to do. I'm still basically an optimist, but I don't think I'm very good at the how-to's."

Mike was right, as I came to learn over the next several sessions. His parents had talked to him about the importance of being a go-getter, but no one seemed to have taught him how to make plans and problem solve as a child. His mind was like a well-charged battery without cables leading anywhere. The talking, at which he was superb, and his sense of energy for goals had masked his lack of planfulness.

Pam: Lawyer Denied

Pam came to therapy because she was in her words, "mad, damn mad." Pam was a thirty-four-year-old lawyer who had just learned she was not going to be made a partner in a her law firm.

"Tell me about it," I suggested.

"I was at the top of my law class and had the pick of jobs. So I took this job with this prestigious firm. I have put in long hours, year after year, and I have done a good job for those guys." Pam was becoming even more agitated as she told her story.

"What do you mean by 'those guys'?" I asked.

"Oh, you see, I was the only women in the firm. So it is a guys' place. I have always been able to find a way to succeed. Up to now, I never thought sexism had touched my life. But I do now. I thought all that stuff about job limits only applied to women who weren't very smart, or didn't work hard. Well, I am smart, and I did work hard, and now they tell me I didn't make partner."

"Is there anything you can do?"

Pam then recounted how this experience of being blocked so completely was a new one for her. Although she had undergone challenges to reaching her goals before, she always had been able to come up with solutions. This time she felt overcome with anger and a sense of injustice, but she was so flooded with these feelings that she was unable to think clearly about what to do next. This was what brought her to therapy.

Lack of Waypower Overview

Clearly determined to pursue her goal of becoming a partner in the law firm, Pam recently had encountered an enormous block in her pathways to this goal. She was angry at this impasse. Overcome with hostility, she also was frustrated because she could not solve this problem. Unlike the case history of Mike who had a general and long-standing inability to engage in planful thinking, however, Pam's loss of waypower thinking was fairly recent and ascribed to the blockage in her career path as a lawyer.

For Mike and Pam, any full-scale hopefulness was hampered by problems in thinking of potentially successful ways to reach their goals. In many instances, therefore, what appears as frustration or anger associated with a particular performance arena can be understood as chronic or acute deficiencies in waypower thinking. Thus, to understand the emotionality manifested as anger, one should focus on the underlying pattern of waypower thinking toward goals. In these two cases, however, these individuals were not totally devoid of waypower thoughts because they did manage to seek psychotherapy. Many people, of course, do not make this important step. Additionally, if people experience low waypower thinking over a very long time, they also are likely to lose their sense of willpower. In chapter 4, I discuss how hopeful thinking can be drained over time when people are blocked repeatedly from their goals. Likewise, chapters 5 and 6 show how goal blockages can be overcome in children and adults.

LITTLE WILL, BIG WAYS

If you scored 9 or less on the willpower subscale, but your score on waypower was 12 or more, you may find yourself partly stuck in the pursuit of goals for different reasons than those described in the previous case histories. Your mind is literally full of workable possibilities about how to reach your goals, but you are low on the sense of willpower to try these mental leads. This low willpower may reflect a long-term deficiency in believing you have the starting or staying capacity to attain goals, or it may reflect a more short-term deflating of mental energy because of some recent setback. If you have this low willpower/high waypower Hope Scale profile, parts of the following case histories may apply.

Ann: "The Fire Isn't There"

Ann was a thirty-one-year-old, single, career-oriented women. After finishing college with a double degree in graphic design and business, she found a job with a large department store. As a buyer for the women's wear department, she was responsible for choosing fashionable women's apparel. What Ann chose, other women bought. From outward appearances, she was a success. But there was trouble in this paradise. She had been hiding something for a long time, and it was getting worse.

"When did it start?" asked her friend as they stepped into an elevator. Mabel was an older women Ann had come to trust and respect.

"College. I was such an impostor.[3] I did the work, and I knew how to play the game." Ann was beginning to reveal her long-harbored secret.

"I don't get it," said Mabel. "You did fine, didn't you?"

"Yes, yes. It was all so structured though. They basically showed you how to get decent grades." Ann recounted how she could find ways to do OK in college. But inside, it had always been very hard for her to get motivated.

"Is it any different now?" asked Mabel. "I mean, it has been years since you left college."

"Sure, I'm even more of a phony now. I know how to do all the buyer things. It's not like I don't know what to do. But the fire isn't there. Hell, Mabel, I don't think it has ever been there. I'm only going through the motions, and I'm not doing anywhere near what I could do if my heart were in it."

"Don't you like your job?" asked Mabel.

"You know, that's the strange part. I think I do. I'm not tired of the job. I'm just tired. I'm not sure that I can do this anymore."

"You can do it," comforted Mabel.

"I wonder." Ann's voice trailed off as she exited the elevator, leaving Mabel behind.

This case typifies a person who has chronically lacked an underlying sense of mental energy or willfulness in carrying out plans to achieve goals. Ann always has wanted more mental spark to do the things she would like to do. Note that Ann is not totally devoid of willpower, however, because throughout her life she has been able to produce enough energy to try some of her excellent plans. What is important to emphasize, however, is that Ann has not stored up any enduring sense of willpower from those previous instances when she has succeeded. In her mind, her previous successes seemed hollow, and her impostor thoughts have deflated her determination.

Chuck: The Idea Man

After graduating from an eastern school with a Ph.D. degree in sociology, Chuck obtained an assistant professor position at a Midwest university that was building a strong, young department. He got the interview largely because of his mentor's glowing letter of recommendation. A quote from that letter especially captured the attention of the recruitment committee. Chuck was, accordingly to his dissertation chair, "so full of ideas and plans to achieve them that he can't fail." This was the sort of comment recruitment committee members loved to hear. In his interview, even though he was quite laid back, he described a dazzling array of future experiments.

When he arrived, his new colleagues and graduate students were filled with anticipation. As the semesters and years went by, contrary to expectations, Chuck never even started most of his scholarly projects. The few projects he did initiate died on the vine. In the six-year period for promotion and tenure consideration, the only thing that Chuck published was his dissertation, which appeared in an obscure journal. Needless to say, he was not put up for tenure. For all his good ideas and plans, Chuck simply couldn't follow through. Everyone was disappointed, none more so than Chuck.

Again, we see that Chuck's good plans were not matched by the necessary willpower to achieve his goals. He was clear about his goals, and he could verbalize impressive ways to reach those goals. He lacked the mental starting and staying power to propel him toward these goals. In this particular case, his parents had rewarded him profusely for his ideas and plans, but they had not gone on to teach and praise him for actually getting started and completing projects. Accordingly, he dabbled impressively in ideas, but not action-oriented thoughts.

Katie: Burned Out Mother

Katie came to the group because she was burned out. Katie was a single parent raising three children; the child support promised by her former husband had ceased. She worked part time and was the legal guardian for her mother, who was in the early stages of Alzheimer's disease. Katie also had agreed to having her mother move in with her.

To hear Katie talk, it was obvious she had always been the one to take care of other people. When she was growing up, as the oldest daughter she babysat for her two younger brothers. Additionally, as the family problem solver, she tried to settle squabbles. She was good at taking care of people and previously had lots of mental and physical energy to get things done.

Something changed, however, on her fortieth birthday. Looking at her tired face in the bathroom mirror, she heard the kids fighting in the other room and immediately sank to the floor crying. In the next days she found it extremely hard to do the normal things involved in keeping the family functioning. Although she had done this stuff for years, Katie finally reached a point where she was out of energy. As she told the group about her burnout, she quickly found understanding and support for what she was going through.

The case of Katie differs from Ann and Chuck in that she previously did have the willful thoughts to carry out her plans, but she simply had worn down over time. She sought the therapy group as a means of recharging.

Lack of Willpower Overview

The stories of Ann, Chuck, and Katie involve people who lack the mental energy to carry out their plans. The dearth of willpower may be of a long-term nature, or it may be a more recent phenomenon. Burnout is a the culmination of willpower depletion. Sometimes traumatic personal news, such as learning that one has the HIV virus, can literally take the wind out of one's mental sails. Many low-willpower people just seem to be going through the motions. Even though at times they can impress others with their ideas (e.g., Chuck) or even their work (e.g., Ann), on the inside these low-willpower people experience the goal pursuit process as a constant struggle. Although such people can talk about how they will get things done, they often are somewhat depressed.

BIG WILL, BIG WAYS

Our last Hope Scale profiles reflect the prototype of the full-blown high-hope person. If you scored 13 or more on both the willpower and waypower subscales, you should be brimming with mental energy and ideas about workable ways to reach your goals. If you have this high-hope profile, you may resonate to parts of the next case histories.

Hobart: A Reporter Making His Own Leads

Hobart Rowen, the noted writer for the *Washington Post*, underwent a cystoscopic exploration of his bladder on March 11, 1991, at

Georgetown University Hospital. When he awoke from his general anesthesia, he found vivid red blood draining into a urinary catheter bag. As he put it, "I didn't have to be a rocket scientist to know that I had a real problem."

"Was it malignant?" Hobart asked his doctor.

"Oh sure," said the physician, "I never had a second's doubt when I saw it."

After other tests, the dean of urology, the head surgeon of the department of urology, the chief medical oncologist, as well as two other urologists held a conference with Hobart. What followed was a review of the proposed rigorous chemotherapy regime, as well as a five-hour operation to remove the bladder and prostate. His routine procedure had turned into a diagnosis of life-threatening cancer.

At the beginning of his intravenous chemotherapy treatments, Hobart reported, "I retained hope and a cheerful perspective. I continued to do my twice weekly column, working at my home computer."

After sensing his original diagnosis of bladder cancer might be incorrect because of the results of other tests, Hobart in his own words, "proceeded to take charge of my own case and get a second opinion at Johns Hopkins in Baltimore."

Johns Hopkins, being one of the three premier centers for urological problems in the United States, afforded Hobart another path to the goal of regaining his health. He energetically pursued this latter option. Once these tests were completed, it turned out he had prostate rather than bladder cancer. As the prognosis was more positive for prostate than bladder cancer, Hobart was further energized. His choice to pursue a second opinion, paired with his mental determination, may have saved his life. Indeed, after hormone treatments, his subsequent blood tests revealed that his cancer was in remission.

As we can see, Hobart advocated a mental activism. His words give a recipe for high hope: "Ask questions. Demand more information. Insist on explanations."[4]

Carla: Grandma Bulldog

To look at Carla, you wouldn't notice anything out of the ordinary. In fact, she described herself as nothing special. To talk with her, or

to see her in action, however, would lead you to a different conclusion — she is a dynamo with an agenda.

Carla is not, however, a captain of industry, a renowned actress, a
leading physician, or a holder of any of the other traditionally ac-
claimed stations in life. She is a sixty-three-year-old, widowed
grandmother with a high school education. After raising her children, she took a counter job at a dry cleaners, where she has worked
for the last twenty years.

In the 1980s, Carla became increasingly upset with what she saw
happening in her urban neighborhood. People living on the streets,
were hungry and fending for themselves.

"I couldn't believe it at first," said Carla. "I didn't want to stop
looking these people in the eyes; I was scared for what I was doing
to myself. I was learning to look away, learning not to care. Somebody had to do something, so I said to myself, Carla, what do you
want? The answer wasn't any big deal, but I vowed that day in 1981
that I wanted to help these street people. I was going to do what I
could to get them some clothes, food, and shelter. That's what I
have been doing ever since."

What Carla did was not easy. She tells it best: "It started by taking whatever money I could save and using it to help. This meant I
had to begin to talk to the street people, which I hadn't done before.
I can't imagine what some of these folks must have thought when a
white-haired, little old woman walked up to them and asked what
they needed." She laughed out loud at this sight. "But, I knew I
could do it, so I did. And people told me what they needed. Sometimes it was food, sometimes clothing, and of course, a place to
stay."

The rest of the story, in brief, is a saga of a person who was going
to help against the odds. "I rarely gave anyone money. No, I'd go to
work to get them whatever was number one on their wish list —
food, clothing, or shelter. I paid for food, clothes, and some rooms
for a night or two. My money didn't go too far in the beginning, but
what I was doing sure felt right. Of course, my kids and grandkids
were scared to death. Here I was spending my evenings and weekends with street people. I tell you, though, the streets aren't mean
because of any of the people I met."

What did Carla do when her own money wasn't sufficient?

"I asked all the local businesspeople I knew for some contributions, but those were slow in coming. So, I drove out to some of the grocery stores and bakeries in the suburbs and talked to lots of store managers about getting bread products, or other foods that they would normally throw away. They were skeptical, but I think my grandmother image helped a little." Carla's laugh emerged again. "And I kept going back, even when they said no. I don't know how many places I went, but I wasn't going to stop. And some of the times I would come back with my Ford loaded up with food. That felt great. I still do this today."

She did the same thing with clothes; she asked her own dry cleaning customers if they had any old coats, sweaters, pants, and shoes that they didn't need. In turn, she gave these treasures to the street people. Carla also hit up local stores for clothing and even went back to the businesspeople in her neighborhood. She tried one thing after another to get more clothes. She was, to borrow a fond description in the neighborhood, one part grandma and one part bulldog.

Her latest mission is to lead a drive in her community to get a shelter for the street people. The shelter also would have food and clothing. This is Carla's big dream.

"Oh, it can happen. There are ways to get it done. I'm excited and more determined than ever. You know, I am the grandma bulldog!" She laughed at herself. This laughter was contagious. So was what was going on in her mind.

High Hope Overview

High-hope people keep their goals clearly in mind and constantly are thinking about ways to obtain them. They interact easily with other people and are willing to take chances to get what they want. Very focused on their objectives, they freely move from one idea to another to facilitate obtaining their goals. At times, as we see in Carla, there is a tenacity in the thinking and behavior. In other instances, such as Hobart's case, options are openly considered and tried. Both Carla and Hobart are quiet fighters for what they want. In summary, high-hope people are very active in their thinking, and they almost always believe that options are available to their goals.

WHAT HOPE SAYS
ABOUT YOU

This section introduces you to the psychological characteristics that go along with having a higher level of hope. The subsequent conclusions typically are based on one or more research studies we have conducted on the particular characteristics.[5]

Optimism

We routinely have found that overall Hope Scale scores correlate positively with measures of optimism.[6] Interestingly, optimism usually relates more strongly to the willpower than the waypower component of hope.[7] Thus, optimists are more likely to have a sense of mental energy for their goals, but they may not necessarily have the waypower thoughts. These findings support what I said in chapter 1 about the similarities and distinctions between hope and optimism.

Recall the case of Mike, the DJ. He had a high willpower/low waypower profile in that he was actively thinking about his goal of becoming a social worker. Interestingly, in his own words, he was an optimist, but he did not think in ways to obtain his goals. In this sense, he was a frustrated optimist.

Perceptions of Control

Based on the prediction that higher-hope people want to exert personal control in their lives, we correlated the Hope Scale with an overall measure of the desirability of control, a person's decisiveness, preparation in anticipation of stress, leadership, and avoidance of dependence.[8] The resulting positive correlation between these two scales suggests that hope is tied positively to perceptions of control. No surprise here.

In another study, we correlated Hope Scale scores with a source of control scale. This well-known psychological measure uses a continuum of beliefs about where the power in one's life resides. At one end of the continuum, those who have an internal source expect to control their own destiny (the captain of the ship perspective); at the other end of the continuum, those who have an external source expect to be controlled by powerful outside forces and people.[9] As you may expect, higher-hope people score toward the internal source of control end of the spectrum.[10]

These control perceptions are especially significant in the case history of Hobart, the man who took charge of the course of diagnoses and treatments for his cancer. Indeed, if one talks with high-hope persons, it is apparently that they perceive themselves controlling their lives. This is not a Rambo-like bravado, however, but a quiet sense of self-direction.

Perceived Problem-Solving Ability

Because one of the cornerstone components of hope is waypower thinking, hope should relate to an individual's perceived ability to solve problems. Accordingly, we have administered the Hope Scale along with an index of problem solving and found that the two were highly related.[11] Furthermore, although perceived problem solving relates to one's overall hope, it is especially related to waypower thinking.

The problem-solving way of thinking of high-hope people becomes especially evident during times when they are experiencing difficulties in their normal ways of achieving their goals. Under such circumstances, higher-hope people become very task-oriented and turn to alternative ways to get what they want. In interviewing them, I noticed that high-hope people anticipate problems whereas low-hope people do not. It is as if the higher-hope individuals understand there will be roadblocks; at times they even plan ahead for them. This is analogous to the backup systems built into our space shuttles in anticipation of possible difficulties.

Competitiveness

Competitiveness involves testing oneself in comparison to other people. Among male and female athletes, higher hope has related to greater competitiveness. Higher-hope people enjoy working hard and gaining a sense of physical mastery. In turn, high-hope people look forward to testing themselves against others. What is interesting, however, is that among this same sample of athletes, no relationship was found between higher hope and the desire to win in competition with others.[12] This suggests a motivational picture of high-hope people that mixes social comparison as a testing grounds for one's competitive performance with a lack of concern about necessarily winning.

High-hope persons evidently are not caught up in the winning-is-everything mentality, but they are drawn to the competitive arena. Why, if not to win? The answer is that high-hope persons appear to enjoy the process of testing their skills, and the competition provides an invigorating challenge. For example, although competing against a standard such as a time in a distance run is quite concrete, it does not give a vivid sense of feedback about one's performance as is the case if one is lined up alongside several other runners. Likewise, the pleasure for the high-hope athlete is more in the process than the outcome. This latter logic is similar to a seemingly paradoxical mindset I have gleaned from interviewing high-hope people in general. Although they are goal-oriented and set high goals (as we see later in this chapter), they are more attracted by the process of moving toward their goals than they are by the actual attainment. High-hope people also prefer situations that stretch their skills; in our society such tests often come in the form of interpersonal competitions. Finally, high-hope people are attracted to other people and enjoy interacting with them; competition is one standardized form for doing this in our society.

Self-Esteem

In chapter 1, I stated that self-esteem should reflect one's level of hope. If you are a high-hope person accustomed to willful and planful thoughts about your goals, you generally should experience positive self-esteem across a variety of situations.[13] Indeed, our data support this speculation.[14] The robustness of hope in predicting self-esteem is illustrated in a study with teenagers, many of whom had undergone traumatic physical injuries when they were younger.

In this study, the higher-hope teenagers had the higher self-esteem.[15]

Higher-hope people think positively of themselves because they know they have pursued their goals in the past and can do so in the future. Their favorable self-evaluations are not necessarily public displays of pride. On the contrary, there often is a quiet self-respect and dignity. Recall Carla, who in an almost self-effacing manner went about her quest to help street people. At the national level, the present emphasis on self-esteem typically rests on a public display of self-worth. In my estimation, such public self-esteem is overemphasizing the importance of external audiences. Let us not forget that, by definition, self-esteem is for the individual's internal rather than the external audience. I get the impression that the self-esteem of higher-hope people is of this private type.

Positive and Negative Affectivity

Yet another characteristic that should go along with hope is positive affectivity. Positive affectivity is a mental state characterized by full concentration, engagement, and high energy. It is a way of thinking in which our minds are interested, excited, strong, enthusiastic, proud, alert, inspired, determined, attentive, and active.[16] Higher-hope people experience such a positive affective state as evidenced by our correlational findings.[17]

In watching and interacting with higher-hope people as they go about their activities, I sense they are fully engaged with particular goal pursuits. They literally are immersed in their activities and clearly energized by what is happening. At times, high-hope persons' surprise and delight in trying different solutions or pathways to reach their goals intensifies their positive concentration and sense of interest. Furthermore, there is a childlike enthusiasm to the high-hope person's approach to what he or she is doing. As an example, consider Carl, a seventy-two-year-old retired electrician, who spends four afternoons each week volunteering at the hospital. "It's always different here," said Carl. "I mean I get to meet so many nice people from all over. And my time spent here helps people, and me. . . . Why, it's like I'm a big kid."

The flip side of positive affectivity is negative affectivity, a general state of subjective distress including nervousness, contempt, anger, fear, and guilt.[18] This negative mindset should not be characteristic of high-hope people, and this is what we have found — high hope relates to less negative affectivity.[19]

The particular negative affectivity emotions of low-hope people warrant some elaboration at this point. In the context of hope theory, feelings of anger and hostility indicate that people believe they are being blocked in the pursuit of their goals. Whether it is other people, outside forces, or the perceived lack of waypower thinking because of personal deficiencies, low-hope people may be hostile because they cannot get what they want. The anger of high willpower/low waypower people, for example, arises from their inability to get around the impediments in their lives. More generally, people profoundly blocked in the pursuit of their important goals may experience a sense of anger and despair. (See chapter 4, "The Death of Hope.")

The guilt experienced by low-hope people reflects their insight that they are expected to pursue their goals, but they are not able to do so. In the words of a low-hope person, "I know I'm supposed to get to my goals, but I'm not very good at getting it done."

The fear of low-hope people is derived from the fact that they neither cope with nor avoid the negative things that happen in life. For low-hope people, the future is scary because it keeps tumbling down on them with one aversive outcome after another. Indeed, the world is a frightening place from the low-hope perspective that bad stuff may engulf one at any moment. Such fear undoubtedly is related to a perceived lack control in the lives of low-hope people, as we discussed earlier.

In my work with low-hope people, their negative emotions appear to stem from their intensive self-analysis of some aspect of the goal-pursuit process. Perceiving they are not very good at the goal game, they fall into a cycle of self-examination of their deficiencies. In my work with shy clients, for example, they know that they are expected to carry on a conversation or keep up their end, but they report being unable to meet this goal expectation. Therefore, they are caught in a painful awareness of how poorly they are doing when they are in interactive situations with other people. What such people tend to do is to focus on their shyness, which only increases their inability to interact.

Anxiety and Depression

Anxiety is a subjective state of worry about specific events. Although high-hope people are not necessarily immune from anxiety, they should be inoculated by their willpower and waypower mindset. Using two different measures of anxiety,[20] we have found that higher-hope people are less anxious.[21]

Depression is a pervasive, negative mood that does not necessarily have a focus. Higher-hope people are alive with mental energy and ideas about reaching their goals; as such, they should not be depressed.[22] We have found support for this hypothesis in both psychiatric inpatient and outpatient samples of people, as well as with college students.[23]

Depression was obvious in the earlier case history of the artist Isabel. She lacked any sense of goals in her life, and she increasingly was sinking into a state of mental inertia and confusion. She had not always been this way, but her depression had worsened over the course of several months. A breakup with her boyfriend seemed to precipitate the profound sense of worthlessness and self-doubt. Her lack of willpower and waypower, as well as dearth of goals, fueled this depression. This is an instance where the person's introspective thought patterns contributed to the depression. This type of depression should be distinguished from bipolar mood swings with biological underpinnings.

A milder, depressionlike appearance can accompany individuals who have a high sense of waypower thinking related to their goals, but lack the willpower. Recall the case of Ann, the clothes buyer, whose general malaise had been a long-standing problem. Or, the case of Katie, the young mother suffering from burnout. The probability of improvement for low willpower/high waypower persons is more favorable than for low willpower/low waypower persons because the former are lacking in one rather than two key components to goal-directed thinking. This is not to suggest, however, that the low willpower/high waypower person does not suffer psychologically. On the contrary, to know how to get where one wants, but not to be able to initiate and sustain action produces a mixture of anxiety, dysphoria, and bewilderment. If you are looking for tips about overcoming these depressionlike symptoms, chapters 6 and 7 should be helpful.

Summary of High-Hope Characteristics

In summary, the prototypical high-hope person appears to exhibit optimism, perceptions of control over one's life, perceived problem-solving ability, a preference for competition (but not winning itself), high self-esteem, and positive affectivity. Additionally, compared to low-hope individuals, high-hope persons are not as likely to manifest negative affectivity (including hostility, fear, and guilt), anxiety, and depression.

WHAT HOPE SAYS ABOUT YOUR GOALS

The previous section explored what hope tells us about our psychological makeup in general. At this point, we turn to a detailed discussion of what hope reveals about goal-related thinking in particular. Because you are similar to other people who have scored low or high on the Hope Scale, we can make some useful observations about the number and difficulty of your goals, as well as how you experience these goals. These conclusions are based on what we have learned from various research projects aimed at understanding the differences in the goals set by persons with varying Hope Scale scores.

How Many?

My initial hypothesis was that higher-hope people, because of their facility at setting goals, have more arenas in life in which they establish goals. To test this hypothesis, we performed an interview study on Lawrence, Kansas, residents in their twenties through forties. There was an equal number of men and women, and the sample was predominantly white, middle class, with a typical education level between some college and a college degree. In addition to completing the Hope Scale, people were asked about their goals in six life arenas (family of origin, friendships, marriage or intimate relationships, health, employment, and spiritual development). As expected, higher-hope people reported they had more goals across these life arenas.[24]

These results support an observation I have made in talking with high-hope people. When it comes to goals, they do not put all their eggs in just one basket. As investors in goals, their portfolios are quite diversified in that they have a range of objectives for the different parts of their lives. They are not narrow in their focus on goals, and they are able to move attention from one goal to another with relative ease. This multiple goal approach of high-hope people is advantageous when the circumstances make a given goal truly impossible to achieve. In such instances, high-hope persons can switch to other goals already on their mental agendas. Indeed, this flexible pursuit of alternate goals may keep hope alive when one goal is unreachable.

A good example of this multiple goal approach is shown in the words of Sue, a woman who came up to me after I had given a speech on hope. She informed me that she had gotten a very high score on the Hope Scale, which I had shown in my talk. She then went on to talk about her goals: "You know, I have always gotten kidded by my friends because I have so many goals. I've got a bunch of things I'm shooting for at work. But the rest of my life is filled with goals, too. Whether it's relationship, exercise, or fun, I have things I am aiming for." Sue then went on to recount how she could move from one goal to another, especially if she were stuck on one.

How Difficult?

Another idea I had about high-hope people was that their willpower and waypower thoughts may enable them to take on more difficult goals than low-hope people. In looking at this question in studies involving goals that college students establish for themselves, we have consistently found support for this hypothesis. For example, when we gave students a fairly difficult warm-up task that supposedly was to precede the subsequent tasks they were to perform (e.g., analogies, sentence-completions, spatial reasoning), we found that higher-hope people reliably selected more difficult tasks for the second part of the experiment. Hope continued to indicate the choice of more difficult tasks even after we statistically removed the effects of these students' optimism scores and their high school grade point averages.[25] These results obviously suggest that hope is a very powerful predictor of the difficulty of goals that students undertake.[26]

Although high-hope people set more difficult goals and they have a greater number of such goals, they do not seem at all burdened by this load. On the contrary, the goal game seems to be fun for high-hope people. I build on this idea next.

In the Eye of the Beholder

Beyond the issue of whether high-hope people set more difficult goals, a next logical question is how people of varying levels of hope think about their goals as they pursue them. In psychology, this notion is captured by the term *appraisal*. Here is what we have found: First, we have measured the degree to which people expect to attain their goals. As predicted, higher-hope people believe they will be more likely to obtain their goals than low-hope people.[27] Furthermore, this happens even when high-hope people encounter initial impediments to their goals. These latter findings relate to the fact that high-hope people have more positive thoughts when they encounter stress than do low-hope persons.

Second, higher-hope people appear to have a more positive, challengelike mental set when they pursue their goals, as compared to a negative, ambivalent set for low-hope people. To see if people differ in how they view their own goals, high- and low-hope persons were asked to set one-month and six-month goals in the various areas of their lives. Remember that these people set their own goals. Next, people were asked whether they were focusing on the consequences of succeeding or failing on their goals, their perceived probability of attaining their goals, and their emotional state as they considered their goals. For both the one-month and six-month goals across the various life arenas, the higher-hope people consistently had more positive appraisals on all three questions. That is to say, the high-hope persons focused on success, had a high perceived probability of obtaining their goals, and evidenced positive emotions.[28]

These appraisal results give us an important insight into the minds of high-hope persons. Even though high-hope persons select more difficult goals than low-hope people, they do not see it this way. Indeed, these seemingly difficult goals of high-hope people are seen as challenges, successes waiting to happen. Likewise, the positive emotions are part of this mental set. Qualitatively, high-hope people experience their goals differently than do low-hope people. High-hope people appear to embrace their goals. As a high-hope person once told me, "Life is like a giant game board and you might as well have some fun with it."

The choice of goals that are stretches, as well as the challengelike appraisal of these goals is revealed in the words of Jeanne, a new assistant professor: "What a chance this assistant professor thing is. I have six years to show what I can do, and the freedom is enormous. It's up to me. During these coming years, I will publish articles and probably one book. And I'll do a first-rate job in my teaching. What I'm trying to say is that I'm going to set some tough goals. But, I'll make it." One can easily discern the high-hope goals and thoughts in these words. Contrast this with Ralph, another beginning assistant professor. "Oh, I suppose I'm smart enough, but I don't know about this tenure thing. I'm already thinking I'm not doing enough. I feel like I'm being thrown into this big competition with all the other new assistant professors. There's a record playing in my head asking, How are you doing? I guess I've put myself into this race, but there is not much joy in it."

Summary of High-Hope Goals

High-hope people operate with several goals in their differing life arenas, and they typically set difficult goals for themselves. Our studies show they embrace their goals and view them as welcome challenges that are a normal part of life. High-hope people use their goals as mental touchstones for success; they go after their goals and think they will obtain them. In short, high-hope people are bullish investors in life goals, and they expect to obtain excellent returns on their mental investments. Low-hope people, on the other hand, appear to be used by life goals; they are bearish investors who do not actively pursue goals and are more concerned with protecting themselves from losses.

HOPE AND REACHING
GOALS

If higher-hope people set more difficult goals and appraise these goals more positively, the next question pertains to actual success in meeting goals. In several studies, we have given the Hope Scale to entering college students and have followed their subsequent academic performance. In every study we have performed, Hope Scale scores taken at the beginning of the semester have significantly predicted final grades obtained at the end of the semester.[29] In fact, even if we remove the influence of how well students do on their first set of college examinations about six weeks into the semester through statistical procedures, Hope Scale scores still predict final grades.[30] This is a remarkable finding because first examination grades count for approximately 25 to 30 percent of the students' final grades. Additionally, in one study we obtained students' high school grades; when the influence of these previous grades was removed statistically, Hope Scale scores still significantly predicted first semester college grades.[31]

My point is that hope is more than one's record of previous academic achievement. Although one would expect some slight positive correlations between high school grades and Hope Scale scores, which we have found, hope is more than this record of achievement.[32] Also, we have given people a standardized test of intellectual functioning and have found that Hope Scale scores are not correlated with IQ.[33] Overall, therefore, the academic performance benefits of high hope are not simply differences in previous records of scholastic achievement or intellectual ability.

If the mindset of hope cannot be equated with basic intellectual ability, can it be equated with physical ability? In other words, can hope provide any increase in our understanding of athletic performance beyond what we already know because of physical talent? In a test of this question, the members of seven of the Big-8 women's track and field teams were given the Hope Scale, and their coaches rated each woman's pure natural physical ability. Thereafter, the subsequent athletic performances were recorded. Results showed that the hope of these women predicted their actual athletic performance (i.e., higher hope related to better performances). What is especially noteworthy, however, is that hope significantly predicted actual performance beyond the coaches' ratings of natural physical abilities.[34]

Our society has long been preoccupied with the importance of the intelligence and physical ability concepts. Along with physical attractiveness, high intelligence and physical talent are the most desired attributes in our society. Based on our findings, however, an even more important activity lives in our minds — hope. This conclusion should be welcome news for many of us. After all, our basic intelligence and physical capabilities have been set by genetics, but we can do things throughout our lives to enhance our hope if we choose to do so.

REACHING GOALS WHEN
LIFE GETS TOUGH

Higher hope should benefit us especially when things get difficult, when some sort of roadblock appears as we pursue our goals. This section briefly describes six studies showing how high hope works when we encounter difficulties.

The Bad Grade Scenario

Consider a study we did to find out what high- and low-hope college students say they would do when they encounter an obstacle to their grade goal. In this study, we were interested in what they would do if they were taking a course for which they had set a grade goal of B, but got a D on the first examination (counting for 30 percent of their grade). We also had control groups of high- and low-hope students who were not given the D grade feedback, but were merely told that they had a B grade goal. All students were then asked to list the strategies they would use to get their grade in the course (a measure of waypower), as well as how certain they were of using the strategy and having it work (a measure of willpower). Compared to those given no grade feedback, the low-hope people given the negative grade feedback tended to have less situational willpower and waypower, and the high-hope students given the negative grade feedback tended to exhibit more situational willpower and waypower. In fact, under the stressful negative grade feedback, the high-hope students reported much higher hope (willpower and waypower) than did their low-hope counterparts.[35] The bad grade feedback elicited a certainty on the part of high-hope students that they could invoke such adaptive strategies as going to talk with the professor, outlining their notes and readings, adopting specific times each day to study, and hiring a tutor. To turn a twist on an old saying, when the going gets tough, the hopeful keep going.

The Traumatic Injury Scenario

In another test of how people cope with even more profound stressors, men and women who had experienced traumatic spinal cord injuries completed the Hope Scale and were examined for their level of depression and reported impairment. Patients with higher hope reported significantly lower depression and impairment related to their injuries. Both willpower and waypower were related to better adjustment in the month directly following the injury, but over the subsequent months the elevated sense of waypower evidently was related to sustained adjustment.[36] Adaptive waypower-related strategies for spinal cord injuries included proper physical exercises, avoiding injurious movements, anticipating stressful events, and obtaining assistance from others. In the months after the spinal cord injury, therefore, the ability to make plans in relation to the debilitating injury was the especially effective part of the hope mindset.

Another study explored the role of hope in teenagers with a previous history of traumatic burns.[37] One of the markers of adjustment for teenagers in general, and especially those recovering from burns, is the number of behavioral problems they exhibit. Results showed that the teenagers with higher hope had fewer behavioral problems.[38] Equally important, this high hope and low behavioral problems relationship remained when the influences of perceived disability, social support, and social status were removed through statistical procedures.

Taken together, these two studies with teenagers and adults suggest that how traumatic injuries are handled is moderated by one's level of hope. That is to say, one's willpower and waypower thoughts in relationship to goals are important factors in the positive recovery from acute physical injuries.

The Arthritis Scenario

For readers who may have some form of acute or chronic arthritis, the pain and suffering associated with this disease needs no introduction. For those of you without arthritis, suffice it to say that it is very painful. To find out what would predict overall adjustment of arthritis sufferers, the Hope Scale was administered along with an index measuring several aspects of adjustment, including upper extremity functioning, lower extremity functioning, affect, symptom severity, social interaction, and overall health perceptions. For all of these markers of how the patients were coping with their arthritis, higher hope predicted better adjustment.[39] Obviously, this suggests that the coping with the pain in one's joints is related to what is going on in the mind, and vice versa.

The Stressful Job Scenario

Two other studies illustrate how hope protects us in times of job stress. One of the most stressful jobs, day in and out, is that of nurses working in an acute burn care unit. What enables these nurses to cope, particularly given that they must face enormous amounts of on-the-job stress? One answer is hope. In this regard, the Hope Scale was given to burn unit nurses along with measures of reported alienation and burnout. Results showed that high-hope nurses handled the stresses of their job more effectively in that they reported significantly less burnout and alienation.[40]

John Anderson of the American Psychological Association has been conducting workshops throughout the United States with workers who daily deal with patients who are HIV-positive or who have AIDS. He uses a modification of the Hope Scale to make the content of the items applicable to persons with the HIV-positive diagnosis and to people with full-blown AIDS, as well as the original Hope Scale. These two measures have emerged as positive predictors of how workers successfully deal with the stresses of their jobs.[41] In other words, persons with higher hope were coping better with the psychological and physical demands placed on them in their various work settings.

Together, these studies suggest that high-hope people are able to continue their travels on the roads of life, and this is especially so when such roads become bumpy and seemingly blocked. I discuss how hope may help us to cope in the next section.

HOPE TO COPE

As we have seen, higher-hope people accrue advantages in a variety of life arenas, including stressful ones, and they manifest a sense of well-being in their lives. The question now turns to what these high-hope people seem to do naturally to cope so effectively.

All of the subsequent tips are based on what we have found in our studies of high- versus low-hope people. Although one always should be cautious about overinterpreting correlational results — and I would like these studies to be replicated and expanded to other subject populations — I believe that we have a useful operator's manual of the basic coping skills of high-hope people.

Minimize the Negative

Higher-hope people do not perceive that events in their lives are as disruptive as do lower-hope people. Even though a high- and low-hope person may be describing the same stressful event, it simply is not the same.[42] The mindset of high-hope people enables them to endure, to have a sense that things will pass. Further, things don't snowball, building from a small to a big problem. Psychologically, higher-hope people appear to cut stress off at the pass.

As an example of minimizing the negative, consider how two people approach the same stressful event differently. Bonnie and Jack were advanced clinical psychology graduate students approaching the last and biggest requirement to obtain their doctorates — the dissertation. Bonnie, the epitome of high hope, saw this project as the light at the end of the tunnel. She acknowledged that the dissertation project by necessity was a big one, but she saw it as being just the next step. If she kept at it, she knew she could handle all the work, and she dove into her dissertation with a sense of challenge. Jack, on the other hand, was low in hope. He saw his dissertation as the last and probably fatal hurdle he would have to jump to get his degree. He could not see himself getting over this barrier, and it seemed higher and more difficult as he procrastinated starting. Any light at the end of the tunnel for Jack was an oncoming train that was about to run over him. The semesters rolled by, and Jack became nervous if he even thought about the dissertation. Bonnie completed her Ph.D., and Jack to this day is an A.B.D. (the pejorative, nonexistent degree of All But Dissertation).

Look Outward and Problem Solve

Instead of beginning to worry and ruminate about themselves, higher-hope people concentrate on the situation at hand to see what needs to be done. Thus, an advantage of high hope is giving attention to the task rather than to oneself.[43] Related research has shown that people who begin to think a lot about themselves may initiate a counterproductive cycle in which they increasingly become convinced they are inferior people who cannot cope.[44]

By focusing outward on the particular goal, higher-hope people become especially effective at forming plans about how to cope.[45] If there are impediments to a given pathway, they think they can generate other ways to get what they want.[46] Thus, not only are higher-hope people unencumbered by disruptive thoughts about themselves, but when focusing on a problem they also have a mindset that they will solve it.

In 1992 thousands of Americans lost their jobs due to a continuing recession. Support groups for out-of-work people sprang up, and it was in the context of one of these meetings that I observed the markedly different mindsets of Carol and Jacqueline. Carol, who was a low-hope individual, was the group worrier. To hear her, things weren't going to improve, and she complained about her plight. One of the other group members made a good-natured attempt at humor with Carol, suggesting that she was a member of the Whiner family in the "Saturday Night Live" skit. She missed the humor, wondering out loud if she really might not be worth hiring. Jacqueline, on the other hand, was clearly on the high-hope end of the continuum. She seemed interested in the other members of the group, and she made suggestions about where they might look for work. Jacqueline's most meaningful advice for herself and others was that they would have to look for lesser jobs than they had previously held. This strategy was proposed until the economy improved. In fact, this advice worked for several members of the group.

Call on Friends

Higher-hope people report they are not lonely.[47] In interviews I have held with high-hope people, they appear to have a social support network they can call on in the good and the bad times. This is not a user perspective in which one person derives all the benefits of the friendly support, but a give-and-take reciprocal relationship. In fact, higher-hope people are very facile at taking the perspective of other people.[48] This means that the high-hope person can forgo an egocentric analysis of an interpersonal transaction (e.g., What's this mean for me?) and attend to the views of other people. This perspective-taking should enable the high-hope person to deal more effectively with the multitude of relationships encountered in life.

The affinity of high-hope individuals to other people makes them more likely to be called on for leadership. I know a psychologist, let's call him Al, who never aspired to any administrative positions. But, his natural liking and ease with people, and his willingness to listen and talk, made his opinions especially valued whenever the group was making a decision. Further, when serving in subsequent administrative roles, Al continued to talk with his colleagues about various matters. His natural problem-solving style and his willpower helped the group to get things done. I once remarked to Al that he didn't seem to experience a sense of separation and loneliness that is sometimes typical of leaders. "How could I be lonely when I enjoy talking with all of you people?" Al replied rhetorically.

Higher-hope individuals are people we like to have around us. Their high hope is, in part, likely to be a source of sustenance to their friends and loved ones. If I had to list the most prevalent characteristic of the low-hope people I have seen in therapy and work settings over the years, it would be their inability to connect with people. Low-hope people don't seem to be able to initiate and sustain relationships. And, if low-hope persons do have relationships, they take a somewhat dependent role. Further, just being around other people doesn't solve the problems of a low-hope person. I am reminded of this poignant observation of a former client: "I'm never as lonely as when I'm in a group of people." The presence of other people only reminded this low-hope person of her perceived outsider status. Indeed, research has shown that lower-hope people report having problems establishing intimacy and friendships, and that the loneliness occurs especially when they are around others.[49]

Laugh

Higher-hope people use humor to cope with the nuisances and blemishes of life.[50] They are able to laugh at the things happening around them, and perhaps more importantly, they are able to laugh at themselves. This is especially true when they are stuck, trying to find some way to solve a thorny problem. A good laugh is energizing and allows us to put things in perspective. After all, is our particular goal really *that* important? Are we really *that* important?

To see the humor in one's predicaments places the high-hope person in the throes of the larger existential ridiculousness of much of life. A sense of the absurd, similar to the perspectives taken in "The Far Side" cartoons of Gary Larson, fills the minds of high-hope people. High-hope people can take things very seriously when it is appropriate to do so; even so, such intense goal pursuit is often punctuated with rowdy bursts of humor. Remember the previously described case of Carla, the grandma bulldog.

Pray

Among religious people, higher hope is related to prayer. Although overall hope relates to prayer, this appears to be mostly due to the willpower rather than the waypower component.[51] In other words, prayer is a means of increasing one's mental energy or willpower;

it is less related to the waypower thinking of finding pathways to one's goals.

To date, no experiment has examined whether high-hope people are more religious. It may well be that prayerlike thinking, rather than religiosity, is associated with higher hope. For example, one of the potential ways prayer enhances the religious person's sense of mental energy is through a recharging of the mind and body. This is also true for people who are not necessarily religious but practice meditation. In the process of becoming quiet and clearing the mind of other thoughts, the praying (or meditating) person shuts off the draining processes associated with attending to various daily stressors. Beyond lessening the depletion of mental energy, we also can gain refreshment from focusing on some simple and familiar thoughts. For example, this may be a particular prayer such as the Lord's Prayer, a rosary, or a mantra. What is important is not so much the particular content of the prayer or prayerlike activity, but the communality of benefits that accrue from such mental rest. Prayer and prayerlike mental activities thus provide a day-by-day renewal that is important when people return to the rigors of coping. In many ways this is analogous to the need we have for sleep as a time to replenish ourselves after periods of wakeful exertion.

Exercise

There is some evidence that higher-hope people are more likely to exercise than are low-hope people.[52] As we have repeatedly had to relearn inside and outside of the field of psychology, the body and the mind are connected. The most obvious transfer is that the physical energy resulting from exercise may infuse us with mental energy.

Part of the benefit resulting from exercise is that it provides a time to clear the mind. In this way, exercise is similar to the processes inherent in meditation or prayer. Another benefit of physical exercise is a physiological high when the post-exercise person experiences the pleasant effects of endorphins. Exercise done repeatedly also has the side effect of providing exercisers with more actual physical energy to employ in daily activities. As may be obvious, exercise should enhance the person's sense of willpower, although there also may be some benefits related to waypower thinking.

Beyond these reasons why exercise and higher hope may go hand in hand, I would add a comment made to me by a sports psychologist: "Exercise is a metaphor for life. You set goals, go after them, and feel good on the way."

Watch Health

Hopeful people may take better care of themselves than do low-hope people. They not only are aware of behaviors related to health problems (e.g., smoking) but also may be more willing to do self-examinations (e.g., skin or breast examinations) and consult professionals.[53] Additionally, higher-hope people may have more ideas for taking care of themselves should they get sick. In other words, they can generate and pursue many options for regaining health. (Recall the case of Hobart, who actively participated in his course of treatment.)

Health is a goal that in many ways supersedes all other goals. If we are not healthy, we are not able to pursue the other goals of life. Although some may take their health for granted, high-hope persons evidently do not.

Aging Gracefully

One of the major coping tasks of adult life is to deal successfully with one's aging. The noted developmental theorist Erik Erikson has suggested that middle adulthood is a stage in which the person must deal with the crisis of generativity versus stagnation (see chapter 3 for more discussion of his work).[54] According to Erikson, the adaptive mindset called generativity involves a continued desire for making things happen, often by investing oneself in the welfare of younger people (e.g., mentoring a beginning worker, or helping children). By using a psychological scale measuring this propensity toward generativity, researchers found it to be more typical of higher-hope people.[55]

Erikson also suggests that the crisis of the late adulthood period involves the resolution of the dilemma pitting ego integrity against despair. The adaptive resolution involves the integrity of maintaining spiritual beliefs, along with some appreciation and sense of peace about what has transpired in one's life (even in instances of difficult lives). Using a self-report measure of this self-integrity notion, research has shown that higher-hope people are more likely to have such thoughts.[56]

One issue we must all face is our own mortality. Some people in their later years become very distressed about their demise. This does not appear to be the mindset of high-hope people, however. In this regard, higher-hope people exhibit a neutral acceptance of their deaths; they affirm such items as "Death is simply part of life" and "I don't see any point in worrying about death".[57] The coping of higher-hope people, as they age, appears to rest on an ability to engage themselves in life goals while acknowledging that their tenure as living beings is limited.

The Hope and Coping Connection

The mindset of higher hope appears to render its benefits through processes involving the mind and body. In the sheer cognitive realm, higher-hope people minimize the negatives they encounter and simultaneously turn their attention outward to the situations at hand. As high-hope people face various situations, they are adept at problem-solving and may enjoy a good laugh at their own expense as a way of coping. Further, they have friends with whom they can share their goals and problems. Prayer or meditation activities appear to restore the mental energy of high-hope people. They engage in preventative health maintenance activities, including physical exercise. Lastly, they continue to focus on life goals as they age, and they are not preoccupied with their own demise. Overall, the active thinking of high-hope people is balanced by physical activities that help "to keep hope alive."[58]

THE HOPEFUL GENDER?

You, Column 1 or 2?

Which one of the following two lists contains more adjectives that apply to you?

Column 1	Column 2
active	affected
adventurous	affectionate
aggressive	anxious
ambitious	attractive
autocratic	complaining
course	curious
competitive	dependent
courageous	dreamy
enterprising	emotional
forceful	fearful
independent	gentle
inventive	mild
logical	religious
objective	self-pitying
progressive	sensitive
robust	sentimental
rude	sexy
self-confident	soft-hearted
severe	submissive
stern	superstitious
strong	tactful
tough	talkative
unemotional	weak

These two lists contain the stereotypical views about the two genders. Column 1 reflects the stereotypes associated with men, and column 2 reflects those associated with women. The men usually are described by instrumental traits which they use to act independently and accomplish things; women are described more in expressive and communal terms, portraying them as being concerned with caring for others and expressing feelings.[59]

Surprise Results and Two Interpretations

Given this backdrop of male and female characteristics, as well as a society in which the forces of sex-role appropriate behavior and sexism are still operative, from the very beginning I expected men to have higher Hope Scale scores. At this point, the scale has been given to thousands of men and women of differing ages, backgrounds, and educations, and the results have been extremely consistent. We have never found any differences between men and women in the overall Hope Scale score, or on the willpower and waypower subscale scores.[60] That is, in our previous research we have always found that both men and women are quite hopeful.

The positive spin on these findings is that both genders, on the average, may have truly equal amounts of this important mental set. Indeed, I believe we have probably overemphasized the differences between the genders. Seduced by the obvious physical and historical role-related differences, we have not attended to the overwhelming similarities of women and men. In a time of social change, in which the rights of women are increasing both de jure and de facto, perhaps women and men truly are thinking similarly about their life goals.

There is another way to consider the similarity in hope scores, however. When I talk to college students and young adults about hope, the females in the audience often argue that of course they have the same level of hope as their male counterparts. Their time has come, they say. But I am troubled by another interpretation, albeit a speculative one, of the equally high Hope Scale scores of men and women. What we do not know is whether the goals toward which willpower and waypower are applied are different for men and women. Women in our society still are expected to bear and raise the children and to oversee the home. Men, on the other hand, have more freedom and are encouraged to pursue goals outside of the family. Perhaps what we are seeing, therefore, is the result of the glass ceiling; women do not really expect to have many of life's goals open to them. Ironically, if you truly perceive that many goals are beyond your reach, you may not even think of certain goals as being attainable. In other words, women may limit their goals to those left open to them. Thus, women may report high hope for those goals that are allowed. In this sense, hope may placate women, as well as others in our society for whom many goals are completely out of reach. This is a disturbing interpretation because while in the short run hope may contribute to women's sense of self-esteem in pursuing the available goals, in the long run it may only prolong sexism because some goals are not made more available.

THE COLOR OF HOPE

In the process of developing the Hope Scale and sampling large numbers of college students over the years, I noticed something about people who were reporting low scores. Low-hope people appeared to be disproportionately represented by African-Americans, Hispanics, native Americans, and Asian-Americans. Persons of color may perceive that their goals are not as readily accessible as goals for Caucasians. Even in instances where we have attempted to lessen the forces of overt prejudice, there may be covert barriers to reaching desired goals. As such, the waypower, as well as the driving sense of willpower, may not develop in the minds of persons of color. This may prove to be an example where the environment has had profound effects on the hope of large segments of our people.

To explore these possible racial differences in hope, we recently completed a survey of students from various ethnic groups at the University of Kansas. The African-American, Caucasian, Hispanic, and Native American students all exhibited higher hope than the Asian-American students.[61] One highly speculative inference, based on a conversation with an Asian-American psychologist, is that the Asian-Americans may have refrained from rating themselves highly on the Hope Scale items because of cultural emphases on modesty. Certainly, by sampling only college students, we may have selected high-hope people and as such any racial differences may be masked. Another possibility is that persons of color lower their goal standards because of the forces of prejudice. If this is true, when persons of color take the Hope Scale, they may score relatively high while thinking of goals that are not as elevated as those envisioned by Caucasians. This may be an instance of persons of color settling for less when they think of their goals.

This explanation for the lack of race differences is similar to the one that I posited for the lack of gender differences. Obviously, this study needs to be replicated. We need further studies using representative samples of Americans from various racial groups. Then, by controlling for socioeconomic factors and education, as well goals, we can begin to get a clearer picture of racial differences in hope.

This racism issue, like the sexism one, is re-examined in chapter 3 on the development of hope and chapter 4 on the effects of blockages on hope. For now, the data are insufficient to answer the question of whether there are racial differences in hope.

WILL YOUR HOPE CHANGE?

Having spent our time in this chapter on issues related to the importance of measuring hope, you may be wondering whether it changes over time. The answer is, it depends.

The It's Pretty Stable Answer

If the question is whether your score on the Hope Scale today would be the same if you retook it in several weeks or months from now, the answer is probably. When we gave the Hope Scale to people over intervals of up to three months, the scores remained relatively stable.[62] (Using a correlation statistic to measure this consistency over time, we have repeatedly found relationships of a .8 magnitude [with 1.0 being a one-to-one correspondence].)

This consistency of hope over time as measured by the Hope Scale supports my assertion in chapter 1 that hope is an enduring pattern of thinking about oneself in relation to life goals. What you hope now probably is what you will hope in the future, unless you begin to utilize some of the tips for raising hope in chapters 6 and 7.

The strictest test of whether hope changes over time would come by giving the Hope Scale to the same people as they age through their twenties, thirties, forties, and beyond. This longitudinal approach has not been tried because the scale is relatively new. We have, however, given the Hope Scale to different groups of people ranging in age from their twenties through forties. Using this cross-sectional approach, we have not found any differences in hope as related to age, which lends further credence to the stability of hope over the life span.[63]

The But It Can Change Answer

Does all this mean that your hope will not, or cannot change? Absolutely not. What it means is that for most people, most of the time, hope is quite stable. This leaves room for some of us to change a lot, and for a lot of us to change some. As we see in the later chapters, naturally occurring and human-engineered events can move our hope up and down. The key thing to remember here is that hope is a *relatively* enduring mindset established in most people by age 20.

The Here and Now Answer

One way to see if hope can vary over time is to use a measure that emphasizes what you are thinking in the here and now, rather than asking people how they generally are (this latter approach is used in the Hope Scale you took earlier). Using this here and now logic, we have developed and validated a State Hope Scale, with items measuring willpower and waypower in the present, ongoing time frame.[64] If you would like to get an idea of your hope at this very moment, try this new scale shown below.

State Hope Scale

Directions: Read each item carefully. Using the scale below, please select the number that best describes how you think about yourself right now and put that number in the blank provided. Please take a few moments to focus on yourself and what is going on in your life at this moment. Once you have this "here and now" set, go ahead and answer each item according to the following scale:

1 = Definitely false   2 = Mostly false   3 = Mostly true   4 = Definitely true

_____1. If I should find myself in a jam, I could think of many ways to get out of it.

_____2. At the present time, I am energetically pursuing my goals.

_____3. There are lots of ways around any problem that I am facing now.

_____4. Right now I see myself as being pretty successful.

_____5. I can think of many ways to reach my current goals.

_____6. At this time, I am meeting the goals that I have set for myself.

To score this scale, merely add your responses on all six items. The scores can range from a low of 6 to a high of 24. If you are interested in your subscale scores, willpower is the sum of the responses to the three even-numbered items, and waypower is the sum of the three odd-numbered items.

If you were to take this same scale each day for a week and write a brief description of the events that happened on each of these days, you probably would find variations in day-by-day hope. Equally interesting, the state hope you report should reflect your appraisal of those events that are transpiring in your life each day.[65] Additionally, if you were to receive some positive feedback about a performance that is important to you, your state hope would increase; conversely, if you were to receive feedback that you had not done well, your state hope should drop.[66] Lastly, by thinking of some recent event in your life where you succeeded in pursuit of a goal, your state hope should increase. On the other hand, you can lower your ongoing hope by recalling an instance where you failed to reach an important goal.[67] Research studies have supported all of these assertions.[68]

These day-by-day fluctuations in state hope are best thought of as the variable base on which our more enduring mindset of hope is built. In other words, the daily variations in hope contribute to our overall subjective estimate of hope. In this sense, big hope reflects an ever-expanding analysis of our small hopes right now. Although our big hopes certainly are more malleable and reactive to situational events in childhood, as adults we still are open to change in overall hope.

MEASURING HOPE IN OTHER PEOPLE

So far, we have been concentrating on what the measurement of hope means for you. It may have occurred to you along the way that the other important people in your life also have some level of hope. Perhaps you are drawn to others with a high level of hope, or just the opposite, you may find yourself surrounded by low-hope people. This topic is relevant to your hope in that the more people you have in your life who are high in hope, the greater is the chance that you also have high hope.

How would you analyze the hope of those important people with whom you interact, whether this be in the context of a romantic relationship, a family, or a work setting? Obviously, you could reproduce the Hope Scale and ask the key people in your you life to complete it. This may not be possible for a variety of reasons. There is another solution, however; you can rate the hope in the other person. You can use the modified version of the Hope Scale for this assessment.

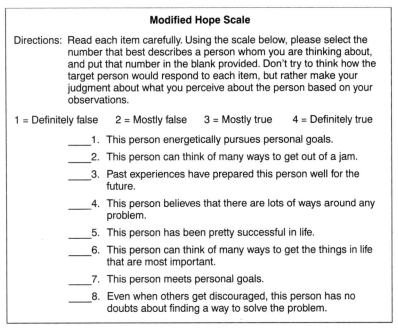

Modified Hope Scale

Directions: Read each item carefully. Using the scale below, please select the number that best describes a person whom you are thinking about, and put that number in the blank provided. Don't try to think how the target person would respond to each item, but rather make your judgment about what you perceive about the person based on your observations.

1 = Definitely false   2 = Mostly false   3 = Mostly true   4 = Definitely true

_____1. This person energetically pursues personal goals.

_____2. This person can think of many ways to get out of a jam.

_____3. Past experiences have prepared this person well for the future.

_____4. This person believes that there are lots of ways around any problem.

_____5. This person has been pretty successful in life.

_____6. This person can think of many ways to get the things in life that are most important.

_____7. This person meets personal goals.

_____8. Even when others get discouraged, this person has no doubts about finding a way to solve the problem.

The scoring is the same as for the Hope Scale you took in chapter 1. By adding the responses to the four odd-numbered items, you have the willpower subscale score for the target person; similarly, by adding the responses to the four even-numbered items, you have the waypower subscale score for the target person. The overall hope score is the sum of these eight items.

In our work, we have found a moderate correspondence between the hope that an individual reveals through completing the Hope Scale, and the hope generated if someone knowledgeable about that same person does the rating.[69] Although hope is a mindset, there probably are cues an observer can pick up. This makes sense because the whole premise of the theory is that the hope in the minds of people is translated into actions involving the goals in their lives. Of course, if we listen to what people say, this also gives us leads about what is going on in their minds.

Given the ideas about the measurement of hope we have covered in this chapter, now you should be better able to assess the levels of hope in yourself and important people in your life. If you are interested in the measurement of hope in your children, the Children's Hope Scale is in the next chapter.

A FINAL ASSESSMENT: HOPE IN YOUR OWN WORDS

Perhaps the idea of completing psychological measures about hope strikes you as being too artificial, even contrived. If you are averse to the measurement approaches I have outlined so far, I would suggest that you already have revealed your hope in the things that you have written or said. Your diary, letters, poems, telephone conversations, as well as almost any written or audiotaped format wherein you have disclosed information about yourself may serve as a naturalistic index of your hope. Look for those sequences in your writing where you describe your goals and merely gauge the quality of willpower and waypower that you exude toward these goals. This approach, though crude, can certainly tell you whether your words, and therefore you, are emitting a low or high level of hope. In fact, when using several judges who have rated the willpower and waypower for goals as evidenced in the words of people, a researcher found high interjudge reliability as to whom the low- and high-hope people are.[70] Examples of people whom I perceive as occupying each end of the hope spectrum may illustrate this for you.

Molasses

In a compelling autobiography, psychologist Norman Endler's hopeful thinking was dashed by a profound depression stemming from biochemical factors. In *Holiday of Darkness*, Endler writes about this depression that was to lift after several months:

> My wife wanted me to buy a new summer suit which was on sale. I refused by saying, "What do I need it for; I'm not going anywhere and will be staying indoors. It's a waste of money." After a while she stopped arguing with me and treated it as a lost cause. Obviously, I would rather sit around the house all day. . . . In general, the excuse I gave for my inactivity was fatigue — extreme, sometimes to the point of exhaustion. I was too tired to make decisions and felt as if I had a huge weight on my back that wouldn't allow me to achieve anything. Had anyone told me I would ever feel this way, I wouldn't have believed it. It's just inconceivable and one cannot really appreciate the feeling unless one has experienced it. No matter how long I stayed in bed and slept, I never felt rested and refreshed. . . .When I did get out of bed I was lethargic. I was as slow as molasses.[71]

Advice on Aging for Little Mopers

At the other end of the spectrum, surgeon Richard Selzer offers his high-hope prescription to himself for handling the aging process in his *Confessions of a Knife:*

> Faced with the inevitable, you can do two things. You can sit in a dark room, hearkening to the thutter of snare drums, or you can adopt a good-natured posture and go about your business. The latter seems better. There is quite enough gloom in the world without your shedding more. And there is a wonderful camaraderie about aging. Come, come, little moper, look around. All the rest of us are doing it too. Except for a few liars and dissemblers. . . . It simply won't work to deny the condition to one's friends. Think of the fun you can have drawing attention to each other's bunions and dewlaps. The trick is to find someone to get cozy with, someone to whom your warts and knobs and droopery are dear, who will understand about your bronchitic scarf. For, oh, the calmative power of love! In the profusion and prodigality of the body, who is to say where beauty lies?[72]

Like these words of others, your words should reveal a story whose themes involve the components of hope. Not surprisingly, our words mirror the thoughts in our minds. Whenever we pause to consider those thoughts, we also have undertaken a mental assay of our hope.

CHAPTER THREE

The Development of Hope

The young...are full of passion, which excludes fear;
and of hope, which inspires confidence.

—Aristotle, *Rhetoric Book II*

BEGINNINGS

Mandy: A Little Voice of Hope

From the mouths of babes, I thought after listening to Mandy, my toddler-age neighbor. She was an unexpected messenger bearing news about the makeup of hope. My guess is that she was a little under three years old when she first began talking with me.

What did we talk about in those days? What seemed to interest Mandy, of course, was Mandy. She recounted a growing sense of mastery over her world. One day, Mandy was listing the things that she could do. You know, little kid things like talking, hollering, walking, jumping, using the potty, and so on. She was full of the "I can's" as her mind exuded energy, excitement, and empowerment. From the beginning, I liked her spunk.

But there was another side to her chatter. Mandy seemed to take pleasure in telling me about how she was going to do things. I almost could see the wheels whirling in her mind as she plotted how she would accomplish her goals. It was as if she was saying in her

language, "I'll do it like dis." On one occasion, her waypower thinking surprised me. Holding a ball and bat, she announced her desire:
"I wanna bat." "How?" I asked. "You teach!" she exclaimed. She was
charting new frontiers and finding pathways; her mind was brimming with possibilities.

It was fun to listen to Mandy. Her enthusiasm and unfolding
sense of wonder and adventure were contagious. Almost fearless,
she was a fountain of hope.

Over the Years: What's to Come

Mandy typifies the high end of the hope continuum. Her mind is
filled with a seemingly endless supply of high hope. But what will
happen to her over time? Will events in her subsequent years dash
her hopefulness? Or, will Mandy and others like her continue to
have hopeful thoughts? In this chapter I explore how hopeful, goal-
directed thinking provides the essential framework — mental building blocks of sorts — for children's successful interactions with their
environments. Although you may get ideas about how to increase
your children's level of hope in the present chapter, this is not my
goal. Rather, I want to lay the groundwork for grasping how hope
develops in our formative years. Later, in chapter 5, I describe in
detail what parents can do to raise the hopes of their offspring.

Of course, this chapter is also about you. Indeed, some of us have
grown up with less hope, and some with more. Whatever our adult
hope may be, it was built in our childhood years. The following
pages may spark memories of places, events, and people that played
major roles in your childhood. Let's journey back to those times.

BUILDING BLOCKS: THE
INFANT TO TODDLER YEARS

A newborn is superbly equipped to absorb information, to begin the
lifelong expedition during which the ongoing goal is successful
engagement with the world. Although the newborn obviously is not

as facile at interacting effectively with the world as she will be in later years, she is far more adept and active in perceiving, understanding, exploring, and manipulating events than we previously thought.[1] The notion of infants as helpless is somewhat overblown. Parents and grandparents of newborn babies know this intuitively, as we marvel at the alertness and live wire qualities of our offspring. All the essential mental and physical building blocks are there at birth, and these processes are continually augmented and used throughout the life span. The ensuing sections describe the components of hope theory to help you understand fundamental developmental processes.

What's Out There: From Sensing to Perceiving, Quickly

In an insightful analysis of the developmental tasks of newborns, Michael Schulman makes a compelling case in *The Passionate Mind* that we come into this world with an intense need to know "what is out there."[2] For a moment, I'd like you to perform a mental simulation to recapture the infant's perspective. Suppose we blindfolded you, put cotton in your ears, and placed you in a padded space suit cutting off sensory contact with the outside world. Next, we transported you to an environment foreign to you, say a desert, and at midday we remove the space suit and other paraphernalia. Blinking at the bright sunlight, your senses are assaulted by this new environment. Your eyes dart around, surveying the details of this world; you hear the sounds of the desert, the wind blowing; the sand brushes roughly against your skin; your mouth is dry, with a slight taste from the perspiration dripping onto your lips. Lastly, you faintly smell the delicate fragrance of a nearby cactus flower. You are alive and active in sensing what is happening. This is precisely what newborn babies are doing, although for them the experience is even more novel because previously they have encountered only one other environment — the womb.

From the moment of physical birth, infants constantly use their senses of sight, hearing, touch, taste, and smell to take in information about the world around them. My granddaughter, for example, has been a looker since the time she was born. Her eyes seemed to watch anything that moved, and she was especially fascinated with faces. Anyone who has cared for an infant knows the strength and importance of the prolonged shared gazes. Visually, newborns survey their environments, quickly learning to recognize what is familiar— say, Mom's face—and what is not, say the face of a visiting stranger.[3] In this example, while Mom experiences a tender moment with her baby, something else with special meaning has occurred: The infant's brain has organized and recognized the input. Raw sensation of the shapes and forms, therefore, has been supplanted by the mind's perception that this is Mom's face.[4] Sensation becomes perception when the infant's mind organizes and comprehends the input.[5]

The other senses offer infants many other what's-out-there perceptual lessons. Let's take hearing next. Human voices beckon our attention. Three-day-old infants not only move their heads in attending to incoming sounds but within a few days after birth they also use the speaker's voice as a source of identification.[6] I was skeptical of this until it was demonstrated to me. While writing this section of the book, I finished work and walked home in a blowing Midwest snowstorm. As I opened our family room door, my three-month-old granddaughter looked up and began to cry loudly. Covered in snow, I must have looked odd to her. When I called her name and continued to talk with her, she stopped crying. Apparently she perceived that the strange person covered in white flakes was familiar. As I kept talking, she grinned widely. My voice helped her understand it was me, albeit a snowy version.[7]

One of the more acute senses of newborns is smell. Among infants only a few days old, for example, the smell of mother is preferred over the scent of other women.[8] The infant's nose evidently knows when mom is nearby.

The touching of objects also quickly becomes a fascinating ritual for babies. Whether it is the softness of Mom's breast or the roughness of Dad's beard, the infant's tactual interactions take on primary importance. Often, newborns put objects in their mouths for further tactual stimulation.[9] Once babies are capable of crawling, of course, parents know only too well the absolute fascination they have with touching and holding everything in reach. Although at times it appears our offspring are on search and destroy missions, remember that these hair-raising activities are part of the normal process children go through as they learn to identify things.

What Things Go Together:
Discovering Linkages

Again, I borrow Schulman's insights about what leads to what. The basic lesson here is that children sensing the external stimuli become fascinated with an even more complicated perceptual phenomenon — what events appear to go together. Contrary to the speculations of noted Swiss psychologist Jean Piaget,[10] infants probably are able to process linkages from the moment of birth.[11] In other words, the vigilant newborn notices that certain things co-occur and, consequently, certain stimuli are linked together in the infant's mind.[12] Such connection insights are based on the newborn's understanding of time. That is to say, as babies learn how certain things are connected (this follows that), they also acquire anchors for comprehending the chronology of happenings.

Perceiving linkages over time contributes to a fundamental additional insight: The stimuli in our world are not chaotic or random. There is some order to comprehend and, as such, much of the early work of newborns is to recognize such recurring patterns.[13] Likewise, the baby learns to make important predictions because of these recurring patterns.[14] Perhaps an example may clarify this prediction-like process. A hungry newborn quickly learns what leads to feeding. In the crudest connection, the newborn arrives at the following mental equation: Mom equals food. The mere appearance of mother, for example, calms the hungry infant who anticipates receiving milk. By the time she was two months old, my granddaughter knew that being taken into the kitchen was the step before getting her milk.[15]

Infants are especially attentive to environmental cues when they experience negative events. When newborns are hungry, cold, or wet, for example, they are keenly aware of the sequence of external environmental events because such events portend signals for help. Indeed, the infant probably apprehends such linkages at the earliest possible time because of basic survival issues.

By the end of the first year, thinking has progressed to the point that babies definitely can anticipate events, plan, and do things on purpose; thus, they are employing intentionality.[16] Additionally, I would suggest that sometime between the first and second year, the toddler's thoughts about pathways are revealed by a simple observation: Depending on whether activities are proceeding toward the attainment of goals, the baby displays varying emotions.[17] When babies perceive movement toward their desired objects, for example, they smile and coo; conversely, when the desired goal is blocked, they become upset and cry. This is consistent with my reasoning in the first chapter that emotions are a result of our successful or unsuccessful pursuit of goals. What is noteworthy in the present context, however, is that such emotions indicate babies are assessing their movement along the pathways toward their goals.

Goals

The perception and linkage lessons are refined as the baby begins to point out objects in the environment.[18] Pointing suggests the baby recognizes objects, and equally important, it implies that the young child has conceptualized a goal of sorts.[19] Pleasure attends this pointing game, especially when the baby begins to attach words to the objects. (This is a wonderful time to teach your infants the names of the things to which they are pointing.) There is another, and even more essential inference to be derived from this pointing game. From many possible objects, the child is selecting one. Whether it is a toy, a food, or mommy, the young child is signifying that he wants the object targeted by the chubby, little pointing finger. This form of pointing, perhaps amplified by the naming of the object,[20] reflects thoughts to engage a nearby caretaker to get the desired object.[21] To help with these lessons, go ahead and help your baby to look at and touch the coveted objects.

As the what's-out-there and what-things-go-together processes unfold, the fundamental process of setting goals also is being established. As I argued in the introductory chapter, human beings are intrinsically goal-directed. While our perceptions tell us what is out there, and what events seem to follow each other, our minds constantly focus on selected objects as goals. With the ability to perceive such linkages to goals, the baby has acquired waypower thinking. But what about the child's sense of personal willpower? I turn to these developmental processes next.

Recognizing the Self

Acquiring knowledge about our selfhood is an extremely important developmental task occurring during the infant-to-toddler stage.[22] When does this process begin?[23] Self-recognition evolves consistently over the first several months, and often is in place by twelve to twenty-one months.[24] A mirror experiment illustrates an infant's ability to recognize self. If a small red dot of rouge makeup is placed on the nose of a baby, those over one year old consistently touch their noses when they see themselves in a mirror; babies younger than one year old do not, suggesting they lack the necessary self-recognition skills.[25] Try this experiment with your baby.

Around eighteen to twenty-one months, the toddler undergoes a psychological birth when she begins to use the word *I*.[26] This use of self pronouns documents the infant's revelation of distinctiveness. Likewise, the naming of body parts further signals knowledge of self (e.g., "Where's Drew's nose?"), as do statements about internal states such as thoughts and feelings.[27] Finally, many of us have played the recognition name game with our toddlers. The young child gleefully points to himself when asked "Where's (toddler's name)?"

Recognizing the Self as Instigator

With the increasing self-awareness, the developing child arrives at a momentous insight: I am the originator of some sequences of events. At this point, young children realize they are the sources for events that happen subsequently. Consider the following experience of a young girl named Emily:

> And then an event did occur, to Emily, of considerable importance. She suddenly realized who she was.
>
> She had been playing house when it suddenly flashed into her mind that she was she . . .
>
> Each time she moved an arm or leg in this simple action, however, it struck her with amazement to find them obeying her so readily. Memory told her, of course, that they had always done so before; but before, she had never realized how surprising this was.[28]

It also is revealing to examine the content of children's speech from ages two to three, where the referents often pertain to the toddler's capacities, volitions, and activities.[29] Here are some examples:

I'm taking my shoes off. (boy, age 2 years, 10 months)
I do so, hm? I do la, la, la. (girl, age 2 years, 10 months)
Me too, (I) want..., (I) won't..., Me do it. (boy, age 2 years, 11 months)
I can..., No, I can do it myself. (girl, age 2 years, 8 months)
I *can* do it! (girl, age 2 years, 7 months)[30]

This natural speech of toddlers suggests a future orientation. More important in the present context, the way children say things indicates that they see themselves as the creators of some sequences of actions and that these actions lead to some short-term goals.[31]

Depending on the environment in these first two formative years, varying thoughts about one's willpower to produce movement toward goals should result. Even for toddlers with relatively deprived circumstances, the basic insights about personal willpower are established in the context of the available environment. In other words, the nature of the developmental process is such that most children acquire some sense of being the source of actions. For certain children, unfortunately, the ensuing years may crush this important sense of willfulness. (See chapter 4 for a discussion of the death of hope.)

Putting the Hope Building Blocks Together

The processes discussed so far are part of the natural learning occurring from birth to age two. Although I have discussed the five developmental steps in separate sections for purposes of exposition, these processes co-occur and build on each other during this early period. You can see the approximate times when these five hope building blocks are activated in the chart on the next page.

From birth, the newborn's senses are engaged fully with processing and perceiving the relevant stimuli in the environment. Likewise, the infant's capabilities to link events occurring closely in time also appear to be active and continuous from the moment of birth.[32]

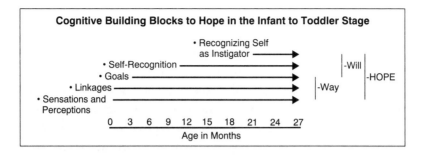

As these perceptual and linkage lessons continue, the developing infant begins to select certain objects as goals. As can be seen in the chart, the perceptions and linkages that lead to goals form the basis for waypower thoughts.

What about willpower thinking during this formative period? As the insights about self-recognition blossom, so too does the comprehension that one is the source of action in the waypower sequence. Therefore, two-year-old toddlers know that they can initiate actions toward a goal. Together, thoughts of selfhood and self as an instigator toward a goal yield a sense of personal willpower.

As shown in the chart, the waypower thoughts occur somewhat earlier than the willpower thoughts. By age two and a half, however, the toddler's thoughts fully involve the components of hope—mental willpower and waypower for goals. Indeed, these basic components of hope are built on over the subsequent childhood and adult years.

STUMBLING BLOCKS AS BUILDING BLOCKS FOR THE INFANT AND TODDLER YEARS

Hope not only provides a framework for understanding how newborns navigate the normal challenges of the first two years but it also applies when young children encounter blockages to their goals. As adults, we experience barriers almost daily; how we handle such occurrences by using hopeful thinking is probably a result of our childhood experiences with impediments. Stumbling blocks are essential childhood experiences that train us to think hopefully.

Barrier Work

The role of impediments is most obvious when toddlers are confronted with concrete, physical barriers standing between them and desired goals. Since the earliest experimental studies on this topic, results indicate that children become upset when encountering barriers to their goals.[33] A typical approach is to place a toddler in a room with a desirable goal (e.g., a toy), whereupon a barricade is erected to prevent the child from reaching the goal. The results are predictable to those of us who are parents. Because of the goal blockage, a full-scale tantrum, including whining and aggression, often erupts.

Another important finding, however, comes out of such research. In particular, toddlers consistently prefer the blocked object to other readily available objects. In other words, the desirability of the restricted goal is enhanced in the child's mind. At least in the short run, therefore, the net effect of barriers is to increase the toddler's fascination with the prohibited goal.[34] Does this sound familiar to you parents? How many times have you taken something from your toddlers, for example, only to find them going into a frenzy to get it back?

The barrier research also yields clues about how toddlers may use caregivers to help them struggle with barriers. In one version of this research, two-year-old toddlers were exposed to a barricaded toy, but there was a critical difference from earlier research — their mothers were present. Instead of the tantrums found in previous research, the toddlers looked at their mothers and made gestures apparently aimed at getting their assistance in removing the barrier to the toy.[35] Caregivers are allies in helping infants get what they want, and it is natural for the child to turn to the mentor for guidance in such difficult circumstances. When your toddlers are struggling with some sort of blockage, get down on the floor with them and help find a way around the block. Don't try to remove the blockage for them, however, because an important part of their learning is grappling with solutions to their problems.

If you have a toddler, you may be asking why your child seems more intent on starting a good fight than on wanting your mentorship. The answer is that we caregivers often are perceived as the barriers. The terrible two's are legendary exactly because our two-year-olds become enraged and increasingly covetous of those things prohibited by parents. When we adults say no to two-year-olds, we erect psychological barriers. Of course, we parents need to say no to establish a sense of boundaries and discipline in our young children. To the child these no situations reflect the psychological barriers that parallel the physical barriers of the research studies. What we adults may fail to realize is that rebellious pursuit of prohibited goals is a normal part of learning to handle barriers. Indeed, some amount of such behavior needs to be tolerated to augment our offspring's hopeful thinking in the face of opposition.

Immunization

The mindset that results from grappling with barriers is analogous to an immunization process. That is to say, by dealing with the difficulties and blockages related to one's early childhood goals, the young child may be protected in future encounters.[36] Slowly, with some successes in handling impediments, children come to think they can handle such problems.[37] Hope is not only part of the normal thinking processes in childhood but it also especially is fostered when children successfully deal with impediments to goal-directed actions. The key for parents is to avoid intervening with and removing all the obstacles in the lives of their children. Rather, the caregiver's task is to help toddlers wrestle with the blockages in their young lives.

Perhaps the best evidence for the existence of protective, immunizationlike thinking is found in those young children who thrive in spite of environmental circumstances such as family discord, poverty, and parental mental illness. This ability to cope successfully with such adversities is called resiliency.[38] Through people (e.g., a role model, a friend, a teacher) whom they may call on in stressful goal-blockage situations, resilient children learn how to handle problems successfully. Emerging from their transactions with adversity, resilient children — like high-hope children — think they will be prepared to handle similar future events.

Waiting

One last issue in regard to the lessons learned in dealing with obstacles is the necessity of waiting at certain times. In the newborn-to-

toddler stage, there are many highly desired goals. Like the proverbial kid in the candy store, the coveted objects are everywhere for the baby. Because of limited skills, or because of physical constraints imposed by the environment or caregivers, however, it may not be possible for the baby to move toward the desired goal. Thus, any effective goal attainment at that given time is precluded.

This topic has been called *delay of gratification* or *frustration tolerance* in the psychological literature.[39] These are instances in which we must take time out to get what we want. Young children can learn these skills, and they acquire elaborate self-distraction techniques for changing the waiting into a more enjoyable experience.[40] Included here are such distracters as singing or talking to oneself, covering the eyes, and playing with hands and feet. Perhaps those infants who have larger repertoires of distraction techniques grow up to be higher-hope adults.

The Legacy of Obstacles

Successful handling of difficult transactions begets children empowered to find solutions to future problems. Because of impediments, children at times must wait before any progress toward the desired goal is possible. Part of a hopeful mindset in such circumstances is to curtail one's thoughts toward a given goal until a future time. In other instances, hopeful children actively think about how to pursue the desired goal in spite of the obstacle. Rather than letting the problems get to them, therefore, children's hope gets to the problems. Indeed, the problems become the mental testing grounds for strengthening hopeful thinking.[41]

A good obstacle example involved an Easter egg hunt I witnessed. Toddlers, each accompanied by a parent, were to find eggs in a small field. As an additional twist, children were blindfolded, thus making the egg hunt more difficult. One little girl, with her father in hand, timidly took a few steps, feeling the grass with her hands. When she asked her dad for help, he replied, "No, no. You have to do it." The only other advice that he offered several minutes later was, "Hurry up!" Another little boy was having difficulty finding eggs, when his mother said in an exasperated tone, "Oh, I'll do it." She proceeded to put eggs in her son's basket. These two examples strike me as parental recipes for low hope in offspring. Contrast these with two other partnerships more conducive to high hope. One daughter and mother set out, with mom's encouraging words, "You can do it." Later, this pair wandered by, and the mother offered the praise, "You are doing great. Just keep it up." Lastly, a son-father combo appeared to be in good communication. The father told the son, "It's OK. . . . Ask for help if you really need it." When the son did ask for help, the father gave hints such as, "You're getting closer." These latter two children were being schooled in how to handle difficult situations.

As noted in chapter 1, the beneficial effects of hopeful thinking should be apparent especially in those instances when there are impediments to goals. Moreover, in chapter 2, several research studies illustrate how high hope in adults is positively related to coping in stressful circumstances. It should come as no surprise, therefore, that the child's early transactions with obstacles form the foundation of a hopeful mindset.

ON CONNECTING:
THE ATTACHMENT FACTOR

If the infant has a secure attachment to one or more caregivers, then the hope-related learning in the building block stages should be facilitated. Usually, of course, mother is the source of such continued and intense interaction with the baby. According to attachment theory, there are evolutionary advantages for newborns remaining physically close to their caregivers.[42] Mom and Dad, for example, will protect the young child. Additionally, the caregiver's dependability and responsiveness instill a psychological security in the baby.[43] Accordingly, the child internalizes a mental representation of these responsive and accessible caregivers, and comes to think of herself as being accepted and loved. With such felt security, there are both short-term and long-term benefits. In the presence of mother, for example, a one-year-old explores goals in the environment, using Mom as home base.[44] Moving to the long-term benefits, secure early attachments contribute to an adult mindset of empowerment and goal-directed behavior.[45]

Erik Erikson, the noted developmental and life stage theorist, arrived at similar conclusions about the importance of attachment.[46] Namely, he suggested that infants should develop a continuity and dependability about their environment if they have quality relationships with primary caregivers during the first two years.[47] Further, Erikson suggested the infant's major task during year one is to answer a simple question: Do I trust or mistrust the world? In particular, he posited that children trust the world as a good place if attentive primary caregivers meet their needs for contact and caring.[48] Hope, according to Erikson, results as the child adopts a sense of trust rather than mistrust during this critical phase. Assuming that secure attachment and trust are established, Erikson also reasoned that the next task for the toddlers in the second year is to begin thinking about their autonomy.

Secure attachment to a caregiver provides the infant with a model for effective goal-related activities. Additionally, the infant has a superb coach from whom to learn the basic components of hope. Such a caregiver not only exposes the infant to visual stimulation but also is facilitative and sensitive to the infant's needs. Attentive, goal-directed thinking is more likely to develop for an infant under such tutelage. The responsive caregiver also produces an environment where the linkages among events are consistent and easily learned (i.e., what goes with what). Likewise, because of the dependability and sensitivity of the caregiver, the baby learns that he is an entity separate from the caregiver. Indeed, the good parent fosters the development of self-awareness in the child. Further, through the stable, trustworthy feedback delivered by the attentive caregiver, the baby should become more knowledgeable about his ability to make things happen (i.e., the instigator of events).[49] Lastly, attachment is both a matter of the sheer time spent with the toddler by the caregiver and the interactive quality of that time.

Let me illustrate the points I raised in the previous paragraph about attachment through examples I witnessed on separate airplane trips. First, there was Jenny and her mom. I would judge Jenny to be about thirty months old. She was taking her first airplane ride. Mom described the loud engine noises at takeoff, and how they would be pushed back in their seats. "And, I'll hold your hand," said Mom. Jenny and Mom were both excited and chattered away through the entire flight. Mom enjoyed how Jenny experienced things for the first time. She even took Jenny for a walk around the plane, all the while answering her questions or pointing out things. Jenny got scared when the landing gear went down, but her mom comforted her with a big hug and an explanation as to what was going on. Jenny and her mom were clearly connected and trusted each other.

At the other extreme, consider the interactions of Teddy (age three) and his mom. Mom put Teddy in the seat next to hers, fastened his seat belt, and said, "Now, just sit there and be quiet. Mummy is going to sleep" (which she did). Teddy was obedient but his big eyes and trembling little hands revealed his fear at several points in the flight. Mom was oblivious, however, to what was happening in Teddy's mind. If there were things he wanted, one would never know because he sat quietly throughout the entire flight. No words or touches were exchanged. Teddy did not share whatever thoughts he had about things he wanted to do or learn. In many ways, he was flying alone.

Attachment builds an environment where children learn to think of themselves as successful in the pursuit of goals. Furthermore, the benefits of attachment should be especially apparent when developing children face blockages to their goals.[50] Lastly, because hopeful thinking often must involve activities and outcomes related to other people, having a secure interpersonal foundation should benefit the child throughout the years.

THROUGH THE AGES: THE PRESCHOOL YEARS

Having examined the impressive mental accomplishments of the first two years, I move the hands of the developmental clock forward to the preschool years (ages three to six). In exploring those issues that especially pertain to hope, I use less detail than I have for the previous birth to age two period. This is because the later developmental periods solidify or undo the basic hope lessons acquired in the critical infant to toddler stage.

Let's continue with this developmental hope journey by first examining the preschool years. From ages three to six, the preschooler's brain expands from 50 to 90 percent of adult weight.[51] Minds are literally growing during this period, but I focus on the thoughts in those minds. Of course, preschoolers also talk and talk. I begin with this latter issue to explain the major hope lessons of the preschool period.

Language and Objects as Symbols

From ages three to six, there is a mental explosion in the number of words in the typical child's vocabulary. While the two-year-old may know somewhere around 50 words, the six-year-old's mind is filled with more than 10,000 words.[52] Much more than sheer word power, however, is being stockpiled in the child's mental arsenal during this period. In comparison to the two- or three-word phrases of the two-year-old, children from ages three through six increasingly begin to string together several words,[53] acquire grammar rules, and utter more complex sentences.[54] What is happening here with language and hope? Obviously, thinking and language are inextricably intertwined.[55] How, for example, could one think without some label system such as language as an underpinning for thoughts? It is impossible. Language gives the child a system of symbols for building mental maps of the world; language also becomes the critical tool for conceptualizing the elements in one's world.[56] These key elements, in terms of hope, are thoughts pertaining to goals, as well as thoughts about oneself desiring those goals. The words also become the means for understanding the pathways to desired goals (i.e., waypower thoughts), as well as our appraisal of motivation to pursue those goals (i.e., willpower thoughts). By necessity, therefore, the developing child begins to think with more precise language to become effective at goal attainment. Although I have yet to perform the experiment, my hunch is that verbally facile children are also likely to be high in hope. As we impart word power to our children, so too are we instilling hope.

There is more, however, to the role that language plays than merely serving to identify objects involved in our goal attainment. Words and language also serve as a means of communicating and interacting with one's environment. Hopeful thinking, when distilled to its essence, involves thoughts aimed at getting to our goals.

Because we are social creatures from the very beginning, language becomes the vehicle for learning how to achieve our desires in the context of the group.[57] Whether it is for the purposes of internal mental dialogue, or for interactions with others, the three- to six-year-old child who has attentive role models acquires hope-related language skills.

Vivid examples of language and parental influence can be seen in almost any supermarket, where a parent is wheeling around a three year old in a shopping cart. A typical scene goes like this: Turning down an aisle, little Johnny starts jumping up and down, hollering, "I want, I want." He points excitedly to shelves laden with all kinds of chips and bread products. "Settle down a little so I can understand," says Mom. "Now, use your words to tell me which thing you want." Johnny quiets down, realizing he needs to try another approach to get what he wants. "I want crackers," he says. "Good, that helps me," says Mom. Johnny in this instance has learned to use words to reach his goal. This is a crucial lesson. He will use this process for the rest of his life.

While language provides a symbolic representation of objects, preschoolers learn to use actual objects as symbols. In this way, preschoolers acquire another hope-related lesson. Play and pretend activities with objects often are obsessions for preschoolers. The complexity of the pretending increases during these years, as the child transforms a given object into an imaginary one.[58] With this accomplishment, we are witnessing the power of the child's mind to turn tangible objects into intangible mental representations. Once objects no longer have to be what they appear, the preschooler can perform mind experiments with action-directed sequences. Such pretend play is important work for preschoolers. Indeed, for Erikson, the key cognitive asset to be derived from the preschool period is a sense of initiative at taking on new play activities.

There is a park in the middle of our town where parents bring their preschoolers to play. It was here I saw a fascinating lesson in symbols and hope-related thinking. A four-year-old boy was holding a plastic airplane that had lights, made noises, and generally looked remarkably realistic. He played with it for a few minutes and then handed it to his dad. He looked bored, when all of a sudden he jumped up and said, "I'm a jet." Thrusting his arms backward, he made jet noises and ran off flying around the park. After awhile, he had some other boys and girls flying with him. Tiring of this activity, he turned himself into a race car. He was off again. He could transform himself, through the power of imagination, into different objects. Where the plastic replica of the airplane appeared to shut down his flexible play thoughts, his mind was a transformer that could turn his body into endless objects. His play became hopeful in that he was energized and had plans to reach his goals. For instance, at one point he announced that he was an airliner taking passengers, who were to line up behind him.

Scripts

The specific building block lessons of the first two years are broadened in the preschool years, where the young child acquires mental representations of a series of events. In other words, based on experience with the various rituals of childhood, the preschooler develops mental scripts as to the people, events, and actions that go together. Scripts are mental snapshots, or perhaps even more aptly stated, short movies, that outline what is to be expected.[59]

During the preschool period, the scripts often involve things to avoid. For example, parents teach five-year-old Alex, "Now, what do you do if a strange man or woman offers you a ride? Well, you run to the other kids or tell a grownup you know." These protection scripts are often used by parents in our modern world. Another script might be, "What do you do in the morning to get ready for school?" The parent then coaches the child in a sequence involving such events as "Go to the toilet, brush your teeth, and make your bed."

Once scripts are learned, they contribute to hopeful thinking in at least two ways: First, to the extent preschoolers have constructed accurate mental scripts for a variety of situations, they are better prepared to reach their goals in those situations. Second, the more similarities the preschooler can recognize in scripts across situations, the more general principles she acquires about goal-directed thinking.[60]

The developing language skills, often honed through verbal interactions with the primary caregivers, enhance the narrative thinking of children.[61] Stories become mental scripts for children to recall what has happened and to shape expectations about what will happen in the future. Indeed, sometime toward the end of the preschool years, the child's mental scripts form autobiographical memories that can be recalled in adult years.[62]

Although scripts guide the preschooler though situations, at times they may limit the goals that are the endpoints of action sequences. In two instances — gender and race — scripts may operate in just such a fashion.

One of the major preschool scripts involves what is acceptable for girls and boys to do. In this regard, psychologist Sandra Bem suggests that preschoolers are taught the prevailing societal roles deemed appropriate for girls and boys.[63] By age four, for example, preschoolers can clearly identify girls things (e.g., flowers, butterflies, etc.) and boy things (rough things, tractors, etc.).[64] Once these boy or girl scripts become part of children's mindsets, they choose the sex-appropriate activities from available options. At age three, boys and girls appear to exhibit similar patterns of play; but by ages four and five, the girls are playing with dolls and the boys are engaging in more rough-house activities.[65] By age six, girls and boys appear to express stereotyped ideas about what is appropriate for each sex to wear, do, or feel.[66] These early scripts are consistent with the point that I made in chapter 2 that girls and boys may be aiming toward differing goals.

Another script in the minds of preschoolers involves race. Although there is no research specifically aimed at understanding the goals held by preschool children of different racial groups, studies on the preferences for dolls are informative. In the earliest studies, African-American and Caucasian three year olds were asked to give their reactions to dolls representing both racial groups. Results of these studies showed that preschoolers of both races could distinguish between the dolls; moreover, children of both races preferred the light-skinned doll.[67] Subsequent studies have replicated these findings,[68] and have shown similar results with Native Americans.[69]

These studies have been highly controversial because they can be interpreted as indicating that children of color have lower self-esteem. Although I do not think that self-esteem is the key issue, my interpretation should be even more disturbing to a society purporting to promote equality of opportunity. Namely, my conclusion is that such preferences actually reflect instances in which the

African-American or Native American preschoolers are selecting the Caucasian doll because that doll has more attractive roles available to it. In a study with Native American children, for example, the preschoolers who had rated their racial group doll more negatively said they had done so because that doll wouldn't be able to undertake the same roles as the Caucasian doll. As a case in point, one Native American child said that the white doll definitely would be the teacher, but there was no way that the darker skinned Native American doll would be a teacher because she would have to be an aide.[70] These preschoolers, unfortunately, already were putting a cap on their goals because of scripts they had learned. Again, as with the scripts for gender, the levels of hope itself may not be different, but the acceptable goals may be.

Attending to the Perspectives of Others

To obtain one's goals and develop hopeful thoughts, children increasingly need to understand and attend to what other people around them are thinking. Although toddlers at times must attend to surrounding people, they are quite egocentric.[71] Likewise, preschoolers generally prefer to see things from their perspective.[72] There are, however, some increases in the preschooler's perspective taking. By age four, for example, the preschooler can think about the thoughts of other people.[73] By age five, the child is able to comprehend the visual perspective taken by another person.[74] (Recall the results discussed previously in chapter 2 where high-hope persons reported that they were more facile at understanding the perspective of other people.) Additionally, between three and six, the child learns some lessons in turn taking. Relatedly, the delay of gratification lessons of the infant to toddler stage continue as preschool children know that they must wait in line or share.

The preschool child also begins to take into account what the other person may be able to understand. In dealing with even younger infants or toddlers, for example, preschoolers simplify their speech to be better understood.[75]

When dealing with adults, the preschooler increasingly must comprehend the rules. What society wants, as promulgated through caretakers' teachings, is part of the mental equation as children weigh their desires against those of the system. By listening to the perspectives of the bigger people, preschoolers find out how to navigate to meet their goals.

These ideas about preschool children attending to others are consistent with my observations in chapter 2 that high-hope adults enjoy and are effective at interacting with other people. Hopeful thinking clearly has a social flavor to it. Consider the following social bartering interchange between two five year olds:

Rochelle: "I want your big box of crayons."

Susie (frowning): "Nope."

Rochelle: "Come on, please."

Susie (still frowning): "No way."

Rochelle: "OK, how about I give you some baseball cards for 'em, 'cause I know you like them" (a lie).

Susie (shaking her head): "No, don't like 'em that much."

Rochelle: "OK, I know you love my stuffed dog. What about it?

Susie (smiling): "It's a deal."

THROUGH THE AGES: THE MIDDLE YEARS

Relative to the preschool years, the middle years (ages seven through twelve) are a period of continued expansion, both in physical size and scope of activities.[76] Erikson calls it the time for industry. Exploration abounds in this period. Not only are the bodies and turfs of middle childhood expanding, but the minds of children also exhibit a parallel growth of hopeful thoughts. Indeed, although the expansion of body and space is impressive, the thoughts undergirding this newly won independence are the benchmarks of middle childhood. This section explores two broad categories related to hopeful thinking in the middle school years.

Mental Boosters

The child in the middle years adds greatly to the storehouse of knowledge that he can call on for goal-related activities. Through physical exploration, children expand their mental maps of the world. Whereas the skin is the boundary of the infant, and the immediate area surrounding the home is the boundary for the preschooler, the child in the middle years explores the neighborhood and town more generally. He also obtains some notions of larger geographical areas involving states, nations, and planets. Much of this knowledge base is experiential as the child in the middle years sets out to explore the neighborhood. Physical exploring goes hand in hand with hopeful thinking, and parents should encourage such behavior whenever possible. I can still recall the sense of empowerment I felt as a kid during this exploration phase. Because we moved to a new town frequently, each time I would set out on my bike to explore the new turf. I would be gone for hours, sometimes getting lost, but somehow making it back to my house. I know now that these excursions were frightening for my parents, but I thank them for not putting me on a leash! Because of the realistic concerns about the harm that may come to our children in modern America, we parents obviously need to identify places where such important exploration can occur safely.

In addition, middle-years knowledge is expanded by modes other than direct experience. For example, language and reading add to this information base. Unlike the preschool years where the child was learning to read, in the middle years the child is reading to learn.[77] Reading becomes a tool for acquiring the information base for hopeful thoughts. Although I have yet to test this hypothesis, my guess is that higher-hope children read more than do lower-hope children. Much like the high-hope child exploring the world physically during the middle years, the avid reader is doing the exploration through the pages of books.

Just as reading skills add to the knowledge base related to hopeful thinking, so too do mathematical skills. During these middle childhood years, for example, the child moves from understanding mathematical questions, to knowing how and when to apply given strategies for solving the questions.[78] Not only do the premises of such mathematical questions contribute to hopeful thinking, but the terminology bears some similarities. Mathematical questions are posed as problems (i.e., a goal with barrier potential), which in turn call for solutions (i.e., waypower thinking); moreover, operators are symbols that indicate an active mathematical process (i.e., pathways with inherent willpower properties). If your children are drawn to mathematics, praise them as they expand their skills in this area. My point here, and one that I elaborate in the subsequent chapter on nurturing hope, is that any learning arena where your child can experience a sense of success is a superb source of hopeful thinking.

Another prerequisite to more effective goal-related thinking is an increased memory capacity. The reason is that we need as much relevant information as we can get to set appropriate goals and to think about how to reach them. To imagine one's goals more clearly as well as the necessary ways to reach those goals, the child in the middle years can hold more information in the mind than her preschool counterpart. Furthermore, the time taken to retrieve and process the relevant mental information decreases during these middle childhood years.[79] Hopeful thinking is built on successful goal ventures; to the degree that developing children recall previous similar experiences, they can employ that information in any present setting. Indeed, one of the memory lessons good teachers or parents impart to children is to ask them, when they encounter a problem, whether they can remember how they handled any similar situations.[80] If your children are stuck, have them think about any similar instances in their young lives.

One last mental booster that kicks in during the middle years is when children are able to understand and talk about their memories and thinking processes.[81] These skills are important for hopeful thinking because they enable children to discuss goal-directed thinking with other people in a coherent and defensible manner. Take a ten-year-old named Corky, for example. During his preschool years, Corky's dad spent a lot of time with him. Because of increasing work commitments, however, dad was spending less and less time with Corky. At age ten, Corky remembers that things used to be different with him and his dad. So Corky, with his middle childhood memory and goal capacities, says to his father, "I want my old dad back!" This insightful plea serves to reinvest the father in spending more time and paying attention to Corky. Memory-based goal skills, as shown by this example, are important because other people may have some say in the achievement of our goals. This latter point leads us to the second general issue of middle childhood — the individual as a goal-directed being in a social context.

The Egocentrism-Social Interaction Balance

Unlike the infant/toddler and to some degree the preschooler, the middle-years child no longer can get by without considering the perspectives of other people. If children in the middle years do behave in a totally self-centered manner, they probably hear the nearby adults saying, "Act your age." Peers won't put up with it either, as they shout some variant of "Grow up!" Beyond these rebuffs, however, an even more essential lesson is being imparted in the middle years: Totally egocentric children do not get what they want.

What is going on here? Is it the demise of self-interest? Certainly not, because adults still strongly attend to their points of view about the perspectives of other people.[82] The answer for the child in the middle years lies in paying more attention to the rules and social conventions for goal-directed activities. If the preschool years yield some lessening in the egocentric perspective, this process definitely intensifies in the middle years as children attempt to balance what they want within the context of their social contacts. Given the increases in general mental capacities just described, the child in the middle years understands that other people are part of goal-directed scenarios.[83] Unlike the toddlers or preschoolers who make the world fit their conceptions, children in the middle years must balance their objectives with those of other nearby important people.[84]

The rules and social conventions learned during the middle years provide frameworks for reaching objectives. The rules may allow the child to reach the goal alone (e.g., competitions where there is one winner) or, in other circumstances, encourage group efforts to achieve objectives (e.g., competitions where the members of a team are winners).[85] Sometimes, of course, the children in these middle years use the rules or seek to modify them to obtain their goals. Success at such maneuvers, however, involves a sensitivity to those adults or peers who must agree to such changes.

It is noteworthy that social problem solving, which bears striking similarities to hopeful thinking, begins in the middle years. The initial step in social problem solving is to identify a goal, whereupon the goal is considered in the context of the social situation. Thereafter, children produce and evaluate various strategies to attain the goal. Assuming the child truly wants the goal, he implements the strategy perceived to be the best and evaluates the outcome in the social context.[86] I saw a touching example of this at a baseball practice of ten-year-old boys. Tony got hit on the helmet by a pitched ball during batting practice. Scared and crying, Tony threw down the bat and bolted to his mother sitting in the bleachers. After several minutes of comforting, Tony had calmed down. His mother then asked a critical question, "What would you like to do now?" Tony came up with three possibilities — going home, staying in the bleachers with his mother, or going back out and practicing. After mulling over the pros and cons of each, including what would be best for him and what the guys would think, Tony decided to go back to practice. The guys gave him a cheer, Tony grinned, Mom sighed in relief, and the episode had a hopeful resolution.

Nowhere is the adaptive resolution of the mine/thine equation more apparent than in the friendships formed in the middle years. The developmental cornerstones of such friendships involve communication, reciprocity, commitment, conflict resolution, and positive emotions.[87] Although the number of friends appears to diminish relative to the preschool years, children in the middle years may have one best friend with whom they interact especially closely.[88] It should come as no surprise, therefore, that good social relations and friendships are routinely reported by high-hope adults in our research. As I discussed in chapters 1 and 2, friends are a source of willpower and waypower thoughts; moreover, the communication of high-hope people is two-way in that they enjoy facilitating the goal-directed thoughts of their friends. That is to say, the friendships of high-hope people appear to be based on a "You win, I win" rather than a "I win, you lose" mentality. I return to this important topic in chapter 7.

One last issue related to the mine/thine equation pertains to how children compare themselves with other children. Although preschoolers engage in some of this social comparison, by age nine or ten it is well in place.[89] Furthermore, the outcomes of such social comparisons differ for preschoolers and children in their middle years. Preschoolers are pleased with their outcomes irrespective of how those outcomes compare with those of their peers. For children in their middle years, however, doing better or worse than one's peers results in positive or negative assessments of oneself.[90]

It is interesting to speculate about the resolution of this social comparison process for high-hope children. In a study of high-hope adults, we have found that they are not antagonistic and hostile in their interactions with others.[91] This indicates that high-hope adults navigate the social comparison process of middle childhood and approach others positively.

THROUGH THE AGES: THE ADOLESCENT YEARS

As adults, we often have vivid memories of our adolescent years (ages thirteen through eighteen). This may be because of our enhanced teenage capacities to record events mentally, or perhaps because the adolescent years are closer to our adult perspective. Of course, our recollections also reflect the fact that these wonder years were filled with happenings of import. The passing of the torch into adulthood occurs, in part, because adolescence provides the finishing touches on hopeful thinking begun in childhood. I explore two major hope-related issues of adolescence next — relationships and sexuality and solidifying one's identity.

Relationships and Sexuality

Sexual maturation imparts a new and expanded agenda for adolescent thinking. As the primary sex organs of adolescent girls and boys become functionally mature, the previous middle childhood patterns of relationships with one's peer group change. By the time of late adolescence, girl-boy pairing is typical.[92] Throughout this process, the adolescent is acquiring the societally scripted norms for sexual expression, and the underlying sexuality increasingly occurs in the context of exclusive relationships.[93] Although it would be an exaggeration to conclude that the thinking of adolescents revolves entirely around matters of sex, such thoughts certainly are prevalent.

More generally, an emerging goal for many adolescents is to secure a relationship in which their sexuality plays a principal part. Although boys and girls are attracted to one another for biological reasons to increase the probability of successful mating, the point in the present context is that this issue represents a large-scale testing ground for thinking about and obtaining two interrelated goals — relationships and sexual expression. These two goals preoccupy the thoughts of adolescents and young adults. Related to this issue, our data suggest that compared to low-hope people, high-hope persons describe themselves as being more effective in establishing such interpersonal relationships.[94]

Solidifying Personal Identity

The key issue for the adolescent, according to Erikson, is to form an identity rather than continue in a state of confusion about who and what one is, and where one is going. To resolve where one is psychologically, I would reason, means that the mind has a vision or template for the future. The initial stages of adolescence, however, may thrust teenagers into a confusing insight. Namely, they may find themselves acting and thinking differently in varying situations. Because of the importance of peers and the inconsistent roles demanded in varying groups, the young teenager may experience more contradiction than coherence. With time, however, late adolescence produces greater perceived stability across situations.[95]

The personal identity insights of late adolescence often relate to choosing a career (e.g., I'm going to be a [fill-in-the-blank]) and in this sense are related to work role-playing.[96] Unfortunately, the opportunity to practice adult work roles is limited, and the available jobs overwhelmingly are for minimum wages.[97]

The societal norms for career goals deemed appropriate and acceptable for adult women and men often are internalized by adolescents. Evidence gathered in the 1970s suggested that high school counselors steered men into occupations that required more education and less supervision and that paid better,[98] but discouraged female students from pursuing "male" career goals.[99] More recent studies, however, indicate that women have comparable educational aspirations and, in prestige of career and commitment to that career, women actually score higher.[100] Compared to men, high school women also are more likely to consider nontraditional careers, along with having interests in home-making activities.[101]

There is more to personal identity than job trajectory and gender-related occupational or career expectations. For example, the late adolescent with a coherent sense of personal identity can describe his political beliefs, appearance, physical and mental abilities, psychological characteristics, and preferences about a variety of matters. As such, a solid foundation of selfhood offers a good platform for goal-directed thinking. Personal coherence serves to clarify the important goals in one's life; in turn, having specified goals increases the probability that the adolescent has the necessary will- and way-related thoughts to pursue those goals. If you have teenagers, ask them to talk about themselves. This bewilders them at first, in part because their views of themselves and their world still are in flux. But stick with it, because they would like to make sense of themselves and their world, and such informal discussions can help that process. They are able to talk about some things and typically appreciate your interest if you are not too pushy. Don't expect miracles, however. Your teenager may prefer to talk about some things only with peers. Likewise, at times we parents may need to wait until our teenagers want to talk with us.

THROUGH THE AGES: FAST FORWARD REVIEW

This is a brief synopsis of the developmental contributors to hopeful thinking. We all went through certain steps in forming our thoughts about goal-related activities. The components of hopeful thinking, including the approximate times at which they begin, are in the chart on page 103. View this chart as a series of developmental steps; in a cumulative sense over the formative years these steps contribute to willpower and waypower thinking about the goals in one's life. If you have children, you can judge how they are doing in regard to the appropriate developmental steps for their ages. If your child needs further attention to one or more of these steps, you can attempt to help them by using the specific tips in chapter 5. Also, the Children's Hope Scale later in this chapter is a validated self-report instrument for measuring your child's hope.

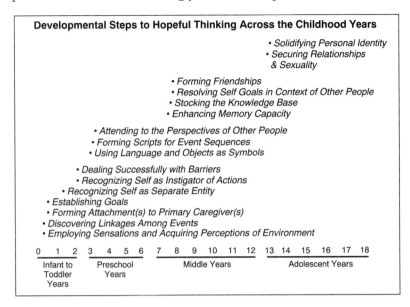

As you examine the steps in the chart, do you find that you still have difficulty with one or more of these issues? As an adult, if you have unresolved problems related to one or more of these steps, you now have clues as to why your score on the Hope Scale may be low. In other words, each of these steps contributes to your level of hopeful thinking as an adult. If you do have low hope, you can turn to chapter 6 for suggestions about raising it. Indeed, my subsequent hope-inducing tips relate to improvements you can make in one or more of the developmental steps.

THROUGH THE AGES
BACKWARDS: PARENTS
AND CHILDHOODS
REMEMBERED

Another way to understand the development of hope in childhood is to question adults about their recollections of this early period. Although one must be cautious in interpreting such retrospective data because of the ravages of selective memory, it is instructive to explore the views about parents held by low- and high-hope young adults as they reflect on their childhoods. These recollection data augment the inferences derived from the previously described research conducted on children during the various developmental periods.[102] Furthermore, note that hope is a future-oriented mindset based in part on our remembrance of the important people and events in the past. As a former client of mine put it, "Hope is my rope from the past to the future."[103] Or, in the intriguing words of existential philosopher Gabriel Marcel, hope is "a piercing through time . . . a kind of memory of the future."[104]

Characteristics of Mothers and Fathers

This section looks at the most common shared qualities of mothers and fathers as remembered by high-hope offspring. Several general characteristics often apply to both parents of high-hope people: First, such parents are energetic and determined as they think about future events. This sounds, obviously, like the willpower component of the hope model. Included in this set are such descriptors as "Was future oriented," "Accentuated the positive," "Really believed that things would work out," "Was a determined person," and "Seemed to have a lot of mental energy for whatever they wanted to do."

Second, both parents are capable of finding ways to get what they wanted. This is similar to the waypower component of the hope model. Included in the descriptors for this set of characteristics are "Was an enterprising person," "Was a flexible person," "Would channel efforts to effectively reach his or her goals," and "Was able to find ways to get what he or she wanted."

Perhaps as a derivative of these two goal-directed cognitions of parents, the high-hope offspring described their parents as being successful at what they did. This success was tied to a willingness to stand up for one's ideas. Independence and autonomy thus accompanied the offspring's perceptions of the parental success. Relatedly, these parents were portrayed as having high self-esteem in that they were happy and had positive images of themselves. As a final note, high-hope children reported that their parents took care of their health and exercised.

Overall, the parents of high-hope offspring are relatively successful, autonomous, and happy. In short, they appear to be models for hope in their children. Listen to the words of a prototypical high-hope adult named Spencer, as he describes his parents: "Oh, what can I say, but that they were good models. I mean, they were each pretty successful and busy in their lives, but they always seemed to have time for me. My dad's motto was 'Can do!' and my mom's motto was 'Can do, too!' This was our little family joke. They weren't fanatics or anything like that! Anyhow, they were upbeat people and could usually get what they wanted. Oh, but I shouldn't forget to mention that they both worked real hard . . . but they played and had fun also."

Lessons Taught to Children by Mothers and Fathers

Beyond the general modeling provided by the parents, were specific lessons taught by both parents? We have surveyed high-hope people about what they have learned from their parents. One important lesson such parents give is instructions about how to handle blockages. Specific teachings here include such phrases as "Taught me how to minimize the negative things that happened," "Taught me to think of things as challenges rather than failures," and "Said that when things got tough, I shouldn't worry so much." These lessons evidently sink in. Recall from chapter 2, for example, that high-hope people do appraise their goals in a positive, challengelike manner; this is especially so when they encounter obstacles.

Parents evidently imparted their when-things-get-tough lessons in a comforting and supportive manner. In particular, high-hope offspring especially endorsed the descriptors of "Was emotionally supportive," "Comforted me," and "Said he or she was proud of me." Furthermore, the parents were dependable and "Could be counted on if I had a problem." Lastly, the parents fostered autonomy and "Encouraged my taking responsibilities."

Together, these parental lessons suggest a consistent, supportive stance in which children are given tips about how to deal with difficulties. This latter lesson may be similar to what I described earlier in this chapter as mental immunization processes. Parents play an important role in this immunization process in that they recognize blockages inevitably occur in life, support their children during hard times, and give them ideas about how to handle the difficulties they encounter. Along with the support and mental immunizations, autonomy lessons may be the logical third leg to this hope-related trilogy delivered by both parents.

The lessons taught by parents of high-hope adults are captured in the words of Meg: "The biggest thing I remember about my parents is that they taught me to do things for myself. But, I always knew they were there for me if I got in a jam . . . which I did. If I did foul up something, they would talk with and not at me. 'Now, how could you have done this differently?' was my dad's favorite question. He and I would brainstorm about different ways I could approach the problem in the future. My parents let me make my own mistakes, but they were big on the learn by your mistakes rule — you know, don't make the same mistake twice, and all that. I did some pretty stupid things . . . and some pretty neat things, come to think of it. They were always there supporting me through all of it. That's what I remember."

Lessons Taught to Children Particularly by Mothers

We have found some lessons that high-hope offspring attribute mostly to their mothers. Before discussing these, I should emphasize we have not found lessons that high-hope offspring attribute mostly to their fathers. In other words, mothers have special lessons for their high-hope children. If fathers do begin to play more active roles in the child-rearing process in the future, they undoubtedly may impart special high-hope lessons. For now, however, the mothers fulfill this important role.

According to our high-hope adults, their mothers encouraged them to set goals. One particular message delivered by mothers to their daughters and sons was the importance of taking care of their health. Recall that high-hope parents took care of their own health.

Mothers also provided the greatest instruction in willpower and waypower thinking. One common willpower lesson is summarized in the phrase "Encouraged me." The waypower thoughts conveyed by mothers include such phrases as "Taught me the ways to achieve my goals," "Taught me how to problem solve," "Emphasized problem solving," and "Emphasized the importance of being flexible." Although high-hope adults describe both of their parents as having will- and way-related thinking, mothers are the ones remembered as expressly cultivating these thoughts.

High-hope adults also describe their mothers as the parents who delivered the discipline. Moms not only were depicted as giving the punishment but also were seen as doing this in a consistent fashion. Additionally, in such discipline-related interchanges, mothers were said to "Expect respect, but not total obedience." Likewise, in the process of decision making, mothers apparently fostered independence. For example, high-hope adults state that their mothers "Allowed me to make decisions about things whenever possible," and "Believed in letting me try things for myself." Not only did mothers establish boundaries for appropriate behavior but they also fostered autonomy in the offspring. These findings mirror what I said earlier in the chapter about the importance of providing limits and saying no to our toddlers while being supportive and instructive in regard to their goal pursuits when faced with obstacles.

High-hope adults report that their mothers used an open communication style for teaching these lessons. Particular items applied to mothers are "Listened to my ideas and thoughts," and "Talked with me, not at me." Thus, these mothers appear to use messages that are consistent in both content and manner of open communication.

Perhaps the basis for all these teachings is that mothers are perceived as the ones who spent the time and were interested in the children. Items such as "Spent time with me," and "Was interested in what was going on with me at school" exemplify this notion. One final statement is noteworthy from the perspective of high-hope adult offspring: "In her own way, she was a hero to me."

Janet, a high-hope adult, describes her mother in the following manner: "Mother really raised us kids. I don't know how she did it. It's not that my dad was a jerk, or anything, but he was not really there for us. It was Mom who always was around to give us support and kick our butts if need be. And we could talk about almost anything . . . and fight and make up. She was very open and loving. I wish there was some way I could repay her for everything she has given me. I only hope I can be half as good a mother as she was."

Mother, at least in the recollections of high-hope people in our research, is the primary mentor who cultivated the particular lessons related to a hopeful mindset.[105] She spent the time, listened and communicated well, and provided the goals and the accompanying willpower and waypower lessons. Mother also conveyed the boundary lessons involving discipline for things that should not be done, as well as the stimulation to take responsibilities and try things that may not have been tried previously. Related research on parenting styles reveals that clear standards and boundaries foster goal-directed thoughts in children, when delivered in the context of affection.[106] This point echoes my observations earlier in this chapter about attachment processes as part of the building blocks of hope.

MEASURING CHILDREN'S HOPE

As I reasoned in chapter 2 on the measurement of hope, assessment is important to help us understand this mindset. This is especially the case with children, where the foundations are being laid for hope in the later years. This section discusses our work in measuring children's hope.

Contrary to the measurement model of other researchers in which hopelessness has been the focus, we set out to develop and validate a self-report measure of children's hope based on the positive, goal-directed thoughts pertaining to willpower and waypower.[107] Our efforts resulted in the Children's Hope Scale, which can be given to children from ages eight through sixteen.[108] A child with reasonable reading skills can take the Children's Hope Scale with little or no adult interaction. If the child has difficulty reading, however, it is helpful to read the items aloud and to record the answers in the appropriate boxes.

Scoring and Norming

To score the Children's Hope Scale, merely add the scores on all six items (i.e., none of the time = 1; a little of the time = 2; some of the time = 3; a lot of the time = 4; most of the time = 5; all of the time = 6). Accordingly, total Children's Hope Scale scores can range from a low of 6 to a high of 36.

Children's Hope Scale

Directions: The six sentences below describe how children think about themselves and how they do things in general. Read each sentence carefully. For each sentence, please think about how you are in most situations. Place a check inside the circle that describes YOU the best. For example, place a check (√) in the circle (O) above "None of the time," if this describes you. Or, if you are this way "All of the time," check this circle. Please answer every question. There are no right or wrong answers.

1. I think I am doing pretty well.

O	O	O	O	O	O
None of the time	A little of the time	Some of the time	A lot of the time	Most of the time	All of the time

2. I can think of many ways to get the things in life that are most important to me.

O	O	O	O	O	O
None of the time	A little of the time	Some of the time	A lot of the time	Most of the time	All of the time

3. I am doing just as well as other kids my age.

O	O	O	O	O	O
None of the time	A little of the time	Some of the time	A lot of the time	Most of the time	All of the time

4. When I have a problem, I can come up with lots of ways to solve it.

O	O	O	O	O	O
None of the time	A little of the time	Some of the time	A lot of the time	Most of the time	All of the time

5. I think the things I have done in the past will help me in the future.

O	O	O	O	O	O
None of the time	A little of the time	Some of the time	A lot of the time	Most of the time	All of the time

6. Even when others want to quit, I know that I can find ways to solve the problem.

O	O	O	O	O	O
None of the time	A little of the time	Some of the time	A lot of the time	Most of the time	All of the time

---

In samples of several hundred children who have taken the Children's Hope Scale, the normal or average level of hope is 25. An average score suggests that the child thinks hopefully a lot of the time. As is true for adults, most children in middle childhood to adolescence are toward the hopeful end of the continuum.

If your child scores 29 or higher, this suggests a level of hope in the top 15 percent of scores. Children scoring in this high range apparently think they have both the willpower and the waypower to achieve their goals most of the time. If your child scored 21 or less, he is in the lower 15 percent of scores. Children scoring in this low range think they have willpower and waypower for their goals some of the time. Note, however, that even low-hope children are reporting some degree of will- and way-related thinking.

The willpower subscale score can be obtained by summing the three odd-numbered items, and the waypower subscale score is the sum of the three even-numbered items. As such, the willpower and waypower subscales each can range from a low score of 3 to a high of 18. Average willpower or waypower scores, are about 12.5, suggesting these separate thoughts are operative a lot of the time. Scores of more than 15 suggest that the child is in the top 15 percent in willpower or waypower; scores of less than 10 suggest the bottom 15 percent level of thoughts in the two components of hope.

Although most children evidence equal levels of willpower and waypower, some children may have relatively higher scores on one of the components. As a parent or teacher, such information can give clues about where to focus lessons in helping children to enhance their hopeful thinking. I discuss how to nurture children's willpower and waypower in chapter 5.

Gender Differences

As with the adult Hope Scale in chapter 2, we have yet to find any significant differences in the scores of girls and boys on the Children's Hope Scale. Although the goal-directed thoughts of young men and women in our society appear to be relatively equal in our research, the unanswered question is the actual comparability of the goals themselves. In other words, we do not know whether the equal hopeful thoughts reported by men and women are applied to similar goals. With this caveat in mind, however, at this point your child's score on the Children's Hope Scale is not gender-related.

Hope over Time

We have given the Children's Hope Scale over a one-month period and found that the scores appear to be quite stable (e.g., correlations of .7 to .8, where 1.0 reflects that children are obtaining the same scores both times). These findings parallel those for the adult Hope Scale and reflect the fact that, by middle childhood, one's goal-directed thoughts are relatively consistent across time.[109]

Rating Your Child's Hope

If you would like to rate your child's hope, you can use the Children's Hope Scale with a slight modification. Wherever the pronoun *I* appears in each of the six questions, just substitute *he* or *she* and then mark down your impression of your child using the six-point continuum. As with the Children's Hope Scale when taken by the child, the parents' rating version yields scores ranging from a low of 6 to a high of 36.

In two studies, we have found that the parents' ratings of their children's hope correlate modestly (correlations in range of .35 to .50) with the offspring's actual scores on the Children's Hope Scale. Camp counselors or teachers also can rate the child's hope, although the relationship is not as strong as that obtained by parents. This latter finding makes sense in that parents have a much better understanding of their children's hope-related thinking.

One potential exercise parents can try with the Children's Hope Scale is to compare their ratings with the actual self-reports of their children. Are you able to predict your child's hopeful thoughts accurately? Were you more or less accurate on the willpower or waypower items? On what particular items did you and your child agree or differ? Assuming that hopeful thinking is important, do you know your child in regard to this mindset? The chance to make this comparison may provide you with insights about your child's willpower and waypower thinking.

Before leaving this section on parental rating of hope, one last finding is worth mentioning. We have found that parents' actual hope is related positively to their ratings of hope in their offspring, and to a lesser extent, the offspring's actual scores on the Children's Hope Scale. In short, hopeful parents think that they have hopeful offspring. Assuming, as I have argued, that the hopeful mindset is learned, and assuming that the parent is a principal early source of such learning, it follows that parental hope begets offspring hope. Recall the recollection data, wherein high-hope adults remember that their parents also had high hope. I return to this issue of modeling in chapter 5 on nurturing hope in children. Another explanation for this relationship, however, does not emphasize that hope simply is transmitted from parent to child. It may be that a reciprocity of hope develops wherein the parent and offspring mutually influence each other.[110] This cuts both ways, of course. Parents and children who do not think they can attain their goals perpetuate low-hope mindsets in each other; conversely, children and parents who do think that they can attain their goals reinforce high-hope thoughts.

What Goes with Children's Hope

The guiding question in this section is the degree to which knowing a child's score on the Children's Hope Scale enables us to make predictions about that child's coping as measured by other scales commonly used with children. To answer such questions, we administered the Children's Hope Scale along with a variety of other instruments; our findings follow.

One prediction is that higher hope in children should relate to less reported depression. Our research supports this proposition.[111] As I have argued on theoretical grounds, we would be well advised to consider children's sense of unsuccessful goal-direction as the underlying factor that drives negative emotional states, including those such as profound depression. A related prediction is that the child's hope should predict perceived competencies in specific arenas, as well as an overall sense of competence and self-worth. In a test of this proposition, we found that scores on the Children's Hope Scale correlated positively and significantly with perceived competence in scholastics, social matters, athletics, physical appearance, and behavioral conduct, as well as global self-worth.[112]

To test the competency component of the competency-hope relationship in a different manner than through the child's own report, we used a behavioral checklist completed by parents. This checklist reports the parents' appraisals of the number of sports and nonsport activities, job performance, the number of organizations, the number of friends, contacts with friends, and performance in school.[113] The children's self-reported competence and their competence as rated by parents correlated positively and significantly with higher scores on the Children's Hope Scale.

Using an index of children's source of control, we hypothesized that higher hope should relate to greater internal as compared to external thoughts about the controlling forces in one's life. In support of this point, we have found that children who are internals (i.e., believe they control things in their lives) are higher in hope than externally controlled children.[114]

High-hope children, we reasoned, should evidence fewer problems in comparison to their low-hope counterparts. Using a checklist that parents completed about their children, higher hope children were judged as having fewer problems.[115]

In summary, the findings with the Children's Hope Scale reveal a pattern of predicted relationships with other measures similar to those produced by the adult Hope Scale. We have found that compared to lower-hope children those with higher hope report less depression and an elevated sense of self-worth, as well as an internal source of control; moreover, based on judgments made about them by their parents, higher-hope children manifest fewer problems in coping with stressors and more competence in general.

CONCLUDING THOUGHT: HOPE FOR THE STARTERS

Hope is rooted in experiences empowering children's goal-directed thinking. Important caregivers and the surrounding environment mold childhood hope. The first two years of life allow most children to have a base of hopeful thinking. Newborns are predisposed, I would submit, to acquire basic will- and way-related thoughts for their goals. Reflexes available at birth, including grasping, rooting, sucking, and orienting to stimulation, are hard-wired responses facilitating goal-directed action. The infant's mind also appears to be primed to develop goal-directed thinking.[116] In turn, adults have a protective, responsive reaction to newborns. Crying infants attract care. Survival of the offspring is a priority. For all of these reasons, our beginnings are likely to be hope inducing. This is the good news on the viability of starter hope. The bad news is that some infants do not subsist in hope-inducing environments; moreover, even if some hope is instilled, the events in the lives of some children and adults may erode it. I discuss these instances of the death of hope in the next chapter.

CHAPTER FOUR

The Death of Hope

While there's life, there's hope.

— Terence, *The Self-Tormentor*

INTRODUCTION

Sunday Morning, Coming Down

Staring at the bedroom wall, my head hurt. Must be the sinuses again. My mind was sluggish. Unfortunately, coffee didn't deliver its normal lift, so I leaned back in the kitchen chair and contemplated what was happening. Nothing captured my imagination. I plodded over to the bathroom medicine cabinet, looking for the aspirin. They tasted nasty as I had difficulty swallowing. Three hours later, lacking any relief, I was back on the unmade bed. The aspirin hadn't been the wonder promised in the ads. It was a struggle to think. The telephone rang, and running for it I hollered at the dog as I tripped over her. The phone stopped ringing, so I plopped down on the couch, dreading the hours that stretched ahead. Falling in and out of a nap, my headache worsened. I couldn't think of a thing I wanted to do. No, that's not true. I wanted to eat, but it was such a hassle to go out, and there wasn't anything in the house worth fixing. I stared out the window, frustrated at the snowy/rainy day keeping me inside. I was stuck. Nothing seemed worth doing. What about the work I brought home? Who was I kidding, I couldn't touch that stuff. Television? Surfing through the channels only made my head hurt more. Off with the TV, and on with the misery. Slow, slow . . . time going by. By the end of the day, much of my normal hope was gone.

This was how a Sunday went recently when my family was away. In the evening, I took out the State Hope Scale shown in chapter 2. Fumbling for a pencil, I completed the six items. Low on willpower and waypower thoughts, my score verified the obvious: I was low on state hope. A bad day.

A Preview of the Demise of Hope

Most of us have had days like my Sunday. They are part of life. Hope dies, at least for a day. For some of us, however, the death of hope extends into days, weeks, months, years, or a lifetime. This chapter traces how this happens. We explore the lives of children and adults who have descended into a psychological deathlike existence in which hope has been trampled. Some consider physical death as the solution for such hopelessness. Whether psychological or physical death occurs, however, one's hope plays a determining role. The following pages chart this dark journey involving the underside of hope.

PSYCHOLOGICAL DEATH

Definition

Psychological death results when goal-directed thinking diminishes to a point of vegetablelike indifference. In psychological death, one is left in a relatively enduring state of mental apathy toward life goals. Assuming the child or adult had some initial level of hopeful thinking, then the death of such thoughts transpires in a stepwise fashion. This demise of hope usually involves the move from hopeful thinking, to rage and despair at the blockage of goals, to the ending point of apathy about goals in general. Before tracing this progression, let's examine some of the factors that influence our sense of being blocked.

The Dimensions of Goal Blockages

Over the course of life, our goals often are blocked. Such goal blockage may vary along several important dimensions: First, blockages may occur for the more important goals. Impediments to more important goals elicit greater frustration because such goals reflect important aspects of our public and private identities. Right now, for example, I'm more perplexed by hindrances to writing a good book than by the obstacles in getting the roof on my house repaired.

Second, blockages that apply to more of our goals upset us to a greater degree. For example, in the past two years, I have undergone three surgeries, four hospital stays, and chronic pains that have precluded pursuing many of my goals involving family, work, recreation — even simple bodily functions. Although these health problems have not been life threatening, they have immobilized me on several fronts. I have been outraged at my situation.

Third, hindrances of a larger magnitude produce greater frustration. This follows because big impediments are harder to overcome than small ones. My recent health problems are examples of impediments that have loomed large. As in my experience, large impediments also may detract one from the pursuit of multiple and important goals. Other large impediments would include one's loss of a job or a divorce.

A fourth dimension of goal blockages pertains to whether they continue to thwart goal pursuits over time. Enduring blockages stymie our goal efforts not only now but also in the future. As a young boy, for example, I could not learn to identify colors correctly. Although I had been told I was color blind at an earlier age, for some reason this did not sink in until I was eight years old. I recall how mad I was because I would never be able to identify colors.

From Hope to Rage

Although my personal examples probably do not apply to you, they illustrate how the beginnings of psychological death involve blockage of important goals, as well as impediments that are large, recurring, and impacting on multiple goals. Our reactions to such profound goal blockages produce a form of anger called rage. Rage conveys the sense of strong anger; further, rage has a focus. In the present context, rage reflects the emotional reaction when we are thwarted in the pursuit of a strongly desired goal. Much of the rage we see in our society reflects the first stage of the demise of hope.[1] For example, because of the influences of such profound blockages as unemployment or prejudice, hope often is supplanted by rage.

Whether the rage progresses to despair and apathy, however, is related to the level of dispositional hope and the nature of the goal blockages. Higher-hope persons should be less likely to experience the sense of anger and rage at goal blockage because of their effective thinking patterns during such circumstances; they find alternative waypower, or perhaps different goals. Moreover, when higher-hope persons do experience this focused anger, they should resist moving to the apathy stage because of their sense of determination and capacity to solve the impediment to their goals. Nevertheless, even high-hope people are not impervious to the ravages of goal blockages. When goals remain blocked, rage should result for most people. Confronted with blocks to their goals, the rage may last for a few minutes, or it may span days, months and, in some cases, years.[2] On the positive side, rage suggests that people still are fighting with the impediments to their important goals. Given strong and enduring impediments, however, the rage eventually decreases and so too does the individual's hope.[3]

From Rage to Despair

We cannot maintain the aroused cognitive/emotional experience of rage indefinitely. If the blockages remain strong and continue in spite of willpower and waypower thinking, the rage may give way to a despair and cynicism about the previously desired goals. I am reminded here of the life of quiet desperation exemplified in the character of Willie Loman in *Death of a Salesman*.[4] Sensing that he would never make the big sale and reach the heights of business success about which he had dreamed, Willie was defeated.

Despair reflects a capitulation to the perceived blockages to one's important goals.[5] Unlike rage, wherein one still is grappling mentally with the blockage, despair reflects a depression-related state of immobilization. Although despair, like rage, involves some

investment in the seemingly unobtainable goal, despair signals more
of a resigned inaction. Rage is an active, outward expression of goal
blockage; despair is a passive, inward expression about the possible
insurmountable nature of that blockage.

From Despair to Apathy

Eventually, an extinction process may set in so that we no longer
consider the previously desired goals to be tenable. Despair thus
tumbles into apathy. Willpower and waypower thoughts about
goals abate. Additionally, thoughts about the goal itself evaporate.
Despairing people still think about the goal, but apathetic persons
no longer care. When goals in one or several important life arenas
have been abandoned, a more general apathy supplants the earlier
hopeful thinking.

The later stages of the death of hope are remarkably similar
to the diagnostic criteria for major depressive episodes. Barring an
organic basis for such depression,[6] the following nine markers indicate a major depressive episode.[7] To meet the diagnostic criteria, the
person needs to manifest at least five of the following:[8]

1. Diminished interest in activities most of the day, and over days.
2. Psychomotor restlessness or retardation.
3. Loss of energy and fatigue.
4. Inability to concentrate and focus.
5. Depressed mood most of the day, and over days.
6. Worthlessness feelings.
7. Thoughts of, or attempts at suicide.
8. Weight loss or gain.
9. Insomnia or hypersomnia.

As can be seen, this list contains markers that either directly
indicate a lack of willpower (items 1, 2, and 3) and waypower (item
4), or feelings (items 5 and 6), thoughts (item 7), and behaviors
(items 8 and 9) that are by-products of blocked or unsuccessful goal
pursuits. That is to say, the collapse of hopeful thinking undergirds
depression. As discussed in chapter 3, we repeatedly have found
strong relationships between lower hope in children and adults and

elevated levels of depression. For people who are truly depressed, a minimalist mental existence ensues; moreover, they abandon hopeful thinking involving the pursuit of important and difficult goals in favor of simplistic and unfulfilling ones. Next, I explore how this loss of hope happens in both children and adults.

PSYCHOLOGICAL DEATH: THE INFANT TO TODDLER YEARS

At the close of chapter 3, I suggested that the loss of hope may take two general forms: First are the newborns who, for a variety of reasons, do not have a care giving environment that facilitates hopeful thinking. On one hand, this is not a loss of hope because such infants never acquired it. On the other hand, these children are a loss to society because they could acquire hopeful thinking if they were given the appropriate environmental support. The second loss of hope involves children who do learn some level of hopeful thinking, but the events of their young lives serve to trample it.

Lindy: Hopes Lost from the Beginning

Lindy and her twin sister Letitia were born two months prematurely. Letitia did not survive more than a few days. Burdened with grief over the death of their daughter, parents Martha and J. R. donated enough money to have a rocking chair placed in each of the units where Letitia had stayed. These chairs reflected their attempt to keep Letitia's memory alive.

Lindy's first weeks were spent in several neonatal intensive care units. Eventually, Lindy was discharged and the parents turned to raising her and the other children. When Martha went back to the intensive care units, she was angered that the rocking chairs were nowhere in sight. At one hospital the chair had not been purchased, and at another it had been broken. These events intensified Martha's despair.

J. R. worked as a manual laborer and put in extended hours for minimal pay. Martha's hours also were long and engulfing. To earn extra money, she cared for neighborhood children. Further, Martha's aging and sick mother-in-law, as well as her unemployed sister, were living with the family. Adding to the load were four children ranging in age from four to seven. It was in this crowded environment that Lindy competed for her share of the attention. One wonders if she got it, however. She was constantly ill, which necessitated many visits for treatment. Understandably, the health care professionals sensed that Martha seemed preoccupied with other matters and was not attending to Lindy.

Cared for by her brothers and sisters and a mother who was overloaded, Lindy's environment for mental stimulation was impoverished.[9] Not surprisingly, her thinking did not develop at the normal rate. Physically small and shy, by age three she had only very simple language skills.

Neglect: Hopes That Never Sprouted

Lindy did not acquire the willpower and waypower thoughts that characterize children in more nurturing environments. There are, though, no villains in this story. Indeed, the parents were living under circumstances that would stretch all of us to the point of physical and mental exhaustion. In American and other societies throughout the world, this scenario is not unusual. Whatever the reasons for the inattention to newborns, however, the unfortunate bottom line is that they do not obtain basic instruction in hopeful thinking. The legacy of such neglect is that the essential hoping process never comes to life in these young minds.

The case history of Lindy echoes several points made in the previous chapter on the development of hope. In particular, hope in the first two years lies fallow if the child does not make a solid attachment to a primary caregiver. Without an attentive mentor, newborns are confused about how to identify and obtain their goals. Likewise, they are mentally malnourished and lack direction. For hope to flourish, parents need to spend significant amounts of time with their children. Indeed, our research reveals that low-hope adults report that their caregivers did not spend much time with them. Relatedly, low-hope adults report they were not supported, nurtured, or given guidance during their early years.[10]

Neglect entails the caretakers' failure to deliver one or more of the following to their children: shelter, clothing, food, education, medical care, protection, and supervision.[11] Of the total number of child abuse cases, statistics suggest that fully half are due to neglect.[12] Although the types of neglect are varied, the magnitude of this problem is severe. The caregivers of neglected children appear to be engulfed in survival activities such as maintaining food and shelter. Relatedly, physical neglect is more prevalent in families that are poor, chaotic, and socially isolated.[13] Further, half of these caregivers are single parents, and more than 40 percent are unemployed.[14]

Research on neglect shows an aftermath laden with a lack of hope for children. Neglected children are more passive and apathetic, and less persistent. Perhaps most noteworthy in the present context is that neglected children are less enthusiastic (similar to the willpower component) and flexible (similar to the waypower component).[15] Neglected children also experience more behavior and academic problems.[16] Even more disturbing, when compared to physically abused children, neglected children exhibit a variety of deficits, including delays in cognitive development and academic performance,[17] social isolation,[18] and lowered confidence in facing new tasks.[19] Thus, neglected children demonstrate more deficits than those abused.

Although impoverished economic circumstances increase the chances of child neglect, it can occur in the context of affluence. Money alone does not assure that the caregivers attend to their offspring, nor does it necessarily follow that purchased relationships such as nannies produce sufficient time and psychological investments in children. The primary caregiver must not only be there for large amounts of time but also attend to, interact with, and stimulate the developing infant. In other words, hopeful thinking may be stymied when the caregiver does not truly engage the infant. At the risk of invoking a cliché, this latter notion is captured in the phrase *spending quality time.*

Hope remains dormant when the time spent with the infant is not attentive, not interactive, and not evocative. Without a caregiver's presence, the world of events and inanimate objects does not make sense readily to the infant; with a nonattentive caregiver who is present, the infant also must struggle with the perception that people are unresponsive. Thus, from the perspective of the infant, the caregiver becomes part of the more general noncontingent and confusing environment.

Abuse: Hopes Intruded on by Caregivers

Another devastating pattern involves active caregiver abuses. Let's begin by examining those physical abuses where caregivers use excessive physical violence that injures children.[20] Similar to neglect, factors related to physical abuse include single-parent status,[21] unemployment and poverty,[22] and social isolation.[23]

The tragic paradox is that the abused infant is subjected to assaults from the very caregiver who provides human contact. Rather than being a source of stability and support, however, this caregiver's feedback shuts down the developing infant's goal-directed thinking. Instead of pursuing the developmental goals that should fill the first two years of life, therefore, the abused toddler must be preoccupied with avoiding the onslaught of the parent. In this atmosphere of terror, hopeful thinking, quite literally, lies beaten down.

Abuse by the primary caregiver also can shut down the baby's receptivity to people in general. Attachment and social support are shunned because the infant learns that interactions with people are aversive.[24] Unable to reach out to others, the abused toddler is isolated further, and the mental building blocks of hope remain in disarray. Not surprisingly, physically abused children also have difficulties with self-control,[25] and aggression toward other children.[26] Lastly, problems in general thinking processes appear. In particular, physically abused children evidence early deficits and delays in learning.[27] These children may be frozen in a perpetual state of hostility against others, and this continues into adulthood, where those abused as children perpetuate abuse onto others. Not only does physical abuse destroy hope in one generation but it also may do so across generations.

One other category of child abuse — sexual — warrants our attention. This type of abuse typically involves the adult's commission of sexual acts on a dependent child incapable of informed consent.[28] Such sexual abuse is perpetrated against children of all ages (including infants), with girls being victimized more than boys.[29]

The long-term repercussions of early sexual abuse in the first two years are not documented, although abuse occurring later in the developmental sequence has deleterious implications for behavior problems, aggression and anger,[30] and psychological disturbances such as depression.[31]

In summary, basic will- and way-related thinking are not fostered in neglected or abused babies. Even if such babies do acquire some semblance of goal-directed thinking, their problems are compounded because they do not get much instruction in how to deal with barriers to one's goals. Therefore, when such toddlers are confronted with obstacles, their thoughts center on the impassability of those barriers and the futility of applying effort to surmount them. For such a low-hope toddler, goal-directed thinking generally is eschewed; moreover, in the rare instances in which goals are entertained, the likelihood of being blocked looms over other thoughts. The end result is a toddler who sometimes is angry and aggressive, and at other times appears very passive and depressed. (See footnote 1 for a description of how people may move back and forth between the anger/rage and despair/apathy stages.)

Of course, neglect and abuse are not limited to the first two years of the child's life. These killers of hope may continue throughout the childhood years, leaving a wake of impoverished goal-directed thinking. On this point, at least three factors should influence the loss of hopeful thinking in later child and adult years: First, the earlier the neglect or abuse occurs in the developmental sequence, the more profound should be the repercussions on diminished willpower and waypower thoughts. Second, the more severe the neglect or abuse, the more marked should be the retardation of hopeful thinking. Third, the longer the neglect or abuse are inflicted on the child, the more intractable should be the resulting low-hope thought pattern.

PSYCHOLOGICAL DEATH: THE PRESCHOOL TO ADOLESCENT YEARS

The previous section described very young children who have little basis for hopeful thinking. Unfortunately, unless people and events intervene to change this pattern, the ensuing childhood years only continue this low-hope mode of thinking. On the other hand, some children acquire basic willpower and waypower thoughts only to have them disrupted by people and events encountered subsequently in childhood. This section explores the demise of hope in children from the ages of approximately three through eighteen (the preschool, middle, and adolescent years).

Tim: Angry Aftermath of Parental Loss

Tim's early childhood was very happy. He was outgoing, talkative, and playful during his toddler days. An only child, his parents enjoyed watching him grow up. Elementary school was a breeze, as Tim relished the new information and the interactions with the other children. He especially delighted in recounting his daily feats to his mother, Janice. Indeed, Janice and Tim had a specially close relationship.

When Tim came home from his second-grade class one day, he found his mother sitting on her bed, crying. "Mommie's sick, real sick," she said. The rest of this story is a downhill slide for mother and Tim. Janice had liver cancer that had metastasized, and she endured thirteen pain-filled months before dying. Tim saw his previously vital mother slip away. To protect Tim, Janice's illness and death never were discussed in the home. For similar reasons, the father decided not to take Tim to the graveside services. On the outside Tim tried to be brave. Inside, he was terrified. He ached with pain; his normal, talkative, and happy self turned angry, angry at not being able to understand what was happening. He was angry at his mom for dying, angry at his dad for being alive, and angry at losing his best friend. He also was angry at all the silence.

Tim became belligerent with his teachers and the other kids in the third grade. He spent hours sitting in the principal's office as punishment for fighting. His relationship with his dad, which previously had been loving, became very distant. Dad and Tim were both grieving, but neither would talk with the other. Tim became disinterested in his school work, and his grades deteriorated. His mood was unpredictable, varying between angry and sullen. No one seemed to make contact with him.

Loss through Parental Death

Tim's case history shows the potential detrimental effects of a loss on a child's thinking. Loss as an instigator of decreased hope usually involves the removal of a previously valued relationship from the child's life. The two most typical losses are the death of a parent and parental divorce. Before elaborating on these losses, however, let's see how these blockages can be understood on the dimensions described earlier in this chapter. Recall that the child's relationship with the primary caregiver is an ongoing, vital source of willpower and waypower toward goals. When the parent is gone, the resulting blockage involves goals that are both important (e.g., nurturance, learning, etc.) and varied (e.g., involving family, school, and other arenas). Moreover, this loss represents a blockage of large magnitude because the child has counted on the parent for help in goal-related activities. Lastly, given that the caregiver cannot be replaced, the loss endures over time.

As I have noted earlier, attachment is a key factor in the rise of hope. In the present context, I would add that attachment often is critical for the fall of hope. Tim obviously had a positive attachment to his mother, and her death became even more devastating because of this bond.[32] In addition, the lack of openness and communication between Tim and his father served to freeze Tim in bereavement. That he was not allowed to go to the graveside services only made matters worse by making it difficult for him to get closure on Janice's death and to proceed with the goals in his young life. Grieving children such as Tim may slide into a recurring pattern of aggressive, negativistic behavior.[33] Likewise, declines appear in concentration and general academic performance.[34]

Beyond the hope-diminishing effects occurring in the first several months after parental loss, research also reveals that the early loss of one's mother increases the probability of adult depression when subsequent life stressors are encountered.[35] In further analyses of these latter findings, G. W. Brown and colleagues have found that the lack of affectionate care following maternal loss predisposes such children to depression. These researchers also conclude that the major cognitive factor contributing to this vulnerability is a thought pattern of helplessness; that is, children no longer think they can reach their goals.[36] Evidently, the death of a primary caregiver diminishes the children's sense of nurturance, which in turn undermines their propensity to think hopefully about goals.

Loss through Divorce

The events surrounding divorce follow a typical sequence. At the time of separation, both the adults and children experience strong distress. There is hostility between the adults, mixed with depression and anxiety. Overextended and exhausted, the adults' parenting suffers. The amount and quality of time spent with the children diminishes during this period, especially for the mother, who most often is assigned custody. Mothers, by necessity, must gain or continue employment under these circumstances of reduced monetary resources. The other tasks related to running the household also typically fall on the mother, who must find the resources so that the children are supervised after school.[37] From the child's perspective, this represents a big change in mom.

The issues surrounding father's visits with children raise ambiguities for all involved. For the child, questions abound about how this new procedure is supposed to work. Sometimes, the children perceive that dad has abandoned them. Although there certainly are instances in which these arrangements work favorably, the more common result is that the visits are painful for everyone.[38] The stress for the children is compounded when parents take years to deal with the aftermath of the divorce.[39]

Longitudinal studies have followed the children of divorced parents to ascertain their short-term and long-term coping compared to children whose parents were not divorced. In the short-term, divorce causes a combination of anxiety and sadness in children. Oppositional behavior and an inability to focus attention are common, as are dependency and lapses into periods of inactivity.[40] Not surprisingly, school performance also suffers.[41] Relative to girls, boys appear to fare more poorly in that they are prone to behavior problems. These generally negative short-term effects of divorce are tempered if the remaining family unit is perceived by the child to be supportive, and if the father still is involved with the child.[42]

Five years after divorce, one study has shown that 40 percent of children still exhibit depression of some magnitude.[43] Perceived rejection by the father is a common problem, although this is not the sole cause of the depression. Good relationships with both the noncustodial and the custodial parents moderate the negative impact of divorces.

A ten-year follow-up of children after divorce has revealed that 50 percent still were experiencing a sense of strong rejection by their fathers. Half of the boys, and a quarter of the girls were described as doing poorly; in particular, they were experiencing depression and unhappiness with their relationships. These children of divorces also were less likely to attend and graduate from college, a fact that may be an unfortunate financial fallout of divorce. Lastly, many of the children still had vivid negative memories of the divorce, and the majority reported that it had adversely influenced their lives.[44]

One conclusion from the divorce literature is that the family unit is an exceedingly important factor in the maintenance or collapse of hope-related thinking. Divorce is devastating for most children in the short run, and in the long run troubling implications remain, especially in the area of relationships.[45] These findings highlight the importance of the child's attachment to caregivers. When this is severed, the child often continues to fantasize about the departed, noncustodial parent. The child apparently loses more than just a parent, however. In particular, children may abandon ideas about the viability of a relationship as a goal for themselves.[46] More generally, the child may lose a sense of nurturance that forms a basis for goal-directed thinking. This demise of the child's hope-related thoughts results in part because the divorced custodial caregiver often does not have the necessary time and energy to attend to the child.

Barry: Young Teenager Out of Control

Barry, a fourteen-year-old eighth-grader, was expelled from school for fighting and threatening the other students. He was awaiting sentencing on one count of aggravated assault; further, he had a pending shoplifting case. Wandering the streets in the late evening hours, Barry was approached by policemen in a squad car. He responded with a defiant and mocking sneer to the officers' questions.

When the police delivered Barry to his home in a middle-class neighborhood, his mother answered the doorbell. "Not again," said Barry's mom. "What now?"

By this time Barry's dad had stumbled into the front hallway, looking bewildered at this latest spectacle. "We have tried everything with him. Why don't you just take him?" was dad's bitter question.

"Can't do that, sir," said the officer, "because he is your responsibility." After the police left, the father threatened to discipline Barry. The rest of the family, including a twelve-year-old sister and ten-year-old brother, all began to shout. They had heard this all before; everyone knew no family rules were consistently applied. Chaos was the norm, and when things got especially bad, no one supported anyone else. Even when something good happened, there was no praise dispensed. It was every person for himself or herself.

"I'm leaving," said Barry.

"Go ahead," said Barry's younger brother.

Barry shot his brother the finger and walked out the front door into the night. He had no idea where he was going. The tears rolled down his face, unseen in the darkness.

A World without Boundaries, Consistency, and Support

Barry's case combines several forces that undermine hope in children of all ages. Because of the cumulative effects of these factors, the erosion of hopeful thinking becomes especially apparent in the teenage years. One such factor is a family where there are no rules or structure.[47] In this environment, the child does not learn what consequences to expect. In fact, either the rules may not be articulated, or if they are discussed, they change for no apparent reason. In our recollective research data on low-hope people, they report having relatively little structure or guidelines for appropriate and inappropriate behavior. This phenomenon is akin to the confusion that little children experience as they cry "No fair!" in regard to how a game is being played. This retort often reflects that the child does not understand the rules. In this ambiguous game set, just as in the larger game of life, it is difficult if not impossible to play, much less to reach a goal. Confusion is the enemy of hopeful thinking.

Beyond a family context in which the rules are vague, an equally impactful problem emerges when the rules are not consistently applied and enforced.[48] Consistency of rules across time and situations provides an order and predictability for the developing child. Without this consistency, the pursuit of goals is unpredictably interrupted.[49] Further, research suggests that discipline must be applied in a well-balanced fashion to clarify rule infractions. Otherwise, children are left without a real sense of the boundaries applying in their lives. Again, returning to our recollection data, we have found that low-hope people describe childhoods in which they were not consistently disciplined. Obviously, such discipline needs to be applied early and over the course of the childhood years so that it can have an effect in the teenage years. In the case of Barry, the rules and application of consequences were rarely or haphazardly applied, and he basically was defining his behavior irrespective of the family. Without consistent family discipline, aggressive and delinquent behavior are more likely.[50]

A final characteristic of Barry's case is the chaotic family where there is little or no support for each other. The lack of nurturance and the generally ineffective communication patterns in a family deprive children of a sense of accomplishment. Successful goal pursuit is met either with indifference, or perhaps hostility. In our research on low-hope persons, we have found that their families typically do not communicate support. Likewise, low-hope people describe their families as being uncaring and unresponsive to their needs and accomplishments.[51] Other researchers have suggested that nonnurturing, discord-filled families are destructive of hope-related thinking in children.[52]

If the adolescent also is unable to establish a sense of social support outside of the family, hopeful thinking is even more unlikely.[53] Barry may not have been adept at establishing social support among peers or teachers. If so, Barry's experience would mirror what research indicates — that the inability to make such extrafamilial contacts is associated with reduced hope-related thinking.[54]

Lacking rules, consistency in the application of those rules, as well as the support and communication with family and friends about accomplishments, the teenager is left in a bewildering maze of self-doubt, confusion, and anger. Unfortunately, many teenagers are the living proof of this recipe for the loss of hope.

Lucy: Word Imperfect and Withdrawal

Lucy was the middle child. Her older sister, a National Merit Scholar, had gone off to continue her academic accomplishments at a private college on the West Coast. A younger sister in the second grade had a bubbly personality that drew people to her. The mother was a successful senior partner in a large and prestigious law firm, and her father was a managing editor of an urban newspaper. Lucy's parents were verbally facile people who made their livings and based much of their worth on the exchange of words. Her sisters also evidenced this flare for language and words. Everyone fit in the family except Lucy.

Lucy sometimes wondered if she had been adopted because she did not share the family penchant for language. Reading, spelling, grammar, writing, and speaking were tortuous for her. During her earlier years, Lucy compensated through sports and art. This worked reasonably well, but as she got older it was apparent she could not excel in the courses based in reading and writing skills. Unfortunately, this included almost all courses.

By her junior year in high school, Lucy was struggling just to pass her courses. Her teachers and word-prolific parents pressed her to no avail. No longer in the supportive atmosphere of grade school and junior high, her frustration deepened and she began to withdraw further. She spent hours in her room, listening to music. Her parents were baffled at her unwillingness to try her best. Seventeen years old, Lucy felt powerless in a world dictated by written and spoken words.

Although Lucy might have been diagnosed as having some form of learning disability or language disorder,[55] this is not the point of her case history. The point is that her difficulties with words and language were magnified because she lived in a family and a society where these factors were valued greatly. Within this context, this young teenager's goals appeared beyond her reach. Her response was to shut down and avoid anything related to the aversive activities where she was judged to be lacking.

You Don't Have It, but You Should

Lucy's case is an example of a more general dilemma in which children find themselves blocked in the pursuit of valued goals. In our society, goals related to intellectual matters are highly rewarded. Other valued societal goals include physical attractiveness, athletic prowess and success, and social popularity and status. Children in the preschool to teenage years become increasingly adept at discerning these valued goals. Likewise, thoughts of what they don't have but should have often frequent the minds of children. For a child who lives where physical achievements are the only rewarded goals, the keenness of the competition and the lack of high ability are external and internal factors that may serve as roadblocks. Beyond the level of competition and ability, however, it is the child's interpretation of these factors as being insurmountable that provides a major impetus for the demise of hopeful thinking.

Consider the perceptions of a teenage girl taught by our society and the media that the standard of physical attractiveness is pivotal and further that being thin is the only real standard. This, of course, produces a cycle in which the young girl makes desperate attempts to emulate the slender models. Even if the girl is thin, she may think she is not. This mindset typifies eating disorders, in which the you're not thin enough, but you should be message becomes so ingrained that hopeful thinking is supplanted by anxious and despairing feelings.

Obviously, everyone cannot be a stellar student, incredibly attractive, an outstanding athlete, and popular. For the developing child, however, these standards often are held out as the only valued ones. Although children may want to exit the carousel in which they are confronted constantly with these goal standards, we parents and society more generally do not let them get off. Some children, listening carefully to these messages, become caught in a downward cycle of social comparison and conclude they are inferior to the idealized high standards. Research consistently reveals that forced comparison with superior standards demoralizes and depresses people, and children often are the unfortunate recipients in such invidious comparisons.[56]

PSYCHOLOGICAL DEATH: THE ADULT YEARS

Forces impacting on childhood hope may have repercussions that transcend the years. The childhood effects of neglect, abuse, loss, lack of family structure and support, and insufficient skills or talents leave their marks on the thinking patterns of adults. Such childhood events may portend adult inadequacies in goal-directed thinking. These aftereffects of the childhood death of hope are not the focus of the present section, however. Rather, let's look at the events that deflate an otherwise adequate level of hopeful thinking during the adult years. If the events covered in this section occur to adults in addition to those discussed for childhood, the demise of hopeful thinking should be even more profound.

David: What Will I Do without Her?

Married to Kitty for thirty-one years, David was a salesman who had worked the road for years. David needed considerable attention when he came home on the weekends, and he looked forward to the care that Kitty showered on him. Kitty, a fifty-two-year-old woman whose two children were out of the house, had gone back to college to finish her degree. She still found time for David, however, and he became her big kid. He would tell her about his week; she was the only person with whom he had any in-depth contact. David was strongly attached to Kitty, and depended on her for human contact. Kitty, on the other hand, was cultivating a widening set of friends through her college course work, and this was a threat to David. He was angry and jealous of her new life, and she was somewhat guilty about not attending totally to his needs.

While she was driving home from her afternoon class, a truck broadsided Kitty's car at an intersection. By the time David got to the hospital, Kitty had died from massive head injuries. David sobbed uncontrollably, and his grieving continued for months. He was lost without Kitty and thought about her constantly. He could not imagine life without her. This void could not be filled in spite of the efforts of their children and friends.

David described the unfairness of this accident and his grief as if it had happened a week earlier. In fact, it had been twenty-one years since Kitty's death, and David was a seventy-three-year-old man frozen in a time capsule of suffering and remorse. When asked about the possibility of dating other women, David bristled and pledged that there was only one woman for him. Asked about his future, David said he had none. Psychologically, he died when his wife did.

Connections Lost

The death of one's spouse is one of the most devastatingly stressful events for the widow or widower.[57] Data even suggest that the mortality rate soars in the first six months after the death of a spouse.[58] The prognosis for many survivers is a return to the level of hope-related thinking characteristic for them before the death of the spouse.[59] The focus here is on those others who continue to wallow and suffer for years because of spousal loss.

David gives us a glimpse of how a loss can permanently devastate subsequent goal-directed thinking. For one thing, the destabilizing effect of spousal loss is more marked if the death is seen as unexpected and unfair, such as an accident.[60] David's perception of the injustice of the loss kept the psychological wounds open. Additionally, if the widowed person had a dependent, enmeshed relationship, the death of the spouse may produce long-term decreases in hopeful thinking.[61] In David's case, his existence centered around Kitty, and he could not engage himself with other people after her loss. Such inability to make human contact is yet another factor contributing to sustained low hope.[62] In short, the death of a spouse is more likely to kill hope in the surviving spouse when this human connection is strongly established, broken unexpectedly, and yields a survivor incapable of reconnecting with other people.[63]

When shattered, the sense of interconnection between two people provides a serious and sometimes enduring threat to the survivor's identity.[64] Separation and divorce are other events that may cause such hope reduction.[65] On this point, research has shown that divorced persons score lower on the Hope Scale.[66]

Divorce obviously is a stressful event, and the downturn in hopeful thinking is made more enduring by the presence of several factors: First, most people see themselves as being less likely to get divorced than the average person; moreover, people believe they will work much harder than others to make their marriages successful.[67] This perception, known as *unique invulnerability*,[68] eventually must confront the fact that approximately half of the people who marry divorce at some point in their lives.[69] The psychological devastation of divorce should be magnified by the degree to which persons previously believed it wouldn't happen to them. Indeed, for persons who have not anticipated the divorce or breakup, the loss of hope-related thoughts is even more marked.[70]

Second, if the person is the one left, rather than the one leaving, there are more short- and long-term decreases in hope-related attitudes and beliefs.[71] In the words of country singer Robert Earl Keen, Jr., "Leavin' never hurts as much as bein' left behind."

Third, when the divorce places one partner in a particularly burdened financial position and enhances the pressures of child care and general daily living, then hopeful thinking may decline in both the short term and long term.[72] This effect appears more commonly for women because they typically are responsible for child care and have fewer financial resources than men. My conclusion is buttressed by the observation that women are paid less than men in American society and by the disgraceful reality that nonpayment of child support is widespread.

For all of these reasons, divorce may portend serious threats to the process of hopeful thinking. I do not question the fact that in many instances, divorce is appropriate, and that it may produce positive results in peoples' lives. Rather, my point is that we are inherently social creatures, and the loss of social connections often damages hopeful thinking.

Although social connections are enormously important in forming one's identity, our identities also may be tied very strongly to work or career. Persons who lose their jobs are left questioning life goals and purposes.[73] Having spent much of one's adult life cultivating a record of achievement, the termination of employment, whether for capricious or valid reasons, can have traumatic effects on hope. Related to this point, for each 1 percent increase in the unemployment rate nationally, there may be as much as a 4 percent increase in first-time admissions to mental health facilities.[74] People who love their work are truly fortunate, unless they are disconnected from that work. Then, such people may plummet into a prolonged state of lowered hope.

Lisa: Only and Lonely

"I can't do this college thing," said Lisa.

"You mean the schoolwork?" I asked.

"No, no . . . it's not that. I can't talk with people. Can't do all the social stuff. You know, the dormitory parties for freshmen, the sorority rush, the dating scene . . . or just talking to the others in my classes. In fact, I'm a mess when I'm around people."

"So, what do you do?" I was trying to find a little more about her behavior before exploring her thoughts.

"Stay in my dorm room. My roommate calls me 'Lisa the loner.'" Lisa looked hurt.

"How does that make you feel?"

"Sad, but it's the truth. I am a real loner. Why, I'm probably the only girl in my dorm who is like this." Lisa was fidgeting, avoiding eye contact. It was excruciating for her to talk.

"What do you mean when you say you are the only one like this?"

"I'm just not like the others. It's real frustrating. What can I do?"

Lisa sat quietly for much of the remaining time in our first session. If I didn't speak, she didn't either. The silences were awkward. At the end of the session, I doubted she would come back. She didn't, and yet another connection was not made in Lisa's life.

Connections Never Made

I believe that Lisa exhibited a classic case of loneliness. Loneliness is characterized by a deficiency in social relationships, a subjective sense of being unable to make contact or connection with people, and an unhappiness with this state.[75] Lonely people experience their environments as being filled with people with whom they cannot make this important human connection.

Lisa found herself in an environment filled with other first-year college students, but this only heightened her frustration and sadness at not being able to talk with any of them. New situations such as the beginning of college can be especially difficult, with lonely persons thinking they are very different and worse off than other people.[76] I call this perception *unique vulnerability* to signify the person's belief that he is not coping well and that everyone else is. Note that Lisa described her plight as if she were the only one with difficulty in making contact. In point of fact, college dormitories are filled with beginning students experiencing the loneliness of being away from home for the first time; moreover, many of these students also are uncomfortable in meeting large numbers of new people. Unfortunately, the lonely person does not know this and may become all the more immobilized in her thinking and actions because of the shutdown in communication with others.

In our research, we have found that lower-hope people report being more lonely.[77] Low-hope and high-loneliness people report that they have not experienced a nurturing and warm relationship with their parents; moreover, higher loneliness has been found in adults whose parents divorced when they were young.[78] Loneliness also appears to follow losses involving the death of a spouse, divorce, and separation.[79] These findings again highlight the importance of early and later attachments. For the lonely adult, however, the difficulty in establishing these later attachments precipitates and sustains less hopeful thinking.

When faced with stressors in life, some people are unable to talk with others. They literally keep things bottled up and have no one with whom they can share. Research has shown consistently that persons who cannot confide their problems suffer psychological consequences that mirror low-hope thinking.[80] Such people appear to remain mentally stuck at the stressful blockage they have encountered. Relatedly, we have found that low-hope people do not perceive they have confidants with whom they can speak about personal matters.[81]

In psychology over the last decade, the importance of social support has received enormous attention. The earliest results from this research suggested that people who do not have friends or relatives whom they can call on in problem situations are likely to suffer psychological symptoms that indicate a loss of hopeful thinking. Although the importance of lacking a social support network should not be underestimated, more recent research suggests the person's perception or interpretation is even more critical. In other words, even if you have friends or relatives with whom you can interact during stressful events, what matters most is whether you think you can really talk to and make connections with these sources of potential support.[82] People who think they cannot connect with other people not only may have lost one of the major goals in life but also cannot benefit from such interpersonal contact in the face of ongoing life stressors.

Whether it is conceptualized under the rubric of loneliness, inability to confide in another, or lack of perceived social support, the conclusion is the same: The unconnected person is at risk for losing hope.

Kelly: Rape of a Mind

"I can remember it very clearly," said Kelly. "As I got off the elevator in the basement parking garage of our building, I felt this sharp object in my back. I started to turn around, but he told me to keep looking ahead. His voice was low and sounded mean. He pushed me over to a corner of the parking lot where a van was parked. He shoved me in the back and closed the door. I tried to scream, but he put a knife to my neck. Then my worst nightmare began."

"How do you mean?" I asked.

"Oh, well, the physical part was so demeaning. He did everything to me, always sticking the knife on me. I felt helpless. But the worst part was the whole verbal thing about me 'wanting it,' and being a 'prick teaser.' After about an hour, he tied me up, gagged and blindfolded me, and drove somewhere. I thought he was going to kill me. Instead, when we stopped, he came into the back of the van and raped me again and again. He told me to get dressed. More driving and then the van stopped."

"What happened?"

"Well, he told me that if I said anything about this to anyone, he would come and get me for good. He said that he knew all about me and could find me whenever he wanted. At that point it was late at night, and he opened the back of the van. Pushing me to the pavement, he threw my purse at me and closed the door. I noticed I was in the side alley of my apartment building, so he did know where I lived! I ran to the building and locked myself inside my apartment. Sitting on the shower floor, I ran the water over my body for hours trying to get any remnant of him off me."

Kelly was a fifty-four-year old woman who was a member of a therapy group when I heard this story. This rape incident had occurred some fifteen years earlier, and she had been affected profoundly by it. Although Kelly had told a girlfriend about the trauma, she basically had been in a state of terror and despair for years. She was having nightmares about it, and although she knew the threat of this rapist returning for her was unlikely, she was frightened and anxious whenever she when out. She felt imprisoned in her apartment, even though she long since had changed her place of residence. On that day over a decade ago she had lost control of her life, and she wanted it back.

Victimization

After writing about this former case, I opened our college town newspaper. Traumas were the standard fare of the headlines. Local and distant members of humankind had been subjected to natural disasters stemming from floods, earthquakes, and tornadoes; killings related to interpersonal disputes between two people and two nations; accidents involving automobiles, airplanes, bicycles, and buses; serious illnesses such as cancer and AIDS; and, physical assaults motivated by robbery or no apparent reason at all. It had been a horrendous day for many people. These traumatic events assaulted not only the bodies of the victims but their minds also.

The prevalence of trauma has added a four-letter acronym to our lexicon. The diagnosis of PTSD for post-traumatic stress disorder applies to thousands of people, including Kelly. Unlike the stress that results from more common relationship, health, and financial difficulties, PTSD is triggered by extreme events (e.g., a threat to the life of oneself or a loved one) that elicit profound helplessness and fear. Additional symptoms lasting a month or longer include hypervigilance, avoidance of situations associated with the original trauma, and vivid reexperiencing of the stressful event.[83]

One point to be emphasized about PTSD is that, regardless of the nature of the trauma, it leaves mental scars. Indeed, the mind of the person with PTSD is, in the most profound sense, the victim of the trauma. Persons with PTSD no longer think with willpower and waypower for their goals. Instead, their minds often are frozen by the traumatizing event. The trauma, as relived in the mind, becomes an all-encompassing blockage. In terms of the dimensions of blockage, the traumatizing event for the person with PTSD is large in magnitude (this is so by definition); the trauma serves to block goal-directed thinking for important life goals; it incapacitates the person across a range of goals; and, it endures over time. With all four dimensions of goal-blockage operative, one can see how such victimization of the mind epitomizes the death of hopeful thinking.[84]

At times, as in the case of Kelly, there are no physical traces of the traumatizing events, but the event becomes a roadblock etched in the mind. In some instances, physical injuries remind the victim constantly of the traumatizing event. Related research shows that people experiencing profound psychological problems associated with their physical injuries are low in hope.[85] Although traumas dampen hope for most people in the short run, for persons with PTSD, there are long-term repercussions. Minds victimized for years by such traumas are drained of hope.

Bob: Dead Wood

"When I first started teaching, I was a ball of fire. Fresh out of college, I thought I could make a difference. I had seen so many high school teachers who were out of gas, tired, and I was adamant that I wouldn't be like them."

I was seeing Bob, a forty-seven-year-old high school geography teacher. He came for this session after his daily schedule at the high school was finished at 5:00 P.M. "What happened to you?" I asked.

"Damned if I haven't turned into the very thing that I despise. I'm like a zombie. All my enthusiasm and high ideals are gone. I'm exhausted. I have classes that are much too large. I teach six sections two days a week, and four sections three days a week. Maybe if I had smaller classes . . . No, that isn't the only thing. The kids don't want to learn geography. Hell, I spend most of my time trying to keep order and discipline so that I can be heard. It's not the way I thought it would be. Worst of all, I don't even like the kids any more. They are just sort of noisy, self-centered, spoiled brats. I can't believe I feel this way."

"So, what are you going to do?" I asked.

"Oh, well, I'll keep at it. Have to. But I'm not really there when I teach. I'm just putting in time until I retire. I hate to say it, but I've turned into the proverbial dead wood. Who wouldn't? You should see what I have to go through each day."

Burnout

Bob was tired mentally and physically. His job, like those of many people who work in constant contact with people, had turned into distasteful drudgery. It is important to highlight the fact that Bob was not always this way, however. In the beginning, he was filled with hopeful thoughts. One cannot burn out, therefore, without previously having been on fire.[86]

Psychologist Christina Maslach defines burnout as a "syndrome of emotional exhaustion, depersonalization, and reduced personal accomplishment that can occur among people who do 'people work' of some kind."[87] Emotional exhaustion, which appears to be the most robust of the three markers of burnout, reflects a sense of being overextended and drained by one's work.[88] Depersonalization involves a cynical and negative view about one's clients, including distancing and a loss of concern. The lack of personal accomplishment reflects a sense of lowered competency and productivity.

Because of their cynicism and negative demeanor in regard to work and colleagues, it is tempting to dismiss those suffering from burnout as a people who have been bitter and mentally exhausted throughout their lives. Nothing could be farther from the truth. In the beginning, they often are the idealistic ones drawn to the helping professions (e.g., mental health workers, teachers, social workers, physicians, nurses, etc.). Such people also start their careers with lofty goals. They throw themselves into their careers but, especially if they are working in bureaucracies, they typically encounter roadblocks to their goals. They experience more and more failure. Such failure can produce a perceived lack of personal accomplishment, which is one of the markers of burnout; the emotional exhaustion and the sense of depersonalization follow over time.

One of the primary researchers on the topic of burnout, Ayala Pines, has suggested that burnout can be understood as an instance in which one's important work-related goals are frustrated by blocking circumstances. For example, the goal of most teachers is to convey information and stimulate thinking, but the large class sizes and need to attend constantly to discipline may block this goal. Therefore, it is not just stress, but also the goal blockages that actually cause burnout.[89]

Nurses should be especially vulnerable to burnout. Researchers have studied the mindsets of nurses to test the proposition that burnout could be understood as a manifestation of the loss of hope.[90] Those nurses experiencing the least hope as measured by the Hope Scale also had the highest emotional exhaustion and depersonalization and the lowest sense of accomplishment on the Maslach Burnout Inventory.[91] Furthermore, results revealed that, for those who had been nurses for a long time, the lack of a sense of accomplishment especially predicted low hope. Burning out, therefore, reflects our repeated perception that we have been unable to reach important goals. Burnout is the extinguishing of hope.

Diane: Alcoholic Nonanonymous

It all started in high school. Diane drank a beer or two with the guys. It made her feel less anxious and seemed innocent enough. She never thought much about it until college, where there was plenty of beer and other liquor at the various social functions. Nervous at the prospect of these events anyway, Diane found that the social drinking was the norm and made these occasions more bearable. She wasn't certain about what to say at parties, but when fortified with a glass of gin (her drink of preference by junior year), she at least could talk.

In her senior year Diane met Ed at one of these parties. Their relationship grew, and Diane was forced to go to more parties because Ed was the president of his fraternity. Increasingly, she had her favorite drink of gin neat prior to going out. She was a very beautiful girl, and her life centered around her relationship with Ed, who was quite a catch according to her roommates.

Married after graduation, Diane was called on to serve as the hostess for Ed's parties. He was on the corporate fast-track, and Diane was along for the exciting ride. The problem was that she was drinking more to fortify herself for these social functions. By their third year of marriage, Diane was consuming at least a fifth a day. Over time, she needed larger quantities of booze to numb her for the endless socializing.

When Ed confronted her about the excessive drinking, Diane protested that she could quit. But she couldn't. She behaved more and more erratically, and her appearance deteriorated. Eventually, Diane informed Ed of the real problem — she was an alcoholic. The booze was her problem. For two more years, Diane excused her behavior by telling Ed and anyone else who would listen that she was an alcoholic. Continuing to self-medicate her deepening despair with liquor, Diane believed that an alcoholic deserved some pity. At the very least, she reasoned that Ed should cut her some slack. He did. He packed his bags and left.

Purchasing Faustian Bargains

Goethe's famous literary figure of Faust tried to make a bargain with the devil. I believe that people make similar, ill-advised deals when they advocate psychological symptoms and labels as excuses for not performing well. In the beginning stages of this Faustian bargain, the process seems relatively benign.[92] Diane, for example, worried about how she would be able to cope with social situations effectively, and her initial strategy was to have a few drinks. This was a socially acceptable behavior; should Diane make a faux pas, she could invoke a the-booze-made-me-do-it excuse. In moderation, this worked but over time Diane slowly increased her alcohol consumption. The gin became a part of her life, so much so that she eventually embraced the label of alcoholic. At this point, she no longer harbored the notion that she had control of the gin; it had control of her. (My guess is that the etymology of the phrase *demon rum* derives from similar tales in which the rum takes over and supposedly drives the abnormal behavior of imbibers.)

This scenario is not a hypothetical one. My colleague, Ray Higgins, has conducted studies suggesting that heavy social drinkers increase their consumption of alcohol when doing so can serve as an excuse for potentially poor performance in an upcoming arena.[93] Excuses that people make in anticipation of an important upcoming performance, especially when one is uncertain about the outcome, are extremely seductive. This is contrary to the usual notion that an excuse is something we say to ourselves and others only after we have had a failure experience. That is to say, people may begin to give their excuse in anticipation of not doing well.[94] Because of the seductiveness of this process, people may use their excuse more over time. This strategic use of excuses in anticipation of upcoming failure-inducing situations has been called *self-handicapping*, signifying that the protagonist actively embraces the impediment.[95] A growing literature suggests that people use all types of self-handicaps, including procrastination and lack of effort, as well as psychological symptoms such as hypochondriasis (reporting of physical complaints) and anxiety. The demise of hopeful thinking occurs over time as such self-handicapping people increasingly seek the cover of the anticipatory excuse at the expense of the important goals in their lives.

This analysis is not meant to deny the seriousness or problematic nature of mental health problems including alcoholism and drug addictions. Rather, my point is that a self-handicapping cycle may be reinforced at several levels. First, the new self-handicappers may use the excuse for the first time and find that it protects their underlying competence. Diane, for example, still could harbor the belief that she was socially competent if she made social errors while drunk. Friends may even lend support and sympathy to such handicaps. Among college students, it is "Yeah, you were really wasted. It's OK."

If chronic self-handicapping persons eventually seek the help of a mental health professional, they receive a label (diagnosis) for the difficulty and may become even more wed to the now reified problem. A self-fulfilling prophecy may set in; the person and those around him expect the label to be confirmed in behavior (whether it is depression, alcoholism, etc.). Once diagnosed, less may be expected of the person (After all, Diane is an alcoholic). In fact, such labeling can get the person out of trouble should they break the law (e.g., alcoholism is a recognized extenuating circumstance by jurors). Both the intrinsic and societal reinforcing properties of adopting the label work together to increase the display of the accompanying symptoms. The endpoint of this Faustian bargain is that the person is living a life in which the symptoms and label are reaffirmed, and there is little room for normal thinking and behavior. Unfortunately, such a life precludes any thoughts about meaningful pursuit of important goals. Indeed, hopeful thinking is largely abandoned.[96]

Two Cases of Racism: 1952 and 1969

It must have been sometime in the summer of 1952. I was standing outside the window of the dime store in downtown Council Bluffs, Iowa, looking at the incredibly tempting jars of candy, when I noticed another kid about my age also eyeing the treats. I remember asking him if he wanted some. He nodded his head.

"Let's go in and buy some," I suggested to my new companion.

"Can't," he said, backing away.

"Why not?" I asked.

"My people can't go in there," he replied.

He was African-American. Looking back, this was my first inkling that goals were not equally available to all people.

Seventeen years later, in 1969, I was a second-year graduate student, getting ready to go on a peace march protesting the Vietnam War. Starting down Westend Boulevard toward downtown Nashville, Tennessee, our group was growing in numbers. After walking with us for a few blocks, one of these late joiners peeled off as we approached a group of police.

"Why are you leaving?" I hollered.

"I'd be the first one arrested," he answered.

He was Hispanic, and he knew that while we Anglos could, he could not protest with relative impunity from the authorities. Again, the message was that some goals are not as accessible to some people because of their race. Déjà vu 1952.

Discrimination, Prejudice, and Isms

Discrimination, when applied to people, means that we make differential judgments about persons based on some salient characteristic. Race, gender, and age are examples of such discrimination. The importance of discrimination made along these dimensions is that people may have prejudicial thoughts attached to the poles of the continua (i.e., black versus white, male versus female, young versus old). As such, the mental act of discrimination is unbiased, but it may be followed by biased judgments that people in power make about what goals are deemed appropriate for the person who is the target of the prejudice. In other words, because of prejudice the playing field is not level when it comes to goals. Discrimination, however, is neutral. When it is followed by prejudice, the process becomes an exercise of power so that one targeted group is not allowed access to the valued goals. By definition, therefore, discrimination with prejudice is antithetical to the furtherance of hopeful thinking among those who are the target of the prejudice. This is not to suggest that members of the targeted group cannot sustain hopeful thinking, but rather that the societal forces are aimed at undermining such thinking (sometimes called *uppity* thinking).

My first academic exposure to this topic occurred when I read *Black Rage* by William Grier and Price Cobbs.[97] Their thesis is that the history of prejudice against African-Americans had created a profound mistrust, suspiciousness, and anger at the larger American society. For the Caucasian, this anger often is interpreted as raw delusional paranoia. In the present context, however, such anger to broad-scale goal blockage is not delusional; it is an expected response for any person or group against whom there is strong, long-standing, and continuing prejudice.[98]

Consider the following incident recounted by Bill, a middle-aged, successful businessman being seen in psychotherapy. One of his major problems was the anger he was feeling about his treatment as an African-American. Bill had taken a white client to an expensive restaurant in New York City. When he greeted the maitre d', the man ignored Bill and asked the white guest if they had reservations. After the meal, the waiter put Bill's charge card and the check in front of the client. Furious, Bill nevertheless completed the paperwork and continued to talk as if nothing had happened. Walking outside, he shook hands with his client on the major deal they had struck. This should have been a positive moment portending a fat commission and possible promotion for Bill. Instead, he was filled with rage as he saw the white client immediately hail a cab, while he stood at the curb unable to accomplish the same task.[99]

Knowing that it is not socially appropriate to express such anger and that it may be dangerous to do so, the African-American may purposefully appear to be calm and collected.[100] Kenneth Hardy, an African-American family therapist puts it this way, "There is really no great mystery to how the game must be played: don't be too assertive, defer to the white man, suppress your own will, remember that the white man's needs are always more important than your own. Don't display intense emotions, especially anger. Don't make yourself scary to whites. Above all, know your place."[101]

In chapter 2, I presented the two lists of characteristics deemed acceptable for women and men. Although these lists are of equal length, there are less acceptable roles for women. If women try to venture into roles not traditionally seen as female, they encounter prejudice and resistance.[102] As one example, consider work. Beginning with the process of obtaining a job, when qualifications are equal, research shows that women are less likely to be interviewed.[103] Further, women are especially unlikely to be hired when the evaluators hold gender-role stereotypes, and when the qualifications of the applicants are ambiguous. I would call this *access prejudice*.[104] Once hired, women also experience *treatment prejudice*.[105] They are paid less than men, and this disparity remains when one controls for counterexplanations (e.g., percentage of time working, length of time working, type of occupation, etc.).[106] Inherent in these data is the glass ceiling that appears to limit the advancement of female employees.

Taking racism and sexism together, I believe that in terms of goal blockage prejudice decreases hopeful thinking for the targeted members of these groups. How can this assertion square with our findings that there generally are no differences in Hope Scale scores between racial groups and between the genders (see chapter 2)? Likewise, how can my assertion about the death of hope as a function of prejudice hold when recent studies have found no differences in self-esteem between racial groups and between the genders?[107] The answer to this puzzle is that the person who is the focus of prejudice probably does not entertain the same goals as people who are not targets of prejudice. As I reasoned in chapter 2, for persons impacted by prejudice, the end result may be that they settle for lower goals and report their willpower and waypower as being anchored to those goals. In such instances, I would expect that the members of the targeted groups may not move into the despair and apathy stages, but they may still have considerable anger in those instances in which they think about the inequity of their goals. In the degree to which increasing proportions of persons who are the target of prejudice are unwilling to settle for inferior goals, there is profound rage and despair if the barriers to the desired goals are not lifted. Further, those individuals most concerned about equal goals experience the biggest decrease in hopeful thinking if there are not forthcoming changes.

There may be other isms worthy of comment in regard to the demise of hope, but I would like to make some brief remarks about only one other — ageism. Although you may or may not be a member of one of the aforementioned targets of prejudice (e.g., an African-American or female), there is one group that we all usually join — the elderly. The march of time brings with it societal restrictions as to what is expected and allowed for older people. Whether it is employment, interpersonal behaviors, or health-related activities, the older person is strongly encouraged not to think about or undertake certain goals. I am reminded of a story about a 100-year-old man who went to his physician for a pain in his right knee when he went walking. When the physician lectured him on the fact that he shouldn't be exercising so much given his age, the old man snapped back, "My left knee is 100-years-old too, and it doesn't hurt." Many older people, however, do not have the spunk of this centenarian, and their hopeful thoughts are thwarted unnecessarily. In these cases, the mind expires before the body.[108]

Crowding: The Big Squeeze

At the societal level, any of a myriad of blockages may impede our pursuit of goals. Such blockages may include the seemingly minor events of being cut off in traffic and having to wait in line, to the more major loss of a job and poor living conditions. We increasingly hear of people who are enraged about something in their lives, and manifest their anger in overt acts of aggression against property and persons. A common force amplifies this anger and aggression — human crowding. Crowding is a subjective experience in which we have less space than we would like.[109]

The increasingly crowded conditions under which people live produce stress.[110] Why? Given that there are shared and oftentimes limited numbers of reachable goals, crowding serves as an inherent impedance for many people. With increased numbers of people, there is anger and frustration because others are perceived as "getting in our way."[111] The critical anger-inducing mechanism of crowding, according to psychologist Judith Rodin and her colleagues, is that density decreases one's underlying sense of control. Research supports this hypothesis. In one study involving a crowded elevator, for example, those who were standing farther away from the buttons felt out of control and aroused.[112] Additionally, in an environment such as a college dormitory, increases in crowding evoke distress and perceptions of loss of control.[113]

As a test of this crowding phenomenon, recall the last time you wanted to get somewhere, and found yourself blocked in a long line of other people or cars. What happened? Research suggests that any hopeful thoughts were replaced by frustration and anger.

PHYSICAL DEATH

Hopelessness and Lethal Thinking: To Be or Not To Be

In perhaps the most widely recognized soliloquy in Western literature, Hamlet's thoughts turn to a fundamental question:

> To be, or not to be — that is the question:
> Whether 'tis nobler in the mind to suffer
> The slings and arrows of outrageous fortune,
> Or to take arms against a sea of troubles
> And by opposing end them.[114]

Based on this portion of the quote, Hamlet still is entertaining the to-be solution to his suffering. Our previous discussion of psychological death suggested that people maintain their participation in life, albeit in a state ranging from anger/rage to despair/apathy. Although such people are profoundly blocked from important goals and have undergone a psychological death of sorts, they are still alive and, in the sense of Hamlet's dilemma, they are on the to-be end of the equation. Their prototypical thoughts are captured in the top To Be portion of Figure 4.1.

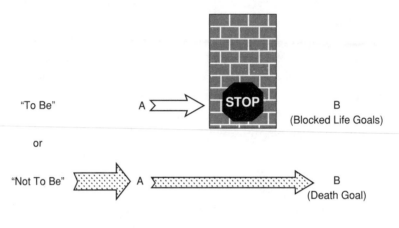

Figure 4.1

Lest Hamlet be too vague in his view about death as a potential goal, however, he immediately asserts:

To die, to sleep—
No more, and by sleep to say we end
The heartache and the thousand natural shocks
That flesh is heir to. 'Tis a consummation devoutly to be wished.

This is the not-to-be solution illustrated in the lower half of the figure. That is to say, the person no longer wants to pursue the previous important life-related goals that are blocked, but rather begins to think about death as a goal.

Not-to-be thoughts result when the normal goals related to living no longer are perceived as tenable. Faced with profound goal blockages, over time people give up on their usual goals. This sense of being blocked and frustrated — hopelessness — is the catalyst that unleashes the goal of dying.[115] The factors that magnify the impact of the perceived blockages, and therefore increase the probability of hopelessness and death-related thoughts, are the same ones I discussed earlier in this chapter. Namely, impediments perceived as being difficult to overcome now and in the future, and those applying to one or more important goals, should be particularly lethal in shutting off to-be thoughts. Under such thinking, not-to-be thoughts appear the logical choice.

Research on the processes associated with suicidal thinking suggests that three general qualities contribute to the not-to-be goal.[116] First, suicidal people are frozen in an unbearable here and now and cannot think about any changes in the future. Second, the suicidal person thinks very rigidly and does not consider alternative means to achieve blocked goals.[117] Third, suicidal persons become polarized in their thinking. Although all people at times may think dichotomously, the suicidal person is especially likely to perceive the world in absolute terms (e.g., none, always, never); thus, that one perspective is held as the only valid one. In this perspective, the suicidal person may become fixated on the not-to-be goal.[118]

Lethal Acts: Death by Commission or Omission

The person without hope for life goals may settle on death as the desirable goal. Once this death goal is seriously considered, the individual may enact lethal self-directed behaviors varying from acts of commission to acts of omission. Perhaps it is easiest to describe the acts of commission, those routes we often associate with suicide. For example, a person takes a handgun, aims it at the temple above the right ear, and pulls the trigger. This self-directed act of commission terminates a human life. The usual modes for such suicides are firearms, poisons, drugs, car exhaust, hanging, jumping, and cutting. Less obvious means include automobile accidents and drownings. In the 1990s, the topic of suicide has been complicated by suicidal assists. These reflect instances wherein the suicidal person is given instructions such as from the Hemlock Society and implements related to self-inflicted death such as Dr. Jack Kevorkian's suicide drug machine.

Beyond this type of suicide, a form of self-induced or self-accelerated death involves acts of omission. Omission-driven approaches to death represent acts wherein the person chooses not to engage in some course of action or treatment that would prolong the life span. In these instances, the person typically experiences a profound sense of giving up. As a case in point, the person suffering from a painful and debilitating cancer may elect not to have chemotherapy. Similarly, the unwillingness to eat, to protect oneself from hypo- or hyperthermia, or to adhere to a treatment regimen may accelerate the process of dying.

Self-induced deaths by both commission and omission are included under the definition of suicide employed by present-day thinkers. For example, a leading figure in suicidology, Edwin Schneidman, defines suicide as "a conscious act of self-induced annihilation, best understood as a multidimensional malaise in a needful individual who defines an issue for which suicide is perceived as the best solution."[119] Whether through acts of commission or omission, however, the mindset of hopelessness triggers this fatal solution. I explore the role that such hopeless thinking plays in the deaths of children and adults next.

PHYSICAL DEATH:
THE CHILDHOOD YEARS

Cliff: "Never Been Anybody at All"

Cliff Evans, a grade-school boy, tapped his bus driver on the shoulder and quietly asked to be let off. Once off the school bus, he collapsed in a snow bank by the side of the road. He was dead. The school principal asked the boy's favorite teacher to inform the parents. Here are the teacher's words:

> I drove though the snow and cold down the canyon road to the Evan's place and thought about the boy, Cliff Evans. His favorite teacher! I thought. He hasn't even spoken two words to me in two years! I could see him in my mind's eye all right, sitting back there in the last seat in my afternoon literature class. He came in the room by himself and left by himself. "Cliff Evans," I muttered to myself, "a boy who never talked." I thought a minute. "A boy who never smiled. I never saw him smile once."

The big ranch kitchen was clean and warm. I blurted out my news somehow. Mrs. Evans reached blindly toward a chair. "He never said anything about bein' ailing."

After school I sat in the office and stared bleakly at the records spread out before me. I was to close the file and write the obituary for the school paper. The almost bare sheets mocked the effort. Cliff Evans, white, never legally adopted by step-father, five young half-brothers and sisters. These meager strands of information and the list of D grades were all the records had to offer.

Cliff Evans had silently come in the school door in the mornings and gone out the school door in the evenings, and that was all. He had never belonged to a club. He had never played on a team. He had never held an office. As far as I could tell, he had never done one happy, noisy kid thing. He had never been anybody at all.[120]

Andrea: "I Miss My Daddy"

Andrea was a six-year-old girl when she first entered the psychiatric unit. She had tried to kill herself by running in the street in front of an oncoming truck. Previously she had several "accidents" involving suspicious burns. When asked why she had run into the street, she said she wanted to die. Her reason was "I miss my Daddy."

Andrea's father had died two years earlier in a car accident, and she wished to join him in heaven. Her mother had been severely depressed after the death of the father, and she spent long hours crying. Finding it difficult to care for Andrea, the mother often was angry with her. In the weeks before the suicide attempts by Andrea, the mother had been particularly depressed.[121]

Donald: "Why Don't the Others Like Me?"

At the time of admission to a psychiatric inpatient facility, Donald was twelve years old. He had taken a large number of his mother's tranquilizers. Previously, he had threatened to kill himself by jumping out of a window. In fact, he had a history of overdosing on the tranquilizers he found in the medicine cabinet. When asked about his attempt to kill himself, Donald said he was angry and sad because of the teasing at school. Lacking any friend, he was the target of ridicule. He would fight with the other kids, but desperately wanted to be liked by them. "I am very lonely. Why don't the others like me?" These words formed the theme of his hopelessness.[122]

These childhood case histories reveal the death by omission to commission dimension. Cliff appears to be more toward the omission end of the continuum, with his physical demise being the result of a continued mental withdrawal. Although the exact cause of death is not specified, one gets the impression that his desire to live evidently expired. Andrea, running in front of an oncoming truck, and Donald, with his ingestion of tranquilizers and threats of jumping out a window, are clearly more toward the commission end of the self-inflicted death continuum. There would have been no ambiguity about the causes had these acts resulted in the deaths of Andrea and Donald. Whatever the nature of their death-related activities, however, each of these children had a sense of hopelessness.

Risk Factors, Hopelessness, and Suicide

Cynthia Pfeffer, an expert on the topic of childhood suicide, has written that "death has a specific meaning to the child and this meaning is associated with a solution to the child's perception of overwhelming distress."[123] The overwhelming distress relates to some problem or problems the child cannot solve. The context for this stress is often a family where children are unable to meet their goals. For example, families in which children do not perceive themselves to be part of a cohesive unit, and families where there are conflicts, are associated with suicidal thoughts and behaviors as the solution for escaping this situation.[124] This negative family environment may result because the parents are divorced or separated, or perhaps because of abuse.[125] For Andrea and her mother, the death of the father had left the family in an upheaval. The sense of loss in the context of the family, as well as the inability to make contacts or connections outside of the family, increase the probability of the child's suicide. In Cliff's case, he never made contact in his family or school. With Donald, the hopelessness reflected his inability to make friends at school.

One method of studying the risk factors for childhood suicide is the psychological autopsy. In this approach, detailed analyses are conducted of the lives of the children who commit suicide in comparison to a matched group of living children (i.e., the families had the same race, income, religion, educational background, etc.). Extensive interviews are conducted to pinpoint the characteristics of those families where the child commits suicide. Using this methodology, one exemplary study found that childhood suicide was associated with parental absence, abuse, a family history of suicide attempts by other family members, and depression in family members.[126] Additionally, the parents do not share warmth and affection for each other,[127] and the home life is either insecure, hostile, or both.[128] Indeed, the factors that increase the chances of attempted and completed childhood suicides are similar to those eliciting psychological death in children. Hopelessness is the communality between psychological and physical death.

Having discussed factors associated with hopelessness and suicide in children, let's turn to more focused questions. Namely, if we have an index of the child's hopelessness, can suicidal ideation and behavior be predicted? Furthermore, given that depression and hopelessness are positively correlated, does hopelessness add anything beyond depression when we are trying to predict suicide?

Psychologist Alan Kazdin and his colleagues were the first to investigate systematically the relationship between childhood hopelessness and suicidal tendencies. To examine this issue, it was necessary to develop a short and valid measure of childhood hopelessness. What resulted was a seventeen-item, true-false self-report measure for children from age seven and beyond. The content of the items reveals a sense of being blocked in the pursuit of one's important goals, both in the present and in the future (e.g., "I might as well give up because I can't make things better for myself" and "I don't think I will get what I really want").

In the initial study with the Hopelessness Scale for Children, the suicidal thoughts and behaviors of sixty-six children who were in at a psychiatric care facility were determined on the basis of information obtained at admission and through independent psychiatric evaluations. Results showed that children with suicidal ideation and attempts had reliably higher hopelessness than did children without such tendencies.[129] Subsequent studies generally have replicated this finding.[130] Thus, in regard to the question of hopelessness and suicidal tendencies in children, there is a positive relationship.

The second question about hopelessness involves whether it is a better predictor of suicidal tendencies than depression. The initial study introducing the Hopelessness Scale for Children found that hopelessness was positively related to three different measures of children's depression. Although depression predicted suicidal tendencies in these children, when the effects of hopelessness were removed by statistical procedures, depression no longer related to suicidal tendencies. As we already know, hopelessness predicts suicidal tendencies, and in this first study it did so even when the influence of depression was removed by statistical procedures. This latter result is worth restating: Hopelessness appears to be more important than depression in predicting suicidal tendencies in children.[131]

PHYSICAL DEATH: THE ADULT YEARS

Mr. Wright: Treatment and Hopes Lost

Mr. Wright had been diagnosed with cancer that had spread to various parts of his body. In the face of this untreatable disease, however, he was infused with a desire to live. When he learned of a new drug, Krebiozen, that was being given to persons with a more favorable prognosis than his, Mr. Wright implored his physicians to give him this experimental drug. After one injection, his condition improved. With continued treatments, most of the traces of his cancer had disappeared. Two months later, however, conflicting evidence about the effectiveness of Krebiozen was published. Concerned that Mr. Wright's physical condition had returned to its previous grave status, his doctor decided to employ a placebo on the chance that improvement would occur again. The doctor told Mr. Wright that previous shipments of Krebiozen were made ineffective by incorrect storage techniques and that it indeed was effective. Thereafter, Mr. Wright was given the treatments from a new batch of the drug (actually water), and he evidenced even more pronounced improvement in his cancer (as traced by objective indices such as a radiograph) than the first time. For two months he was free of symptoms. Then the American Medical Association pronounced that Krebiozen was ineffective as a cancer treatment. Several days later, Mr. Wright was readmitted to the hospital under rapidly deteriorating conditions. His faith and hope depleted, he died two days after entering the hospital.[132]

The Case of Mrs. Kay: The Loss and Alcohol Mix

The police found Mrs. Helen Kay, age seventy-three, at 4:00 A.M. below a beach pier. Slumped over, holding an empty pint of whiskey, she appeared to be dead. But, she was still breathing. How did she get to this point in her life? The incidents leading up to this suicide attempt center around the loss of her husband and an increasing use of alcohol.

A graduate of Radcliffe, Helen had married Harold Kay, a lawyer. Their marriage was a happy one, with three successful children. The only signs of problems were her occasional depressive moods and her propensity to take responsibility for bad things that happened to her husband and children. Harold Kay was forced to retire at age seventy-two, having been diagnosed with both cancer and Alzheimer's disease. For the final three years of his life he was bedridden, but Helen was constantly at his side. In a moment of horrific insight, Mrs. Kay realized he no longer recognized her. Finally, after repeated discussions with family members and physicians, Mrs. Kay allowed her husband to be moved to the hospital, where he died the next day.

His death was almost unbearable for Mrs. Kay. During the funeral, she frequently stopped the eulogy to proclaim her responsibility for his death. As the casket was lowered into the grave, she tried to throw herself on the lid.

After an unsuccessful attempt to live with her son's family, she moved to an apartment near the beach. Although other widows lived nearby, she withdrew from interacting with people. If she did say anything to others, it was in a sulking and complaining tone. Her new friend was the bottle. Only a social drinker previously, she later sought the numbing effects of liquor during long bedside vigils for her husband. At the time of her suicide attempt, Mrs. Kay was drinking herself to death.[133]

Ralph: Writer's Block and Russian Roulette

Ralph, age forty, was admitted to a psychiatric unit with depression, feelings of despair, and suicidal thoughts. He was a social isolate and lacked social skills. A writer by profession, Ralph reported that the biggest stressor in his life was his constant struggle to obtain work as a writer. Although he occasionally did get articles published, he often felt like a failure. The frustration of Ralph's life is revealed in this lethal, recurring ritual. Sitting at his typewriter in the throes of writer's block, he would take out a partially loaded revolver and play Russian roulette.[134]

These three adult examples involving suicidal behaviors, like the cases with children, highlight the acts of omission-commission dimension. Mr. Wright, no longer able to believe in the cancer drug, appeared to shut down his fight to live. Of course, he would have died of cancer, but his mind may have let this happen more quickly in the end (an act of omission). For those interested in other examples of act of omission suicides, I recommend Viktor Frankl's classic *Man's Search For Meaning*.[135] In this moving account of his three years in Auschwitz, Dachau, and other Nazi concentration camps, Frankl describes a pattern where the prisoner who had lost any goal for living simply would give up and die. Refusing to eat, wash, or get dressed, such prisoners sat down and waited to die. To quote Frankl, "There he remained, lying in his own excreta, and nothing bothered him anymore."[136] In another instance, a prisoner was convinced that the war would be over on March 30. As this date came without any end of the war in sight, the prisoner became ill and died.

Returning to the other cases I have described, Mrs. Kay is somewhere in the middle of this continuum in that she stopped taking care of herself (an act of omission), although she also increased her drinking to a dangerous level (an act of commission). Ralph, with his Russian roulette, is clearly toward the act of commission end of

the continuum. Let's look at what leads such adults to these potential ends next.

Risk Factors, Hopelessness, and Suicide

The trail of lethal influences in adult suicide can be traced back to
childhood experiences. Childhood abuse appears to be a common
theme in the lives of adults with suicidal tendencies.[137] Another
powerful childhood antecedent is parental loss through death,
divorce, or separation.[138] Additionally, the family lives of adolescents
and adults with suicidal tendencies are chaotic, nonsupportive, and
disinterested.[139] As discussed earlier, the childhood aftereffects of
hopeless thinking are carried into adulthood.

What events catapult the adult toward suicide? It is noteworthy
that the arena for the greatest pleasures and satisfactions in life —
interpersonal relationships — is also the source of enormous misery,
hopelessness, and sometimes suicide. Suicidal intent and behaviors
have been associated with all of the following relationship-based
issues: poor communication,[140] inability to form warm and interde-
pendent attachments,[141] conflicts and quarrels,[142] separations because
of difficulties,[143] breakups with more lethality for the one being left
behind than the one leaving,[144] and, death of spouse.[145] Analyses of
the content of suicide notes also reveals themes involving disturbed
interpersonal relationships.[146] Whether it is due to problems related
to the establishment, maintenance, or the loss of relationships, the
person faces higher suicidal risks. Recall that Mrs. Kay's spiral into
suicidal tendencies was initiated by the loss of her beloved husband.
Note, however, that losses of a seemingly less serious nature (e.g.,
difficulties in a relationship ranging from poor communication to
quarreling) also elicit suicidal activities. We humans view attachment to others as extremely important, and when our relationships
are blocked in some fashion, the repercussions are serious for both
our mental and physical welfare.

Victimization, especially after sexual assault, and spousal abuse
also increase the probability of suicide.[147] Furthermore, although it
typically may not be thought of as victimization, the person who
contracts a terminal disease or a serious injury is at increased risk for

suicide. Included here are higher suicide rates for persons with AIDS, cancer, and spinal cord injuries.[148]

Yet another blockage with suicide-eliciting properties is the loss of meaningful work.[149] For some, this workless travail continues as they are unable to find suitable employment for years. The case of Ralph highlights this issue. A writer by profession, he was unable to support himself and his family. Often, the unemployed come to think of themselves as unlikely ever to secure appropriate employment. This is a blow to the pocketbook and the identity.

Lastly, alcohol and drug abuse are suicide risk factors.[150] Here the literature suggests a very consistent pattern: Alcohol and drug abuse greatly increase the probability of attempted and successful suicides. In the case of Mrs. Kay, for example, her suicidal tendencies were more serious because of her alcohol consumption. Although people may or may not die because of the direct effects of the drug, there also are increased accidents when they are under the influence.[151] Drug usage often becomes an escape from an untenable situation. In the beginning, the escape may be short periods of highs; with repeated use, the escape may be death.

The risks for adult suicide all generally involve important goals. Whether it is interpersonal relationships, meaningful employment, or physical health and safety, our pursuit of these central goals is sometimes prohibited. The blockages we encounter produce stress and, assuming the impediments remain, our thoughts may plunge into hopelessness. This hopelessness in adults may unleash suicidal thoughts and behaviors.

Aaron Beck and his colleagues have developed the Hopelessness Scale to have a short, self-report measure of the negative expectations adults hold about their present and future situations. A twenty-item, true-false index, the Hopelessness Scale measures thoughts of being blocked in the pursuit of goals both now and in the future. Two items are "I might as well give up because I can't make things better for myself," and "I never get what I want so it's foolish to want anything."[152] Using this scale, researchers have consistently found that hopelessness is related to suicidal intent and ideations,[153] as well as to completed suicides.[154]

The more stringent test of the Hopelessness Scale involves the question of whether it predicts suicidal tendencies more than related measures. The obvious first candidate for comparison to hopelessness is depression. Results of many studies show that although these two variables are positively related, hopelessness more strongly predicts suicidal intent.[155] The importance of hopelessness also is revealed in a study of suicide attempts among drug abusers; namely, hopelessness more strongly predicts suicide attempts than does actual drug usage.[156]

These findings with adults parallel those obtained with children: Hopeless thinking is critical in the chain of events that leads to suicide. A child or adult who thinks that his or her present and future goals are blocked has reached a potentially lethal conclusion.

THE PARADOX OF SUICIDE
AS THE LAST HOPE

I close this chapter with the seemingly paradoxical conclusion that suicide, in the end, may reflect manifestations of the last hopeful thought. Blocked in the pursuit of goals related to living, people are filled with despair and search for a goal that removes them from the unbearable traps. Death is that final goal. Although one may quarrel with the decision to pursue death, I do not want to become entangled in that debate.[157] Rather, my point is that suicidal people become mentally activated and energized to find a way to obtain their goal—death for themselves. Indeed, it is clinical lore that helpers should become concerned about a suicide attempt becoming lethal when three indicators are present: First, the person begins to describe his or her death in concrete terms (the goal); second, the person appears to have a surge of energy (willpower thinking); and third, the person has specific plans about how to accomplish the deed (waypower thinking).[158] Although hopelessness sets the mental stage for suicide by fixating the person on the goal of death, the will- and way-related thoughts complete the fatal sequence. Ironically, therefore, the principles of hopeful thinking apply to suicides.

CHAPTER FIVE

Nurturing Hope in Children

Listen to the MUSTN'TS, child,
Listen to the DON'TS
Listen to the SHOULDN'TS
The IMPOSSIBLES, the WON'TS
Listen to the NEVER HAVES
Then listen close to me—
Anything can happen, child,
ANYTHING can be.

— Shel Silverstein, *Listen to the Mustn'ts*

INTRODUCTION: A TALE OF TWO CITIES, AND MORE . . .

My mother had that look on her face. "Again?" I asked. "Again," said Mom. When I was growing up, we moved. I mean, moved a lot. My dad's sales job involved one transfer after another. By the time I finished high school, I had gone to a dozen or so schools across the United States. Childhood was quite a trip, as we constantly were getting ready for the next move. Something special, however, always made the move with us. That something was hope, and my parents taught me how to keep it alive.

Looking back, I am thankful my childhood was filled with many of the ideas about engendering hope that fill this chapter. Of course, kids don't pick their parents, so it was by the luck of the draw I had such an environment.[1] For those of us who are parents now, or plan to be in the future, the task is to pass hope to our offspring. This chapter offers tips about producing a hope-inducing environment for our children.[2] Likewise, if you would like to reflect on the hope-inducing properties of your own childhood, the subsequent pages may bring back memories.

GOALS

The lessons for instilling goals in children build on their natural desire to know what is out there. Of the many challenges encountered by children, it is crucial for them to learn how to locate desired targets. In the infant's earliest days, of course, she must identify sources of food and comfort. Additionally, as the childhood years unfold, an equally essential skill is to identify goals that may bring satisfaction and growth. This section contains suggestions for filling young minds with hope-related goals.

Getting to the Point

If you are the parent of an infant less than one year old, notice your baby focusing on nearby objects. As described in chapter 3, this is a basic part of the perceptual process. Particularly good attention grabbers are mobiles, music boxes, and soft stuffed animals (for vision, hearing, and touch, respectively). Put these near your infant's crib so he can appreciate them. Watch your infant carefully so you can know when she is searching for one of these attention grabbers. During these occasions, your baby is establishing rudimentary goals. In responding to your children's cues and fulfilling their desires to make the mobile move or crank up the music box, you are reinforcing the goal-directed attention process. One of the keys in this process is that you need to spend time with your infants and watch for instances in which they are focusing on nearby objects.

My general advice is to make sure your infant's environment is rich with stimulation. By doing this, you help to encourage the search for desired objects. Notice that your infant responds to novel things introduced into his world. Young or old, we all like a certain amount of stimulation. Be careful, however, not to introduce too much new stimulation because this may overwhelm your baby. At the other extreme, as I pointed out in the previous chapter, children should not be understimulated through neglect.

Around one year of age, your child probably points at things. This is an exciting time, and I would urge you to join your offspring in a game called *What's out there.*[3] When your one-year-old points a little finger at something capturing his or her attention, ask, "What is it?" Then, give your child the answer, "That's a picture." Next, follow this with the related question: "Can you say picture?" You may sound like Mr. Rogers here, and you can get tired of doing it, but hang in there because it is important for your child. Also, kids love this game once they catch onto it. My granddaughter, for example, roams around our house asking, "Whoz it?" Once we name it, she tries to say the word, and often wants to hold or touch the desired thing. Go ahead and let your children touch such objects until they tire of them, and then move on to another goal object. By doing this, you are teaching your children to explore, to map out goals in their small worlds, and to apply words to those goals. Delightfully soon, for example, your child will learn the names of the earliest and most coveted goals — Mommy and Daddy — as well as the other important people and things in her environment.

Along the way, your baby is learning a fundamental lesson about the importance of asking questions. Praise your children for asking questions and they will ask even more.[4] Of course, if you answer their questions, it is only fair that they answer yours. Vary your questions so your children have to use all of their senses. Create an atmosphere for your child where question asking is a good thing to do.

Another game you can initiate with your child is one I call *Show and tell.* The key here is that you call your child's attention to something, and then you say a little about that thing or event. It helps to imagine you are a tour guide. "Look at that!" says Dad, and the infant's eyes turn to the stuffed bear. "That's a bear . . . bears go grrrrrr," continues Dad. The child's other senses, especially sound and touch, can be used in variant games of *Listen to this* and *Feel this.* Put some enthusiasm into these games, and your child will become more interested in this identification process.[5] If you are tired and not in the mood to invest some energy, remember how interesting and important this identification process is to your little one. Animated parents and teachers invite the child to the wonders of exploration. As child psychologist Michael Schulman puts it, "Perhaps the best advice one could give a parent is, show your child everything. Actually, 'show' is not a strong enough word. One wants to *celebrate* the world for your child."[6]

One of your jobs as caregiver is to teach toddlers the words that apply to their goals. Words become a way of conveying to others what your child wants, and this skill is crucial for communicating precise thoughts about goals. On this point, recall from the developmental chapter how important language is as a tool for hopeful thinking, especially as the young child is attempting to communicate her desires. Sometimes we need to coach our children to put words to their desires about interpersonal matters. Recently, for example, Nana (my granddaughter's name for my wife) was playing with our one-year-old granddaughter, when little Drew extended her arms and uttered, "Ugh!" Nana said, "Say *up*," and then picked up the baby. In a few days, I noticed that Drew had begun to utter "Up" when she wanted to be held.

With young children, many goals involve their desires to have the bigger people do something for them. As an example of what not to do, consider my behavior with our first child. He merely would grunt, and as a new parent I would scurry around trying to get him things. What I wasn't doing was to use these occasions as opportunities to teach verbal skills to my son. In other words, as a well-meaning parent, sometimes you can work so hard to successfully respond to your children's desires that you are not teaching them to use words to specify their wants. As I got more experience, I let my son send off more clues about what he wanted, and I began to teach him to use words to clarify what he wanted. When you sense that your child wants something, therefore, help him to put words to these desires. Children are wonderful at sending out nonverbal cues about their desires, so understanding what they want is not a daunting task.

Yet another refinement in this goal specification process is to teach your child to say, "I want _____" (the child then fills in the blank). Your children may learn to specify without any I want tutoring on your part. In fact, they may use it so frequently that you are tempted to squelch it. My advice, however, is to reward your children for verbalizing their I want desires, although you cannot fulfill all of them. For instance, "I'm glad you told me you want a banana, but you will have to wait until we get some at the grocery store."

All Points Considered

As our children learn how to specify their goals, it also is important to expose them to another goal-making lesson. In particular, instruct your youngster to consider several other attractive goals in addition to the primary one. Children, especially when they are very young, may not want to consider any goal other than that one. The American tradition of making quick decisions contributes to this problem of one-goal thinking. This let's-get-on-with-it mentality, when pushed to an extreme by parents, produces children who pounce on one goal, often any goal. My sense is that higher-hope children, through the help of their parents, have learned to slow down this process so they can consider several goal options before selecting one. Although at times you may become impatient as your child decides on a goal, don't hurry this process. If you do, you are teaching your child to be impulsive, to not take the time to consider alternatives. This may contribute to low hope in your children because in their rush to select one goal without a consideration of several, they may choose goals that are unsatisfying or inappropriate.

Another problem of one-goal thinking is that children often find that their only goal is unobtainable. A societal emphasis on persevering toward a goal contributes further to this one-goal thinking. Perseverance toward a truly unobtainable goal, however, especially when there are alternative desirable and obtainable goals, is not characteristic of high-hope children and adults. My sense is that although hopeful children persevere in their pursuit of goals, they also demonstrate flexibility and switch to other attractive goals when necessary.

If your children are relatively young, you may have to help them generate optional goals. Sometimes tantrum behaviors reflect that young children have not learned to generate alternative goals. In such instances, as a caregiver you need to teach your children about the importance of being flexible in their goals. Watch how a mother does this effectively in the following interchange:

Tommy (a five year old): "I want to play with Barry."

Mom: "Barry isn't home now. Anyone else you would like to play with?"

Tommy (upset because his neighborhood pal is gone): "No!"

Mom: "Well, who are your other friends outside of our apartment building?"

Tommy: "Oh, Bobby's down the street, and Zach lives over near school."

Mom: "Why don't you give one of them a call and see if they can come over?"

This mom helped to expand the category of friends when Tommy limited his desires to a good friend who lived in the same building. Parents need to continue these lessons in lateral goal thinking into the middle and adolescent years because older children also become unduly restricted in their goal thinking. Even when the desired goal may be obtainable, it is a good exercise to have your child consider alternative goals before settling on one.

You may find your children so filled with goals that they are confused about which one to pursue. This is opposite to the problem of the child who is stuck on one goal. For example, a girl may want to play with each of several friends, but this is not possible at one time. Perhaps your child may have several fun things he would like to do, but he can only do one. Or, there is gift dilemma, where the child can select only one toy from among several desired ones. The key lesson in all these examples is to have your child talk about the pros and cons of each goal and to compare the alternatives. Then, if your child can rank the goals, this should clarify which one is desired most strongly. You can help in this process by asking your child to think about which goal is most important and why, which is second in importance and why, and so on. It also is helpful to suggest that at some future point your child may have the opportunity to pursue one of the goals not selected first. This tends to take the heat off the present goal decision. But when it gets down to the actual decision about a goal, let them make it, and praise them for going through the deliberation process.

Pinpointing

The labeling and elocution of desired goals continue throughout childhood, especially if the growing child interacts with people who teach such goal naming. It is helpful if children learn to use more precise words to identify what they want.[7] I would suggest avoiding such parental favorites as "Do your best" and "Give it a good try," however, because while well-meaning, these vague encouragements do not have the hope-inducing properties of more specific goals. I have worked with parents, for example, who were adamant that they would not put pressure on their children. These parents adopted this approach because they believed their parents had put too much pressure on them. Acting on this no-pressure premise, the parents emphasized that their children just do their best. Their children, however, were baffled by this instruction because they often were unclear about their goals. In other words, in their well-intentioned desires to not push their children, the parents were not providing the critical instruction in helping their offspring to specify goals. Research on this point shows that clearly specified goals not only enhance hope-related thinking among individuals previously unmotivated[8] but also result in more positive outcomes.[9]

Why are more specific goals helpful to your child? I believe specific goals are beneficial because children can readily comprehend their meaning. Concrete goals give children a clear benchmark for their subsequent efforts. In contrast, the more general do-your-best statements are difficult to understand because children often do not know what their best is. Having precautioned against vague statements as goals, however, I would endorse a statement such as "You gave it a great effort" as a means of conveying love and support. Further, if you have helped your children to specify their goals, it is appropriate to encourage them with do-your-best statements.

As your children grow, the precise formation of goals continues to be important. Additionally, older children become more adept at discerning the subcategories defining a larger goal. That is to say, children learn to form discriminations within categories. As an example, five-year-old Paul says, "I want to play ball." At age nine, he says, "I want to play football." By age thirteen, Paul asserts, "I want to play quarterback." Or, the "I want candy" evolves into "I want a Snickers." This process of discriminating within a goal category is refined throughout childhood and continues into adulthood, where it is called *specialization*.

Sometimes we need to do a little detective work to pinpoint exactly what our children want. We would do well to borrow a technique from psychotherapy, where therapists often use the emotions of the children as clues to their underlying goals. A good practice as a parent, therefore, is to follow the emotions. By doing this, we may find what our children really want. As an example of this process, consider the following interchange between a therapist and a nine-year-old boy who was referred because of irritability and passive aggressiveness.

Therapist: "You seem to feel angry."

Child: (Seems to agree but says nothing.)

Therapist: "Can you tell me why?"

Child: "The kids at school make fun of me."

Therapist: "Oh, in what way?"

Child: "They say I don't try in sports, and that I'm no good in baseball."

Therapist: "And this kind of hurts your feelings . . . and makes you feel angry with them."

Child: "No, I don't care. They're not my friends, so I don't care what they say."

Therapist: (Pause) "Well, I wonder in what ways you might like me to help you."

Child: (Pause) "I'd like to have more friends at school."

Therapist: (Pause) "On the one hand you're saying you don't care about them, and on the other you're saying you would like them to be your friends."

Child: (Begins to cry quietly.) "I do want them to be my friends."[10]

One of the keys in helping your children to specify their goals is to make sure you are listening to them. An example is the case of Candy and her mom. Candy, a teenage girl, came to therapy because she and her mother didn't get along. Candy was trying to focus on what goals she wanted as she began the dating process. Her mother construed this as Candy having gone boy crazy. In reality, Candy desired some advice and clarification about what she wanted to get out of dating. Mom wasn't listening to her daughter's real desires and jumped to an incorrect conclusion. My major intervention was to teach Mom how to hear what her daughter was saying. When mother began to do this, she was able to help her daughter clarify goals about dating and other matters in her life. Throughout the developmental sequence and especially in the teenage years, our children may want to move from vague goals that are inherently unsatisfying to more specific goals that are reachable and rewarding. As parents, we need to be attuned to how we can help in this pinpointing process.

Goal Stretching

Once children have a clear notion of how they did previously in a given area, encourage them to base their upcoming goal on this previous performance. One key point is *goal stretching*. In goal stretching, children set goals somewhat more difficult than their previous level of accomplishment. A little coaching on your part can encourage your offspring to set their sights a little higher. This goal-setting stance is characteristic of high-hope people. It also is worth noting that other researchers have found that this goal stretching approach leads to better subsequent performance.[11] I am not talking about turning our children into zealots who are perpetually chasing upwardly spiraling goals. In fact, caregivers who are too pushy may see their efforts backfire. Rather, I am suggesting that a modest improvement on the child's previous standard should result in a sense of challenge. Another advantage of this approach is that it is based on the child's level of performance rather than that of other people.

Stretching should be rewarded for a multitude of goals in young children. Case in point: Fourteen-month-old Molly is sitting in her high chair, and Mom introduces a new tool — the fork. Molly tries to hold the fork and gets some food into her mouth and some on the floor. "Good job!" exclaims Mom. "Now, see if you can get a little more in your mouth." Consider another major event in childhood — learning how to ride a bike. Dad runs alongside five-year-old Jimmy's bicycle, holding the boy up. Then the fateful moment arrives, and Dad lets go. "Keep peddling, keep going . . . you're doing it!" shouts the father. The boy goes a few feet and falls. Dad says, "Good work . . . now see if you can stay up a little longer." Whether it is using a fork, riding a bike, or any of the other many stepping-stones of childhood, the child is learning and obtaining a positive challenge because the goal is a stretch.

The goal stretching for older children should occur in the context of important goals. Here is an example: Fifteen-year-old Perry is starting the ninth grade. School is not easy for him, and he comes home after the first day with a perplexed look. "What's wrong?" asked his mother. After some further talk, Perry disclosed two things: First, after he had joined a club, he found out the club was having a contest to see who could sell the most Christmas cards and supplies (the profits going to the club). Perry really didn't think this contest was important, so he asked his mother if he could just sell a few Christmas items and not put in much effort. His mom said, "Sure, if it's not that important to you." The second problem Perry was weighing was how difficult his courses were going to be and what he should aim for in terms of grades. His mom's advice was to pick out one course that really interested him and try for an A in it. "OK," said Perry, "but what about the other courses?" "Last year you got mostly C's and B's," said mom, "so what do you think you could work for this year?" "I'll shoot for B's in the rest of my courses," said Perry. What has transpired in this interchange is that Perry has decided not to stretch himself by setting a high sales goal for the club that is not very important to him, but he is setting concrete and difficult goals for the more important ninth-grade courses.[12]

If your child has a learning disability, physical problems, or seemingly is not talented in particular areas, you have a normal kid like the rest of us. Goal stretching is especially effective with such children. If a particular activity is difficult for your children, do not conclude they cannot learn. Rather, look for whatever the child can do and build on it.[13] Likewise, keep the learning goals concrete and reachable. Remember also, the goals should be your child's, not those of other children or your parental goals. If your child is in school, this may mean you have to keep track of the goals the teacher has for the entire class. Talk with the teacher, and formulate stretch goals that your child can attain. With such goals, learning is almost always possible. Whatever you do, do not turn off the goal-setting process because your child will follow your lead.

If you can help your children set their goals according to these suggestions, you probably will find at least two additional benefits. First, children who can clearly articulate stretch goals also begin to think of pathways to their goals.[14] Likewise, stretch goals focus the attention and enhance the sense of willpower to reach the goals.[15] To think about such stretch goals, therefore, may mobilize will- and way-related thinking in our children. This should come as no surprise, however, given that the target of willpower and waypower thinking is goals.

Undoing Dueling Goals

Sometimes your child's goals may conflict with each other, and she does not perceive this. In such instances, the caregiver needs to point out the conflict. Although this can happen to children at almost any age, in my experience the teenage years especially produce such conflicting goals. I once saw a sixteen-year-old boy named Brad, who came to therapy because of feeling anxious and strung out. Both he and his parents were unhappy about what was happening to him. When I asked Brad what he wanted, he said he would like to get good grades and eventually go to college. When I asked about other goals, Brad informed me that he wanted to be friends with Tony, who was one of the tough guys at school. Tony, it turned out, had disdain for anyone who studied and got good grades. Bingo. If Brad were to be friends with Tony, he had to get lousy grades. But, Brad wanted to get good grades. At this point, I confronted Brad with his choices: either study and get good grades or befriend Tony and get poor grades. His first choice was to be friends with Tony, and he therefore stopped studying. Brad felt even more anxious and conflicted, however, as he pursued this option. After three weeks of trying his initial choice, he decided it was more important to study and get good grades. He kept with this goal, and stopped trying to live by Tony's rules. With this decision, Brad's anxiety lessened.

In Brad's case, the goals truly were incompatible, and as such he was in a state of turmoil trying to reconcile them. Sometimes, however, our children may be conflicted about holding two goals that society says are antithetical but which in point of fact need not be. For example, American culture promulgates the following false antitheses to children:

— One cannot be athletic and intelligent.
— One cannot be beautiful and intelligent.
— One cannot be heavy and attractive.

There are other such false dichotomies, but my point is that we should disabuse our offspring of goal fallacies that cause undue distress. There are enough antithetical goals to confuse our children without adding to the list with societal misconceptions. Whatever the source of such false antithetical goals, they are harmful to the child's welfare.[16]

Goals From Within and Without

Childhood is a time of immense interest in how one is doing relative to others. In fact, social comparison is well in place by age ten. As such, we may find our children not marching to the beat of their own drum, but rather setting their goals according to the perceived standards of others. Such comparison to others sets up a dangerous cycle when taken to extreme, however, because children increasingly come to define their worth in relation to others. It is useful to take a cue from high-hope people about this issue. High-hope people consider the relevant external standards as provided by other people, but they pay attention primarily to their own standards in setting goals.

We cannot and should not try to have our children avoid all social comparison, of course, but what kind of goals may be more conducive to hopeful thinking? The answer lies in having our children attend first and foremost to their own standards and then to any other relevant input about the goals of others in similar circumstances.[17] Children know roughly how they have done in particular arenas of their lives; if they do not, we adults can help them to judge their goals for the future.[18] Earlier I suggested that one of our duties as parents is to help our children as they formulate goals. Indeed, our research shows that high-hope adults describe their parents as being very helpful in forming and selecting goals.[19] If our children are pursuing goals for which they lack the basic capabilities, however, it is the parents' job to lead them gently back to those things for which they do possess the requisite talent and interests. Likewise, in these latter circumstances, parents may want to help their children explore other goals.

Although it may be obvious that we parents influence our children's selection of goals, we cannot and should not dictate goals to them. In the context of group therapy, I recall the father who had set all the goals for his son through high school. The father even had the son begin a premedical course of college study after deciding his son should be a doctor. Not surprisingly, when away from home at college, the boy revolted and dropped out of school. Likewise, the son stopped communicating with his father. I still can remember the father's ironic words, "I was only doing what was best for him." The moral is that parents can guide and facilitate goal setting, but we should not dictate our children's goals, especially as they get older.

Recall the previously discussed case of Lucy, the teenager who could not perform well in the language-related activities valued by her parents and the school system. Unable to pursue the usual language goals related to reading and writing because she lacked the talents, she had withdrawn into a depressionlike state of low hope. To make matters worse, her parents were clueless about what talents and interests Lucy possessed. Her parents, like a lot of us, just assumed that their offspring would have the same goals they had. In this case, I suggested that the parents spend time talking to Lucy and listening to what she wanted to do. Eventually, the parents realized that their daughter enjoyed working outside with plants and greenery. These interests, plus her artistic talents, led Lucy to pursue a career in landscaping design. This case, as well as the previous one involving the father dictating a medical career for his son, show how important it is for us as parents to be sensitive to what our children want to do with their lives.

The guidance of parents is needed especially as children grow into their teenage years, where the influence of peers becomes very strong. During these later years teenagers need to be reminded of their role in forming goals. One of the reasons for doing this is that, depending on the particular peer group, the goals conveyed to our teenagers may differ widely from day to day. Although teenagers feel they lack any good sense of setting goals, in reality they typically can produce a more stable and appropriate set of goals than the volatile peer group.

For example, I worked with a mother having problems with her daughter's conformity to peer pressure. The focal point of the problem was her daughter's desire to wear the in things as defined by her teenage peer group. The daughter was constantly chasing the latest clothes fad of her group, and the mother couldn't afford all the outfits. The solution that eventually worked was to give the daughter a budget to buy her own clothes. This forced the daughter to settle on her tastes and preferences for clothes because she couldn't pay for the clothes reflecting the rapidly changing tastes of her peer group. This example shows how the child can be given some responsibility in setting goals, and in doing so must arrive at personal goals in the context of the peer group. Given the fact that many of the goals of teenagers involve the outlay of money, this budget technique can foster personal goal setting for differing problems.

A Goals Checklist

To summarize what I have said so far about facilitating the development of adaptive goals in our children, I offer the following tips:

Do

✓ Help your babies to identify and name desired objects in their environment.
✓ Teach your offspring to use words to specify precisely what they want.
✓ Listen carefully to your children so you can know what they really want.
✓ Make sure your children consider a few attractive goals before settling on one.
✓ Instruct your children in making stretch goals that build on previous performances.
✓ Help your children to match their goals with their talents.
✓ Show interest and ask about your children's goals.
✓ If your children have conflicting goals, show how this can be a problem and help them select one goal.

✓ Remind your children to set goals they want, rather than seeking things others want.

✓ Whenever possible, let your children make the decision about their goals.

✓ Praise your children when they make goals for themselves.

Don't

✓ Overwhelm your children with too much stimulation.

✓ Anticipate and fulfill your children's desires without also teaching the words signifying those desires.

✓ Assume your children can learn to identify goals without your coaching.

✓ Ignore your children when they ask questions.

✓ Rush your children when they are selecting a goal.

✓ Foster vague goal-setting by saying "Just do your best," or "Give it a good try."

✓ Confuse your children with too many possible goals.

✓ Second guess your children's goal decisions.

✓ Push your children to extremely difficult goals.

✓ Encourage your children to select goals that are more for you than for them.

WILLPOWER

Assuming your children have developed their goals along the previously discussed lines, this section presents ideas for enhancing childhood willpower in thinking. Children have a natural enthusiasm for goals, and it is our job as caregivers to cultivate their determination to pursue those goals. Such willful thinking involves children's beliefs about their power to start and sustain movement toward goals.

The Who Did That? Game

Recall that chapter 3 discussed the importance of the one- to two-year-old's revelations about selfhood and the self as instigator of actions. Developmentally, insights about self appear before the thoughts about one's capacity to initiate actions. To foster self-recognition, a good starting place is to ask your baby to point to a body part. For example, after asking "Where's Sue's nose?", you can point to the correct location. This is a specific version of the point-ing game discussed earlier in the goals section. It can be expanded to the more general question, "Where's Tommy?" The mirror can be a good prop for helping children to identify themselves.

Once the self-recognition lessons have progressed, somewhere between twelve to thirty months of age children are awakening to the fact that they are the forces causing things to happen. This is the birth of willpower thinking. A good game to play with your youngsters is to have them do something enjoyable and then ask, "Who did that?" They delight in telling you they did it. For exam-ple, two-year-old Bobby is asked to throw a rubber ball to his dad, which he does. Then Dad asks, "Who threw the ball?" The child proudly says, "Bobby threw it." Or, suppose Dad says to Bobby, "Let's run across the park," and they do. Dad then asks, "Who was running?" Bobby, looking a little perplexed, replies, "Daddy." "Who else?" asks Dad. "Well, Bobby was!" exclaims the toddler. Whenever you do something with your children, let them tell what part they played. In fact, it is a good practice in general to ask kids what they can do. Around age three, children are expanding rapidly their repertoire of skills, and they are more than happy to tell you about these. The answers to this question include, among others, talking, taking off shoes, throwing a ball, and running.

Of course, children do not stop learning about their capabilities to initiate action sequences at age three, so parents also should continue asking about these willpower revelations. Children of all ages enjoy being asked what they have learned, and it serves to rein-force such thinking. In other words, continue to ask your children what they have learned today, and praise them for this learning process. The who-did-that? game for the young child becomes a credit game for older children. By this I mean that caregivers should pay attention to the activities that older children initiate as well as those activities they sustain. Most importantly, we caregivers should acknowledge or give credit to the child for these activities.

Sometimes we may take our children's starting and staying power for granted and say nothing. If we praise them for these actions, however, it adds to their sense of willpower. For example, suppose fifteen-year-old Kent has gotten up faithfully and made his 8:00 A.M. junior high class all year. His parents should be certain to compliment his willpower. In my experience, it is common for problem children to perceive that their caregivers never praise them for the things they do right. Remember that it may be hard for our children to think well of themselves if we caregivers do not praise them.

Little Voices in Support

If your children are low in willpower, there may be harmful thoughts playing constantly inside their heads. These negative inner voices are pounding the I can't message into the young minds. Children with this I can't inner voice are undermined when they think about starting a task.[20] Furthermore, even if the child does get started toward a goal, the I can't voice sabotages any thoughts to sustain efforts. This voice is the enemy of hopeful thinking.

Before explaining how you can undo these I can't thoughts, let's look at some things that well-meaning parents inadvertently may do to contribute to this negative thinking in children. As I already have noted, parents may not pay sufficient attention to their child's goal-setting thoughts. Without clear and appropriate goal thoughts, our children are more likely to lack willful thinking. Parents also can step in inappropriately and take over things their children are trying. Two phrases I would advise against saying are "You can't do this," and "Oh, I'll do it myself." Likewise, we may take our children's efforts for granted and not remember to praise them. Even worse, we may give criticism that we think is helpful, when in reality our kids experience such feedback as mentally deflating. All of these parental behaviors may build the I can't voice into the minds of children.

If you suspect your child is flooded by the I can't voice, you can ask about it in a gentle and supportive manner. It may be that this voice is an accurate scorekeeper because the child has not experienced many successes. If so, you need to work so your child can begin to experience some successes. Sometimes, however, the I can't voice comes to life because of one failure experience that sticks in the minds of our children. Talk with your child and try to find out why the particular experience has remained so important in her thoughts.

Another possibility is that your child may have experienced mostly successes, but pays more attention to the occasional setbacks. In this case, you can review the child's successes and see how he reacts to these events. If your children discount their successes, you have hit upon a crucial process that drains willpower. Depending on the age of your child, you need to discuss how they don't seem to own their successes.

After talking with your child about accentuating the negative over the positive, begin to offer special praise for positive behaviors. As an additional lesson, teach your child to change the I can't tape's content. At first, you may want to see if he can change the I can't to Sometimes I can't, but often I can. Have him practice out loud and then instruct him to use this new phrase instead of the old tape that was running in his head.[21] (This tape analogy is one that children today can grasp because of the prevalence of audiotapes in our lives.) After awhile, suggest to your child that it is time to change the tape again. This time you may ask him to substitute a new tape that says, "I can."[22] When this new voice takes hold, children experience an increase in their willpower.

Much like the little train in the children's book that eventually comes to say, "I think I can," willpower thinking can be learned. Several years ago, I coached a little league team of ten- and eleven-year-old boys. My team included all of the kids who had not made the other teams. At the first practice, one boy wouldn't even volunteer to hit during batting practice. Later, I took him aside and asked about practicing hitting. Looking down and kicking the dirt, Doug said the fateful words, "I can't . . . hit." I had an idea. I asked Doug if he would change what he said to, "I can't hit, but I can swing." He looked at me puzzled and said, "Well, yeah." So I had him say it a few times. Then I asked him to stand in the batter's box and say, "I can't hit, but I can swing." He repeated these words, looking all the more bewildered. I then put a bat in his hands, and asked Doug to be certain not to hit the ball when I pitched it to him. Doug laughed and said he could do this for sure. Much to his surprise, he hit a few of the pitches. I sent him home with a new tape to play. I told him to practice saying "Maybe I can hit." By the end of the season, Doug had a tape of "I can hit" playing in his head. Further, he readily volunteered for batting practice. Indeed, he became one of the most determined batters on the team. (Incidentally, our record was 0 and 10, but the kids improved, had fun, and perhaps learned some lessons about hope.)

Containing the Negative and Spreading the Positive

Suppose your child has difficulties learning in some areas, but has strengths in other areas. For example, your daughter may excel in sports but not in English. Or, your son may be doing very well in English, but struggling in science. So often our children's thoughts are ruled by what they cannot do, rather than what they can. In fact, our children sometimes may be so absorbed by one bad outcome that they catastrophize and conclude they are all bad. Such temporary irrational thinking has to be handled before a parent can go on to emphasize the positive.

Here is one technique for limiting your child's negative thoughts about herself. Draw a circle and put some other smaller circles inside the big one. Working with your child, label each small circle with the various characteristics and skills the child possesses. Then, show that just because there is one "bad" circle, it doesn't spoil all the other good circles that make up the child. If you can conclude this circle exercise with an outrageous analogy, all the better. For example, you might say to your teenager that she wouldn't junk an expensive portable stereo just because a battery is dead. Similarly, you suggest she shouldn't trash herself when only one thing goes wrong.[23]

Only the rare superkid is accomplished in everything. Our children's unevenness is part of their specialness. So, what can we do to enhance our child's overall willpower? Instead of letting the difficult areas define your children's sense of accomplishment, build on their strengths. Let what your child can do spread in importance.[24] As a parent, accentuate and value your child's assets. Make that particular facet of your child's life even more prominent, both in the time your child spends on it and the praise that you deliver. Our task as parents is to promote the attention and extra learning opportunities to maximize the positive.

When your child is low on willpower because of difficulties in other areas of life, remind her of her determination and success in another area of strength. This is an approach I have used with older children: Have your child make a deposit in a mental bank account when she enjoys an activity and does well at it. A parent's praise also can be deposited in the Mental Bank of I Can-Do's. This account is filled with mental can-do's that a child may withdraw when he is feeling down. Such withdrawals are a ready source of willpower.

Barrier Boosts

A critical factor in hopeful thinking is how children deal with obstacles to their goals. By bestowing barrier boosts, parents help their children overcome barriers. During the very early years, caregivers play an important role in fostering a sense of determination as children tackle goals and their associated barriers. It is one thing to have determined thoughts when our goals are unencumbered, and another when our goals are somehow blocked.

What can caregivers do to increase the chances of children maintaining their willpower in the face of barriers? The first lesson is to normalize the fact that the child is being blocked. For a very young child, this is a difficult concept to grasp, but stick with it. The key is to show your youngster that all of us run into roadblocks to what we want, and this is just part of life. You might give examples of how other children they know have encountered obstacles. Or, you can talk about how you, even as an adult, have come upon roadblocks. Children also enjoy hearing about the tough spots that their parents faced when they were young. Talk about times that you were stuck and include instances when you struggled successfully and unsuccessfully with impediments. Of course, do not overdo or continue to repeat these stories about the old days because your children may tune out. A second lesson is to point out how your children have kept trying to get what they wanted when encountering blockages in the past. Often children forget or do not give themselves credit for their past perseverance; reviewing these experiences is a source of renewed determination.

Third, teach your children that these tough barrier-laden situations are best thought of as challenges rather than failures waiting to happen. As discussed in chapter 2, high-hope people not only think this way but also describe their parents as teaching this challenge perspective.[25] Say to your child "Life puts these barriers in our way so we will keep alert" or "Obstacles make things more interesting for us. Why imagine how boring it would be if we always got what we wanted without any trouble." These barrier boost little voices in kids' heads help solidify the I-can tapes.

When children are young, you need to be there to help deal with problems. Parents possess a powerful additional means of sparking willpower — encouragement. A few statements such as "You can do it," and "You know I'm behind you," go a long way in imparting willpower thinking, especially if you tie such encouragement to a specific goal the child is pursuing. Whatever the age of your children, offer your support. Sometimes simple encouragement to stick with their goals is helpful to the children experiencing difficulty. Such support is important for children of all ages. The spirits of children are enlivened at times by the mere thought that their parents, or important role models, are behind them when things get tough. In looking back at their childhoods, high-hope adults report that their parents not only taught them what to do when encountering obstacles but also provided support to their offspring.

When children are very young, parents may intervene and offer concrete help when they encounter obstacles. Over the years as children age, we need to intercede less and less so that they develop their own willpower to overcome obstacles. Indeed, we are undermining our children's willpower when we continue to solve their problems. I remind you of Ann described in chapter 2. Ann didn't seem to have any mental drive or willpower in her job as a clothes buyer. During her childhood, her parents stepped in and handled her problems. By watching and talking with her parents, she developed pathways thinking, but she never acquired much of a sense of her own willpower.

Another barrier boost worthy of discussion is laughter. A good laugh, especially if it is at one's own predicament, can clear the mind of a sense of being stuck. Such humor is refreshing because it enables children to stop a continuing cycle of negative thinking about their predicaments. Laughter also gives one a spurt of mental energy.

How can we teach our children to have a sense of humor about themselves, especially in those times when they are discouraged and feeling stuck? One possibility is that the parent and child together make up a story that forms the essence of the child's actual situation. Then, the parent can try some humorous twists to explain what happens to the protagonist in the story (who, of course, is the child). Soon the child may be joining in with even further messes encountered by the hero of the story. Exaggeration of the hero's plight also is a good means of igniting the humor. Likewise, puppets are useful aids in this exercise with younger children.

You may think of other approaches to increasing the natural propensity of your children to find humor in their lives. Of course, if we are able to invoke humor at our own parental fallibilities, our offspring may model our behavior. Because much of humor is based on human foibles and predicaments, our job as parents is to help our children find the absurd in situations. Often this discovery means your children gain some perspective on themselves; with this new perspective comes renewed willpower. It is important to guide this perspective-taking, of course, without making fun of the child (e.g., You're such a baby) or discounting feelings. Yet another barrier lesson involves sitting tight. At times, the child's pursuit of a goal may be blocked by something in the situation. For the young child, this might mean that some other toddler is using the swing in the park; for the teenager, it may mean that dad is using the family car. Or, the child may not have the skills necessary to reach the goal; for example, the toddler does not know how to use the swing, or the teenager doesn't know how to drive. Whatever the nature of the blockage at the given time, the child needs to learn how to wait until the desired goal may be reached.

When one does not learn to wait, mental energy is vented in the form of frustration. Teach your young children various distraction techniques so they can handle this waiting. These techniques can be anything from singing to playing with one's hands, as well as counting or identification games. If your children are rather impulsive and get frustrated when having to wait, or when confronted with a barrier, you may want to teach them the turtle technique.[26] This starts by telling a story of a young turtle who talked to an older and wiser turtle about how to handle things when he was not getting what he wanted. The old turtle suggested putting his head down between his shoulders, closing his eyes, and keeping his arms close to his body. This is doing the "turtle." When a child gets in the turtle, she tenses and relaxes her muscles and even can think about how to solve her problem. Of course, children encouraged to try these exercises learn to channel their energies when they cannot get what they want immediately.

Young children must learn how to handle delay of gratification because they face many instances of this challenge during their lifetimes. For older children, the waiting may necessitate their switching to other more reachable goals. If the waiting is necessary because children do not yet have the requisite skills to pursue their goals, this becomes a prime time for learning the particular skills. Waiting that is filled with activities, especially if those activities contribute to your child's eventually reaching the coveted goal, is most palatable to children.

One last barrier boost lesson involves the instance in which your child is truly stuck and cannot surmount the barrier. In such moments, teach them that this happens to all kids and adults at times. You also may want to use the goal lesson of abandoning the truly unreachable goal and substituting another.

Encourage Process, Not Just Product

Even though high-hope people are goal-directed, they enjoy the process of getting there as much as the actual arrival. This is one of the seeming paradoxes I initially had difficulty disentangling when talking with high-hope people. Goals certainly capture the attention of high-hope people, but this largely seems to be true because such goals offer a marker for progress or mastery occurring along the way. This means that we still need to help children clearly articulate their goals. Additionally, however, we need to promote the child's sense of movement or growth toward a goal. If we teach our children to monitor their progress, for example, they experience their growth more vividly.

If your child is low in willpower, it may be that he is making comparisons to the outcomes of other kids. Rather than these social comparison-based goals, performance goals are more satisfying. It is more useful if children establish their own goals and note their progress toward them. You may have to help them make charts where they can plot day-by-day improvements. If the goal is spelling or word meaning, for example, place a growing list of the child's vocabulary on the refrigerator door. If the goal is to have fewer tantrums, placing stars on a calendar for tantrum-free days may be effective. Whatever means of charting you devise should enable your child to see the progress being made. Such charts do not and should not lead to perfectionistic goals, but they do illustrate positive movement to our children. This perception of positive movement engenders willpower.

It also is helpful to instruct our children about the importance of understanding or learning itself, rather than gaining approval solely for some praiseworthy end product.[27] Unfortunately, our schools often emphasize the product and ignore the process. From elementary to graduate school, children end up chasing the almighty grade and do not revel in the learning itself.[28] Children focusing on end goals try not to make errors. Part of learning, however, is based on a willingness to take risks and make mistakes. This trial and error approach is critical to the discovery process. If we teach children that it is normal to make errors along the way to their goals, they are likely to be more energized for the process.[29] (This latter point is similar to my earlier one about normalizing barriers that are encountered.) At times in American society, we are so focused on the product that we become impatient with the errors that are necessary as progress and learning occur.

When we impart such impatience to our children, we are not rewarding the learning process, or appreciating the gains being made. To stifle errors and to rush goal pursuits in children is to take the fun out of the process. Indeed, the process is the energizing part of goal-pursuits for the young and old. Therefore, instead of heaping praise on our children only when they obtain goals, we must praise their willingness to undertake tasks and make errors, as well as praising their involvement and pleasure along the way. These latter characteristics build a child's willpower, perhaps more so than the actual goal attainments. Because of the societal emphasis on the end product, we parents need to provide a counterpoint about the critical role of the process of pursuing goals.

An example of how to change from emphasizing the end product to emphasizing the process may be helpful at this point. I once saw a young teenage boy named Phil who was depressed and lethargic. As we talked, it became apparent that the boy's father had extremely high expectations that Phil should be a winner in sports. The father was a former athlete who experienced some success in high school, but did not excel in college. The son had considerable talent and interest in sports, but he felt enormous pressure to win for his dad. Feeling worried and insecure about producing to his father's satisfaction, Phil withdrew into a shell of depression and inactivity. My role in the process was to help the dad see how he was placing undue pressure on his son. Because Phil said he enjoyed sports, we worked out a contract where having fun and participation was the emphasis in any sporting activities. The father agreed to this and came to realize that he was reenacting a win script his father had put on him. One of the more telling insights occurred when the father told about how bottled up and defeated he felt when his father behaved in a similar fashion. Most importantly, the boy became more active and successful in his sporting activities and came out of his depression. Not only were the son's spirits lifted in this process but the father also appeared buoyed by no longer having to impart the old family win script. (I discuss the winning versus performance emphases further in chapter 7.)

Rechargers

Sometimes it is obvious that our children are discouraged and their willpower is depleted. As described in the previous chapter, all of us may experience down times. It is important for caregivers to explain to children that such times are normal. Even high-hope children have periods when they are not experiencing their typical degree of motivation. We need to teach our children that such down times may result because of illness or physical exhaustion. In other words, if children have been playing or working very hard, they naturally experience a slowing down period where they are in need of both physical and mental recharging. One way of showing children the necessity of such recharging time is to discuss how we all need sleep. Children, like adults, go in bursts of physical and mental energy, and then slow down to renew themselves. For young children, fussiness often signals the need for a nap. As a parent, be firm about nap and bed time. Likewise, as your children get into their teenage years, enforce a quiet time after some point in the evening (say,

10:30), and insist that your children are off the telephone and the stereos and televisions are turned off.

Another means of energizing the minds of children is to make sure they are getting enough physical exercise. Although we may think that children by their very nature are active, many are not getting enough physical exercise. Physical exercise builds the child's stamina to undertake the learning tasks that are an essential part of development. A child who is physically fit is more alert mentally and willing to explore and tackle tough jobs. If your child is experiencing boredom and sluggishness, more physical exertion may be needed rather than rest. With the increased propensity to watch television and play video games, many children in our society need the stimulation of physical exertion. A good way to start this habit is to exercise with your child. This shared exercise can be through games, or activities such as jogging or riding bicycles. Likewise, research suggests that high-hope people enjoy the competition of organized sports; participation in such activities helps to increase your child's determination.[30]

Yet another recharger for your children involves moving to new goals. Sometimes your child may be tired of pursuing a goal and needs a break. This is the all-too-familiar boredom, in which the child's mind no longer is engaged. Psychologist Ellen Langer would call this state *mindlessness*.[31] In terms of hope, I conceptualize this as being low in willful thinking.

Consider another related instance in which your child lacks motivation. If your children are nearing the completion of a goal, do they seem paradoxically less motivated? As I discussed earlier, children may enjoy the process of getting to a goal as much as the actual achievement. In such instances, tell your children to take a break and try something else that captures their attention. This is similar to the sense of recharging that adults experience on a vacation. Even though we may work harder on vacation than in our regular jobs, because it is something different we are refreshed when we return to our routine.

Another version of recharging occurs when our children reach their goals. They experience some satisfaction with the attainment of their goals, but they may be down for a period until they get a new project or goal. This new goal enlivens their minds and renews their willpower to undertake the new task. One way to ensure that your offspring experience this new goal recharging is to help them set the stretch goals described earlier. Although stretch goals are difficult, they are not unduly so; children can complete them and take time to appreciate their achievements. Thereafter, they are more likely to experience the surge of willful thinking that accompanies a new goal.

Before closing this section on rechargers, I must warn parents against becoming activity enforcers with their children. Over the last decade in my group therapy experiences and talks, I have encountered more parents who compel their children to participate in one activity after another. The children are required to take special lessons before and after school, as well as on the weekends. The parents' motive is to make their children well rounded. The net effect, however, is that the parents are tired from having to haul their kids to all of these activities, and the children also are exhausted. My advice to such parents — and to you should this pattern be evident in your family — is to leave your children plenty of free time to relax and enjoy childhood.

A Willpower Checklist

Having touched on the major approaches for enhancing our children's willpower thinking, review these willpower tips in the following checklist:

Do

- ✓ Take every opportunity to make your children realize that they were the ones who made something happen.
- ✓ Praise your children whenever they show determination to get what they want (assuming it is a goal condoned in the family).
- ✓ Teach your children to have positive mental tapes playing in their heads about how they can do things.
- ✓ Help your children accentuate their strengths and minimize their weaknesses.
- ✓ Emphasize that roadblocks are a normal part of life and are to be anticipated.
- ✓ Tell your kids about roadblocks you encountered in your childhood and how you coped successfully and unsuccessfully with them.

✓ Suggest that barriers should be viewed as challenges rather than preludes to failure.

✓ Coach your children to recall how they have overcome previous barriers when they encounter new roadblocks.

✓ Help your children to laugh at themselves and their predicaments.

✓ Teach your kids how to be patient and to wait when they are not getting what they want.

✓ Encourage your offspring to enjoy the process of getting to their goals, rather than concentrating only on the outcome.

✓ Point out that being mentally drained sometimes is normal, and that we need to recharge when we feel this way.

✓ Allow your children to take time-outs from their goal pursuits.

✓ Make sure your children are exercising and getting enough rest.

Don't

✓ Assume that your children know when you are proud of their goal-directed efforts and achievements.

✓ Dwell on weaknesses or failures.

✓ Tell your child "You can't do this" or "I'll do it myself."

✓ Overdo your stories about your childhood successes at overcoming difficulties.

✓ Abandon your children when they face difficulties.

✓ Make fun of your children or discount their feelings.

✓ Intervene and try to solve all the problems of your children.

✓ Prescribe to your children how involved and motivated they should be for particular goals.

✓ Commit your children to so many activities that they don't have free time to relax.

WAYPOWER

Pathways are the mental means to all the wonderful things our children desire. We can teach children how to achieve their goals and how to solve problems, but these lessons are not enough.[32] Some experience with successful planning and problem solving is necessary as a foundation, but the real key is that children believe in their capabilities to produce these mental road maps. If children believe they can come up with effective routes to get what they want, they have an advantage in achieving those goals.[33] In this section, I describe what we can do to build our children's trust in their way-power thinking.

Little Links

In the developmental chapter, I suggested that children begin to make this-leads-to-that linkages from the moment of birth. This section presents things we can do to help our infants with these crucial links. By teaching our newborns to participate in such linkage exercises, we are laying a foundation for beliefs in their way-related thinking. The common element in these exercises is that they teach infants the rudimentary causal formula of this is followed by that.[34]

Because you are doing a lot of diaper changing anyway, watch how your infant participates in this process. When your baby is only a few months old, take advantage of any natural behaviors and work them into your routine. For example, when baby Eddy thrashes about when you take off his diaper, let him do this for awhile as you clean him, then when he has his legs spread, put the diaper on. All the time, talk to Eddy and thank him for putting his legs out so the diapering is easier. After awhile, you will notice that Eddy puts himself more quickly into a position to be diapered. In other words, he anticipates the ritual and participates in it.

One relatively straightforward lesson in linkages can be conducted with infants at three months. Tie a string to something that makes noise, such as a little rattle or bell, and make sure your infant can see the noise maker. Then, loop the string around the infant's ankle or arm. What happens? Your infant starts moving the string to make the noise. This is an early example of a lesson that the children repeat many times over their childhoods. As parents know, children love to find out how to make noises.

The basic lesson in the previous example is about pulling something. This lesson has several variants. If you tie a string to an object, or put a toy on a piece of cloth, babies can readily learn to pull the desired object toward themselves by using the cord or cloth. You may have to show them a few times, but they catch on. When babies begin to crawl, and even more so when they begin to walk, they love to pull things that make noise. These clackers or poppers may be anything from a duck to a race car.

Another pulling lesson comes when you hold your six-month-old by the arms and gently lift her up to a standing position. In our family, this game is called *so big*. At first, the baby limply lets you pull her up. After a few repetitions, however, notice the baby stiffens her legs to make the pull-up easier. Later, the baby also begins to pull with her arms. Throughout this process, of course, it is helpful for the parent to keep up a constant stream of chatter about what is transpiring.

A related lesson to pulling that uses the opposite principle is bumping. Here, the babies learn they can push things. Food on the high chair may be an early thing to move. Or, they can knock down blocks built in front of them. They can push a large rubber ball back to Mom. They can learn bumper-cars and hit one object with another. Drums can be hit to make noise. In our house, we use the pots and pans; our granddaughter loves to hit them with a wooden spatula. The options for bump lessons to be learned are almost endless, but again I would emphasize the importance of the caregiver making a big deal, verbally and nonverbally, about these feats.

Another good game to play with your baby is an early version of hide and seek. Here, of course, the object is to find where the desired object is hidden. At first, you have to be pretty obvious about where you are hiding the object, say under a cloth directly in front of the child. Again, praise your baby when he finds it. "There it is!" is a phrase that we exclaim when the prized object is found. The searching behavior of the baby is a basic component of early pathways thinking. (Incidentally, the pursuit of the goal object and the impediment offered by the cover are directly analogous to the principles of hope theory.)

Throughout this first year, therefore, our offspring may develop many linkages with our help. Sometimes we parents may act as if we want our babies to be quiet and inactive. Although this is understandable to give parents some rest, it may contribute to low waypower thinking in offspring. If your apartment or house is filled with the noises of blocks, clackers, pots, balls bouncing, and caregivers' positive proclamations about these events, some excellent pathways are evolving in the minds of babies.

Bigger Links

As your child moves into toddlerhood, the what-leads-to-what lessons continue and increase in complexity. Somewhere around age two or three, your child pounces on a most-used word. What is it? Probably you would guess that it is *no*. My sense is that this word is second on the usage list. My nominee for most used is *why*. At times little ones may rattle off the why's so easily that it may appear they are not really interested in the answer. Don't be fooled, however. I think they are. Why? is an invitation to teach our children about the causes of things they have seen or heard. Don't worry about giving technically correct or totally understandable answers to this barrage of questions, but do the best you can. Also, be prepared for the child's asking a similar question again, as the quest continues.[35]

Toddlers enjoy learning the sequence of events. If you can play games repeatedly with your children, they quickly learn what happens next. Nursery rhymes usually are constructed so your child can anticipate some of the verses. The stories in books stimulate your child's waypower thinking. Favorite songs also offer an auditory means of learning the sequencing of events. As you watch something being built, describe to your toddler how one thing follows another; this offers an excellent visualization of temporal sequencing. One of my fond memories is taking our youngest son to get donuts on Saturday morning. Once we had our donuts, we would go outside to eat and talk. Over several months, we watched the construction of a nearby building in our downtown area. In retrospect, the why questions from my young son about what was happening in the construction of the building forecast his subsequent interests in carpentry.

During toddlerhood, your children have some favorite toys and may play with them for hours. For example, at this age I had a wooden peg set. I could pound the pegs in with a hammer, turn the thing over, and pound the pegs in again. This is one of my very earliest memories, and I recall playing with this pounding set for long periods. If your children have toys that similarly enthrall them — from Lincoln Logs to Legos — let them play as long as they want. Likewise, encourage your children to use their creativity to transform objects for their enjoyment. You don't need a fancy toy, but rather a childlike imagination to play. The pleasure in the toy is probably due in large part to the toddlers' sense that they are producing something. If your children make something, especially if it is for you, proudly display it. I still have such clay figures, drawings, and paintings scattered around my house and office.

In the toddler to preschool period, children acquire many skills that depend on an understanding of causality.[36] Let's take potty training as an example. My belief is that children basically train themselves when they finally understand what leads to what. In other words, all the good attempts to put children on the potty and tell them to go, miss the important point that they may not have learned the bodily cues as to when it is time to urinate or defecate. When your children are aware of these cues, perhaps through your guidance, then they can successfully undertake this toilet training milestone. Be prepared, of course, for accidents while your child is preoccupied with playing. These accidents are to be expected, and you may even prepare your child for them by describing how Sneaky Pee or Sneaky Poop may catch them.[37]

What should be emphasized in this toilet training example, as well as in the other lessons, is the importance of understanding the linkages among events. That is, your child has developed a clearer understanding of If-then linkages: *If* I feel a full sensation and pressure, *then* I am going to pee. This leads to the related planful thought: *If* I feel a full sensation and pressure, *then* I better get to the toilet.

During this preschool period, our children become better at predicting what will happen, and they begin to have planful thoughts about what they will do thereafter. Anything you can do as a parent to increase your children's awareness of such if-then linkages helps them not only to understand causality in general but also to increase their thinking about finding pathways to their goals. Talk with your preschoolers about upcoming events and find out how they are anticipating things that are going to happen. Likewise, you can stimulate you child's if-then thinking by asking what-if questions.

Stick with these if-then lessons, and your children will grasp the linkages that enable them to learn potty training, as well as other necessary childhood skills. Do not, however, criticize your children because they have not learned something quickly enough. Equally devastating and conducive to low-waypower thinking is the exasperated parent who utters such comments as, "You're never going to learn this," "Everyone else your age knows how to do this," or the classic "When I was your age, I could do this." Such statements further block our children's learning of waypower thinking.

Sometimes your youngsters may have incorrect perceptions of what is going to happen, and you can help them obtain more accurate views. For example, five-year-old Penny is scared of starting kindergarten. Her mom asks what will happen when she goes to kindergarten, to which Penny replies, "I won't be able to learn all the stuff." Instead of immediately trying to rebut Penny's perception, the mother reviews with Penny all the things she does well. Penny agrees, and adds, "But I can't read very good." By now, the issue is narrowed from all the stuff to reading. To this, mother asks, "Is there anything you want to do this summer to get ready?" Penny thinks awhile and says, "I want to read lots of books." Mom agrees. The inherent logic of this plan is, *if* Penny can improve on her reading, *then* she will be able to learn all the stuff. Accordingly, Penny isn't as frightened about starting kindergarten.

The worst thing Mom could do in this example is to minimize Penny's concern. Well-intentioned parents can make the mistake of saying, for example, "It's no big deal, you will do just fine." What we parents fail to realize is that it is a big deal to our kids. In such instances, the child deserves advice or guidance about an effective route for meeting the desired goal.

Building Skills and Believing

There are basic skills pertaining to scholastics (e.g., language and mathematics), athletics, and social matters on which the child is evaluated throughout the school years. Because our society dictates these areas of competence either formally or informally, parents can be certain their children are aware of the importance placed on these skills. We have found that higher-hope adults do perform better in the scholastic[38] and athletic arenas.[39] Likewise, children with higher hope are rated as being more competent in scholastics, athletics, and social matters.[40] Therefore, there is a skills base for higher hope. This suggests that to foster higher hope in our children we need to facilitate their acquisition of skills in these arenas.

A full discussion of how to teach scholastic, athletic, and social skills is beyond the scope of this book. However, I have some comments and suggestions about these skills. To aid parents, Appendix A (at the back of the book), lists books that provide excellent advice about fostering learning in these three arenas. (See also footnote 32 in this chapter, where I list books used to teach problem solving to children.)

A few words are warranted about the major scholastic skills, language and writing. To specify one's goals, as well as the pathways associated with those goals, both language and writing skills are critical to our children. As they grow, for example, our children are called on to communicate clearly what they want to accomplish and how they are going about it. In this context, written and spoken words are essential tools or symbols. This latter lesson is worth imparting to your children — language is something that they can use throughout their lives to help them get what they want.

Suppose your daughter, Marcy, loathes reading and writing but loves working with younger children. Her goal is to start a day-care center when she is grown. When Marcy turns fourteen, she decides to begin baby-sitting. To start, she needs to get the word out about her availability as a sitter. You suggest distributing a flyer to all the apartments in your building. Marcy is motivated to do this, but she asks for help in making the flyer say what she wants (i.e., words as pathways). You and she work on this, and you point out how language is useful to her. Eventually, Marcy gets several clients and, to her surprise, some of the kids want to be read to. The children enjoy this, and so does Marcy. Marcy also finds that some of the children are interested in learning how to write, so she helps them with this process. For Marcy these language-related activities are pleasant in this context. Perhaps more important, she learns that reading and writing have a major impact on her eventual career aspirations of working with children.

If you bring this lesson about the importance of language to life with your children, they are more likely to understand and embrace language-related learning. Talk with your child about how she is going to reach her goals. Show her how she needs to communicate her plans to you. Find topics for reading that match your daughter's interests. Encourage your children to take any oral communication courses offered at their schools. Good communication necessitates the use of language as a tool. Use the learning modes to which your children are most responsive. For example, our youngest son could learn better by hearing things first. Our daughter, on the other hand, liked to read. Whatever you can do to show your children that language is a vital thing, do it. Twenty-first-century jobs will demand language skills, and our children must understand this fact.

The skills related to social interactions also are important to your children's development, largely because our thoughts about ways to achieve our goals almost inevitably involve other people.[41] We already know that high-hope individuals enjoy interacting with people, and they listen to the perspectives of others.[42] A good starting point in teaching your children to interact well with others is to convey the importance of listening.[43] To interact in the true sense of this word, your children need to know what other people think and what they want.

How can you teach these listening skills? Periodically, ask your child to repeat what you have said. When you are shopping, ask your child what the clerk said. Tell your children what you thought they said (turnaround is fair play). In part, you also are expanding your child's memory. With teenage clients who were shy, I suggest that the first and biggest step in interacting is to ask other people about themselves, or just to learn to listen to others. Rarely do children realize how important it is to hear and understand what another person is saying. Other people love a good listener, and as such the shy teenager who listens to others can count on being included in activities.

Another lesson taken from high-hope people is that they have give-and-take relationships in which both parties gain things from the interchange. In parenting, teach your children how to share, help their friends, and ask for help from those friends. For adolescents, the initial contacts for friendships appear to be formed at school, but the closeness of such interactions are solidified outside of the school context.[44] Therefore, any time you can arrange activities so that your children can be with their friends in your home environment, you are fostering closer friendships.

A last social interaction skill your child needs is the ability to compromise with friends to arrive at shared goals and pathways. Sometimes your child may be low in hope because he cannot compromise. Such inflexibility in children reflects thinking that is low in waypower. Suppose your seven-year-old Sandy is playing with another boy, and an argument begins about how they are going to do something. The other boy runs off mad, and Sandy stomps in the house crying. Do not try to do anything at this point. Rather, wait until Sandy has cooled off and then get his sense of what happened. Next, point out how this has happened before (assuming it has) and ask Sandy what he could do differently in the future. If he suggests a compromise, praise him and ask him to try it. More likely, you will have to teach Sandy that a compromise is a way two people get what they want. Any stories you may have about your doing this in your childhood (or your adult life) may help. You may have to repeat these lessons about compromise, but keep at it because it helps children have more satisfying interactions with their playmates. I also discuss the importance of compromise in relationships in chapter 7.

Athletics provide physical activities where children learn about individual and group goal pursuits. Thinking about pathways involves plays and routines that children learn to score (i.e., move toward a goal) or prevent another from scoring (i.e., blocking movement toward a goal). Research shows that college students involved in varsity athletics have significantly higher waypower subscale scores on the Hope Scale than do other college students,[45] but this may be due to self-selection rather than the fact that sports instill waypower thinking.[46] Certainly, coaches attempt to train their athletes in flexible, goal-related thinking. Likewise, team sports impart a cooperation among children in the pursuit of common goals. With all the preparation and practice entailed in athletics, a child learns to be both determined and planful. Remember the case of Phil described earlier in this chapter? Phil's have fun approach to his sports involvement not only increased his will-related thinking but also raised his waypower thoughts about reaching common goals with his teammates. For these various reasons, we parents should encourage our children's involvement in sporting activities.[47]

As important as the actual performance in the aforementioned areas may be, what your child perceives about his or her competence is more important. Recall our research showing that children with higher hope also perceive they have more competence in the scholastic, athletic, and social areas. This self-perception of competence is a key to maintaining high hope in children. In other words, a child may have all the competence and skill in the world, but still not believe it. Many successful children think of themselves as impostors unable to come up with ideas about reaching their goals.[48] Such uncertainty by children results when parents have intervened too often and found the pathways solutions for their children's goal blockages. These children are left with low-hope mindsets of being impostors because they do not think they are capable of producing routes to their goals. High-hope children, however, do not think this way.

How do high-hope children get these positive beliefs about their waypower skills? Our research suggests that it starts at home.[49] When your children are every young, they may run into roadblocks because they lack a skill. This is where the skills training I discussed earlier can be taught either by the parents, teachers, or coaches. For children to believe in their waypower thinking, we must let them try their new skills on their own. If one route to a goal doesn't work, the child may need more skills training. Increasingly, however, we must allow our children to come up with possible solutions on their own. In this process, it is helpful to let your children make their own decisions as soon as possible.

In all the aforementioned activities, be willing to spend lots of time talking with and listening to your children as they express their ideas about how to reach their goals. Perhaps most important, show that you believe in your children's growing waypower thinking. Say to your daughter or son, for example, "Keep trying and you probably will find a way to handle this problem." In this context, also make it clear that you are there to provide advice and support if needed. If you openly doubt decisions your children have made about how to pursue their goals, they also harbor doubts about any pathways to their goals. Of course, we parents often experience concerns about our offsprings' choices, but we must trust them to make these pathways decisions.

Movies of the Mind

To enhance waypower thinking, teach your children to form a vivid mental picture of how they are going to reach their desired goals. There are several versions of this movie of the mind, all of which share these basic components: First, there is a leading woman or man, or girl and boy in the present context. Second, there is the happy ending, which is where the girl or boy wants to get. Third, there is the story showing how protagonists get to their goals. In other words, movies of the mind are mental rehearsals of how we are going to achieve our goals.

Movies of the mind involve scripts for those situations where children learn what to do in given circumstances. In chapter 3, for example, I talked about the morning script for the child who is getting up. Scripts involve a ritual or sequence of events that parents often teach their children. Children may have some apprehension before they are to do something for the first time. Examples here would be getting a haircut, going to the dentist, going to the doctor, beginning kindergarten, or starting junior high. Parents can help the child by providing a word picture of how things will go in these particular situations. When children actually undergo these experiences, they naturally modify the script somewhat and carry these scripts around in their minds. Talk with your children about their experiences and have them tell their stories in chronological order. If your children somehow are distorting their experiences, particularly in a negative fashion, help them get scripts that are more positive and helpful for achieving goals. The hopeful script is one in which children focus on the various things they can do to reach their goals. Worry scripts, on the other hand, focus on what can go wrong and how lousy the child will feel.[50] What happens with such scripts is that they can become self-fulfilling prophecies in which things actually happen the way the children have practiced them mentally.

Mental practice for an upcoming goal event enables children to plan what they will do.[51] For example, thirteen-year-old Matt may play out the following scenario in his mind: OK, I'll ask Sally if she has a time to talk after lunch, just before fifth period. And if she doesn't, I'll ask her when we can talk. But if we can talk after lunch, then I'll just go ahead and ask her to go to the dance with me. No, I'll ask her if she is planning on going to the dance. Yeah, and if she says she is, I'll ask her if she is going with anyone. If she says she has a date, I'll say, "Great, I'll see you there." If she doesn't have a date, then I'll ask her. Parents can help their children by talking about these mental simulations, especially if they can give ideas about things that can be done when obstacles are encountered. Notice that Matt has worked one such potential barrier into his mental practice.

Research shows that such mental practice has positive effects on performance in the actual situation, and these beneficial effects are more marked when people strongly imagine themselves in the situation.[52] If you use some of the tips I have given about waypower thoughts, your child's mind should have several possible routes to desired goals. By encouraging them to practice these possible routes mentally, your children become more flexible and successful in their actual goal pursuits.

Doable, Small Steps

As your children grow, they are expected to undertake larger goals, as well as those taking longer to attain. Unfortunately, such goals can be daunting to children. Two high-hope lessons, however, provide related pathways for reaching these goals. One lesson is to have your children begin by tackling what they can do. Large, long-term goals often have several parts a child cannot perform at the beginning of the goal sequence. Typically, the doable part of a goal sequence involves the first step. The second lesson is to coach your child to think through the remaining steps to the long-term goal. Children need to learn how to break down a goal into obtainable subgoals. This is an instance where goal-setting is tied to waypower thinking in that the subgoals are a route to the end goal.

Because what is doable often is related to a first subgoal, parents should teach their children to divide things into steps. One technique I would recommend is to print the end goal, in the child's words, on a piece of paper. Then, place that piece of paper on the floor a few feet away from the child. Next, ask the child to think of her task as making stepping-stones that need to be accomplished on the way to the end goal. Do not do the child's work for her, but have patience as she comes up with these steps. When a step is agreed on, ask the child to print it and place this piece of paper somewhere on the stepping-stone path to the goal. Once the child has come up with several steps, you may want to have her make sure the steps are in the correct order. Next, have the child walk on the stepping-stones and describe what she is doing at each step, as well as how she will know when she has accomplished that step (this is subgoal attainment).

With older children, use more sophisticated means to record the subgoal steps, but keep these steps so the child can refer to them. The partitioning of pathways into several steps has the added advantage of enabling children to monitor their progress, thereby maintaining determination along the way to the long-term goal.[53] Relatedly, you may want to help your children decide on the reward they give themselves when they complete a subgoal.[54] Research shows that such rewards are effective motivators with children[55] and adolescents.[56] Furthermore, findings suggest we need not worry because our children do not go overboard in rewarding themselves.[57]

Failures in Strategy, Not Me

At times a child who is pursuing a goal tries things that do not work. In these instances, high-hope people report thinking that such circumstances are due to their use of the wrong strategy, rather than their lack of ability.[58] Children who are blocked and attribute this blockage to their own lack of talent are left without options in the pursuit of the goal; moreover, such children are left thinking they are bad, or worse yet, just plain dumb. With high hope, however, if one strategy doesn't work, the child can try another. Research consistently shows that this latter type of thinking is conducive to subsequent effective goal pursuits.[59] In other words, children fare better when they focus on the strategy as the problem rather than on themselves.

Therefore, when your child blames herself for not meeting a goal, try to focus her attention away from herself and back onto the pursuit of the goal. Also, don't talk to your daughter about her failures, but rather point out how she just hasn't found the pathway that will work. Additionally, encourage your child to pay attention to the process of pursuing the goal, rather than just emphasizing the end goal (recall the related willpower lessons). This will make it easier for your child to adopt this I-need-to-find-another-strategy approach.[60]

If your child appears to blame himself for failures and is prone to get into a cycle of self-criticism, you can employ the detective technique. Here is how this works: First, ask your child if he is willing to try a different way of thinking. If he agrees, ask him to take on the role of being a detective about his life. As a detective, he is supposed to find out what strategies he is using that do not get him what he wants. Second, tell him you would like a verbal report about these unsuccessful strategies once a week. Third, when he has given a report or two about strategies that don't work, ask for additional information in his next report. In particular, suggest that finding out which strategies that don't work should give some clues about those that work (i.e., effective pathways). Lastly, suggest that a good detective should test out some of the possible strategies that do work. So, ask him to substitute these more effective strategies when an initial one is not effective. After awhile, your child should begin to conclude that his setbacks often call for another strategy. At this point, praise him for learning to apply this adaptive detective mindset to his life.[61]

Before leaving this section, I emphasize that it is not helpful to foster our children's blaming of other people when goal pursuits are unsuccessful. Children and adults are social creatures, and we do not like to be around people who blame us for their setbacks. A child who complains and blames his playmates soon has fewer friends. A blamer of people is like a rotten apple that spoils the social context. Research shows that blaming others does not get the person back on track toward a goal; in fact, it can have quite counterproductive consequences.[62]

Children's Books

In the process of exploring sources for instilling waypower thinking in children, I was drawn to "children's" books. Children's is in quotes because my sense is that such stories are important for children to hear, but the words also deliver helpful messages to parents. Stories have a seductive quality, whether read to or by the child. In one allegory of hope entitled *Crow and Weasel*, the importance of the tale itself is aptly summarized by one of the characters:

> "I would ask you to remember only this one thing," said the Badger. "The stories people tell have a way of taking care of them. If stories come to you, care for them. And learn to give them away where they are needed. Sometimes a person needs a story more than food to stay alive. That is why we put these stories in each other's memory. This is how people care for themselves."[63]

For a list of children's books that teach about various hope-related issues see Appendix B (at the end of this book). There, I list the titles by the topic or problem they address. Under each topic is the name of the book, along with the publisher and a brief description. I selected these books in part for teaching waypower thinking to children, and in part for their readability and attention-holding properties. Most of the books in Appendix B are for the child reader, although I have included a few for adults wanting tips about specific childhood issues.

A Waypower Checklist

The various ideas I have explored for enhancing our children's waypower thinking are summarized in the following list:

Do

✓ With infants, constantly show them how causality works (i.e., This leads to that.).

✓ Supply objects (e.g., drums, pull-toys, building blocks) that, when used, show your youngsters how they are causing something to happen.

✓ Teach toddlers why things happen and have them talk about such linkages.

✓ Listen to you children's explanations or stories about why something happened.

✓ Whenever possible, build your children's skill bases in scholastics, athletics, and social matters.

✓ Instruct your children to have mental scripts about the chain of activities that occur in certain situations.

✓ Use children's stories, nursery rhymes, and songs to teach your children to anticipate how words go together in a sequence.

✓ Help your children break a long pathway leading to a goal into smaller, doable steps.

✓ Teach your children that it is helpful to think about failures as being due to the use of the an ineffective strategy rather than their lack of talent.

✓ Talk with your children about their plans for reaching their goals.

Don't

✓ Get tired of your children's constant why questions and stop answering them.

✓ Suggest that your children aren't learning things as quickly as other children.

✓ Minimize your children's concern about something they haven't learned by saying, "Oh, it's no big deal. . . . You will be OK."

✓ Try to have your children become quiet and inactive in demeanor.

✓ Do all the planning for your children.

✓ Always doubt the pathways your children come up with to reach their goals.

✓ Readily agree with your children if they conclude there are no pathways available for reaching their goals.

✓ Encourage your children to blame other children when goal pursuits are unsuccessful.

TRIPLE PLAYS

Three important principles of parenting are so fundamental that they touch on children's capabilities to form goals and to engender will- and way-related thoughts toward those goals. These processes are attachment, discipline, and modeling.

Attachment

Earlier chapters have explored how attachment is a critical force in the hope process. For all of the previous willpower, waypower, and goal lessons to work, however, parents must establish a firm attachment to their children. This starts with the initial bonding with your newborn and continues through the subsequent close interactions you have with your growing children. From the first moment you hold your newborn, try to respond in a consistent and loving manner to her cries and perceived needs. If you do this, over time your child is more likely to form an attachment to you. With this attachment firmly established, your child has a template for forming other interpersonal relationships in her life.[64] In other words, how your child bonds with you can influence how she forms subsequent relationships with people.

The underlying foundation for the attachment process is that caregivers spend large amounts of time with the developing child.[65] For working parents, this means at least one of the caregivers needs to make a major time commitment to the child. For the single parent, the choice already has been made. One of the reasons divorce has negative effects on children is that the custodial parent's time with the child may be limited.[66] Obviously, this poses a dilemma for a single or working mother who has other demands on her time. My advice for parents experiencing such pulls on their time is to keep your priorities straight. When you are home, make spending time with your child your first priority.[67] For example, your apartment doesn't have to be spotlessly clean and the meals don't have to be culinary delights.

Beyond the sheer amount of time you spend with your child, another aspect of attachment is being attentive and responsive to your children when you are with them.[68] When you are with your child, *really be there*. If your toddler is looking at something, get down on the floor and ask, "What is it?" Help your children describe what they want. Say, "Let's get it," and set off with your child for the desired object. The key in such interactions is being there, being alive and interactive with your child. Imagine you are a personal tour guide to all the unfolding sights and mysteries of the world. Show enthusiasm for the play process. Touch and hug your child as much as possible. Get your hands dirty. Do foolish, playful things. Your young child loves activity, so as tired as you may be after a hard day at work, pump up for your kid's sake. Lastly, keep a line of chatter going with your child.

Being there means being connecting and communicating. As your children get older, keep involved in their activities. When you can, participate directly in their learning. Go to open houses or other activities at school. Talk with your children's teachers. Whenever possible, work with the school and teachers to meet mutually agreed on goals for your children.[69] Don't assume the teachers know more about your children's learning than you do. If you have spent the time and communicated with your children, you are the one who knows what works and what doesn't. In other words, do not abdicate your role as the children's primary instructor when they go off to school.

Discipline

Attachment also involves being consistent and dependable with your child. These latter qualities provide a firm base for your child's risk-taking, and they help should your child undergo some traumatic experience.[70] Part of this consistency and dependability is that you establish the boundaries of acceptable behavior for your child.[71] Be clear about the rules and enforce them. Be careful, however, not to resort to strong forms of punishment involving physical and verbal abuse. If you are a divorced, single parent, or are part of a two-parent team, be sure to follow consistent discipline practices within a supportive context.[72] Although your children may protest, they often appreciate the limit-setting.

Within whatever boundaries you set, as your children grow, increasingly give them as much autonomy and decision-making freedom as is possible.[73] Respect your children's opinions, and ask that they do the same for you. When your children have problems or get in trouble, be there to provide support. Trust your children, and let them know you are on their side. Teenagers especially appreciate such support.[74] If we consistently have disciplined our children, as they grow older, they should be entrusted to apply their own internalized standards of personal conduct. In other words, discipline applied from parents to children evolves into a child's code of self-discipline.

In all of these attachment behaviors and discipline-inducing behaviors, show your love for your children. If you are not a parent, but are a caregiver, teacher, or coach, make it obvious you care about the children.[75] Children learn to have the willpower and waypower thoughts about their goals when they have solid attachments and a sense of boundaries and rules imparted by the important people in their lives. Lastly, children who experience such attachment in the context of consistent and enforced rule structures should make solid connections to other people. Hope has a distinctly interpersonal flavor; children who experience it are more likely to pass it on to their children. This leads to the final topic of this chapter—the modeling of hope.

Modeling

High-hope adults report that their parents served as examples for learning hope.[76] Likewise, a rich history in psychology documents how people learn by watching others.[77] I am reminded here of a caveat for parents: Be careful what you do because you will find your children doing the same thing. Our children soak up what we do and repeat it in their lives. This being the case, we need to give our offspring positive models of hopeful thinking.[78]

Let your children see how you do things. You can start this at a very young age. Children only one- or two-months old watch their parents from their bassinets. Assuming you are practicing the ideas presented previously about fostering attachment, talk to your child about your activities. In such talk, describe your goal as well as how you are going to achieve that goal. Additionally, describe your motivation at various stages of this task.

Once your child is old enough to help, I would recommend a piggybacking technique. Suppose Mom is going to wash the car and asks four-year-old Annie to help. Children are thrilled when asked to help an older person, and they typically participate eagerly. Mom describes to Annie what she wants to get done and how to go about each of the steps involved in washing the car. As they work together, Mom's words of encouragement lift Annie's determination for the task.

At times, we parents think that things can be done faster and more effectively if we just do it ourselves. This may be true, but the long-term lessons learned by a child who helps are well worth any short-term liabilities. Working side by side toward a mutual goal instills children with the perception they can do things valued by adults. If you praise your children for what they have done well, rather than only criticizing the things done incorrectly, they want more of these apprenticelike experiences. Such experiences have a profound impact on children's thinking. They become fond childhood memories and markers of high-hope thinking. As I write this, for example, memories of fishing with Grandpa Gus and my dad came back.

My belief is that children hunger for hope and respond to an environment that allows and nurtures it. I do not suggest it is easy to foster hope in all children. As I noted in the previous chapter, some children have lived in situations where hopeful thinking is virtually extinguished. Whether children have been neglected, abused, deflated by the loss of a parent, ravaged by illness and injury, or have experienced any of the other forces robbing them of hope, however, they still have a chance. That chance, I believe, comes packaged in the form of a positive role model who delivers many of the ideas summarized in this chapter.

One adult role model can have an enormous positive impact on a child. This person does not have to be a parent, given the obvious fact that many children lack any semblance of parents. The role model can be an older brother or sister, an aunt or uncle, a neighbor, an older friend, a teacher, a coach, a therapist, or anyone who is consistently there to talk with and support the child.[79] Only one such adult can make a difference for the child adrift with low hope. Low-hope children are like a small boats lost in the darkness of a threatening sea. A good role model provides a lighthouse of hope for a safe passage.

CHAPTER SIX

Kindling Hope in Adults

It is better to light one candle than to curse the darkness.

— Motto of the Christopher Society

INTRODUCTION: SLAYING THREE MISCONCEPTIONS BEFORE WE START

In talking about and applying the principles of hope theory to the lives of people, I have encountered three misconceptions: First, people conclude that this approach necessitates big changes related to a totally new type of thinking. As I have pointed out at various points, however, we constantly set goals and have willpower and waypower thoughts related to those goals. Usually, we do this without much awareness. Therefore, you definitely are not learning a new type of thinking, but you may become more conscious of how and what you are thinking. At times, some relatively small and yet important changes in the way you think are all that is required.[1]

A second misconception is that to learn hopeful thinking you have to spend most of your time undoing your present counter-productive thoughts. Although at times I give advice about handling your unproductive, goal-related thoughts, my predominant focus is on fostering hopeful thinking. In many instances, the learning of hopeful thinking simply overtakes the negative thinking.

A third misconception is that all of the suggested exercises should work for you. This implies a power and applicability that neither this nor other approaches have. So, don't be dismayed if some of the exercises don't work at first. I do ask that you give some time to each so that it gets a good test. Some exercises work better than others for particular people. Just keep trying and retain the effective ones.

In writing this chapter, I have assumed that you are interested in raising your own hopeful thinking or that you want to help loved ones build their hope. Whatever your focus, my goal is to show how our hopeful thoughts related to goals, willpower, and waypower can be brought to life.

GOALS

Modern culture sends an implicit message that is a combination of "Don't worry, be happy" and "Feel good about yourself." This seductive self-esteem theme leaves us both wondering and wandering; we wonder how we can find the elusive happiness and esteem and wander around trying to find them. If you are looking for happiness and esteem, you will not find them listed under their own names. You are more likely to find these if you look under *goals*. In fact, happier and high self-esteem people are the ones who have concrete and challenging goals in their lives.[2] The philosopher Nietzsche came to a similar conclusion many years ago when he wrote: "Formula of my happiness: A Yes, a No, a straight line, a *goal*." (italics his).[3] Let's look at how you can establish such goals.

Authoring Your Own Decisions

We often set goals without thinking. Indeed, we may have adopted the desires of important other people to such a degree that our lives are ruled by should's.[4] You should be a mother, father, doctor, lawyer, priest, teacher, soldier, carpenter, or architect. You should be a democrat or a republican. You should be a success, or worse, a failure. We adults brought these should's with us from childhood. Throughout our adult years, society also sends messages about what goals are appropriate for particular chronological ages.[5] Likewise, institutions and groups to which we belong have valued goals we are supposed to incorporate.[6] Without awareness, we often let these should's dictate our goal decisions.

This leads to my initial suggestion in regard to setting goals: Be clear you are establishing a goal because it is something you really want. At this point, you may be saying, "Of course I call my own shots." You are an adult, right? Further, if your parents have died, or you have lost a spouse through divorce or death, you may have become painfully aware that you are setting the agenda. Not totally. If most of us think back to our recent goal choices, we probably would conclude that we shared decision making. We inevitably are influenced by the should's placed on us through childhood, as well as by former and present loved ones. Additionally, in ongoing relationships, we need to co-create goals. Indeed, difficulties in relationships often arise because we make important goal decisions without consulting our partners.

So, when do we set goals on our own? My conclusion is that we never undertake goal setting by ourselves because we are influenced by our personal histories and the input we seek from our contemporaries. On the other hand, we always set the goal by ourselves in the instance in which we adopt a goal as ours. At that moment it is important to stop and assess our decisions. We gain control of this process whenever we can shut off automatic, unaware, and mindless decisions, and replace them with greater consciousness.[7]

Practically, what does this mean for you? Obviously, I am not suggesting that you should become highly aware and scrutinize all of your small, daily goals. Many of your practiced habits involving goals serve you well. Automatic pilot is often appropriate for minor goals. If you want to effect a change in some aspect of your life, however, you need to turn off automatic pilot and attend to at least some of the smaller goal decision points. For example, a person with the goal of dieting selects the piece of fruit rather than pie when walking through the lunch line. Likewise, if you want to feel more alive and involved, you need to become more aware of choices about seemingly mundane daily goals. Last and most important, major goal decisions definitely call for your conscious, thoughtful analysis. Choice is fundamental to hopeful thinking, so we need to attend fully to our processing of important goal decisions.[8]

The most powerful psychotherapy exercise I have used to clarify goal setting involves the phrase *I want,* which is to be completed with a predicate. For example, my client George sheepishly asserted, "I want (long pause) to be a success." Sensing his hesitancy, I asked him to complete the stem "My parents want me." He said "to be a success." I then asked George to complete the stem, "My wife wants me" and he chimed in "to be a success." By now George was smiling. When I asked him to complete the original stem "I want," George bellowed out "to have more fun." He laughed loudly at his insight of having defined more clearly *what he wanted.*

Goal Shopping

The next step in effective goal setting is to generate several attractive goals. One good way to do this is to list the important areas in your life. These typically include intimate relationships, family, friendships, career, and recreation. In beginning this process, don't concern yourself with comparing or evaluating these goals; rather, try to include as many as possible. Remember also that these are your goals, not necessarily what you think someone else would want for you. Likewise, try to think only about goals of some importance to you.

One way to develop your wish list is to write the major areas in your life across the top of a piece of paper and list goals under each category. As you think of your goals, you may jump from one area to another; try to have several goals under each category. Some of the goals will overlap, so you may want to group those together. This exercise should take no more than fifteen to twenty minutes. When you are finished with the list, put it away. It is only a first draft, and you need some more time to formulate the goals in your mind.

Let a week or so pass and then take out your list. You probably will find you already have accomplished one or more of the original goals. This is usually a pleasant surprise; we often become so mired in the daily grind that we lose track of how we are meeting some of our goals. Chances are that the goals you have met were fairly short-term ones. Therefore, the remaining goals on your list should be more long-term in nature. Go ahead and rework your list now, adding or deleting any goals as you see fit. Sometimes people do not include goals that may be a reward for them. Try to have such goals in your list. Whatever the treat might be—anything from a walk in the evening to a meal at a good restaurant—strive to include it on your list. Likewise, do your best to increase the number of goals in each arena of your life. That is, don't put all your eggs in one basket. Instead, take a tip from the high-hope people who diversify their goal investments across many areas of their lives.[9] The task is to make a shopping list of as many goals as you reasonably can generate.

For some people, especially those low in hope, this exercise can be quite difficult because they do not think they are capable of achieving any goal, much less several goals. This was true for a man in his midthirties who presented himself to me as being very down and without direction. There was, to hear him, nothing worth doing. After listening to this for awhile, I asked him to say the phrase *There is nothing worth doing* over and over. He repeated this a few times, when he said, "I guess getting some help is worth doing. And feeling better definitely is worth doing." The point of this example is that if you are in the dumps, your goal-setting tends to shut down as you are consumed by your depression. If you are suffering, start with two basic intertwined goals: Getting some help and stopping the pain. Seeking help, whether through a friend or a professional, breaks the cycle of helplessness and goallessness. Likewise, as I discuss later in this chapter, other people often can help us.

Once you make the important step of getting help to solve your problems, ask a question I ask clients. "Where in your life do you feel lousy?" I ask. "Well," my client responds, "I feel lousy everywhere." "But where do you feel most stumped?" I continue. To this, clients usually reel off such comments as, "I can't get along with my boss," "I'm ruining my relationship with my lover," "I'm eating and sleeping too much," and so on. In other words, problems probably are surfacing in several areas of life. Granted, all we are doing here is specifying the different arenas where you feel bad. This is important, however, for identifying goals for improvement in separate aspects of your life. One beneficial side effect is that even though you may feel lousy generally, as you pin it down you may find a few areas in your life where things are working and where you are achieving goals.

Another related means of increasing the possibilities on your list is to try the why-not exercise. I have used this exercise with people to expand their list of goals. Try to imagine some goals that seem a

little far-fetched, possibly even a little uncomfortable.[10] After coming up with one or more of these, ask yourself, why not? I am
reminded of Robert Kennedy's provocative words, "Some men see
things as they are and say, 'why?' I dream of things that never were
and say, 'Why not?'"[11] This simple exercise seems to be quite freeing
to people contemplating new goals.

One last goal-producing exercise is "There's no way I could."
You begin this by saying the stem phrase *There's no way I could,* and
then you add goals that are unthinkable to you. This also can produce a good laugh, which is freeing for the imagination and conducive to goal shopping in general. Sometimes, after coming up
with a seemingly preposterous goal, you may even ask yourself why
not? Rarely do low-hope people produce goals totally beyond their
capabilities. Instead, we often are like the horse with blinders that
can see only those things directly ahead. The purpose of goal shopping is to look around and consider a wide range of possibilities.
Goal shopping opens up one's thinking, and it serves as an antidote
for the shut down thinking of low hope.

All of these goal shopping exercises enable you to slow down the
process of selecting goals. As I noted in the previous chapter on
nurturing hope in children, our society fosters a "Hurry-up, let's get
on with it" mentality when it comes to goals. Such rushing decreases our ability to chose the best goals for ourselves. Therefore, when
you find yourself feeling hurried about goals, it is helpful to slow
down. Haste undermines effective goal setting.

Prioritizing

So far, you have listed a few goals according to categories. Within
each of these categories, go ahead and sort the goals from the most
to the least important. Sometimes people say they are all important.
If this is so, it is no wonder that such people are low on hopeful
thoughts because they feel pulled in far too many directions. If this
sounds like you, you probably have not made the necessary distinctions among the priorities in your life.

One technique is to assign a grade to each goal within each category on your list. Give A's to the extremely important things, B's to

the quite important, C's to the somewhat important, D's to the slightly important, and F's to the unimportant. Being a teacher, I am familiar with the grading scale, but feel free to use any similar system for ranking your goals. When you do this, however, be stringent about those goals fitting in the top category. In other words, be a tough grader. To show you this system, I prioritize my present goals in the chart below.

	Relationship	Family	Work	Health	
A	Listen to and talk more with spouse	Spend more time with children	Improve course lectures	Get rid of stomach pain	A
A	Give more help to spouse	Listen to what kids are saying	Attend to student needs	Eat healthy foods	A
B	Say "thank you" more often	Help in kids' projects	Finish book	Exercise	B
B	Carve out alone time for us	Listen to my father more	Attend to colleague needs	Get sleep	B
B	Plan vacation	Help financially	Review articles	Have wisdom teeth removed	B
C	Remember birthday	Build college fund	Prepare for meetings	Get outside more	C

I would encourage you to write down your priority list because this makes for easier inspection. Often you can get your list on both sides of a 3-by-5-inch note card that fits in your pocket. If you can make such a list and carry it in your head, this is fine also. The key, however, is to think about your highest ranked goals as you spend the hours of your day. Likewise, it is helpful to revise your list at regular intervals. Some people may prefer doing this every week, others may like a biweekly review, and yet others may prefer to redo their lists monthly. When you encounter any of life's inevitable waiting periods (at a physician's office or on the commuter train), work on your priorities list. Wherever and whatever the interval, continue to review your goal priorities.

Initially, you may resist this exercise because you think it is too much work. Granted, this prioritization does take some time—

especially on the first pass through the process. The time involved shrinks, however, as you gain more experience with it. At the other extreme, sometimes a person can get obsessed with such lists. Don't let the list control you, but be sure that you control it. Remember, the list is just a tool to keep the important goals in your sights. Likewise, just a few items on this list warrant your close attention.

Making Bull's-eyes

Once you have prioritized your goals, it is time to clarify further the ones that you have rated as most important. You can do this by carefully describing what each goal entails.[12] Specify only the goals you have rated as extremely or quite important (the A's and some B's). Try to describe each of them so other people could understand. (At times it is necessary to accurately convey to others what you are pursuing.) Use concrete, recognizable markers for your goals. To illustrate, here is a typical exchange that led to goal clarification:

"I don't want to flunk out," asserts Linda, a college sophomore.

"What does that mean?" I ask.

Looking puzzled, Linda replies, "You know, I need to make better grades to stay in school."

"Can you make it more concrete for me?"

"Oh, well . . . no D's or F's. I'm on probation, you know," Linda admits.

"Can you change your goal into a positive one? For example, tell me what grades you want to get in each of the courses that you are taking."

From this point, Linda progressively worked up a grade goal for each of her five courses. Further, we negotiated a contract where she would report ongoing grades to me throughout the semester. If you are low in hope, this latter point may be especially helpful. Namely, once you have committed to an important goal, arrange to check in periodically with someone (a friend, family member, colleague) about your progress.

Other examples include the following specification changes:

— The would-be dieter's goal of "Losing weight" becomes "I will lose ten pounds in two months."

— My own previously mentioned goal of "Spending more time with my children" is sharpened to "I will spend one hour each day with my children."

— The anxious woman's "I've got to get myself together" becomes "I will learn how to assert myself to my boss."

— The middle-aged exhippie's "I've got to stop drifting" becomes "I'm going to the employment agency this afternoon."

— The depressed man's "My pain has to stop" becomes "I'm making an appointment to see a psychologist tomorrow morning."

— The retired woman's "I'm bored" becomes "I will get out and do some volunteer work."

The point is that we need to refine our vague goals into well-specified ones. Such clarity enables us to see how we are doing. Also, clarity propels us out of the low-hope malaise of having vague goals. Likewise, well-specified goals make it easier to generate way-power thoughts.[13]

Occasionally, I have encountered people who resist setting clear goals. In one such instance, a psychotherapy client expressed concern about specifying her goals because doing so would make it obvious when she was not making any progress. She preferred the shelter of vague goals.[14] Unfortunately, vague goals not only provide a shelter but also turn into a prison entrapping any goal-directed thoughts and behaviors.[15] If you are balking at my suggestion about clearly defining goals, your vague goals may be contributing to a pattern of low-hope thinking. Remember that clear goals at least set the stage for successful goal attainment. Vague goals, on the other hand, typically preclude any such sense of attainment.

Another kind of low-hope thinking involving vague goals is worth mentioning. Do you find yourself chasing ill-defined and yet outlandishly difficult goals? Consider the supersecretary. A fifty-year-old woman named Jeanne came to see me because she was tired, anxious, and unhappy with herself. She was an administrative secretary, and she had vague ideas about how she should perform every aspect of her job at the very highest levels. She worked very hard, but because she did not set any clear goals for herself, she always felt she hadn't done enough or hadn't done it just right. Another version of this same vague/high goals dilemma is the supermom who has to do everything well and yet never senses any real satisfaction related to attaining a few important goals. If this vague/high-goal style fits you, my advice is to set a few concrete goals — not too many — and try to reach them. This means less frantic action in your life, and more thought about a small number of important things you would like to accomplish.

Once you have clarified each of your important goals, focus your thoughts on these few targets.[16] In turn, regularly evaluate how you are doing in relation to them. This feedback should serve to improve performance. Knowledge of how we are doing cannot have a positive effect on performance, however, unless we set these well-specified goals as markers.[17] As long as you keep committed to clearly specified and important goals, your hopeful thinking should be more productive.[18] Often, however, we can be seduced by other less important goals and spend most of our time on things that are not really that important. We look at getting off the track next.

Controlling Attention Robbers

If you are spending considerable time responding to surrounding people and events, you probably are not concentrating on your important goals. The next step in goal-setting, therefore, is to improve your ability to focus attention on the things you deem important. The poet Goethe succinctly summarized this lesson when he wrote, "Things which matter most must never be at the mercy of things which matter least."[19] I am not suggesting that you abandon all attention to the immediate emergencies in your family or job, but I do think that most of us can spend more time on our important goals.

The urgent label grabs our attention. It may be a telephone call; a special delivery letter; a meeting; or a family member, friend, or colleague who comes to us. These urgent matters are visible, and they often have short-term solutions. Such hot crises or deadlines demand some reaction on our part.[20] Furthermore, if you are the one others always count on to respond to those things they think are urgent, you will be called on more and more to serve this function. After awhile, your days may be filled entirely with these urgent matters.

Recall my previous descriptions of supersecretary and super-mom. Another goal-related problem that they encountered was a result of their availability and willingness to give to those around them. That is to say, their coworkers, friends, and family assumed that the supers always would be available to help out. In turn, the supers often are very adept at handling the problems brought to them. Does this cycle sound familiar to you? One way to get out of it is to realize that you cannot help everyone. In fact, the more you get into this role, you may become so frazzled that you are not effective in those few truly important instances in which your help is needed. You may find that repeating the phrase *More is not better* can make you more sensitive to your needs and personal goals. I also have found that repeating such phrases as *I am not superperson* helps people to get out of this cycle of attending to others' needs without attending to their own. Some balance is needed.

What else can you do to turn off the unwanted fire alarms in your life? One thing is to keep a journal for a few days about what goals are occupying your time. This way, you can track the investment of your attentions. When you do this, you probably will be surprised and dismayed at how much time is taken up with relatively low-priority goals. The remedy for such attention robbery is to take control of the goals and spend more time on your bull's-eyes.

Many of the things that seem pressing at work and home probably can be put off until later. Better yet, some things can be put off totally. Or, perhaps someone else in the family or work setting can respond to them. Whenever possible, delegate. If you have used the A to F grading system discussed earlier, attend to the A's, perhaps a few of the B's, and an occasional C, but forget the D's and F's. This means you need to begin to say no to some of the demands on your time. One homework assignment I have used with clients is to ask them to say no at least once a week to an undesired request on their time. Once you have said no once, you can up your quota to two, three, or more no's per week. Try it. The people who have, like it. Another means of capturing more time for your goal agenda is to go somewhere where you cannot be disturbed. This is a time-out you can count on each day. Our lives are peppered with many "May I have your attention, please?" seductions, and it is our job to control them rather than having them control us.

Setting Challenging, Yet Doable Goals

Assuming you have implemented my previous suggestions about goals, the last lesson is to set moderately difficult goals. This lesson comes from research on human motivation,[21] goal-setting in general,[22] and the characteristic goal-setting of high-hope people.[23] Goals should not be so far beyond your reach that you are unlikely to attain them. Conversely, goals should not be so easy that you are certain to meet them. In fact, research shows that people believe hopeful goals should involve roughly a 50 percent probability of attainment.[24]

Usually, if higher-hope persons have undertaken an activity previously, the next time they set their goals somewhat higher.[25] Therefore, whenever there is an internal standard available to you, the high-hope way of thinking is to build on your past performance. In the previous chapter on increasing hope in children, I call this process *goal-stretching*. Based on previous research and my experience with fostering hope, I believe this goal-stretching works effectively.

Perhaps you have an area of your life where you would like to make some constructive changes. Many of us probably would agree to this supposition. Or, you may be experiencing a more profound dissatisfaction with your circumstances and have a mindset of low hope. What we all need, as I have suggested throughout this book, are some goals that guide us in our daily lives. If you want more friends, for example, start with a stretch goal of talking a few minutes with a coworker (neighbor, merchant, etc.) with whom you have not previously interacted. Low-hope people may have difficulty in making such contacts, but all it takes is a little step in the beginning. Once you are talking a few minutes to one person, your goal is to add another person. Then, you may want to talk for a little longer with particular people, and so on.

Whether your goal is to lose weight, get more exercise, have more time alone or more time with loved ones, get more rest, improve your health, get along better with your spouse, find a job, feel less nervous, or any of the multitude of other goals that we adults entertain, our hope-inducing journey is based on challenging and yet doable goals. Be careful not to set your goals at such an easy level, however, that you become bored and disinterested. Likewise, avoid making your goals so difficult that you or anyone else would be unlikely to achieve them. This can be as deflating to hopeful thinking as the setting of exceedingly easy goals.

Goals Checklist

The activities I have discussed in regard to goals are summarized in the following checklist:

Do

✓ Be clear that you are setting a goal because it is something you really want.

✓ Try to become more aware of decisions you are making about important goals.

✓ Before settling on your goals, generate many goals in the different areas of your life (e.g., relationships, friendships, career, recreation, etc.).

✓ Rank your goals in each area from those that are most to least important.

✓ Specify your most important goals with concrete and recognizable markers.

✓ Have another person with whom you can check or discuss your progress toward a goal.

✓ Put aside enough time for your important goal or goals.

✓ Set up your life so you are not interrupted by outside demands.

✓ Stretch yourself by setting goals at a somewhat higher level than your previous performances.

Don't

✓ Always set goals that other people think you should have.

✓ Be in a hurry to select your goal.

✓ Be seduced by thoughts and activities that distract you from your important goals.

✓ Become obsessed with attending to and revising your goal list.

✓ Set very easy goals for yourself.

✓ Set exceedingly difficult goals for yourself.

WILLPOWER

Perhaps you are feeling down, tired, and don't have the mental zest you once did. Your thoughts increasingly drift toward refrains such as I've had it, I can't, it's not worth it, and it wouldn't work. Feeling like you have to drag yourself around, you even may have visited a physician, who found no medical cause for your pervasive fatigue. If you have been worn down by the stresses of our modern lifestyle, or have undergone some recent traumatic experience that has sapped your normal mental energy, this section should be helpful. Also, if you scored relatively low on the willpower subscale of the Hope Scale, this section is for you.

Whether your willpower has been chronically low or has been drained by some recent event, the task is to build your determination to get moving toward your goals. You can change your sense of willpower by investing enough energy to try some of my suggestions. These suggestions are aimed at sparking beliefs about your capability to initiate and sustain goal-directed action.[26] Most of us have some potential for action, for it is the rare person whose mental pilot light is totally out. The flame of willful thinking is still flickering, ever so imperceptibly. What follows are exercises to increase these fires of the mind.

Talking Heads

If you pause for a moment and close your eyes, notice that your mind is filled with an ongoing self-dialogue. As an example of this process, let's journey into the heads of two forty-five-year-old women. One woman's thoughts tell her, I feel old; a second woman's thoughts are I feel like I have a lot of good experience. The former words suggest inaction, the latter the potential for action. Instead of the plaintive what's the use, therefore, willful thinking is an internal goal message to ourselves that says let's go for it! Affirmative rather than doubting thoughts buoy the high-willpower person.

What is the content of your inner dialogue? One good way to access this is to list your major thoughts for each of the next seven days. When a thought fills your mind, jot it down under that day of the week. Each time you report a similar thought, put a hatch mark beside it on your list. Do you find a large number of your thoughts are put-downs in which you are telling yourself you cannot so something, or that bad things are going to happen to you? If so, it should be clear that you have low willpower. Don't be ashamed by this insight, for this only deflates you further. Rather, realize that your ability to change starts with this awareness.[27]

To develop a high-willpower internal dialogue, we have to focus on the upcoming positive outcomes. Sometimes this is a matter of making commitments to yourself or others about goals. For example, if you make public statements to your friends about accomplishing something, you also make more determined statements to yourself.[28] Recall the previously discussed exercise of finishing the stem phrase *I want*. When people have stated several goals that complete this I want stem, I then ask them to complete the stem *I choose*. Almost invariably, this is an empowering exercise, because choosing is more active than wanting. Furthermore, to choose a goal and to own it for oneself is more motivating. Remember my earlier suggestion about prioritizing goals? In essence, the *I choose* exercise adds a sense of conviction to the goal selection process.[29] The motivation to reach a goal is enhanced by active choice.[30] If you find yourself wavering in determination, you can say to yourself, "Well, I picked this goal, so I better get on with it."

Another high-willpower self-talk involves statements you make about the nature of the goal. High-hope people appraise their goals in challenges and in doing so concentrate on success rather than failure.[31] Earlier in this chapter I noted the beneficial effects of selecting moderately difficult goals. Instead of thinking of them as difficult, however, think of them as challenges or opportunities.[32] In my work with people, the following self-statements have proven to be empowering: "This _____ (name of goal) gives me a chance to stretch myself"; "It's satisfying to go for something like this _____ (name of goal)"; and, "Sure it's not easy, but I can do it." Use whatever positive spin you can place on your goals as private motivational tapes. Then, play these positive tapes in your head, and turn the volume down on the nay-saying tapes (I can't).

If you have difficulty getting rid of your negative tapes, put aside ten minutes daily to worry expressly about the bad thought such as repeatedly obsessing about doing a bad job. Worry as much as possible during this time, but then dive back into your other ongoing activities.[33] If the negative thought continues to pop up, don't try to suppress it totally because this only makes it stronger in your mind.[34] Do not fret if the negative self-talk does not disappear immediately. These thoughts sometimes have been playing in your head for a long time, and it may take awhile for your new positive tapes to take hold. Be patient and continue to apply these lessons. Increasingly you invite in the positive and let out the negative thoughts from your mind. This reminds me of the landlord exercise. Assume your mind is a large apartment building that you own, and it your job to oversee who lives there. The good tenants are your positive thoughts, and you want to keep these and evict any negative thoughts.

Barrier Beaters

One common low-willpower reaction to impediments involves a surprise thought such as, oh my god, this *can't* be happening! This sort of thought propels the person into an aversive emotional turmoil. If you find yourself constantly being surprised by the barriers you encounter, realize that life throws impediments in all of our paths. So, don't wallow in self-pity and assume that you alone come on such obstacles. Such self-talk as OK, this happens to everyone, I'm not the only person to run onto this roadblock, and other such consensus-raising statements can be very helpful.[35]

Beyond normalizing the fact that you are encountering barriers, the next step is to stop being surprised by these situations. In working with people, I suggest that one does not always have to be the naive victim of impediments. In other words, take some time to see if there is a pattern to those surprise roadblocks in your life. Granted that there are instances in life where we cannot foresee the upcoming problems, I believe that most of the time we are far better at anticipating difficulties than we realize. In this slippery road ahead exercise, imagine you are traveling down a road that represents your future. It is your job to put up precautionary signs in your mind for those places where you encounter difficulties. The importance of this exercise is that you can anticipate problems; the more anticipation, the more likely you are to travel these bumpy roads more effectively.

So, now you are thinking more in terms of impediments visiting all of us, and you have begun to anticipate where in your life such problems arise. But suppose that you still get a rush of unpleasant emotions when confronted with a blockage of some sort. This is where you can use the talking heads dialogue described in the previous section to give yourself some instructions. In other words, you talk to yourself about how to regulate this emotionality.[36] Some helpful things to say to yourself include: OK, now relax and clear your mind; take a few deep breaths; or, I am very upset, but I am in control. Don't lose all of your emotional rush, however, because you can harness it to your advantage by saying I'm up for this, or When things get tough, I get going. Finally, think of these roadblock-laden situations as challenges that provide a good test of your resolve.

One of the ways to rekindle willful thinking is to recall your previous successes. The essence of the past push exercise is to recall former instances where you had the willpower to move toward your goals when facing obstacles. These memories, especially if they are vivid, activate our willful thinking in the present situation. The focus of these memories can be one of two general types: First, you may bring back a similar circumstance from your past where you were able to marshal the willpower to cope with a problem. This can lead to such thoughts as, well, if I did it then, I can do it now! Second, your memory may focus on how you previously weathered the difficult time. Relatedly, recall how former problems eventually passed. This can give you the uplifting insight that your present circumstances also are likely to improve. Obviously, the key to these visits down memory lane is to resurrect the positive about yourself, rather than dredging up the negative.[37] If you have trouble focusing on the positive, try some of the other suggestions for raising willpower in this section.

Another tactic for retaining willpower in the face of barriers is to find humor in the circumstances. Recall from chapter 2 that high-hope people use humor as a coping strategy.[38] How, you might ask, can we possibly find humor when we confront barriers? One approach I have used with myself, as well as with clients, is to try to find the absurdity in the situation. This takes a bit of detachment to view yourself almost like an outside person.[39]

Sometimes when I am lecturing to a class, I know that my examples and class demonstrations are getting in the way of my teaching. During such instances, I stop and ask, "Does this lecture sound as bad out there as it does inside my head?" In fact, over the years I have found that by having some fun with my own difficulties in class, I can get a renewed sense of willpower for my teaching goals. The delightful paradox is that we can get a boost by acknowledging our fallibility. I would suggest placing a sign somewhere in your mind, and looking at it when things seem particularly bleak. That sign reads: *If you don't laugh at yourself, you have missed the biggest joke of all.*

If you can find humor in your daily life, then you are less likely to experience adverse effects when you come on stressful events.[40] In other words, your sense of humor can buffer you against the bumps you encounter. Equally important, once you are confronted with impediments, your sense of humor can make the situation more comfortable.[41] A wonderful case study of this is Norman Cousins' *Anatomy of an Illness.*[42] Cousins, the former editor of the Saturday Review, found himself racked with pain due to a serious collagen disorder. Fed up with his hospital regimen and the pain medications, he decided to try another approach to sustain his mental energies. While in his hospital room, he arranged to watch humorous Laurel and Hardy films and television shows such as "Candid Camera." Cousins credited humor for giving him the necessary determination to fight the disease, which he successfully conquered. What Cousins's story suggests, along with other research findings, is that humor keeps our spirits up both before and after a potential stressor. Find what makes you laugh, and you should have an ally in retaining your willpower during the tough times ahead.

A final means of handling a barrier is to abandon the original blocked goal and to replace it with a new one. Indeed, those blockages that are large in magnitude and enduring over time should make us ask an important question: Should we adopt another goal that isn't blocked? As I have noted previously, persistence in the face of insurmountable barriers is not adaptive and can only lead to the fizzling of one's willpower. Do not construe this advice to mean that you should not persevere in the face of strong obstacles. Indeed, it is the high-willpower pattern to persist up until the point that it appears to be futile. Unfortunately, however, people who otherwise are very competent can become inflexible in their continued pursuit of untenable goals.[43]

What can you do if you become fixated on a blocked goal and cannot seem to give it up? The first step in regoaling is to let go of the original goal that is blocked solid. To initiate this decision, you must acknowledge you are stumped in this instance.[44] In other words, don't let yourself get deflated because of this one blocked goal. Also, to put some distance between yourself and the original blocked goal, tell yourself the goal was so impeded that no one probably could have attained it.[45] Then, back away from the original goal pursuit and do not obsess about either the unobtainable goal or your inability to reach it. The second step is to search for another attractive goal with some of the properties of the original goal. In thinking this way, you stay energized in the context of your new goal.

Perhaps an example may help to illustrate regoaling. I have worked with people who are severely depressed because they have sustained serious injuries through accidents. Initially, such people go through a grieving process about the physical skills lost because of the disability. To grieve and feel depressed is a natural reaction to a sudden physical disability. At some point, however, it is time for the person with the disability to abandon previous goals, the loss of which is fueling the depression. Then, I suggest they adopt other goals not blocked by their disability. Thus, a rabid recreational basketball player takes up wheel chair basketball; the marathon runner who is struck with a back injury pursues swimming. In fact, as we all age and meet the impediments of life, it is necessary for us to let go of some previous goals and find substitutes. Having flexibility in one's goals keeps willpower alive.

Before closing this section on barrier beaters, remember that everyone, including high-willpower people, have times when they are relatively low in willful thinking while dealing with problems.[46] It is normal to be down occasionally. What differentiates people who are characteristically high in willpower, however, is that such people have shorter down times or psychological troughs. You can use the approaches in this section to lessen the impact of impediments in your life. In doing so, you can mirror the approach of high-willpower people who get themselves out of their psychological down spells more quickly.

The Getting-There/Being-There Balance

If you have interpreted any of what I have said to mean that the end-all focus and pulling force of hope is one's goal, then I need to emphasize a mental balancing that also includes the important process of moving toward the goal. Over the years, I have talked with many high- and low-willpower people about this latter process. How they describe their thoughts and feelings is quite different, and I believe there is an important lesson to be shared. Let me summarize what seems to fill the consciousness of low-willpower individuals. Low-willpower people describe themselves as being painfully aware of social expectations about having and pursuing goals; moreover, if they do set a goal, they tend to worry about not reaching it. There is a profound sense of self-evaluation and self-focus among such low-willpower people, and they express doubts they can reach their goals. As one low-willpower person described this to me, "It's like I'm back in school, taking an impossible test. I keep looking at the clock and it's hardly moving. I feel strangely removed and sluggish, almost as slow as the clock." High-willpower people, on the other hand, report getting caught up in what they are doing and losing track of time. They have goals and use these as guides for their journey. When in this state, high-willpower people report feeling full of energy and excitement about what they are learning or discovering.[47]

What does this mean for enhancing your sense of willpower? I would suggest abandoning a sole emphasis on goals and constantly wondering how you are doing relative to that end goal. Rather, try to attend carefully to what you are learning right now, and you will notice you are not static. Let the present capture your attention, and you will find you are drifting naturally toward some long-range goal. The sense of movement is pleasurable. Enjoy it. The long-term goals are like magnets that pull you in a direction, while you control the ongoing journey.

When you reach a goal, allow yourself to experience the satisfaction for awhile rather than hurrying to set the next goal. At some point after reaching the goal, however, you need to find a new one. Indeed, if you do not get a new goal, you may suffer what Nietzsche called, "the melancholia of everything completed."[48] Songstress Peggy Lee offered a melodic version of this same message in her song "Is That All There Is?"

To strike a balance between getting there and being there, many of us need to live more in the present. One approach I have applied to my own life and have used repeatedly with clients is the I'm aware exercise. Concentrating on this very moment, keep completing the *I'm aware* stem with whatever comes to your mind. This exercise gets us more attuned to the here and now, and people find this to be quite invigorating. By living solely in the past or the future, we miss the vibrancy of our ongoing journey. To experience fully what is happening at the moment, you often can find pleasure in your ongoing activities. If you have set moderately difficult and challenging goals, you should be stimulated by new demands on your skills. Also, you need to trust that you will grow and respond to the task at hand. Focus on the ongoing task leading to some longer-term goal, and you will find yourself thinking, I can do this.[49]

If you practice these various suggestions, you can and will follow through on things. It will mean you are a person who not only gets there but also enjoys getting there. This is a very invigorating balance.

Consumption Patrol

Your mouth, depending on what you do and do not put in it, is an important source of mental energy. What we ingest influences what appears in our minds. Let's start with eating. Food is fuel, and we need the proper nutrients to sustain ourselves in the pursuit of goals. Many adults, for example, do not eat well-balanced diets. The surgeon general tells us to avoid too much sugar, salt, and fat.[50] Additionally, it is helpful to eat more of our food earlier in the day. If you do not eat breakfast, for example, I would encourage you to start doing so. Also, try eating several small meals over the day rather than one big evening meal. You need the energy throughout the day, and eating late does not give this boost. What you eat and when you eat can help to contribute to your overall mental energy.

How much you eat also can influence your willful thinking. It is estimated that 20 to 40 percent of all Americans are overweight.[51] If you overeat, the extra pounds you carry are taking away both physical and mental energy. A sluggishness accompanies eating too much.[52] At the other extreme, if you are eating too little, along with starving your body more generally, you are depleting your capacity for willful thinking. Anorexia is a common problem among young adults, especially women. Any available mental energies of persons with anorexia often are poured into their obsession with dieting.[53] Too little, like too much eating, drains our willful thinking. For both over and undereating, the goal is moderation. If you apply the goal-setting tips as well as the other willpower suggestions in this chapter, your food consumption will result in an adaptive weight. This moderate eating also enhances your willful thinking.

Other ingested products also rob us of willful thinking. For example, by drinking many cups of coffee each day or having several cans of soda, you are using caffeine to stimulate your body and mind. Too much caffeine increases your anxiety, and you may be so aroused that you have difficulty focusing on your goals. Likewise, you pay for the caffeine later because you may have difficulty sleeping, which makes you even more tired.[54] So, you consume more caffeine-filled products to get you going in the morning and throughout the day. Does this sound familiar? If so, you are on a carousel that increasingly erodes your ability to think willfully.

At this point, you may be protesting. After all, you know that those few cups of coffee in the morning get you going, as do the two or three sodas in the afternoon. Surely, that which stimulates you cannot rob you of mental energy. As I argue in the previous paragraph, however, caffeine can make us tired. Try cutting back on your caffeine to see what happens. The best approach is to do this little by little. Tomorrow, for example, drink one less cup of coffee or soda, and gradually continue this process of elimination over the coming weeks. Because dehydration can lead to a lack of energy, however, increase your intake of other liquids such as water and juices. In fact, whether or not you are cutting back on your caffeine-laden liquids, it may help your mental energy to drink more liquids.

Do you, like about 30 percent of Americans, smoke cigarettes?[55] If you do, you may be depleting your willful thinking. We know, of course, that we should not smoke because of the long-term health hazards related to cancer and heart attacks.[56] But a short-term liability of smoking is rarely discussed. Namely, smoking is associated with physical and mental fatigue. Such fatigue is a common complaint of smokers, who are twice as likely to report a pervasive sense of tiredness in comparison to nonsmokers.[57] The smoking cycle is similar to that for caffeine. By smoking, you stimulate your body, which in turn returns to a state of lowered energy. In response to this, the smoker has another cigarette, and the cycle continues.

Whether you quit cold turkey, or employ some treatment program, the less you smoke, the more you regain your actual physical and mental energy. Approximately 90 percent of the people who stop smoking do so without the help of a formal treatment.[58] Therefore, try cutting back to see if you experience an increase in physical and mental energy. This process may take several weeks, assuming that you decrease your smoking gradually. You will need to call on your willpower reserves to initiate and continue your withdrawal. If you do this, however, your repayment will be increased willpower in the long run, not to mention better health.

Like the legal drugs of caffeine and nicotine, we also may consume alcohol.[59] Alcohol, when used in large amounts, leaves us physically and mentally exhausted. As a sedative, it also depletes our mental energy reserves by causing loss of sleep, emotional distress, and nutritional deficiencies.[60] Related research consistently shows that alcohol use and abuse are related to a sense of powerlessness.[61] If you have begun to use alcohol frequently in your daily routine and you cannot stop or reduce the drinking by yourself, it is time to seek help.

As you can see, many things passing over our lips influence our willful thinking. Clearly, our body and mind act together. Beyond the physical effects on willful thinking that I have described, we also can suffer psychological processes depleting our willpower. That is to say, if you have labeled yourself as being addicted to overeating, undereating, caffeine, nicotine, or alcohol, you inadvertently may have given up your willpower to change.[62] If you see yourself as controlled by one of these consumption problems and your own efforts to change have not succeeded, I urge you to get up enough determination to seek professional help. In the short run it may seem more draining to try to change, but if you keep at it your willpower grows as you increase your effectiveness at consumption patrol.

Move It

Beyond the consumption patrol issues, there is yet another willpower-raising approach that takes advantage of the body-mind connection. One technique I have used with people lacking in willpower thinking is to ask them to initiate a program of regular physical exercise. I have yet to encounter a low-willpower person following a rigorous exercise regimen. Recall also our research suggesting that low-hope people are less likely to report exercising regularly.[63] Research on the effects of physical exercise shows that regular exercisers have more vitality and general determination,[64] and that aerobic exercise both increases will-related thoughts[65] and prevents their loss in the face of stress.[66]

Aerobic (meaning *with air*) exercises involve physical activities where your system has to resupply large amounts of oxygen over a sustained time. These rigorous exercises involve such activities as walking briskly, jogging, bicycling, swimming, soccer, basketball, tennis, and aerobic dancing, to name a few. If you are a low-willpower person who has been leading a very sedentary life, see your physician prior to undertaking these aerobic exercises.

Once you have the green light from your doctor, begin one or more of these exercises. Before settling on the type of exercise that you like, try several. Some types of exercise may not suit you. Jogging is very popular, and it is often the first exercise people try. It may not be the best for you, however. I once had a thirty-six-year-old client who was a former athlete. As part of his earlier sporting activities, his coaches had pushed him to run for conditioning. When he was older, he found running to be aversive and equated all exercise with running. With him, the key was to find an aerobic exercise that didn't have the associated bad memories. He tried racquet ball, and found that it did not have any of the negative memories associated with running. In fact, he liked it. Some people find running to be boring; if this is your reaction, try other physical activities. You will find one or more that you enjoy.

Whatever exercise you select, start at an easy level. In the beginning, just try to get in good habits about regularly repeating your particular exercise. Then, slowly build up the rigor of your program. You do not have to train like an Olympian. Likewise, do not go out on a weekend and overdo. This only causes pain and potential injury as well as deflates your spirits. Rather, maintain a steady schedule of some exercise that raises your heart rate. Brisk walking is sufficient to generate increases in will-related thoughts.[67]

The reasons for the willpower-enhancing properties of exercise are multiple. First, such exercise increases the level of beta endorphins, which are powerful chemicals producing a natural high.

Second, becoming aerobically fit should increase your overall ability to carry out the tasks of your life, as well as to handle stresses. Third, such exercise fosters weight control and a more positive evaluation of your body. All of these forces fuel our thinking that we can and will pursue our life goals. The common denominator of aerobic exercising is that your mind must send your body a message: Move it. If you heed this message, your body sends a similar message back to your mind.

Eye Lighters

Do you feel down as the days grow shorter in the winter months? During these periods of relatively greater darkness, are you tired and sluggish, and do you have difficulty in keeping your mind focused on your goals? Peggy, who suffered from this winter depression or Seasonal Affective Disorder (SAD), paints a vivid picture:

> It was mid-January. There had been a string of gray days but nothing bad had happened. I hadn't failed any exam or lost a boyfriend, but I felt so weighed down and in such a state of despair that I saw no future for myself. Everything I looked at was wrong. I went down into the basement, found a water pipe, got a piece of clothesline and tried to make a noose out of it, but I was unable to do so. I just didn't have the energy to figure out how to do it properly or the strength to do it. . . . The next day was sunny and I said to myself "Had you committed suicide yesterday, you wouldn't be alive to see this beautiful day," and I felt better.[68]

If you live in the northern hemisphere, you too may lose some of your mental and physical energy between October and December and find it returning in March.[69] This syndrome has gained increasing attention in the psychological literature in the last few years, but in actuality it has a long history dating back to Hippocrates.[70]

Simply put, your loss of mental energy may be due to insufficient light. The research on this topic indicates that the lack of light to one's eyes causes this depressionlike syndrome. So, what can you do about it? In previous centuries people were treated with climatotherapy in which they were advised to move to a sunnier climate.[71]

Obviously, very few of us could afford such treatments. Recent studies make a convincing case for phototherapy, however, which exposes one's eyes to bright lights, preferably for an hour or two in the mornings.[72] After exposure to such light, people respond with increased mental energy, often within the span of a few days.[73] Although the exact mechanism by which this light operates is not fully understood, evidence shows that it works. Therefore, you may want to increase the amount of light to your eyes in the mornings and see if it lifts your spirits. Other treatments, according to physician Norman Rosenthal, an acknowledged expert on SAD, include exercise, diet, sleeping less, and acceptance.[74]

The Pause That Refreshes

For a moment I would like you think about why we go to sleep after remaining awake for approximately 70 percent of each day. The reason is that our bodies need to recharge after expending energy during the waking hours. If we do not get this sleep, we are listless and lack our normal mental energy and willpower. In the pace of modern life, we may attempt to squeeze a few more minutes of wakefulness into our already busy day. What happens slowly over time, unless we revert to the usual eight hours of required nightly sleep, is a depletion of physical and mental zest. I believe lack of sleep is more of a problem than we realize. Therefore, I encourage you to monitor how long you sleep each night for a week. You may be amazed at how little sleep, on the average, you are getting.[75] Remember, the effects of sleep deprivation are cumulative.

To increase sleep, go to bed somewhat earlier over a period of days and see if this enhances your physical and mental energy. Take the case of a middle-aged businessman who lost his usual determination and zest for work. He had built a small business by working extremely hard over the preceding fifteen years, and in the process had cut back his sleep time. When he tracked his sleep for a week, he reported getting a little more than five hours per night. He resisted suggestions to increase sleep, largely because he thought he needed all of this extra time to get things done. Likewise, he was skeptical that sleep was the problem. (If you find yourself agreeing with this man and saying that you don't have enough hours in the day anyway to get things done, you may have fallen into this same pattern.) This man eventually agreed to increase his nightly sleep for a trial period. To his surprise, he experienced an increase in physical energy in general, and his mental willpower in particular. Sometimes all the psychological interventions imaginable are not as powerful as a few good nights of sleep.

Just as sleeping replenishes the mind for willful thinking, shorter mental rests may recharge you during the day. For some people, this means taking a few minutes when you are free from the telephone or the kids. During this time, meditate on some peaceful scene by letting your mind drift to this place. Or, you can repeat a focus word you have chosen and by quietly doing so, block out other thoughts. Another approach is to count slowly backwards from twenty, progressively relaxing yourself. Some people can clear their minds by saying "In" and "Out" as they inhale and exhale. If you are religious, use this quiet time to pray.[76]

Whichever short mental rest technique suits you, be sure to take time each day to practice. All of these rest stops allow your mind and body to recharge. Use your particular rest stop whenever you must wait anyway (before an appointment, while riding the subway, etc.), and you can turn wasted time into the pause that refreshes.

Phoenix Revisited and Other Small Happenings

A host of ills fill our newspapers and television screens and even may visit our lives. Similar to the plagues unleashed from Pandora's box, the bad often looms in our consciousness. Yet, like the early spring flowers pushing upward though a late winter snow, events and individual acts of quiet humanity convince me hope is still alive. Hope is being nurtured, sometimes by the smallest of happenings that never make the evening news. Consider an experience of mine. I don't remember what had gone wrong that day, but I do remember how low I was feeling. Staring out the window in a daze, I was jolted by a loud crash as a bird flew into the glass. Hurrying outside my house, I found a beautiful robin lying motionless on the ground. I sat down in the grass looking at this small lifeless form. Several minutes passed and all I could think about was this poor, flimsy robin. Surely it was dead. Then, the robin began to move ever so slightly. Much to my amazement and delight, it soon flapped its wings and, after a short pause, flew away. It was as if I had witnessed the mythological phoenix, rising from its own ashes. My spirits soared, too.

Although I have seen this bird reviving event a few times over the subsequent years, I still find it uplifting. If you look carefully at the small things happening around you, there may be unexpected and yet very powerful sources of willpower. Indeed, there are extraordinary things happening right in our own backyards.[77] By attending to our environment, we lose the self-absorption that is draining us. Sometimes we simply need to be quiet and watchful.

Up with Prescription Drugs

If you have tried the other willpower-raising approaches and still are low in mental energy, visit a psychiatrist to see if you are suffering from a depression that would be responsive to treatment with antidepressant medication. If appropriate, one of several antidepressant drugs can be prescribed. Most antidepressant drugs raise the level of willful thinking available for focusing on one's goals. In many cases of biochemically based depressions, for example, people report an elevating effect on their thinking when they take antidepressant medications.[78] After you have experienced this mental lift related to the drug, you may be placed on a maintenance dose for several months to sustain your gains. If you begin a course of treatment on antidepressants, be sure to monitor any adverse side effects.[79] Likewise, if you suddenly stop taking your antidepressants, you may experience adverse effects.[80] Therefore, it is important to keep in contact with your physician throughout this treatment process.

If you are given antidepressants, chances are your physician first will have you take a tricyclic. This class of antidepressants often helps you to sleep, eat, and increase your overall activity level. Common side effects are dizziness, dry mouth, weight gain, and constipation. For this and other medications, consult with your physician and pharmacist about the side effects and interactive effects of your antidepressant with other drugs and foods.

If you do not respond with positive mood changes within four to six weeks (or perhaps longer) to tricyclic antidepressants, then your physician's second choice may be monoamine oxidase (MAO) inhibitors. For these drugs, you need to refrain from eating several foods and beverages and taking nonprescription medications such as diet pills and cold remedies. Side effects include dryness of mouth, dizziness, daytime drowsiness, increased appetite, and decreased sexual pleasure.

Another class of antidepressants includes serotonin reuptake inhibitors. These drugs take one to four weeks to act, and there may be side effects of nausea, diarrhea, headaches, and insomnia, among others. Unlike other antidepressants with associated weight gains, these drugs may produce weight loss; moreover, they do not have the dry mouth and constipation side effects.[81]

Lastly, lithium is prescribed if you experience swings of mood. In fact, for such bipolar mood problems, lithium is the preferred drug for prevention purposes.[82] It stabilizes mood within a week to ten days if the drug is taken as directed. Blood tests must be conducted occasionally to monitor the level of lithium.[83]

The benefits of these antidepressant drugs depend in large part on taking them according to the directions. Lack of adherence to medications often is the reason they do not work. If you have gone to the time and expense of seeing a physician and obtaining a prescribed antidepressant, you need to have enough willpower to take the drugs as directed. If you do this, your physical and mental energy may be forthcoming.

Willpower Checklist

As a review of these willpower-enhancing lessons, consider the following suggestions:

Do

✓ Tell yourself that you have chosen the goal, so it is your job to go after it.
✓ Learn to talk to yourself in positive voices (e.g., I can do this!).
✓ Anticipate roadblocks that may happen.
✓ Think of problems as challenges that arouse you.
✓ Recall your previous successful goal pursuits, particularly when you are in a jam.

✓ Be able to laugh at yourself, especially if you encounter some impediment to your goal pursuits.

✓ Find a substitute goal when the original goal is blocked solidly.

✓ Enjoy the process of getting to your goals and do not focus only on the final attainment.

✓ Control your eating, eat several small meals, and eat most of your food early in the day.

✓ Cut back on caffeine-laden products, as well as cigarettes and alcohol.

✓ Consistently get vigorous physical exercise.

✓ Expose your eyes to bright lighting during the winter months.

✓ Rest sufficiently through nightly sleep and daily relaxation.

✓ Closely observe your local world, including the little things happening all around you.

✓ If you are depressed, see your physician about possible antidepressant drugs that may give you a lift.

Don't

✓ Allow yourself to be surprised repeatedly by roadblocks that appear in your life.

✓ Try to squelch totally any internal put-down thoughts because this may only make them stronger.

✓ Get impatient if your willful thinking doesn't increase quickly.

✓ Panic when you run into a roadblock.

✓ Conclude that things never will change, especially if you are down.

✓ Engage in self-pity when faced with adversity.

✓ Take yourself so seriously all the time.

✓ Stick to a blocked goal when it is truly blocked.

✓ Constantly ask yourself how you are doing to evaluate your progress toward a goal.

WAYPOWER

You can have the most specific of goals, as well as the willful determination to reach those goals, and still be stuck. For example, have you been experiencing a sense of frustration lately? Do you feel blocked? If you dissect those feelings, you may be mentally up to pursue something, yet unable to think of ways to get there. Perhaps you came up with one idea about getting to your goal, but found it didn't work. Therefore, you are doubtful about coming up with any other ways to achieve your coveted goal. Maybe you are surprised with how poorly things are turning out because of your inability to plan.[84]

Do any of these statements describe you recently? Or, are you like this a lot of the time? When you took the Hope Scale, for example, did you score low on the waypower subscale? What is called for in these various scenarios is enhanced waypower thinking. You need to believe in your capacity to generate one or more routes to your goals. This section presents strategies for improving such waypower thinking.

Stepping

If you have set a difficult goal and are determined to attain it, you need to think about the necessary steps to reach your objective. Based on what high-hope people do naturally, as well as other research dealing with how people solve their problems, I would encourage you to break a larger goal into smaller subgoals.[85] Therefore, the first phase in what I call stepping is to abandon any ideas about making one big jump to a distant goal. Indeed, almost all of the important goals in adult life take some time to reach. It may help to realize that every major accomplishment of our civilization has involved an extended period in which people have moved step by step to their goals.

Some people profit by planning the entire sequence of steps to an end goal, but in my experience such persons are rare. Most of us prefer to concentrate only on those steps near the starting point. On this point, let's explore the stepping type of planning. This starts with your clearly defining a goal. With this goal fixed in your mind, think about any intermediate steps you need to make. Take some time to clarify these subgoals, just as you did the end goal. It helps if you write down these steps so that you can refer to them when necessary. Once you have a subgoal, jot down some of the things you need to do to reach it. If this list gets quite long, this means you should make another subgoal resting somewhere between where you are at the starting point and the first subgoal. (You also may want to generate other subgoals falling between your original subgoal and your end goal, but usually people prefer to concentrate first on those subgoals close to the starting position.) You can continue in this same fashion until you have several stepping-stone goals along the early route to your final goal. This may sound complicated, but in practice it is not. Basically, the stepping approach involves making several subgoals on the early route to your end goal and continuing this process throughout the sequence.[86]

Let's take the case of Mike, the DJ, whom I described in the second chapter. Recall that he wanted to go back to school to become a social worker. His plan is shown below.

```
Starting Point:    Mike as DJ ------------------------------------> MSW degree

First Subgoal:     Mike as DJ ----------------------BSW --------> MSW degree
                                              college degree

                                     Gaining
Second Subgoal: Mike as DJ ----- admission ----------------------> BSW degree
                                   to college

                                                                  Gaining
Third Subgoal:   Mike as DJ ----- Applying ------------------------> admission
                                   to college                     to college

                                               Getting
Fourth Subgoal: Mike as DJ -------------------- application ---------> Applying
                                               materials            to college

                                                                   Getting
Fifth Subgoal:   Mike as DJ --------------------- Taking---------> applications
                                       entrance exams              materials
```

Eventually, because Mike did very well on his entrance exams, he was admitted to college, which initiated his planning about how to get the funds to attend school. Achievement of these initial subgoals led to his quitting his DJ job and pursuing student loans, as well as part-time work. Mike liked the stepping approach because it offered a way to make concrete goals that seemed doable. Whenever he reached a subgoal, he would savor the accomplishments for awhile, and then turn to the steps for the next subgoal. In this process, he gained confidence in his waypower thinking.

Although I have presented this stepping process as part of waypower thinking, it also relates to the other two components of hope. Because breaking a larger goal into subgoals is the essence of the stepping approach, it is inherently part of the goal-setting process. Likewise, stepping enables us to sense some progress toward a nearby goal and is therefore helpful to our willpower thoughts.

Multiple Routing

Once you have practiced this stepping approach, try another technique to generate several different routes to a goal.[87] In producing several pathways, research shows that we also discover some high-quality routes to our goals.[88] Instead of just one route, therefore, it is to your advantage to produce two or more.[89] When you are able to come up with several routes to the goal, you then have the luxury of selecting the best one. Of course, if this route proves impassable, you already have alternates from which to choose.

If you are low in waypower thinking, at this point you may be wondering if you can't come up with one pathway, how can you possibly produce several? Indeed, if you are feeling highly anxious about a given goal pursuit, you are unable to think effectively about your higher order goals.[90] Sometimes, for example, we become very upset when we are blocked. In such instances, we need to calm down so we are not swamped by our negative emotionality. One means of doing this is to employ the positive self-talk described earlier. Also, you can gain some perspective by getting away from the situation and allowing some time to elapse.

Recall that it is to your advantage to slow down and consider several goals before selecting one. The same advice goes for producing several pathways once you settle on a given goal. Whatever you can do to give yourself some time to think about various ways to accomplish your goal contributes to higher numbers and a better quality of pathways. For example, you increase the chances of producing several workable pathways to a goal if you learn to say "I need some time to think about solutions" to those who are applying time pressures. Sometimes you may have to say this to your boss, and sometimes you must say it to yourself.

Occasionally, even the obvious routes are not obvious. Remember Pam, the lawyer denied the law firm partnership? In her case, once some time had passed and she was no longer frozen by her anger, she began to consider two routes—one being an appeal within her firm and a second involving a formal litigation in the courts. Likewise, she increased her waypower thinking even further when she retained the partnership as a goal, but considered joining another firm or starting her own law firm. This is the regoaling process I discussed earlier. Regoaling is a means of increasing one's willpower; in this case, it also offered Pam new routes to her overall goal.

Rehearsals

Psychologist Hazel Markus describes the concept of *possible selves* as the ability to imagine ourselves in pursuit of a goal in a particular life arena. In her groundbreaking article on this concept, possible selves include, "the successful self, the creative self, the rich self, the thin self, or the loved and admired self, whereas the dreaded possible selves could be the alone self, the depressed self, the incompetent self, the alcoholic self, or the bag lady self."[91] This idea of possible selves is useful in understanding how we think about getting to goals. Although vivid thinking about one's positive goals can and does promote willpower-related outcomes such as task persistence, the mental rehearsals described next more clearly exemplify waypower thinking.[92]

Sit down some place where you can get comfortable and will not be disturbed. Relax and clear your mind of thoughts and feelings. One way to do this is to imagine your mind as a big blackboard filled with many thoughts. Once you have this image, take a mental eraser and wipe it off until it is empty. Next, think of an important goal and then call up the various intermediate steps you have developed using the procedures discussed previously. It is necessary to have some idea of your intermediate steps before beginning your actual rehearsals. During your first rehearsal, go fairly quickly over what you will be doing and saying. It is important here to actually picture yourself in the situation. Once you have finished this first quick rehearsal, go through the sequence of steps again very slowly and play out each step fully. As you do this, keep a positive image of yourself handling the circumstances arising at each step. Instead of watching an image of yourself going through the steps, actually try to get inside your own shoes and visualize things as they would appear as you are performing them.[93] If you want, use a positive name (Courageous Betty or Can Do Dave) as you visualize yourself and engage in self-talk about successfully handling the various stages leading to your goal or subgoal.

As I was writing this portion of the book, I faced a situation where I used this mental rehearsal process. Our family cat, Yusha, was literally on his last legs. He was fourteen years old and had survived many tussles with cars and other cats; he had reached a point where he was clearly suffering. He had to drag himself by his front paws, he had difficulty seeing, and it was time to end his pain. I knew I had to take him to the vet for a lethal injection. This needed to be done, but I had to think through what I would do. So, I rehearsed it in my mind. Sitting quietly in a chair, I wiped out other thoughts and focused on the issue of planning how to do this. First, I would talk it over with my wife, which I did in my mind. I anticipated that she would say it is hard to do this because the cat had been around all the while our youngest son was growing up. In this imagined dialogue, I agree with her but wait to see her reaction. She concurs that it is the right thing to do given the cat's health. Second, in my mind I approach our teenage son about the issue. "How do you think Yusha is doing?" I ask in an imagined conversation. My son readily describes all the health troubles Yusha is having. "Do you think we should have him put to sleep?" I ask in the rehearsal. My son is quiet, and I acknowledge how hard it is. I wait for him to respond. If he agrees, I will ask him to go with me to the vet. If he doesn't want to go through with this right now, I'll honor his wishes and bring it up at some later point.

For those who have pets, whether or not you think you are very attached to them, I can assure you that this is a difficult scenario. Following my general ideas in the rehearsal, I presented this issue to my wife and son. They both agreed it was the right thing to do. Having thought this through in my mind, I was better able to talk with my family. What I hadn't anticipated was how difficult it was for me to actually go through with it when my family told me to take the cat to the vet. I wish I would have given more thought to my role in this final process. Even sad farewells can profit by some forethought.

Remember, this is your visualization, and you are the leading character in this ongoing theater of the mind. You already may do something similar to this mental rehearsal; nevertheless, I would ask you to take this exercise seriously and practice what you will do and say. Such imagining exercises produce positive results by increasing the probability of your effectively handling upcoming events when they actually occur.[94] Furthermore, having rehearsed mentally, you can enjoy the ongoing experience because you know you are prepared. If you are thinking that nothing ever happens like you expect, so why bother rehearsing, you need to realize that such rehearsal actually helps with handling surprises. As is the case for actors in the theater or movies, rehearsal makes us confident and better able to roll with the inevitable surprises.

There is an additional useful aspect of this mental rehearsal process. In your rehearsal, try to anticipate any impedances you may encounter and then plan what you would do in response to these.[95] As you do this, continue to think of yourself in a positive fashion and know that you are not necessarily stymied by encountered roadblocks. In this exercise, do not overdo the mental preparation for handling blockages; merely imagine one or two things that may be potential stumbling blocks you can deal with en route to your goal. I have used this rehearsal process to help people with several issues, particularly those dealing with jobs or interpersonal relationships.[96]

One mental rehearsal that anticipates possible roadblocks involves a talk with the boss. In this scenario, the goal is to get a raise, more perks, a new office, or some job benefit over which the boss has the say. The problem, of course, is that the boss can and does say no to employees. This situation calls for some rehearsal in your mind. Here is one possible sequence: You make an appointment with your boss, asking for a time where the two of you will not be interrupted by telephones or fax distractions. Now, it is time for your appointment. You walk in to see your boss, thinking I'm going to be friendly but firm. After some small talk, you move the conversation to a review of the positive contributions you have made to the company. Watch for the reaction of the boss. OK, the boss is smiling. Now, pop the request. "Based on my performance record, I believe I warrant a 10 percent raise" (or whatever other goal you have here). The boss is taken aback. Remember, you are friendly but firm, so you recount how much business you have brought to the company. The boss is still not warming to the raise idea. Don't waiver, but highlight the various responsibilities you hold at the company. If the boss is stonewalling, in a nondefensive fashion point out how others of similar responsibility and performance levels in the company are paid more than you. Or, if you are willing to risk it, comment on how your worth to other companies may be higher than what you are being paid at your present company. If the boss would like to give you the raise, but the profits don't allow it at this time, say, "Good. I sense that you agree about my being paid more. Why don't we talk about this in six months when the profit picture is more favorable?" Leave yourself options in your rehearsal so that you can either get your raise now, or keep the issue on the agenda for the future. Try this mental rehearsal approach. You may be pleasantly surprised at how it serves you well in those anticipated situations involving obstacles. This is how debaters practice for actual debates, and you can employ it to similar advantage in your life.

Fallibility Insurance

People with high waypower thinking have a perspective on their goal pursuits that is an insurance policy of sorts. In particular, they view errors as part of the process of trying various routes to their goals; and if they do not succeed with one approach, they do not become highly self-critical and conclude they lack the requisite talent. Rather, high-waypower thinkers conclude they did not employ the correct strategy when they didn't succeed the first time.[97] This mindset is characteristic of good problem solvers,[98] as well as good copers in general,[99] and it enables people to attend to helpful steps related to goal achievement rather than dwelling on negative self-focused feelings.[100]

To see how your failures provide cues for thinking about other effective strategies for reaching your goals, go ahead and practice making mistakes in some goal-related activity. Pick a goal that is part of your daily set of goals. Then, do something you know will not work. Often you may feel out of control when a mistake occurs, but in this instance you are in control because you are making the mistake purposefully. When you see that your purposeful behavior does not work, your first thoughts should be of course it didn't work, it was the wrong thing to do. I need to use a strategy that works! This thought sequence is obvious because you know there is another effective pathway. Also, having purposefully planned the gaffe, you are not caught off guard by it.

Let's consider how this purposeful use of an inappropriate strategy works. Suppose you have difficulty giving talks, and your goal is to improve in this area because it is part of your job. One approach is to forsake any attempts at preparation and to just wing it. Not surprisingly, your first attempt at using this strategy results in a disorganized, anxiety-filled performance. What do you conclude? That preparation is critical. You may have known this intellectually, but it may not have sunk in until it was made obvious to you. Here is another variant. To get your talk over with, try to give it as quickly as possible. As you hurry through the talk, it is apparent that you need to slow down. Next time you will do this. This exercise vividly shows you not to use some strategies and sends you searching for better ones.

Now, suppose you adopt a similar thinking pattern for most of your mistakes. The only difference is that you are not immediately certain of the correct strategy, but trust yourself with the thought that you can come up with some workable strategies. Also, consistent with my earlier point, don't be unduly surprised by the mistake. In fact, it is a positive sign if you are making some mistakes. It means you have selected moderately difficult goals, which by their very nature involve some trial and error. Difficult goals mean you are taking risks, and this is part of the challenge you are experiencing. As suggested earlier, feel free to remind yourself that anyone would make similar mistakes on something this hard.[101] If your goal pursuit becomes exceedingly easy, you probably will become bored. So, instead of seeing your mistakes as preludes to disaster, see them as a source of feedback about what doesn't work and, potentially, what does work for the demanding goals in your life. This mindset provides insurance against our inevitable fallibility as we pursue challenging goals throughout our lives.

The low-hope pattern of thinking concludes that mistakes reflect some inherent personal flaw. Whether it is a lack of intellectual, athletic, or any other ability, the low-hope conclusion is that things are going to stay bad because of deficiencies in personal talents. One reason for this is the low-hope person does not see that these strategies would result in poor outcomes for most people. Likewise, after using one unsuccessful strategy, the person low in waypower thinking quits and feels stumped. Are some of these patterns occurring in your life? If so, instead of quitting after one strategy doesn't work, promise yourself that you will try at least one more strategy. By following the suggestions in this section, you probably can generate one more strategy based on what you have found that does not work. You should find that your second strategy will work at least some of the time. This insight begins to increase your belief in the importance of trying different strategies rather than stopping after one setback and needlessly concluding that you don't have what it takes. What it takes often is another approach to your goal, and this lesson is at the core of waypower thinking.

Skill-Based Believing

At times we need to acquire a basic skill that serves as a pathway for our important goals. A personal example illustrates this process. I do a lot of writing, including reports, student feedback, manuscripts, reviews, as well as letters of recommendation and general correspondence. Throughout graduate school and afterwards, I had written by hand on legal pads and begged, bartered, or paid people to type my scribbles. In 1986, I decided to learn how to type to become less dependent on others. So, I got a self-instruction program and taught myself. This fundamental skill enabled me to reach an important goal of efficiently and accurately getting my ideas into the necessary printed form.

Low-waypower people often don't believe they have the necessary skills related to the goals in their lives. Or, there may be one area, such as my typing, where we are caught in low-waypower thinking because we lack a skill. In such instances, our low-willpower thinking is reality-based because we have refrained from getting the necessary training or schooling. Does this describe you? If so, you need to employ the techniques regarding goal-setting and waypower thinking that I have discussed previously in this chapter. In other words, before you gain the benefits of acquiring skills, you need to see such skill acquisition as your goal and get up enough willpower thought to initiate and continue through with it. Goal- and will-related thinking thus set the stage for acquiring new skills which, in turn, enhance our waypower thinking.

The list of possible skills related to various goals is very long, and it is not possible to go into detail here. Therefore, for the particular skills training that you require, go to the directory section of your telephone book, or visit your local library for leads. Likewise, there may be people at the local community mental health center or colleges who can direct you to appropriate resources.

In my experience with people lacking in waypower thinking, one common issue is how to convey their ideas in general and plans in particular, as well as to communicate about their goals and plans in an assertive manner. Because of this difficulty, these individuals may conclude falsely that goals and ideas about how to achieve them are not important (e.g., How can my ideas about how to do this be very important if I can't even talk about them?). With assertiveness training, which can be obtained in group or individual arenas at you local mental health facilities or college, you can learn to get your plans and ideas across to other people.[102]

Whatever training you undertake, stay with it until you truly have the skill mastered. With my typing, for example, there was a period when I would revert to my old handwriting habit because it seemed faster. This tendency to regress to an old handwriting pattern eventually disappeared, however, when my typing improved. When you reach the point of having confidence in your new skill, so too does your confidence in waypower thinking increase. This belief in yourself may be as important as the actual skill. Waypower thinking does have a skills base, so remain open to expanding your skills. It all starts with your acknowledgment that there is something you need to learn. Never be ashamed of this insight.

For your future goals, I would encourage you to increase your skills. If you learn these skills, you are more likely to believe in your waypower thinking. This latter point is worth restating in a slightly different manner: Although your actual skills naturally form a base for your waypower thinking, it is your enhanced perception of being able to find routes to your goals that is critical for successful goal pursuits.[103]

Friendly Exchanges

Low-hope people aren't very good at making and maintaining friends. Recall the research discussed in chapter 2, where persons low in hope generally report feeling lonely.[104] Such people often have difficulty understanding the perspectives of other people and establishing intimate relationships and friendships.[105] Research also indicates that social support is related to positive coping and reports of well-being, but the sheer number of contacts with friends is not the critical factor.[106] Rather, what appears to be more important is that we subjectively believe we have access to people with whom we can talk.[107] Not surprisingly, low-hope people say they don't have friends with whom they can connect.

Do any of these findings describe you? If so, how can you change? A starting point is to put yourself in situations where you meet people. Many low-hope people, like lonely people, have removed themselves from contact by engaging in solitary activities like watching television and listening to music.[108] Turn off the television and begin to talk with people. As discussed earlier, you do not get to your goal all at once. To make friends, you have to be around people. Start by having the subgoal of talking to someone new. You can set the time frame here, with the goal being a conversation with a different person every week or two. Additionally, try to lengthen the time of these interactions. Likewise, try to be with your co-workers, fellow students, or neighbors during those natural break occasions during the day when people gather. It may be difficult to remain in contact with people because you have not gotten into this habit, but stick with it because you improve your interactions step by step. Remember, however, that such friendly exchanges start by you doing a little more to place yourself into interactions with others.

Let's assume that you have begun to put yourself in interactive situations along the lines discussed in the previous paragraph. Now, if you have negative expectations about how interactions are going to go even before they start, you are setting yourself up for failure. You may be worrying about what you will say, for example. This only gets in the way of attending to and following what the other person is trying to convey. Instead of focusing on what you will say, listen to what the other person is saying. People can sense when they are being listened to in an interaction. Additionally, it helps in conversations if you nod or send verbal acknowledgments that you are following what the other person is saying.

Some of your other conversation habits also may need to be altered. In particular, you probably need to ask more questions to make sure you are understanding the other person. Such questions send the message that you are trying to understand. Do not ask so many questions, however, that you come off looking like a lawyer grilling someone on the witness stand. Generally, it also helps to become more active in your conversations, rather than attempting just to get them over with quickly. Lastly, try to become more interactive so that your conversations have a give-and-take quality. If you are shy or uncomfortable around others, you may be asking what you could possibly talk about. I have suggested to clients that they talk about these interaction difficulties in the actual social situation. One client who experienced distress at parties learned that an excellent starting point in conversation was an admission of her discomfort. To her surprise and delight, she found that many others also held this concern about themselves.

The conventional wisdom in psychology is that such friendly exchanges bolster positive views of ourselves.[109] That is to say, friends comfort and stroke each other with words. For example, if you admit to your discomfort in social situations, you may get support from another who feels similarly. The more that you interact with people, the better chance you have of finding with whom you share similar interests and views; this acts as a natural base for building the relationship. By sharing similar views or interests, you are implicitly and explicitly garnering support for your perspectives. As such, friendships help to bolster willful thinking. Perhaps equally important, however, friends give advice about possible solutions to each other's problems.[110] Friends also may pitch in and help us.[111] Not surprisingly, friends are often a first line of help sought when we want guidance about how to achieve our goals.[112] As you form friendships, try to have at least one such relationship where the other person listens to you and gives advice, and vice versa. Such reciprocal relationships fully meet the needs of both parties.

Occasionally, people low in hope — and waypower thinking in particular — form a relationship in which the friend's advice serves to reinforce the negative self-view. That is, the other person's feedback only reinforces the same low waypower type of thinking you have had all along. Such friends, if they also are low in waypower thinking, may turn your interactions into pity parties in which you both conclude there isn't anything that can be done to reach goals. This type of social "support" is not helpful.[113] On the contrary, we need friendly exchanges where we are consoled during difficult times, but where we also give and get tips about strategies that help to reach positive goals. Indeed, an important part of such friendships is sharing aspirations and tips on how to reach them.

Asking for Help

In my experience, it is more difficult for men than women to ask for help. The image of the male automobile driver who is lost but unwilling to ask for directions may be more than an anecdote. This therapy example illustrates the difficulty males often have in asking for help: My client, Gil, had climbed the corporate ladder quickly, and at a young age found himself responsible for overseeing the directions his company would take to reach its objectives. He was experiencing a sense of uncertainty about his ability to handle these decisions, and he felt isolated because he could not ask for help. To ask for help was not, in his perspective, a manly thing to do. Once we explored how this script had been passed to the males in his family for generations, he discussed this issue with his aging father. This helped to loosen the constraints about asking for advice, and over time he learned to solicit suggestions from his employees. He also cultivated a relationship with an older mentor, from whom he could get suggestions about ways to achieve the objectives of his company.

Whether male or female, however, there are instances in life when we cannot come up with ways to get to our goals in the context of relationships, work, or health. In such instances, to ask for help is synonymous with being open to possibilities, which is the essence of waypower thinking.

If your friends cannot offer sufficient advice for a problem you have encountered, call to the local community mental health center or the other appropriate agencies and people in your area. At times we all need the input of others who are very knowledgeable and experienced with the particular problem we are encountering. You may be surprised and delighted at finding how many people have gone through a problem similar to yours. Talk with these people. They should have lots of good ideas for you.

Waypower Checklist

The ideas about developing our waypower thinking are summarized
in the following list:

Do

✓ Break a long-range goal into steps or subgoals.
✓ Begin your pursuit of a distant goal by concentrating on the first
  subgoal.
✓ Practice making different routes to your goals and select the best one.
✓ In your mind, rehearse what you will need to do to attain your goal.
✓ Mentally rehearse scripts for what you would do should you encounter a
  blockage.
✓ Conclude that you didn't use a workable strategy when you don't reach
  a goal, rather than harshly blaming yourself.
✓ If you need a new skill to reach your goal, learn it.
✓ Cultivate two-way friendships where you can give and get advice.
✓ Be willing to ask for help when you don't know how to get to a desired
  goal.

Don't

✓ Think you can reach your big goals all at once.
✓ Be too hurried in producing routes to your goals.
✓ Be rushed to select the best or first route to your goal.
✓ Over think with the idea of finding a one perfect route to your goal.
✓ Stop thinking about alternate strategies when one doesn't work.
✓ Conclude you are lacking in talent or are no good when an initial
  strategy fails.
✓ Be caught off guard when one approach doesn't work.
✓ Get into friendships where you are praised for not coming up with
  solutions to your problems.
✓ View asking for help as a sign of weakness.

RIPPLES OF THE MIND

If you begin to use these techniques for enhancing your thoughts
about goal setting, willpower, and waypower, you may be in for a
pleasant surprise. Because goals, willpower, and waypower are so

intertwined in our thinking, it sometimes is enough to ignite one component, and the others follow naturally. For example, one or two welcome bonuses result when you fashion goals along the lines I have discussed. First, if you are focusing on your goal, you also may be imbued with a sense of determination to pursue that goal. A tough, well-specified goal produces a mental spark. In fact, one ear-mark of a beneficial personal goal is that it mobilizes positive thoughts about effort and persistence.[114] A second ripple of goal thinking is that ideas about how to pursue the goal begin to appear. With the goal in mind, you more easily can produce mental leads about how to attain the goal.[115] By envisioning a precisely defined goal, therefore, we sometimes set into action the natural will- and way-related thoughts appropriate for pursuing it.[116]

In my individual and group psychotherapy work, I have been continually amazed at the power of goals in jump-starting the related willpower and waypower thinking. One Junior-doesn't-live-here-any-more example may illustrate this phenomenon. A young man was working on specifying his goals when he came to a major realization: He no longer wanted to live the life in which he was the replication of his father. Instead of being called "Junior," he decided he wanted to be called by his real first name of Phil. With this goal in mind, he immediately became energized to implement various plans to solidify his own identity, including pursuing a college major and career trajectory of his choice.

Sometimes a surge of willful thinking begins this ripple process. When you truly think I can, what follows as the predicate to this sentence is a goal. This goal provides the target for the willpower thoughts, whereafter waypower thinking is unleashed to channel your mental energy toward the goal. How often, for example, have you experienced an increase in your willpower and quickly searched for ways to direct this toward the newfound goal in your life? I have experienced this and have seen it happen in other people. In therapy groups, for example, if persons are experiencing a lack of willpower for any of the goals in their lives, I ask them to grasp their legs with their arms and to squeeze themselves into the tightest ball possible. Then, I ask these people to repeat the phrase, *I'm stuck.* Almost always, after the person has done this for awhile, he or she unfolds from the stuckness and announces with a renewed sense of mental energy, "I am *not* stuck!" Having felt the physical constraints imposed by themselves, people thus emerge with renewed determination. What is striking, however, is that this willpower does not remain free-floating; people attach it to goals and action plans to meet those goals.

Lastly, full-fledged hopeful thinking may be initiated by the waypower component. This process is illustrated vividly by a forty-five-year old woman in one of my therapy groups. She had raised two children and had been told by her husband that he was leaving her. She was despondent and without direction in her life. To hear her, she lacked any skills or talents. In her words, she "was at the bottom of a big hole." Struck by this vivid image, I asked her to imagine a ladder that she could use to climb out of the hole. When she had this ladder in mind, I asked whether there was anything that she could use as a ladder in her real-life situation. After a pause, she asserted, "I'm going to college!" College was the way out of the hole in her life. With this waypower thinking activated, her depressive thoughts also lifted. In other words, the waypower thought sparked her willpower. Finally, when asked where this going to college would lead, she responded, "To a degree and a job . . . and feeling better."

I do not want to leave you with the impression that by working on goal-setting, willpower, or waypower alone, you always can produce the full-scale hopeful thinking as shown in these case histories. Indeed, sometimes you have to work on two or three of the components. The good news, however, is that as you improve any of the three components, so too should the chances for your overall hopeful thinking improve. When you strengthen your weakest link, therefore, the productive ripples between goal-, will-, and way-related thinking are more likely.

CHAPTER SEVEN

Hope for Relationships and Vice Versa

Hope cannot be achieved alone. It must in some way be an act of community.

—William Lynch, *Images of Hope*

HOPE VISITS LIFE ARENAS

The key word throughout this chapter is *relationships*. Hope is about one's will- and way-related thinking toward goals, but as I have pointed out throughout this book, it also is a mindset that pays attention to people. Hopeful people bring a liveliness to their interactions with others. I am reminded here of psychologist Douglas Heath's conclusion after studying people over decades. Commenting on the common thread of fulfilling lives, he writes, "To grow, we must be in an *alive relationship* with others, whether as workers, partners, parents, or friends" (italics his).[1]

Hope manifests itself in all our important interactions with other people.[2] The very fact that these relationships are significant means we have goals related to them. If we have goals, then hopeful thinking naturally applies. Also, to make sense of other people and their actions, we must come up with inferences about their goals, as well as their willpower and waypower thinking related to reaching those goals.[3] Therefore, we use the components of hopeful thinking when we interact with and try to understand others.

By this point, if you have followed the previous suggestions about goals, willpower, and waypower, you have begun the process of building hope. These lessons also can be implemented in your relationships. Toward this end, this chapter illustrates how hopeful thinking is an interpersonal asset both for you and the people with whom you interact. In particular, I explore how hope relates to more positive interactions between partners in intimate relationships, teachers and students, coaches and athletes, managers and employees, physicians and patients, and psychotherapists and clients.[4] As the title of this chapter implies, hopeful thinking influences our interpersonal relationships and, in turn, those relationships have an impact on our hope.

INTIMATE PARTNERS

Elsewhere I have written about relationships as seen by an observer from afar:

> Imagine for a moment, the impression that a visitor from outer space would have of us as he, she, or it approaches our planet. If the spaceship should happen to tune into any radio station, the music probably would tell the story of two people in the throes of falling in or out of love. If our space traveler would view our television shows, channel after channel would depict members of our species thrashing around in some sort of relationship. Our books tell vivid stories about . . . intense love affairs. And, in listening to us talk, the visitor would hear yet more about our relationships.[5]

From Getting To Know You to Commitment

This observation does not come as a surprise to earthlings, for we have pursued relationships throughout our lives. Our intimate relationships share a typical chronological sequence. In the beginning, two people are drawn together by some common goal-related activity. Think back to how you met the person with whom you have developed an intimate relationship. Chances are that both of you were in the same class, meeting, or social event. Whatever brings people together as a group usually involves shared goals.

Once the first contact is made, the attraction is partly physical and partly psychological. As we get to know our partner more, it becomes apparent that we wish to spend ever increasing amounts of time together, and we rearrange our lives to meet this goal. This means that we may reprioritize our goals, some of which no longer capture our attention because of our new love.

A couple in this infatuation stage is filled with willful thoughts about how to spend time with each other. We think about what our partner wants (i.e., goals), as well as how our partner plans to achieve those goals (i.e., pathways).[6] In fact, we may become so engrossed with each other that we lose sight of other goals relating to friendships and work. We are, so to speak, consumed with hope. Part of our ardor is that we are fascinated by the newness of our partner.[7] The goal of increased intimacy is reached through sexual intercourse for men, and for women it is achieved by talking about the future of the partnership and meeting the parents.[8] In other words, men view sexual relations as signifying intimacy, while women accentuate verbal communication and family ties. The overarching common goal for both partners, however, is the continued existence of the relationship.

If there are difficulties, usually it is because the two partners do not agree on the necessary shared goals involving the progression of the relationship to the next stage (e.g., living together or marriage). The therapy case of Connie illustrates this point. Connie came to see me because she was feeling very depressed and critical of herself. She was a bright, articulate woman in her twenties. The major source of her unhappiness involved her relationships with men, where she felt used. Connie would have sex with a man on the first date, which she attributed to the fact that "they want it." After the first date, Connie's pattern was to see the man for several days or weeks, all the while engaging in frequent sexual relations. She became very attentive and dependent on her new suitors, only to find that they dumped her. She wanted more enduring relationships, but her male companions did not.

After the initial sessions where Connie presented her full story, I asked her to try a therapy homework assignment. In particular, she was to stop dating so much and, when she did go out, she was to say no to any sexual advances. This was going to be tough, she assured me, but she agreed to give it a try. Much to her surprise, she was able to say no and, as she put it, "play hard to get."[9] She also found men still wanted to date her, and she began to feel better about herself as a person who was appreciated for something other than her sexuality. Over time, Connie said she was attracting different types of men, including some who were interested in a long-term relationship. The paradox Connie discovered was that she could reach her goal of establishing a satisfying, longer-term relationship if she slowed down the dating process and didn't rush into physical and psychological intimacy. Eventually, Connie reported she was enjoying her interactions with men more than ever, and she felt fairly confident about establishing an enduring relationship.

The next stage of relationships that involves long-term commitment is one many of us have tried. This means we decide to live together or marry. As a couple, we also undertake further important shared goals such as having children or buying large-ticket items (e.g., cars, houses, etc.). Assuming we both have will- and way-related thoughts for these shared goals, the relationship thrives. Over time the relationship matures and although the initial intensity of sexual attraction may wane, there still may be a bond of shared goals for which both partners have the necessary willpower and waypower. Thus, we move from passionate to companionate love. Perhaps, the most important of these goals is that the partners want to stay together.

Goal Sharing

In reality, of course, relationships are a prime source of difficulties.[10] As may be obvious, relationships change. Instead of the static tranquillity depicted in the 1950s television series "Ozzie and Harriet" and "Leave It to Beaver," it is more accurate to view relationships as dynamic processes constantly in motion.[11] Ultimately, the high rate of divorce in our society results because one or both partners no longer have the willpower and waypower for the shared goals of the relationship. In many cases, people move away from each other in what they want out of life.

In a relationship that could be titled separate lives, the two partners grow apart over time. There are many prototypes of this pattern. Consider the relationship of John and Carol, who fell in love while in college. They enjoyed common friends, and both were active in student government. Married on graduation, they took jobs with ideas of rapid career advancement. Carol, an English major, became an editorial assistant at a middle-sized publishing house. John used his business degree to obtain a beginning sales job. Both poured themselves into their work, finding pleasure at the successes they experienced. When they got home in the evening, they both were tired and talked little about their daily activities. John began traveling more to call on distant clients, and he would be away from home for several days. Carol worked late evenings and weekends to get more done. She aspired to be an editor and enjoyed talking with her coworkers about the various aspects of the book publishing business. Over time, as John and Carol attended more to their jobs, their bond to each other weakened. Their careers were successful, but their relationship was not. The resulting breakup was one replicated frequently in our society.

A second example illustrates how this separate lives theme is played out along somewhat different lines. Shannon and Dennis had dated for two years when they decided to live together after graduating from high school. They both took manual labor jobs at local industries. Enjoying each other's company, the first few years of marriage were filled with mutual satisfaction. After three years, however, things began to change. Dennis wanted to get married and to start a family, but Shannon wanted neither of these things. In fact, Shannon became dissatisfied with her production line job and wanted to take some classes at the local junior college. After completing a few such courses, Shannon decided she wanted to go to college full-time to get a degree in elementary education. "What about having kids?" protested Dennis. "The only children I want to have will be my students when I am a teacher," replied Shannon. She then proceeded to spend more time with her classmates at college, which only threatened Dennis further. When they were together, they shared only awkward silences. When it became clear that all communication had ceased, Shannon moved out for good.

Yet another possibility is that a couple may learn they never really did share common goals. Consider the following example: Patty and Roy had been married for eight months, when she announced the good news about her pregnancy. Looking horrified, Roy exclaimed, "I don't want to have a kid. You need to get an abortion." Patty was surprised at this reaction because Roy had expressed interest in having children when they were dating. When she confronted him with this inconsistency, he replied that he only said that because he knew she wanted to hear it. Patty had taken him at his word, however, and a fundamental assumption about a shared goal of their relationship was incorrect. This misleading message by the husband resulted in a rift that tore apart the relationship. Sometimes in dating, one or both of the partners say what the other partner wants to hear. Depending on the importance of such messages, they obviously can create a devastatingly false premise for the relationship.

Whether a couple has moved to differing goals, or realizes they never had the same goals, the key is that common goals are lacking. For shared relationship goals to develop, one requisite goal supersedes all others: The partners must talk with each other. A minimum common goal for maintaining a viable relationship, therefore, is a willingness to spend time communicating with each other. In the early phases of our serious relationships, we do this automatically. With relationships of a longer duration, however, regular communication may diminish. In this latter scenario, one or both of the partners perceives that the other "hardly ever talks to me."

If such communication is lacking, you owe it to yourself and your partner and to talk about things to see if there is a basis for continuing the relationship. Even if you do not talk much now, there probably was an earlier time when you did. How can you go about beginning such talking again? First, be clear that you both are willing to commit enough time to try to communicate. Second, settle on a regular time period, preferably each day, where you can talk face-to-face with your partner. Make this time free of distractions such as the telephone or the television. For some busy people, this means they literally have to schedule times to relate to each other. For other couples who are around each other a lot but do not talk, this means setting a time and place where the code of silence is broken. At first, this process may be difficult and it is awkward to talk, but keep at it because this provides the basis for continuing the relationship. Remember also that you did something like this when you set up dates at the beginning of your relationship.

As you talk with your partner, listen also. The problem of one or both partners sensing that they are not being heard undermines any success at communication. A related problem in such communication occurs when one partner interrupts or does not reciprocate when positive attempts at communication are made.[12] As long as you are taking the time to talk, you owe it to each other to listen and understand what your partner is saying. To make certain you have heard what your partner said, rephrase it in your own words. Then, check with your partner to see if you have captured the intended meaning. Respect what your partner is trying to say and don't hurry the conversation. This may be hard because you are angry or hurt about something that has transpired previously in the relationship. Don't be concerned about getting to these issues, however, because the focus is on what the two of you have in common now and in the future. My point is to not jump on your partner by dredging up historical squabbles, because this only undermines the communication process. In these conversations, your goals are not to win or prove that you are right; your initial goals are to set up regular communication and to understand what your partner is saying. Additionally, try to get your perspective across to your partner so that he or she has an accurate notion of your views about given matters.

Don't be derailed from continuing such communication if you encounter difficulties. Remember an earlier premise of hope theory that we experience negative emotions when our goals are blocked. In your communication with your partner, you will run into such blockages when your partner has difficulty understanding what you are trying to say. Instead of being seduced by the usual anger and frustration that interfere with communication, use concrete examples to clarify your ideas. Don't talk down to your partner and realize that a certain amount of miscommunication is normal as people interact.

In working with people, I have found that the desire to communicate on a regular basis and to perceive that one is being listened to are basic goals. Because such communication and listening are required before pursuing other relationship goals, it is appropriate that partners initially attend to these. If you attempt such communication without much success, you may want to visit a professional counselor such as a psychologist, social worker, or marriage counselor who can help the process. One of the major roles that this outside person plays is to facilitate each partner getting a point of view heard by the other.

Once you and your partner begin communicating, one pleasant surprise may be that both of you do share similar goals, and the real problem was the lack of communication. If this is true for you and your partner, the important goal is to keep the lines of communication open.

The other possibility is that when you and your partner begin to communicate, you do find that your goals are quite different. Those who do marital counseling frequently hear such laments as "She doesn't want to do anything I like," and "I want _____, but he wants something different." A couple that has this insight has put their collective fingers on the crux of the problem. Assuming that your and your partner truly do have differing goals, this can be resolved in one of two principal manners. First, you can agree on a trade, where you accept something your partner wants and, in return, your partner accepts one of your goals. Suppose a couple wants to spend more time together, but one partner wants to go out to a good restaurant and the other partner prefers a sporting event. The trade solution is to alternate these outings. This "You get yours/I get mine" approach can be applied to a variety of activities engaged in by partners.

A second approach to disparate goals is to have both partners give up their respective goals in favor of common one. In the early dating phase of relationships, couples compromise on their goals frequently. Somehow over time, however, we either forget how to compromise, or we become focused on our goals to the exclusion of our mate's. The essence of this latter shared goal is compromise. For example, for the woman who wants to buy some furniture and the man who would like to purchase a new car, the compromise is to agree to spend the money on a vacation. Or, consider the puppy solution: The man and woman differed about the desire to have a child at a fairly early point in their marriage. The compromise was to get a dog to see how they would handle this increased responsibility.

A telling point for the viability of a relationship often is whether one or both of the partners are unwilling to compromise. When compromise is not attained, especially after lengthy efforts, the irreconcilable differences result in dissolution of the relationship. This may be an appropriate resolution when shared relationship goals are not possible. Before arriving at this conclusion, however, couples need to talk openly and extensively about the possibility of shared goals.

Finding Pathways to Pursue

Once you and your partner have agreed on a shared goal, it is necessary to develop a mutual plan about how to achieve it. Sometimes it is best to negotiate the plans in concert with the goal. As an example, consider a couple who agree to have more sexual relations. For the man this means an increase in the number; for the woman it means longer time being spent when they do make love. As you can see, this couple needs to agree on a plan that is part of the shared goal. One compromise I helped a couple negotiate was that the husband would increase the time in foreplay and holding after intercourse, and the woman would increase the overall frequency and initiation of sex.

When these plans can be discussed in concrete language depicting what needs to be done, partners can arrive at a mutual understanding.[13] Assuming you and your partner have settled on a concrete goal-plan, then both of you must agree to pursue it. This commitment reflects willpower thinking. Unless truly shared commitments are made, one partner may undermine the goal. In marital counseling, for example, one partner may agree to see a professional but may talk very little in the sessions or have other commitments that preclude making the sessions. If you and your partner cannot dedicate yourselves to a given goal after several attempts, I would suggest that you look for another common goal about which you have shared will- and way-related thinking. Don't be discouraged if this process takes a good deal of effort, however, because it is normal to have false starts and miscommunications.

If you are jettisoning a present relationship with the idea that things will be different in subsequent ones, this may be true.[14] There is a caveat, however. Many people exit relationships without giving serious thought to the necessity of compromise in any relationship. Likewise, we lose sight of the fact that we have to expend considerable mental energy in talking and listening if our future relationships are to be successful. Perhaps prompted by this insight, many people today opt not to become involved in long-term relationships. Indeed, if you are prone to forming bad relationships that do not meet at least some of your goals, this may be the best solution to preserve your hopeful thinking. For many people, however, intimate relationships remain as the high-hope ideal to be pursued. As a client once told me, "Relationships are work . . . I mean *lots* of work, but they are worth it."

TEACHERS AND STUDENTS

Our schools no longer are refuges where young people spend time removed from the problems faced in our larger society. Indeed, if we listen to what our children, teachers, and the media are saying, school is increasingly a place where instability, chaos, and violence form an unwanted informal curriculum. My point is not to lament the plight of schools as microcosms of social problems. Instead, against this troubling backdrop I pose two questions that bear on the topic of hope. First, how is it that some schools have students who are active and involved in their education and look forward to what will be happening next in their classrooms?[15] And second, how is it that even in a school where anger and despair are the norms, there may be one classroom where students appear to be prospering? The answer to both of these questions is that school administrators, and even more important, the individual teachers, can and do make a difference.[16] Some teachers are able to create an atmosphere where hope is so apparent you almost can touch it in their interactions with students. Over the years, I have talked to and witnessed some of these remarkable people in action. Likewise, I have interacted with and learned from teachers who are struggling to regain their lost hope. What follows are the lessons in hopeful thinking imparted by these various teachers.

A Role Model for Better or for Worse

If you are feeling burned out and somewhat cynical as a teacher, a frank and open discussion of this may provide the beginnings of change. If you can talk with a loved one, a fellow teacher, or a therapist, one of your insights should be that these feelings do not make you a bad, uncaring person. On the contrary, chances are that at some earlier point in your career you were full of enthusiasm. Remember, you could not burn out if you weren't previously on fire.[17] In fact, burnout is an understandable mindset if you have experienced repeated blockages to your important teaching goals.[18]

Most teachers got into the field precisely because they thought they could make a difference in the lives of children. Keep this thought in mind on those mornings when you dread facing your 8:00 A.M. class or are overwhelmed by the latest classroom problem. Teaching can make a difference in the lives of students, but teachers may not sense this. In part, this occurs because our time is filled up with attending to the more difficult or problem students. Or, by the time students do realize the positive role you have played in their lives, they have moved on to another place and station in life and do not send thanks or good job messages. So, when you are feeling down, remember that right now in your classroom you may well be a hero to one or more of your students, and they are watching and listening to how you respond to the difficulties in your job. Many students live under stressful home environments, and in spite of their outwardly oppositional behaviors, they hunger for a role model.

Goals That Help

In schools today, teachers often report that their first goal is to establish some order and control in their classes.[19] Frequently, effective teaching involves helping students learn how to behave in the classroom.[20] Although I agree with the necessity of order and control, do not overdo this because learning is often a noisy, active process. Without question, however, a basic level of respect among students, from teacher toward students, and from students to teacher is fundamental to a trusting atmosphere where children take risks. Expect responsibility, but not total obedience. As the teacher, you set the tone. Generally, any hypocritical, inconsistent, or sarcastic behavior on your part destroys trust and makes subsequent discipline more difficult. Remember that many children would prefer to be bad than to look stupid. In your interactions, therefore, do not put down students; instead, find ways of making them look good.[21] If we attack a student's dignity, we lose the student.[22] Teaching is an interpersonal transaction, and instructors must attend to the process along with the content of their topic.

If you are a teacher experiencing negative feelings, it may be helpful to trace their source. Sometimes you have set unrealistically high expectations for your students, and you may feel like a failure because your students cannot match these standards. Or, you may underestimate students' abilities and set expectations that are too low. This also undermines the learning process. The solution is to set challenging but reasonable goals for your students. Your negative feelings also may result because you have one goal for your entire class, ignoring the fact that each class is a collection of individuals. Elementary through high school teachers, for example, are confronted with a range of student abilities and experiences that must be taken into account when forming goals for different students. Teachers given the responsibility of conveying information and skills appropriate for average children may lose sight of those students performing either below or above the norm.

Instead of perceiving this diversity as a problem, however, the high-hope approach is to view it as a challenge and to set individual goal contracts with students. For those of you who may be thinking there isn't enough time, my belief is that students occupied by relevant educational goals will not be overwhelming you with discipline problems and other distracting activities. High-hope teachers are very clear about their objectives and convey these to the class as a whole and to individual students as well.[23] In doing this, make concrete and understandable goals and include subgoals along the way to the larger goals. If you do this, both you and your students sense growth. Seeing students' growth provides an antidote for teacher and student hopelessness.

Write down these goals and place them where they can be accessed by both you and your students to serve as a quick reminder of where the students, with your assistance, are going. If it is possible to get the child's parent or guardian to participate in this goal-setting process, it has even more impact. I realize that in this time of single parents and parental disengagement from the school process, it is tempting to preserve one's time by focusing only on the students. It is worth your efforts, however, to engage the students' parents whenever possible.[24]

Waypower: Plan, Plan, Plan

The major waypower lesson of high-hope teachers is captured by three words—*plan, plan,* and *plan.* Preparation characterizes such high-hope teachers. They put in extra hours organizing their material so that it is coherent and engaging to their students. More effective lessons have an overall organization that is comprehensible to students[25]; they also are structured in a step-by-step sequence.[26] In other words, a good teacher breaks up a larger task into smaller subgoals that children can accomplish at each stage.[27] It also is helpful to devise exercises to which you can switch should a given approach not succeed. In preparing these learning exercises, consult with your present and past students about approaches that work and talk with other teachers about their favorite techniques. Additionally, see if your administrator has any money for you to attend workshops and to visit other schools to learn what works for them.

Remember that particular approaches work better with some students and discover whether the members of your class understand materials better in the visual or the auditory mode. For students with learning disabilities, find out the best means of tapping their knowledge and thinking. Likewise, be sensitive to the fact that some students may not be facile at public speaking or reading. Additionally, remain vigilant about how your exercises elicit participation by students of differing racial backgrounds.[28]

Set up learning experiences where a maximum number of students can get involved, but avoid placing an emphasis on winning such as an exercise where one student is singled out and rewarded for the correct answer. Instead of turning your students into grade predators who succeed because of vicious competition in which the losers are pushed to the lower end of a bell-shaped curve, create an atmosphere where your students are more concerned with mastery of the information. In summary, a high-hope teacher constantly must be on the outlook for effective ways to impart information along with critical thinking. These waypower-related activities all rest on a willingness to interact with and listen to students.

Willpower Boosters

High-hope teachers also infuse their classes with enthusiasm to learn the material.[29] In many cases, therefore, you have to be an active, lively role model for your students. One of the means of keeping your students mentally engaged in learning is to have them chart their progress in a record that is accessible to you and the student. Witnessing concrete improvement, albeit small, can be uplifting to students. Don't make such charts a public display, however; they foster invidious comparisons. For this reason, I also believe honor roles are counterproductive to the willful thinking of many students.

Try to stay up psychologically for your work with students, whatever the size of the class. One way to do this is to prepare materials that interest you. Whatever approach you use, in that moment when your class begins, be prepared to exude some enthusiasm for your material and your students. This instructor enthusiasm energizes our students productively. Consider the following vignette:

> While a lecture was going on before a large class, a student in the back row fell unquietly asleep. The professor noticed the defection but continued with his remarks, more in sorrow than in anger. A few minutes later the boy recovered consciousness and blurted out an apology. "No," said the professor, "it is I who should apologize to you — for not keeping you awake."[30]

For years I have taught a large undergraduate psychology course with several hundred students; there have been times when I was woefully down and lacked in motivation as I approached the auditorium. In such instances I have used this technique of psyching myself up: I conjure up the image of a giant slug (the snail-like slimers without the shell). Then, I imagine a big Ghost Buster logo with the slug image in the middle of a circle. This slug buster always works if I need a mental jump start. I recently read about an elementary school in Mt. Diablo, California, where teachers put up such Ghost Buster signs with *Cynicism* in the middle of a red circle. The teachers evidently did this to fight their occasional bouts of low motivation.[31]

Hopeful teaching is a give-and-take affair in which the teacher gets engrossed in the learning process as it unfolds and yet is sensitive to the reactions and needs of students. As you teach, monitor how your class and individual students are becoming involved in the material. As I suggested earlier, establish a trusting atmosphere where students are free to say they don't understand something. Good teachers, although filled with plans and enthusiasm for their teaching, also need to be good listeners. Remain flexible and open to your students. Respond to their questions and work these questions into your lessons.[32]

Care about your subject matter, and care about what happens to your students. If you expect them to learn, the psychological research on the self-fulfilling prophecy suggests your students pick up on these cues and actually learn better.[33] Tell them you are proud of them and display their projects in the classroom. Make the classroom a home for your students.

If you think back over all your teachers, which ones do you remember as having made a difference? Chances are your favorite teachers not only delivered the content of the subject matter but also invited you to the excitement of the learning process. Hopeful teachers do this. (While you are thinking about these former teachers, why not go ahead and send cards or give them a call?)

If you truly think you cannot touch the lives of your students and if you have tried many of the tips suggested in this section, it may be time to pursue another profession. This does not mean you are a failure. Rather, it means teaching was not the career goal for you. Whatever you do, don't just put in the time to receive your retirement package. This is not fair to the children, who suffer because of your discontentment.[34] Equally important, it is not fair to you. Recall the case of Bob, the high school geography teacher who was just marking time until he retired. Over the course of treatment, he felt increasingly hypocritical about continuing a career where he already was dead wood. Because of these feelings, Bob took an early retirement, and pursued his interests in computer software development. His decision, in my estimation, was a hopeful one.

COACHES AND ATHLETES

Suppose sports teams no longer had coaches. After a period of chaos, the athletes themselves would have to come up with a system of self-governance and one of the players probably would take on the role of the coach. Somebody needs to take a leadership role to help athletes form goals, as well as to provide guidance about how to become motivated and prepared for the subsequent competitions.

Beyond this revelation, however, coaches foster hopeful thinking in their athletes. Indeed, an athlete or team with well-defined and challenging goals and active and positive thoughts about how to pursue those goals (willpower and waypower) has a hopeful mindset that translates into high-quality performances. For the coaches to be successful in engendering hope among their athletes, they must establish good communication. Let's start with this point.

Communication is based on the athletes' trust in their coaches. Such trust is built on the athletes' perceptions that coaches are trying to do what is best for them, as much as this is possible in the context of the particular sport.[35] This does not mean the coach and athlete must agree on everything, nor does it mean that the coach cannot have firm rules and enforce discipline for the breaking of those rules. Likewise, a coach does not have to be infallible. Admit your mistakes. If your athletes are to learn and grow from their mistakes, so should you. As a coach who learns from your mistakes, you can serve as a positive role model for athletes.

To build trust, athletes must sense they can talk with the coach and truly be heard. This means spending time throughout the season and off-season talking with your athletes. Keep the lines of communication open. Interestingly, recent books[36] and articles[37] emphasize the importance of the coach's interpersonal communication skills. Such communication forms the foundation so coaches and athletes can set goals and generate the willpower and planfulness to pursue them.

Emphasizing Performance over Winning Goals

Let's assume a coach has a good working relationship with the athlete or the team as a whole. What is the next issue that must be advanced by this coach? The linchpin notion of hopeful thinking — setting goals — is the first task. In our society, and particularly in sports, winning is the glamorized goal. The media, the alumni, the athletic director, and the owners of the team all focus on winning. Of course, we fans only add to this emphasis. Aside from these external pressures, athletes also have similar perspectives because they have grown up with this social emphasis on winning.[38] Winning, however, is an iffy proposition because 50 percent of the teams on a given day lose; for individual sports such as track and field, the probability of losing is even higher. Coaches somehow must do what is best for the athletes. At the same time, coaches know that unless the team or individual athletes win, they may be out of a job. How can coaches set goals under these circumstances?

The solution for the coach is to help athletes set performance-based rather than outcome-based goals. The outcome-based goal of winning, for example, is not under the control of the athlete.[39] Even Vince Lombardi, the former coach of the Green Bay Packers, lamented the misinterpretation of his famous comment that "Winning isn't everything, it's the only thing." In a subsequent interview, he stated, "I wish the hell I'd never said the damn thing. . . . I meant having a goal. I sure as hell didn't mean for people to crush human values and morality."[40] The overemphasis on winning has the unwanted effect of producing stress for the athletes about things that they cannot control.[41] On the other hand, performance-based goals are conducive to a more positive mental set and better performance. Because it is important, I repeat: Performance-based goals actually produce better athletic outcomes, including wins, than do win-based goals.

It is helpful if the performance goals are concrete and measurable, such as times for track events, percentage of free throws made in basketball, or percentage of baseball pitches thrown for strikes. It also is helpful if the coach and athlete set goals based on the athlete's previous performance, as well as at a challenging and yet doable level of difficulty.[42] Although the coach can take the lead in setting these goals, a participatory relationship with the athlete enhances performance because the athletes tend to set even higher goals than the coach acting alone.[43] Lastly, because athletes may be distracted by other thoughts or activities in their lives, the coach must help athletes stay focused on the performance goals.[44]

Waypower: Pathways of the Mind for the Body

Once the coach and athletes have arrived at well-specified and challenging goals, the long-term goals need to be broken down into short-term steps the athlete can aim for along the way. In practices, time should be put aside for each of these subgoals. For each game or meet, the athlete must concentrate on these performance sub-goals. For example, a basketball player may strive to make three assists, to concentrate on the back of the rim during free throw attempts, and to apply defensive pressure so an offensive player cannot drive for an uncontested layup. These subgoals for the game should be buttressed with practice time allotted to each activity. By the end of the season, the subgoals are increased relative to those set earlier in the season. For both individual and team sports, the coach works with the athletes to build the level of skill in incremental steps. Through repetition, skills and performance speeds improve over time, and the athlete's confidence in her pathways thoughts also rises.

Yet another waypower activity is to use mental imagery, where athletes learn to go through the steps involved in the athletic activity in their minds. Recent books on coaching and sport psychology include sections on these mental rehearsal tactics; many colleges have at least one sports psychologist who works with athletes on this skill.[45] These mental tapes are mastery scripts that the athlete develops about the sequence of unfolding events.[46] These mental tapes help athletes perform better.

Willpower: Psyching Up

Included in these self-talk exercises are positive statements about how the athlete can complete the event. Self-talk bolsters the athlete's willpower thoughts about the next aspect of the event. In such self-talk, coaches and sports psychologists teach their athletes not to think about negative outcomes, like losing or choking. Rather, the focus is on affirmative statements about what athletes want for themselves.[47]

In actual competitions, athletes need to see themselves as active, determined, and capable of handling difficulties that arise. Indeed, coaches train athletes to handle problems that may arise in competitions. Because of this preparation, athletes remain energized when the setbacks occur. Coaches also can help nurture an athlete's hope by maintaining a positive approach in practice, the games, and especially during time outs. A good pep talk emphasizes the positive that can happen, rather than dwelling on the negative. Likewise, the best pep talk is the one incorporated into the heads of the athletes themselves. To borrow a coaching cliché, "Every athlete has a hot button, and it is the coach's responsibility to find it and turn on each player!"[48]

Basketball Coach Example

For years I have been a fan of college basketball and the coaches guiding their teams. This is easy at the University of Kansas where I teach. The string of legendary Kansas coaches started with the first, James Naismith, the inventor of basketball. Since then the notable bloodlines have stretched from Phog Allen to the present coach, Roy Williams. Over the last several years, I have read about Coach Williams, listened to his radio program, watched him on television, observed him at home basketball games, talked with his players, and have caught parts of an occasional practice.

Basketball is a microcosm of life: The goal is the goal. That is to say, the participants attempt to repeatedly get the ball in the goal basket. Conversely, the players try to prevent the members of the other team from getting the ball in their basket. When it comes to the coaching of Roy Williams, I believe that his approach can be broken into two basic goal-related components — willpower and pathways — regarding the thinking of his players. First, he is a master at supporting and motivating players. Under William's tutelage, players display a mental fire and energy in practice and games. Second, Williams teaches the passing game where the players are instilled with the belief that they can get the ball to the player who can successfully put it in the hoop. Likewise, team members practice a tenacious man-to-man defense to the point that they believe they can stop the offense of other teams. One final comment about Coach Williams is how he emphasizes the goal of playing hard and applying the offensive and defensive strategies, rather than simply winning. In fact, I have heard him be extremely upbeat when the team has played well but lost and constructively critical when the team has played poorly but won. Finally, while he sets limits and can be firm in his guidance of players, he also listens to and responds to their concerns. Throughout his interactions with his players, it is obvious he respects them and they respect him.

From the perspective of the Kansas basketball players, they think they will do well. No, it's probably more accurate to say that they know they will do well. This is especially the case for an important game, when the score is close, or when it is toward the end of the contest. In other words, under maximally stressful conditions, these players appear to have very adaptive goal-directed thoughts. In postgame interviews, for example, it is typical for Kansas players to mention how they were mentally up for the game, and how they knew they had an offensive and defensive system that would work. This seems to be more than just talk; these guys are true believers in themselves.

For Roy Williams and myriad other successful coaches, the common denominators are the two-way communication between coach and player about their shared goals, and the mental determination (willpower) and planful preparation (waypower) the team members bring to the arenas. The scoreboard takes care of itself when the players have this hopeful mindset.

MANAGERS AND EMPLOYEES

"What's the bottom line?" is a familiar profit question that permeates many businesses. How does hopeful thinking, particularly between managers and employees, enter into this equation? The answer, in large part, is that managers and employees need to have a relationship where they can share a vision about the short- and long-term goals of the business. Once the company and the employees affirm these goals as being for the common good, both the will and the ways to achieve these goals must be cultivated. Furthermore, this is not just a one-time process. Businesses cannot remain static. Indeed, to survive, as well as to thrive, managers and employees constantly must renew themselves through revised goals, along with will- and way-related thinking about how to pursue those goals.

Shared Objectives

The most widely used version of the goal-setting approach within the business world is management by objectives (MBO).[49] MBO involves a collaborative goal-setting process that flows through all levels of a company. At the highest level, the chief executive officer and the top management typically establish and support visions about the future of the company. The various upper-level managers render these broad visions into more concrete goals such as product development, sales projections, and costs. In turn, these goals are translated by the midlevel managers and their subordinates into concrete goals that are realistic, observable, and challenging.[50] At all levels of goal setting, the MBO approach endorses the KISS (Keep It Simple, Stupid) approach.[51]

At the stage where the translation of goals is made, collaborative interaction between manager and employee is critical. If you are a manager, you are accountable to your superiors for the goals that are set and achieved. Likewise, as a manager you know that your employees' performance is under your evaluation. The raw exercise of power in setting goals and evaluating your employees in terms of those goals, however, can backfire because you may kill their hopeful thinking. While your supervisees may go through the motions and do just enough not to be fired, they will not produce the quality and quantity of work of which they are capable. Your real power lies in developing relationships where there is mutual goal setting with employees, as well as shared ideas about plans and motivations to implement those plans.

To build a framework for manager-employee goal setting, the manager needs to spend time with the employees. Although managers and employees do not have to become best friends, there should be familiarity and open lines of communication. If you are a manager, this means you need to interact regularly with your employees about a multitude of job-related issues. Set up your schedule so you can talk frequently with your employees. If your office or desk is far removed from your employees, move it closer so you can routinely mingle with them in the actual work setting.

In your interchanges with employees, listen to them and value their input. The importance of management's listening to employees is emphasized throughout Thomas Peters and Robert Waterman's

In Search of Excellence, which analyzes the characteristics of well-run businesses.[52] When employees sense that their input actually has an influence on goals — that management is listening — they become invested in the goals and energized to pursue them.

Your employees can provide excellent ideas about how to set their work goals when they are knowledgeable about their jobs. As you interact with them about these goals, follow the basic tenets of goal setting in chapter 6. Namely, make the goals concrete, measurable, realistic, and yet challenging. If these goals are clearly articulated and agreed on, you and your employees have markers against which to monitor progress over time.

In the goal-setting process, remember to establish an environment where your employees can reach the goals. Therefore, instead of implementing goals that most employees fail to meet, negotiate goals that many people can successfully attain. A work environment where people experience success not only is more productive but also is a place where absenteeism and loafing are less prevalent. Research on the self-fulfilling prophecy makes a convincing case that when people are treated as if they are going to succeed, they are prone to do so.[53]

Plans with Push

You can discuss plans to reach the goals with your employees, although for more autonomous and skilled workers this may be unnecessary. At Texas Instruments, for example, it is a general policy that those who implement the plans are also the ones to make them.[54] When such skilled employees are allowed to design their own pathways, they may produce more effective individual planning, as well as enhanced willpower thinking to implement those plans.[55] Be careful not to overplan for your employees. This can kill the initiative effective businesses need to be able to move into action and to try things.[56] By moving to action, you and your employees can get feedback about how the plans are working and institute changes where needed.

If you have approached goals in the manner I have suggested, the clear standards leave little room for disagreement about the employee's performance. If employees meet or exceed the standards, they experience intrinsic gratification. Increasingly in the product development and manufacturing processes, managers and employees are making quality control a part of their production goals. Knowing that one has helped to produce a genuinely useful and reliable product is rewarding in itself. The traditional reward for meeting or exceeding a goal is money (either a percent increase or a one-time addition of actual dollars), as well as possible increases in pensions, life and health insurance, and vacations.[57] Equally important, however, is the employer's verbal praise for the job well done. Successful companies continually celebrate their employees' successes. In such activities, the magnitude of the congratulations is not the critical factor. Rather, employees appreciate the simple act of being recognized by management.[58]

Regular periodic reviews of the employee's performance provide an important feedback period, whatever the performance outcome may be. Likewise, it is helpful to have a review sometime during the middle of the performance period to make corrections and suggestions when they are necessary. Managers should consider using the approach that mistakes are to be expected. This is particularly helpful if employees have set their own plans to achieve a goal. You want your employees to be willing to take risks and try new plans. One related suggestion you can make to your employees is that they didn't use the best strategy for the particular goal. This keeps them from dwelling on the negative and increases the chances they will try something that will work.[59] In these feedback sessions, spend as little time as possible on the negative. Punitive words may have some short-term effects, but you have more sustained influence by praising what is being done well. In other words, your employees will want to do more of the praiseworthy activities.

There are two general caveats — the time required and potential misuse issues — associated with this expanded MBO system as I have outlined it. Time may be the most obvious problem. As a manager, you may not believe it is productive to put in the necessary hours to implement and monitor this goals system. Indeed, this system does entail considerable paperwork and record-keeping.[60]

Turning to potential misuse issues, some managers simply set the goals and implementation plans without consulting employees. Likewise, if managers are not comfortable in such interactions, they avoid communicating with employees and derail the whole approach. There also is the possibility of using goals in a quantifiable, verifiable manner that dehumanizes employees. Conversely, the goals may be set so ambiguously that it is almost impossible to measure performance. Or, the manager may use the goal system primarily to wield power over the fate of the employee. Lastly, the sessions may become a tug of war, where a common goal cannot be agreed on by the manager and employee.[61]

The Relationship Solution

If you find yourself in a low-hope work environment, what can you do? The solution typically resides in having both the manager and employee work to improve their relationship. Indeed, managers who lack people skills should be in the minority because interpersonal relations are an integral part of many business activities. If you are a manager in need of such skills, however, you can learn them. Likewise, if you are an employee and lack communication skills, you can get these through training courses offered by private companies or your local colleges. Communication typically starts with listening and often ends with compromise. These two ingredients facilitate manager-employee interchanges whether it is in the context of one manager and one employee, or teams from management and unions.

What I have described is the vertical organization, where employees report to supervisors who, in turn, report to managers, and so on up the hierarchy. As my emphasis on relationships suggests, however, the traditional boundaries of jobs are becoming blurred by the necessary interaction between varying levels of employees. Indeed, many businesses today have a lateral rather than vertical organizational chart. In a lateral scheme, skilled employees from various segments of an organization freely interact for purposes of product development, manufacturing, or sales. Likewise, companies increasingly are abandoning the nineteenth-century production-line mentality of one individual doing a very specialized piece of work, and passing the product on to another worker for the next step. What is beginning to emerge at companies such as Volvo is more of a *product cooperative* approach.[62] This is my term for a system where several people work to produce the entire product, but individual employees may do any or all of the production steps. In this process, teams of workers decide how they will meet their goals and are not constrained to repeat the same task all day. This approach produces excellent worker cohesion, productivity, quality control, and pride in the eventual product. Undergirding this whole lateral organizational structure is communication and cooperation by employees aiming at common goals. These are precisely the conditions where hopeful thinking should thrive.

PHYSICIANS AND PATIENTS

Surveys suggest that many Americans recently have changed their physicians or are considering doing so in the near future.[63] The reasons given, however, don't appear to be related to concerns about perceived competence. Rather, patients are displeased about the nature of their relationships with physicians. Complaints involve perceptions that physicians don't listen very well, are insensitive to patient needs, aren't respectful, and are rather poor at communicating.[64] Relatedly, book-length essays praising the medical proficiency of renowned institutions such as the Mayo Clinic touch on the desire for more in-depth doctor-patient interactions.[65] If we want these interactions to change, some attention needs to be given to the pressures that encourage physicians to behave the way they do.

Forces Against Relationships

The earliest forces pushing physicians away from relationship-related issues date back to the rationalism of the golden age of Greece. Turning away from previous mystical explanations for illness, physicians in the Hippocratic school of medicine were instructed to search for observable causes of illness in patients. Thus, doctors began to discount what patients said and concentrated on measurable symptoms.[66] These beliefs have been transmitted over the centuries to our present society, where physicians want to know the underlying reason for our illness. This is the disease model.

Accordingly, the medical curriculum of twentieth-century physicians focuses almost totally at the causes of diseases[67] and emphasizes science and technology.[68] Medical students are taught to objectify the human body, with the anatomy dissections being but one prime arena for such lessons. The detachment process is intensified further by jargon; patients become "cases," and the person becomes "the gallbladder in room 327."[69] Such detachment also provides physicians with some psychological protection against the pain and afflictions they frequently encounter.[70]

There are other forces contributing to the breakdown of the patient-physician relationship. Whether they are in a bureaucracy or a private practice, physicians often are evaluated and paid according to the number of patients seen. Likewise, given the specialists' imprint on general practitioners, as well as the litigious nature of our times, physicians are spending more of their time in giving and evaluating tests.[71] Lastly, our physicians are a manifestation of our society more generally, where nurturance and compassion are not necessarily valued qualities.

Given these various interrelated factors, it is understandable how physicians spend their available time. Additionally, we patients often contribute to the problem by acting as if we are in a hurry. Thus, we hold physicians to the highest of standards, all the while often wanting a quick answer to our medical problems.

With these strong forces impacting on the physician-patient relationship, where are things headed? Certainly, we still tend to imbue doctors and the medical community with strong power and influence, especially in those times when we are experiencing serious illnesses. My reading of the medical literature suggests, however, that we are in the early stages of changing the traditional relationship model of an active physician and passive patient.[72] Patients have begun to move from a passive doctor knows best demeanor, to a stance where physician and patient are active partners.[73] The first of several reasons for this transition is the commercialism of medical services. We see daily television advertisements for local medical services, and various news and educational shows inform us about the workings of the medical establishment. A second reason is the emerging likelihood of a national health care system in the United States; under this system, more general practitioners should be available to the population.[74] The net effect is a demystification of physicians and medicine, with the nature of the relationship changing toward greater patient involvement.[75]

What role will hopeful thinking play in this evolving physician-patient process? Granted that simply more time spent interacting may diffuse some of the concerns raised by patients, how the time is spent between the doctor and patient is an equally critical issue.[76] This is where the communication can be improved to enhance the patient's sense of hope in dealing with any underlying disease and the associated illness process. The physician's technical skills and detective instincts help to sustain patients' hopes, but so does the implicit message that the patients will help in this healing process. Increasingly, our physician-patient interactions should reflect a partnership aimed at keeping hope alive for positive health solutions. In the closing words of a medical school commencement address, Norman Cousins suggested a similar credo that physicians should impart to their patients:

> Your body will experience a powerful gravitational pull in the direction of . . . expectations. Your hopes are my secret weapon. They are the hidden ingredient in any prescription I might write. So I will do everything I can to generate and encourage your confidence in yourself and in the certainty of recovery.
>
> This is my notion of what a partnership between physician and patient is all about.
>
> Sincerely yours,
> Your Doctor[77]

Seeing a Doctor

Perhaps it may be helpful to walk through the typical steps of a physician-patient interaction to better understand the role of hopeful thinking in this relationship. Initially, patients experience a physical pain of a sufficient quality that they cannot handle it through the normal self-ministrations.[78] The pain may be large, uncontrollable, enduring over time, and unknown in origin; any or all of these factors may contribute to a sense of suffering that prompts us to

seek medical attention.[79] When we see the physician, there is a ritu-
alized exchange of information aimed at finding out what is wrong
(the diagnosis) and how the difficulty happened (the cause). At this
point, the physician and patient share common goals. Because of
what the patient says, the physician may conduct a physical exam
and order related tests. Ideally, these activities reveal the diagnosis
and underlying cause of the patient's pain. The physician then
describes these results in a form understood by the patient.

Assuming the source of the problem is clear, the interplay
between the physician and patient next turns to the treatments
aimed at alleviating it. This is analogous to the waypower component of hopeful thinking. We may be given prescriptions for an
infection, surgery for repair of broken bones or removal of tumors,
exercises to strengthen muscle groups, or instructions about changing our eating habits, to name but a few possible treatments. These
pathways offer avenues for lessening or removing our pain; through
discussions with our physicians, we make a decision about which
treatment to undertake. Willpower thinking becomes involved
when the patient decides whether to undertake a particular treatment plan.

The I'm Going to Get Help Lift

Having laid out the typical steps of the physician-patient interaction, I would like to amplify on each step's implications for hopeful
thinking. Sometimes the healing effect occurs just because the patient anticipates seeing a physician. If this sounds slightly magical,
the underlying dynamics are not. Many patients believe they are
going to improve because of the powers they ascribe to medicine
and physicians. The history of such placebo effects is well documented in medicine, and the term *placebo* has come to denote positive changes people experience without any discernible medical
treatments.[80] In other words, placebo effects are the medical benefits
the patient receives because of positive expectations for change.
Such positive thoughts probably are derived from the importance
ascribed to physicians.[81] Although the public is becoming more familiar with the machinations of medicine, its achievements and
practitioners still are admired. Remember here that patients rate

their physicians as quite competent. This perception alone contributes to hope-related healing effects.

Diagnosis as Goal

The goal when visiting a physician is to arrive at a diagnosis for our pain or discomfort.[82] Toward this end, it benefits us to think well of physicians, especially our physicians.[83] When we go to our physicians, we often are insecure. For this reason, an open and reasonably lengthy interchange should occur so that an accurate diagnosis can be generated, and our hopeful expectations can be sustained whenever possible. To overcome fears and tell about symptoms, we patients sometimes need a warm-up period of interaction with physicians. Additionally, patients must develop trusting relationships with physicians. These factors contribute to the physician's diagnostic acumen and facilitate the patient's eventual understanding of the diagnosis.

Treatments as Waypower

The treatment is analogous to the waypower component of hopeful thinking. During this stage, the physician describes the nature of the treatment options (e.g., drugs, diet, etc.). To improve the chances that patients internalize the treatment plans into their thinking, it is most useful if doctors use an informational approach.[84] Taking this tack, the physician describes the way the treatment will proceed, including the risks involved if the treatment is not instituted, and the advantages if it is. If there are any side effects or negative aspects of the treatment, it is important to describe these so that the patient does not abandon belief in the treatment at some later point because of such unpleasant surprises.[85] Further, if there are two or three equally plausible treatments, the physician should present these options for the patient's consideration. Lastly, the physician should find out if the patient has any difficulties in traveling to the appropriate treatment facility, or can pay for the treatments. These practical issues need to be weighed into the actual decision about which treatment is undertaken.[86]

Making the Treatments Come to Life

At this point, the patient often may ask for the physician's preference regarding the treatments: "Doctor, what would you do if you were me?"[87] In this scenario, the hope-engendering physician reflects the choices back onto patients emphasizing that it should be their decision.[88] If the patient is reticent to make a choice, the physician needs to encourage a commitment to one. Evidence of willful thinking occurs when the patient forcefully states an intention to begin treatment.[89] Willpower thinking is the key to having patients undertake and sustain their treatment regimens. Such willpower is critical, because fully 30 percent of patients do not follow the recommendations for taking medications in the short-term, and noncompliance is 50 percent or higher for longer-term regimens.[90]

Physicians can do several additional things to increase patients' willful thinking for their particular treatments. Sometimes patients are unable to think in a future-oriented fashion because of their absorption in the illness. In such instances, the physician should emphasize how undertaking the treatment may help them to think about future goals.[91] In other words, undertaking a treatment can result in the active pursuit of life goals that previously has been characteristic of the patient. If the patient has family and friends, the importance of the patient to these continuing relationships can be emphasized to energize the patient for treatment.[92] Other patients who have undergone the treatment, or support groups of similar people, also can provide much-needed mental lifts. I also recommend that the doctor's staff members call or write patients about treatment regimens and upcoming appointments.[93] A patient who clearly understands the nature of the treatments, as well as when they are to occur, is likely to think about and actively pursue these treatments. Lastly, physicians may want to add special health care counselors whose job it is to interact with patients and to explain, initiate, and help in the maintenance of treatments.[94] All of these interactions should increase the patient's willful thinking about her treatments.

Three Tough Questions

When I speak to audiences, especially those including physicians, about the importance of encouraging patient hope, the same three questions usually come up. The first concern often is phrased as a comment: "Surely we would rather have a competent doctor than one who merely is capable of hopeful exchanges." This view is based on the faulty assumption that competence and hopeful interactions are antithetical. On the contrary, I believe that competence and hopeful interactions go hand in hand.[95] The best synopsis of this issue is given by noted physician Eric Cassell, who wrote:

> That often-heard question "Would you rather have a technically competent doctor or one who is humane?" is beside the point. A doctor without technical competence would be inadequate and unworthy of trust. Knowledge by itself cannot indicate which patient it is to be used on and how. To be effective, physicians must be adept at working with patients — taking histories, establishing rapport, achieving compliance with regimens that may be extremely unpleasant, being sensitive to unspoken words, providing empathetic support, and communicating effectively. Doctors who cannot do these things are neither adequate nor entirely trustworthy.[96]

Second, others have asked if I am suggesting that physicians should lie when giving serious diagnostic feedback to patients. My response is that lying is not helpful, but being careful about framing one's feedback is. Indeed, words can be just as devastating to people as their serious diseases. Let's take an extreme example. Suppose a physician believes that the probability of a particular patient's dying of a given disease within the next year is 75 percent. Such data are based on averages across people, and therefore the probability that this given patient will die in a year actually are either 100 percent or 0 percent. My suggestion is not to discuss such probabilities. Instead, the physician can acknowledge the seriousness of the diagnosis, but thereafter spend the majority of the feedback time on plans for treating the illness and making the best fight possible. This is where the patient-doctor alliance turns to what can be done to increase the successful treatment outcome.

Given the relative newness of the data regarding the positive relationship between psychological factors such as hope and physical health, it is not appropriate to make the strong form of this argument at this point.[97] However, if serious health-related feedback can be given in a manner so that patients have a challenge rather than a giving up mindset, the physicians' treatments have a better chance of succeeding. Even the most skeptical among us could embrace this view for humanitarian and quality-of-life reasons. In the process, however, the power of the human mind may stretch our present level of understanding. Consider the following true vignette:

> As I was eating breakfast one morning I overheard two oncologists discussing the papers they were to present that day at the national meeting of the American Society of Clinical Oncology. One was complaining bitterly:
>
> "You know, Bob, I just don't understand it. We used the same drugs, the same dosage, the same schedule, and the same entry criteria. Yet I got a 22 percent response rate and you got 74 percent. That's unheard of for metastatic lung cancer. How do you do it?"
>
> "We're both using Etoposide, Platinol, Oncovin, and Hydroxyurea. You call yours EPOH. I tell my patients I'm giving them HOPE. Sure, I tell them this is experimental, and we go over the long list of side effects together. But I emphasize that we have a chance. As dismal as the statistics are for non-small cell, there are always a few patients who do really well."[98]

A last question, and one that seems to represent the deepest concerns, is whether this approach doesn't run the risk of creating false hopes in patients.[99] A related concern is that patients who do not improve may blame themselves and feel guilty for not being hopeful enough. These understandable questions, like the other two discussed previously, implicitly make the incorrect assumption that hopeful thoughts somehow are separated from traditional medical mechanisms of healing. On the contrary, treatments represent the necessary pathways to recovering health. The actual undertaking and completion of these treatments are fueled by patient's willful thinking. Thus, if hopeful thinking is applied to the recommended medical treatments, as I am suggesting, it should not be criticized as being false or guilt inducing.[100]

Mutuality

In summary, I am advocating mutual hope between physicians and patients as they interact.[101] This is a perspective shared by medical writers, one of whom concludes: "The primary characteristic of the situation we find when a patient seeking help interacts with a physician trying to give help is mutual hope."[102] Without hope, both the physician and patient may withdraw—the patient into noncompliance, and the physician into detached unconcern.[103] When it comes to positive health, therefore, hope is an inherently engaging mindset for doctors and patients alike.

PSYCHOTHERAPISTS AND CLIENTS

Although there obviously are many different psychotherapy approaches for facilitating positive change, all of these interventions share an underlying process: They are an interpersonal enterprise.[104] In the preface to the latest edition of his landmark book on the common factors underlying psychotherapy, Jerome Frank concludes that "the success of all techniques depends on the patient's *sense of alliance* with an actual or symbolic healer" (italics mine).[105] This section elaborates on this relationship theme by suggesting that these therapeutic alliances increase the clients' sense of willpower and waypower for the goals in their lives. Simply put, psychotherapies involve relationships that traffic in hopeful thinking.[106] Before developing this point, however, let's look at who goes to psychotherapy, who are the people who conduct it, and whether it works. (My focus is on Western cultures, although I believe other societies have comparable processes by which psychological healing occurs.)

Who Goes into Psychotherapy?

The consumers of psychotherapy are individuals who are experiencing sufficient nonmedically produced pain and suffering that they seek the help of the therapist.[107] This pain typically is not medical in origin, although this need not always be the case. (See chapter 4 for the steps involving goal blockage that cause various kinds of dissatisfactions among people.) Some people may have encountered an impediment only recently; in others, the blockages may have been building for years. Larger, more pervasive, and enduring impediments are the ones that loom in people's minds, and they are at risk of letting these blockages incapacitate them. Even though they may be down, they are not totally without hope. That is to say, although people who seek psychological treatment have concluded they are unable to handle things on their own, they do have sufficient hope to go to a therapist.[108] My point is that most people enter therapy with considerable psychological pain, and hope for its alleviation.[109]

In addition to those people just described are those who do not seek therapy because of psychological distress related to blockages. Such people want to learn more about themselves, to engage in psychological growth. These clients tend to be young, highly educated, and fairly successful in their lives; and they want to continue their quest.[110] Although such people are in the minority among those seeking psychotherapy, they represent a growing phenomenon in our psychologically minded citizenry. Whatever your reasons for seeking psychological help, however, keep in mind that this is an increasingly common event in our society.

Who Conducts Psychotherapy?

The purveyor of psychotherapy is the therapist, who is a "person trained in a socially sanctioned method of healing believed to be effective by the sufferer and by at least some members of his or her social group."[111] In the United States, these therapists typically have received formal training, and they meet licensing and continuing education requirements appropriate to their particular professions. Included here are clinical and counseling psychologists, social workers, psychiatrists, and psychiatric nurses. Additionally, there are marriage and family counselors, rehabilitation counselors, alcohol and drug abuse counselors, and pastoral counselors. A higher percentage of clients are female, while at present the majority of therapists are male.[112] If you see one of these people for treatment at some point in your life, it is very appropriate to ask about his or her educational training and experience.[113] Competent therapists are comfortable talking about their training and experience.[114]

Does Psychotherapy Work?

The answer to the basic question of whether psychotherapy is effective is a resounding yes. In a bellwether review of many differing types of psychotherapy treatments, Smith, Glass, and Miller found that those persons who had undergone treatment were, on the average, 80 percent better off on a variety of outcome measures than were untreated persons with comparable psychological difficulties.[115] Putting these and other similar results another way, whatever the particular form of psychotherapy received, the clients' outcomes were superior to those of persons on a waiting list for the same period.[116]

The next question about the workings of psychotherapy is whether one approach is more effective than the others. The answer is no. Generally, all major psychotherapy approaches appear to help people relatively equally.[117] This finding, coupled with the conclusion that psychotherapy works, has led various writers to conclude that there are facilitative processes common to all psychotherapies.[118] The components of hope theory—willpower and waypower thoughts for goals—provide one such common framework.[119]

Psychotherapy Beckons and Hopeful Thinking Appears

When a client has chosen to seek help from a mental health professional, this decision alone is evidence that the would-be client is not entirely lacking in will- and way-related thinking. After all, therapy represents a viable pathway to the goal of alleviating the distress; the fact that the person makes the appointment suggests some willpower. Once the appointment is made, there may be an additional surge of will- and way-related thinking in anticipation of the first session. (This is analogous to medical patients recovering before they have seen their physicians.)

The client's seeming indecision and impasse ends when the appointment is made; for this reason, I encourage mental health facilities and practitioners to schedule appointments as quickly as possible after the client has made the initial contact.[120] Although a short waiting period may allow the would-be client's hopeful thinking to incubate, elongated waiting periods run the risk of demoralizing clients and decreasing their desire to keep appointments. If you are a client seeking help and you find the waiting period too long, call various local mental health centers to get recommendations about qualified therapists whom you can see more quickly (the footnote has tips about finding mental health care resources).[121]

Relationship Liftoffs: The Hope-Inducing Effects of Early Sessions

Clients attending their first sessions of psychotherapy are primed with hope. At this point, the therapeutic alliance needs to take place so clients perceive therapists as people who acting in their best interests. Trust is a building block of the client-therapist relationship, and this supportive relationship provides the foundation for furthering the client's hopes for subsequent improvement.[122] It is not by chance, for example, that studies of psychotherapy suggest that the most notable part of treatment from the perspective of the clients is whether they are respected and liked by the therapists.[123] Indeed, a long history of psychotherapy outcome research shows that empathic, warm, and genuine therapists are effective in helping people.[124]

Therapists who convey that they both like and respect a client also believe the client is a suitable candidate for treatment. In fact, research supports this observation.[125] Further, these therapists also send hopeful messages about the prognosis of treatment. It is not surprising, therefore, that clients pick up on these hope-related indicators. Indeed, clients who report that their therapists do not like and respect them are prone to drop out of treatment,[126] and are less likely to report they have improved as a result of therapy.[127] Again, clients use these relationship indicators as clues about the hopeful or not so hopeful prognosis of their treatment.

There are important implications of these findings whether you are the client or the psychotherapist in such relationships. If you are a client, and you have sensed a positive, respectful, and warm relationship with your therapist, you want to continue. Conversely, if you have had one or a few sessions with a therapist and do not sense the therapist exudes positive regard for you, and vice versa, discuss this perception with your therapist as an important issue for your continued treatment. (Keeping this concern to yourself only undermines the psychotherapy process.) If you do not perceive any improvement after this discussion, consider looking for a different therapist. Therapists do not always form this trusting, positive relationship with every client, and it may have little to do with you. If you try two or more psychotherapists and do not attain this positive relationship, however, you need to think about your role in this process.

If you are a psychotherapist sensing you do not have an open, trusting, and warm relationship with one of your clients, discuss this with the client. To establish a strong therapeutic alliance, you may have to adhere to the maxim, "I can find something about this person that we have in common and something about this person that I can like."[128] If the relationship does not improve, it is your responsibility to transfer the client to another therapist where this important alliance for promulgating hope may result. There may be occasional clients with whom you do not hit it off; this does not mean you are a bad therapist. If, however, you are not connecting with several of your clients, I would suggest you go into therapy to ferret out the causes of this difficulty. As is the case with physicians, psychotherapists often encounter a good deal of stress and burnout in their careers.[129] If you are not establishing positive, warm relationships with your clients, chances are you are not hopeful about yourself as a helper. Just as hope begets hope, hopelessness begets hopelessness; it is important for the therapists to monitor this mindset throughout their careers.

Forming Goals

The supportive relationship established in the early sessions allows the client and therapist to engage in shared detective work about the goals for treatment. Although clients often begin psychotherapy with vague notions of what they want, and equally ambiguous ideas about what the underlying causes of their distresses may be, it is the therapist's job to clarify matters. At times, we all need someone who listens and offers guidance. Based on my experience, as well as a review of the literature about people who come to psychotherapy, my conclusion is that many clients do not have someone who listens to them and who can help them sort out what they want in their lives.[130]

In forming therapeutic goals, it is important to let clients say things in their own words, and thereafter to reflect back what you have understood them to be saying. In this process, therapists become allies with clients, and convey that they are trying to understand the client's life. During this process, therapists must listen carefully. Although the theoretical biases of the therapist increasingly come into play over the course of treatment, in the beginning it is helpful for clients to tell their stories from their perspectives.[131]

After clients have told their stores, therapists should ask what they want out of therapy. At this point, the therapist helps the client put the goals into a clear and understandable form. Likewise, it is common to prioritize the goals, with the therapist and client agreeing about which important goal to tackle first. Whatever the therapists' theoretical orientations, they have implicit goals for the client, and these goals need to be made explicit as part of the therapy contract.[132] In my psychotherapy work, for example, I continually discuss and clarify the ongoing client goals and make sure that the client and I agree what these goals are. If therapist and client goals are disparate, this should be discussed and resolved. Obviously, it is critical for the therapist and client to agree on the goals to foster a therapeutic alliance.[133] If clients do not sense that the goals are ones they value, the therapeutic alliance is undermined, and the chances for effective treatment diminish. Open communication between therapists and clients should maximize the chances of arriving at common goals. In turn, these goals serve as markers to which clients and therapists can refer in the subsequent evolution of therapy. As noted previously, setting goals energizes people and opens them to finding appropriate pathways.

Pathways for Change: The Techniques

From the early sessions, therapists explicitly and implicitly convey the inherent powers of their therapeutic approaches. In other words, they indicate that the techniques are effective vehicles for facilitating client change. In early sessions, it is fairly common for the therapist to explain how the treatment works. Such introductions engender beliefs that the procedures help clients in learning how to reach their therapeutic goals.[134]

Once the general therapeutic approach and the client's treatment goals have been discussed, it is time to initiate the particular procedures for change. Given the breadth of approaches used by various psychotherapists, it is not feasible to review these techniques. As I have suggested, however, these varying psychotherapies share an underlying premise of moving clients toward therapeutic goals. Professional psychotherapists keep clients focused on their goals, and do not let the discussion wander away from the treatment of the problems.[135] Because of the strength of the therapist-patient relationship, and the expectations the client holds of the therapy itself, the client typically is quite amenable to staying focused on these treatment goals. This point helps clarify how the talk of psychotherapy differs from talk in other conversations. Significantly, this task focus about the ways to reach goals also epitomizes hopeful thinking.

Willpower and Waypower for Change: The Therapist as a Model

Beyond the specific techniques the therapist uses for facilitating change toward treatment goals, the therapists themselves also serve as models for change. In this regard, therapists exhibit a sense of confidence in themselves as helpers who can effectively teach the techniques. For those who do psychotherapy, I would state the obvious: Our clients are watching us for tips about how to solve our problems. This should not be surprising, because research consistently has shown that children and adults are especially prone to emulate those people perceived as powerful and likable.[136] The psychotherapist usually fits this description.[137]

If you are a psychotherapist, your clients will emulate both your willpower for goals and your waypower propensity to come up with solutions. Although I have not given the Hope Scale to psychotherapists, I believe they are, as a group, hopeful people. If you are a psychotherapist lacking a hopeful mindset, try the approaches for kindling hope in chapter 6. Likewise, you may want to consider personal therapy to explore your hopelessness. Psychotherapists are susceptible to the stresses of overwork and burnout, and we must constantly monitor our hope. This is for our own welfare and that of our clients.

The Psychotherapy Alliance and Keeping Hope Alive

Psychotherapy is an interpersonal enterprise aimed at teaching clients how to build or recapture hope in their lives. It is not enough to engender hope in one's clients, however, without considering how to sustain such hope long after the therapist-client relationship has ended. Accordingly, therapists should emphasize that the positive, goal-directed changes have occurred because clients made them work. It is counterproductive and inaccurate as well, to ascribe the changes to the power of the techniques or to the skill of the therapist. For the positive changes to stick long after leaving therapy, the client needs to take credit for them.[138] Likewise, clients must continue using and expanding on the skills and insights gained in psychotherapy and apply these in their important relationships. Having experienced a genuine, caring, and trusting relationship with the therapist, the key is to do this in the other enduring relationships in the client's life. Clients' insights that such relationships can be attained are a source of sustained hope as they leave psychotherapy. For the therapists whose clients leave with this mindset, there is renewed hope for the enterprise of psychotherapy, and for oneself as a participant in this process. Hope, in this sense, is catalytic.

THE YOU SUCCEED, I SUCCEED CAROUSEL

Relationships where the participants make it possible for each other to reach goals produce a caring and yet active environment where things get done. What this means is that people in such relationships experience the full range of positive emotions as they successfully journey toward and beyond their goals. Furthermore, in the process, these relationships add meaning and richness to our lives.

All of this happens because hopeful thinking is woven indelibly into the very fabric of our important relationships.

A common theme runs through all of the relationships touched on in this and previous chapters. Whether we are talking about parents and children, two adults in an intimate relationship, teacher and student, a coach and athlete, an employer and employee, a physician and patient, or a psychotherapist and client, the partners in the relationship have a commitment to setting reachable goals and to facilitating the will and ways to achieve those goals. In other words, one partner helps the other, and vice versa. Often this process is directed toward a mutual goal, and at times it may be directed to help one of the partners to achieve a goal. Even in this latter scenario, however, there may be a reciprocity and a person we have helped, in turn, may help us to meet our goal.

As I come to the end of this book, I would like to highlight the importance of shared goals developed in the context of the relationships we have with each other. Whenever there is a personal goal, a "me" goal, I would ask you also to think of the implications of this goal for the rest of us as a "we" goal. In the extent to which the me and we goals relate positively on each other, much like images in a reflecting pool, then our goals are in synchrony. Picture in your mind the word *me* with the word *we* placed directly on top of it. Once you have this image, as shown Figure 7.1, it is difficult to lose.

Figure 7.1

Each of stands in a long evolutionary line. Looking back, we honor the memories of our ancestors. Looking forward, we have an unknown and yet undeniable impact on our descendants. Individually and collectively, we are time travelers who, for better or worse, are making a difference in what happens next. The link between what was and what might be rests in our thoughts today. If our minds are filled with willpower and waypower for goals profiting only ourselves and not others, we advance the forces of unhappiness, divisiveness, fear, aggression, and destruction. If our minds are filled with hope for shared goals, however, our legacy will be a positive one. The changes necessary for this latter scenario are not easy, but they are doable. It is our choice, and the decision will be made in the most powerful polling booth of all—the human mind. My vote, for what it is worth, is that we can get there from here.

Books to Help Children with Scholastic, Athletic, and Social Skills

Book Title, Author, Publisher	Summary
Scholastics	
Awakening Your Child's Natural Genius: Enhancing Curiosity, Creativity, and Learning Ability Thomas Armstrong, Ph.D. Putnam Publishing, New York, NY © 1990	Over 300 practical suggestions and activities showing how parents can play a pivotal role in helping their child realize their gifts. Describes how parents can encourage the school to provide the types of experiences all children need to develop their inborn drive to learn and create. Includes resources.
Family Matters: Why Homeschooling Makes Sense David Guterson Harcourt Brace & Company, Orlando, FL © 1992	A high school English teacher affirms the powerful role of the family in a child's education.

How to Maximize Your Child's Learning Ability: A Complete Guide to Choosing and Using the Best Games, Toys, Activities, Learning Aids and Tactics for Your Child Lauren Bradway & Barbara Albers Hill Avery Publishing Group, Inc. Garden City Park, NY © 1993	Helps parents identify child's particular learning style and offers advice on selecting toys, activities, and learning strategies to best use this style to improve learning.
How to Teach Your Child: Things to Know from Kindergarten through Grade 6 Veltisezar B. Bautista Bookhaus Publishers Farmington Hills, MI © 1992	Aids parents in home-teaching and school-supplementation by presenting effective teaching methods, reviews of skills, and evaluation guides.
School Savvy: Everything You Need to Know to Guide Your Child through Today's Schools Diane Harrington & Laurette Young Noonday Press, New York, NY © 1993	Offers an in-depth look at how schools work, and provides ways that parents can be involved at many levels — from helping their children to advocating for changes in the entire system.
Teach Your Child How to Think Edward de Bono Viking Press, New York, NY © 1992	Examples, exercises, games, and drawings teach the difference between intelligence and thinking, and provide a step-by-step method for helping children develop clear and constructive thinking.
How Children Learn John Hold Dell/Seymour Lawrence New York, NY © 1983	Explores ways children learn and examines the process of learning to talk, read, count, and create. Shows how to nurture and encourage children's natural abilities.
Is the Left Brain Always Right: A Guide to Whole Child Development Clare Cherry, Douglas Godwin, & Jesse Staples Fearon Teacher Aids, Belmont CA © 1989	Explains different hemispheric functions; presents tests for assessing hemispheric dominance and developmental activities best suited for each.

Athletics

Let's Play Together: Cooperative Games for All Ages Mildred Masheder Green Print, London, England © 1989	Collection of more than 300 games and sports that teach cooperation over competition. Also suited for children with disabilities. (See also Social Skills)

*The Growing Child in
Competitive Sport*
Geof Gleeson, Editor
Hodder & Stoughton, London
© 1986

Coaches tackle the physiological,
psychological, and sociological problems of overtraining, and relate such
problems to the development of
musicians and actors as well.

Joy and Sadness in Children's Sports
Rainer Martes
Human Kinetics Publishers
Champaign, IL
© 1978

Focus on nonschool sports, examines
the good and bad points of sports for
children from preschool to fourteen
years old.

*Beyond X's and O's: What Generic
Parents, Volunteer Coaches and
Teachers Can Learn About Generic
Kids and All of the Sports They Play*
Jack Hutslar, Ph.D.
Wooten Printing Company, Inc.
Welcome, NC.
© 1985

A manual aimed at helping children
succeed at sports. Examines problems
with current sports models, attitudes,
and programs, and suggests a more
helpful philosophy to adopt for
children.

Social Skills

*How to Develop Your Children's
Creativity*
Reynold Bean
Price Stern Sloan, Inc.
Los Angeles, CA
© 1992

Helps teach children to become more
flexible and adaptive thinkers as well
as expressing themselves in socially
acceptable ways.

*Let's Play Together: Cooperative
Games for All Ages*
Mildred Masheder
Green Print, London, England
© 1989

Collection of more than 300 games
and sports that teach cooperation
over competition. Also suited for
children with disabilities. (See also
Sports)

*Getting Your Kids to Say NO in the
90s When You Said Yes in the 60s*
Victor Strasburger, M.D.
Simon & Shuster, New York, NY
© 1993

Describes difficulties of being a
teenager in the 90s by addressing
issues including impact of divorce
and single parenting, drug use and
sex, and media influences. Presents
latest research and advice to help
parents be more compassionate,
understanding, and effective.

*Playground Politics: Understanding the
Emotional Life of Your School-Age Child*
Stanley I. Greenspan, M.D., &
Jacqueline Salmon
Merloyd Lawrence, Reading, MA
© 1993

Helps parents deal with the typical
issues that arise from school interactions: aggression, rivalry, vulnerable
self-esteem, late-blooming, talents,
learning disabilities, problems with
reality and fantasy, and early sexuality.

Books on Children's Hope-Related Issues

Book Title, Author, Publisher	**Target Audience and Content Summary**

Abuse

A Family That Fights
Sharon Chesler Bernstein
Albert Whitman & Co., Morton Grove, IL
© 1991

Audience: Children
Summary: Henry, the oldest child, struggles with his father's abusiveness toward the whole family.

Sometimes It's OK to Tell Secrets
Amy C. Bahr
RGA Publishing Group
New York, NY
© 1986

Audience: Children
Summary: Teaches children the benefits of telling a trusted adult when their bodies have been violated. Gives examples of how sexual abuse might occur.

You Can Say "NO"
Betty Boegehold
Western Publishing, Racine, WI
© 1985

Audience: Children
Summary: Encourages children to be aware of their surroundings and informs them about sexual abuse.

Don't Hurt Me, Mama
Muriel Stanek
Albert Whitman & Co., Niles, IL
© 1983

Audience: Children
Summary: Offers a positive conclusion and possible solutions for a young girl who is abused by her mother.

Adoption

Adoption Is for Always
Linda Walvoord Girard
Albert Whitman & Co., Niles, IL
© 1985

Audience: Children
Summary: Explores the confusion and upsetting emotions a little girl feels when she discovers that she is adopted.

Affection

The Original Warm Fuzzy Tale
Claude Steiner
Jalmar Press
Rolling Hills Estates, CA
© 1977

Audience: Children
Summary: Presents a story analogous to everyday life that encourages children to give as many warm fuzzies (love) as possible.

Alcohol/Drugs

*Good Answers to Tough Questions
About Substance Abuse*
Joy Berry
Living Skills Press, Sebastopol, CA
© 1990

Audience: Children
Summary: Explains the harmful effects associated with drugs. Includes examples of the temptations to use drugs, reasons to reject them, and gives typical "say no" statements.

Alcohol — What It Is, What It Does
Judith A. Seixas
Greenwillow Books, New York, NY
© 1977

Audience: Children
Summary: Educates children about the negative physical, social, and emotional effects of alcohol.

*Living with a Parent
Who Drinks Too Much*
Judith Seixas
Greenwillow Books, New York, NY
© 1979

Audience: Children
Summary: Deals with stopping drinking, detoxication, rehabilitation, expecting the unexpected, etc. Alcoholism within the family is explored.

I Wish Daddy Didn't Drink So Much
Judith Vigna
Albert Whitman & Co., Niles, IL
© 1988

Audience: Children
Summary: Describes how a little girl whose father drinks too much, along with her mom's help, learns to keep his drinking from ruining their lives.

What's "Drunk" Mama?
Al-Anon Publications,
New York, NY
© 1977

Audience: Children
Summary: Examines a young girl's feelings about her father's alcoholism and the negative effects it has on her family.

It Will Never Happen To Me!
Claudia Black
MAC, Denver, CO
© 1981

Audience: Children and Adults
Summary: Identifies the roles in alcoholic families and the generational progression that is characteristic of alcoholism. Offers resources for individual members of the family.

Anger

I Was So Mad
Mercer Mayer
Western Publishing, Racine, WI
© 1983

Audience: Children
Summary: Describes a boy critter who is mad because he keeps getting into trouble. Story teaches anger control and resolution.

That Makes Me Angry!
Anthony Best
Western Publishing, Racine, WI
© 1989

Audience: Children
Summary: Shows how lack of communication can make people angry at each other. Bert and Ernie work out a communication problem without getting into a fight.

Arguing

Every Kid's Guide to Handling Family Arguments
Joy Berry
Children's Press, Chicago, IL
© 1987

Audience: Children
Summary: Explores family fighting and teaches that arguing is healthy, and that both good and bad can come out of it.

Every Kid's Guide to Handling Fights with Brothers or Sisters
Joy Berry
Children's Press, Chicago, IL
© 1987

Audience: Children
Summary: Gives useful tips on how to handle brothers and sisters when they do things that upset a child.

Attachment

The Runaway Bunny
Margaret Wise Brown
Harper Collins, New York, NY
© 1982

Audience: Children
Summary: Teaches unconditional love in an easily understood story. Bunny learns that his mom loves him so much she will follow him anywhere, even if he runs away.

Love You Forever
Robert Munsch
Firefly Books, Ontario, Canada
© 1992

Audience: Children and Adults
Summary: Shows the enduring nature of parents' love for their children, and how that love crosses generations.

I Love My Family
Wade Hudson
Scholastic, New York, NY
© 1993

Audience: Children
Summary: A middle-class black family's annual reunion sets the scene to teach the similarity of experiences among families of different races, good relations between family members, love and respect for elders, and strong family values.

Why Can't You Stay Home with Me?
Barbara Shook Hazen
A Golden Book
Western Publishing, Racine, WI
© 1986

Audience: Children
Summary: Describes how young a girl
can deal with her mother being away
at work. Feelings of being grown up
and autonomous are presented.

Communication

Every Kid's Guide to
Understanding Parents
Joy Berry
Children's Press, Chicago, IL
© 1987

Audience: Children
Summary: Helps children identify
with different kinds of parents and
suggests steps for getting along with
their own parents.

Reaching Out
David W. Johnson
Prentice Hall, Englewood Cliffs, NJ
© 1981

Audience: Children
Summary: Explains the importance of
skills such as self-disclosure, listening
and responding, and expressing one's
own feelings. Teaches communication with others.

Yes, I Can Say No
Manuel J. Smith
Arbor House, New York, NY
© 1986

Audience: Children
Summary: Gives strategies to help
children respond assertively to peer
pressure, compliments, criticism, and
other forms of communication.

Confidence/Self Esteem

100 Ways to Enhance Self-Concept
in the Classroom
Jack Canfield & Harold C. Wells
Prentice Hall, Englewood Cliffs, NJ
© 1976

Audience: Adults
Summary: Contains exercises to help
teachers improve the child's confidence and self-esteem in a nonjudg-
mental environment.

Liking Myself
Pat Palmer
Impact Publishers
San Luis Obispo, CA
© 1977

Audience: Children
Summary: Offers ways for children to
get in touch with their feelings and
encourages expression of feelings in a
tactful manner.

The Good Luck Pony
Elizabeth Koda-Callan
Workman Pub., New York, NY
© 1993

Audience: Children
Summary: A little girl finds the
courage to ride when her mother
gives her a tiny golden pony that
radiates self-confidence.

Crying

I Am Not a Crybaby
Norma Simon
Albert Whitman & Co., Niles, IL
© 1989

Audience: Children
Summary: Gives reasons why people cry (e.g. a sad cry when one is hurt, or a happy cry at a wedding), and stresses that one is never too old to cry.

Death

Someday a Tree
Eve Bunting
Clarion Books, New York, NY
© 1993

Audience: Children
Summary: A young girl, her parents, and their neighbors try to save an old oak tree poisoned by pollution. The girl finally discovers a solution that restores her hope.

When I Die, Will I Get Better?
Joeri & Piet Breebaart
Peter Bedrick Books, New York, NY
© 1993

Audience: Children
Subject: A six-year-old boy tries to come to terms with the death of his younger brother by creating a story about rabbit brothers that closely parallels his own experiences.

Too Young to Die
Francine Klagsbrun
Houghton Mifflin, Boston, MA
© 1976

Audience: Children and Adults
Summary: Based on interviews, surveys and research on death and dying with youth, parents and professionals. Helps parents understand feelings youths may experience. Helps youths understand problems of peers and self.

On Children and Death
Elisabeth Kubler-Ross
Macmillan, New York, NY
© 1983

Audience: Adults
Summary: Offers help to family members of children who are terminally ill. Helps families through knowledge of and preparation for the process of dying.

*When Bad Things Happen
To Good People*
Harold S. Kushner
Schocken Books, New York, NY
© 1981

Audience: Adults
Summary: Written by a man dealing with the pain of a terminally ill child. Helps the person who has been hurt by life to find the strength and hope to carry on.

Good Answers to Tough Questions
About Death
Joy Berry
Children's Press, Chicago, IL
© 1991

Audience: Children
Summary: Explores causes of death
and reasons why people die. Covers
stages of death and feelings of the
dying person, as well as scenarios the
body and spirit may experience after
death.

Dealing with Death
Norma Gaffron
Lucent Books, San Diego, CA
© 1989

Audience: Adolescents
Summary: Discusses biological, legal,
and emotional aspects of death.
Explains ways to deal with the death
of a friend.

Everett Anderson's Goodbye
Lucille Clifton
Holt, Rinehart & Winston
New York, NY
© 1983

Audience: Children
Summary: Tells the stages of grief
and how a boy passes through them
after his father dies.

The Accident
Carol Carrick
Seabury Press, New York, NY
© 1976

Audience: Children
Summary: Explores a young boy's
feelings when his dog dies.

Determination

The Evergreen Wood: An Adaptation
of the Pilgrim's Progress for Children
Alan & Linda Parry
Oliver Nelson, Nashville, TN
© 1992

Audience: Children
Summary: After a long and arduous
journey, Christopher Mouse reaches
the Evergreen Wood, where all the
animals live in peace and safety.

Kids Can Succeed: 51 Tips for Real
Life from One Kid to Another
Daryl Bernstein
Bod Adams Inc., Holbrook, MA
© 1993

Audience: Teenagers
Subject: Tips for teens include goal
setting, maintaining a positive outlook, and trying different approaches
to solve a problem.

Horton Hatches the Egg
Dr. Seuss
Random House, New York, NY
© 1940

Audience: Children
Summary: The story of an elephant
who is loyal, dedicated and determined to keep his word no matter
what happens.

The Day the Dark Clouds Came
Phylliss Adams
Modern Press, Cleveland, OH
© 1986

Audience: Children
Summary: A little robin uses hope,
effort, and determination to overcome her fear of failure

The Little Engine That Could
Watty Piper
Platt & Munk, New York, NY
© 1976

Audience: Children
Summary: After a train filled with toys breaks down, several faster and stronger trains refuse to help. Finally, a little blue engine comes along, and even though he has never been over the mountain, he gets the toys to the children on the other side with determination and encouragement.

Success: What Is It?
Janet McDonnell
The Child's World, Elgin, IL
© 1988

Audience: Children
Summary: Defines success as reaching a goal, finishing a task, and doing the best one can do. Also, gives examples of success.

Disabilities (also see Learning Disabilities)

Little Tree: A True Story for Children with Serious Medical Problems
Joyce C. Mills, Ph.D.
Magination Press, New York, NY
© 1992

Audience: Children ages four to eight
Summary: Although she is saddened when a storm has taken some of her branches, Little Tree draws strength and happiness from the knowledge that she still has a strong trunk, deep roots, and a beautiful heart.

Sarah and Puffle: A Story for Children about Diabetes
Linnea Mulder, R.N.
Magination Press, New York, NY
© 1992

Audience: Children
Summary: Upset by the restrictions imposed by her diabetes, Sarah dreams about a talking sheep who helps her accept her condition.

Brothers, Sisters and Special Needs
Debra J. Lobato
P.H. Brooks Publishing
Baltimore, MD
© 1990

Audience: Adults
Summary: Gives activities and information to help siblings of children with chronic illnesses and developmental disabilities.

Living with a Brother or Sister with Special Needs
Donald Meyer, Patricia Vadasy
& Rebecca Fewell
University of Washington Press,
Seattle, WA
© 1985

Audience: Children
Summary: Provides explanations about handicaps along with support for feelings toward the handicapped sibling.

*Brothers and Sisters — A Special Part
of Exceptional Families*
Thomas H. Powell
& Peggy Ahrenhold Ogle
Paul H. Brooks Publishing,
Baltimore, MD
© 1985

Audience: Adults
Summary: Gives advice on techniques
and services that can help the siblings
of handicapped children in dealing
with family issues.

*My Friend Leslie: The Story of
a Handicapped Child*
Maxine Rosenberg &
George Ancona Lothrop,
Lee & Shepard Books
New York, NY
© 1983

Audience: Children
Summary: Shows a multihandicapped
child, and how she is accepted in
various school settings.

About Handicaps
Sara Bonnett Stein
Walker & Co., New York, NY
© 1974

Audience: Children
Summary: A boy who is frightened of
others' handicaps learns that people
who are different can be good
friends.

Special Parents, Special People
Joanne E. Bernstein & Bryna Fireside
Albert Whitman & Co.
Morton Grove, IL
© 1991

Audience: Children and Adults
Summary: Children of parents who
are blind, deaf, or confined to wheel-
chairs tell how they deal with their
parents' handicaps, accept their circumstances, and benefit from their
lifestyle.

A Very Special Critter
Gina & Mercer Mayer
Western Publishing, New York, NY
© 1992

Audience: Children, Teachers, Other
Adults
Summary: The first day at school for
a little boy in a wheelchair is scary for
him and the other children. Gives
positive examples of relating to a
handicapped child and seeing similarities rather than differences.

Divorce and Stepfamilies

Living with a Single Parent
Maxine B. Rosenberg
Bradbury Press, Macmillan
Publishing Inc. New York, NY 10022
© 1992

Audience: Adolescents
Summary: A collection of first-hand
stories by adolescents with single
parents.

When a Parent Marries Again:
Children Can Deal with Family Change
Marge Heegaard
Wooland Press, Minneapolis, MN
© 1991

Audience: Children ages six to twelve
Summary: Helps process grief surrounding death of a parent and the emotions following remarriage with illustrations that the reader draws.

Helping Children of Divorce
Susan Arnsberg Diamond
Schocken Books, New York, NY
© 1985

Audience: Adults
Summary: Helps teachers and school officials better understand and assist children whose parents are divorced. Also helps divorced parents.

How Does It Feel When
Your Parents Get Divorced?
Terry Berger
Julian Messner, New York, NY
© 1977

Audience: Children
Summary: Examines feelings that children experience when their parents divorce. Emphasizes that many of the negative feelings experienced during the adjustment period will pass.

Daddy Doesn't Live Here Anymore
Betty Boegehold
Western Publishing, Racine, WI
© 1985

Audience: Children
Summary: A little girl named Casey deals with the fact that her Dad still loves her even though he is divorcing her Mom.

Good Answers to Tough Questions
About Stepfamilies
Joy Berry
Children's Press, Sebastopol, CA
© 1990

Audience: Children
Summary: Explains the feelings of stepchildren, including sadness, loss of control, resentment, anger, frustration, fear, jealousy, insecurity, and many others.

Where Do I Belong?
Buff Bradley
Addison Wesley, Reading, MA
© 1992

Audience: Children
Summary: Helps children (eight to twelve years old) deal with stepfamily. Touches on divorce and living through it, and being a stepchild.

Let's Talk About Stepfamilies
Angela Grunsell
Gloucester Press, New York, NY
© 1990

Audience: Children
Summary: Answers questions young people have when experiencing new additions to their home. Alleviates myths such as the wicked stepmother.

Fear

Sometimes I'm Afraid
Jane Watson, Werner Switzer,
Robert E. Hirschberg, & J. Cotter
Crown Publishers, New York, NY
© 1986

Audience: Children and Parents
Summary: A young boy, afraid in many different situations, deals with his fear and gives reasons why he becomes afraid.

Friendship

Caleb's Friend
Eric Jon Nones
Farrar, Straus, & Giroux
New York, NY
© 1993

Audience: Children
Summary: When a storm threatens, Caleb and his friend learn that even if they cannot be together, they will never be truly apart.

Pinky and Rex Go to Camp
James Howe
Avon Books, New York, NY
© 1993

Audience: Children
Summary: By sharing his fear of going to camp, Pinky finds support from his best friend and ends up having a great time.

Friends Forever: Six Stories
Celebrating the Joys of Friendship
Debbie Butcher Wiersma
& Veveca Gustafson
Western Publishing, Racine, WI
© 1992

Audience: Children
Summary: Stories about friendship, brought to life through various characters.

That's What a Friend Is
P.K. Hallinan
Children's Press, Chicago, IL
© 1977

Audience: Children
Summary: Explains friendship in simple language.

Goals

The Man Who Had No Dream
Adelaide Holl
Random House, New York, NY
© 1969

Audience: Children
Summary: Story explains the importance of having goals and dreams. A rich, idle, and unhappy man finds a way to be useful and live a happy life.

Grover's 10 Terrific Ways to Help
Our Wonderful World
Anna Ross
Random House, New York, NY
© 1992

Audience: Children
Summary: Using the philosophy that the world takes care of us and in return, we must take care of the world, Grover gives a list of things (e.g. plant a tree, do not waste, recycle) that children are capable of doing.

Oh, The Places You'll Go
Dr. Seuss
Random House, New York, NY
© 1990

Audience: Children and Adults
Summary: Show the ups and downs that one might encounter in the future. Encourages the reader to persevere and find the success that lies within.

Oh, The Thinks You Can Think
Dr. Seuss
Random House, New York, NY
© 1975

Audience: Children and Adults
Summary: Colorful pictures and silly rhyme encourage use of imagination. Introduces the reader to creative ways of thinking.

Hector's New Sneakers
Amanda Vesey
Penguin Books, New York, NY
© 1993

Audience: Children and Adults
Summary: Explains children's feelings about fitting in and having the right things. Hector's parents cannot afford the sneakers he wants, and he learns that he can be happy without the in shoes.

When I Grow Up
Mercer Mayer
Western Publishing, New York, NY
© 1991

Audience: Children
Summary: A little girl dreams of all the different things she might be when she grows up, such as a mountain climber, lion tamer, or a famous doctor. Exposes both boys and girls to nontraditional roles.

Health/Nutrition

What About Me? When Brothers and Sisters Get Sick
Allan Peterkin
Magination Press, New York, NY
© 1992

Audience: Young Children
Summary: Laura experiences conflicting emotions when her brother becomes seriously ill. Includes suggestions for parents to help.

The Well Child Book — Your Child from Four to Twelve
Mike Samuels, M.D. &
Nancy Samuels
Summit Books, New York, NY
© 1982

Audience: Children and Parents
Summary: This book covers nearly every aspect of growing up, including stress, healing, anatomy and physiology, nutrition and exercise, as well as medical advice.

Every Kid's Guide to Nutrition and Health Care
Joy Berry
Children's Press, Chicago, IL
© 1987

Audience: Children
Summary: Teaches about maintaining a healthy lifestyle by exercising, eating nutritional food and adhering to bodily requirements. Gives tips on hygiene and wearing appropriate clothing.

Individual Differences/Cooperation

Old Henry
Joan W. Blos
William Morrow & Co.
New York NY
© 1987

Audience: Children
Summary: Shows how different kinds of people learn to get along.

The Ugly Duckling
Marianna Mayer
MacMillan, New York, NY
© 1987

Audience: Children
Summary: An ugly duckling spends an unhappy year ostracized by the other animals before she grows into a beautiful swan.

The Rag Coat
Lauren Mills
Little Brown, Waltham MA
© 1991

Audience: Children
Summary: Minna proudly wears her new coat made of clothing scraps to school, where the other children laugh at her until she tells them stories behind the scraps.

Why Are People Different?
Barbara Shook Hazen
Western Publishing, Racine, WI
© 1985

Audience: Children
Summary: Teaches that everyone is different in their own way and encourages acceptance of individual differences.

The Mixed Up Cameleon
Eric Carle
HarperCollins, New York, NY
© 1975

Audience: Children 4–8
Summary: A cameleon goes to the zoo and wishes he could be like the other animals. When this wish is granted, he realizes he cannot be a good cameleon if he's like other animals.

We're Different, We're the Same
Bobbi Jane Kates
Random House, New York, NY
© 1992

Audience: Children
Summary: Explores the physical and emotional similarities and differences among people, and stresses that it is natural for people to be different from each other.

Learning Disabilities

Trouble with School: A Family Story About Learning Disabilities
Kathryn & Allison Boesel Dunn
Woodbine House Inc.
Rockville, MD
© 1993

Audience: Children
Summary: A dual narrative between mother and daughter shows both perspectives of the struggles with the daughter's learning disability.

Sixth Grade Can Really Kill You
Barthe DeClements
Viking Penguin, Santa Barbara, CA
© 1985

Audience: Children
Summary: Helen, a child with a reading disability, struggles with her disability by acting up in school. This portrait of a typical child with a learning disability has a promising conclusion.

*Cross Age and Peer Tutoring: Help
for Children with Learning Problems*
Joseph R. Jenkins &
Linda M. Jenkins
Eric Clearing House, Reston, VA
© 1981

Audience: Adults
Summary: Drawing from a base of
research findings and practical
knowledge, program designs and
strategies for learning disabilities are
described.

*When Your Child Isn't
Doing Well in School*
Ann Thiel, Richard Thiel,
& Penelope B. Grenoble
RGA Publishing Group, Chicago, IL
© 1988

Audience: Adults
Summary: Behavior and mental
characteristics associated with learning disorders are identified. Provides
information that will enable parents
to detect, comprehend, and assist in
their child's disability.

Legal Rights

*Every Kid's Guide to Laws That Relate
to Parents and Children*
Joy Berry
Living Skills Press, Sebastopol, CA
© 1987

Audience: Children
Summary: Explains the legal rights
and responsibilities of young readers
and their parents.

*Every Kid's Guide to Laws That Relate
to School and Work*
Joy Berry
Living Skills Press, Sebastopol, CA
© 1987

Audience: Children
Summary: Describes the legal rights
and restrictions that apply to schools,
and the legal issues that pertain to
work standards for minors.

*Every Kid's Guide to Understanding
Human Rights*
Joy Berry
Living Skills Press Sebastopol, CA
© 1987

Audience: Children
Summary: Informs children about
their rights they possess as well as the
rights of others. Encourages children
to be inquisitive, courteous, and
resourceful in their quest for discovering rights.

Listening

Oh, Bother! No One's Listening!
Betty Birney
Western Publishing, Racine, WI
© 1991

Audience: Children
Summary: Winnie the Pooh and
friends plan a party, only it doesn't
turn out very well because no one
listened when Rabbit read the list
of what everyone was to bring.
Christopher Robin explains that
good listening can help make things
happen.

Understanding
Sandra Ziegler
Children's Press, Chicago, IL
© 1989

Audience: Children
Summary: Teaches children to be
more understanding toward others,
and describes understanding as an
important part of being a nice person.

Making Mistakes

Nobody's Perfect, Not Even My Mother
Norma Simon
Albert Whitman & Co., Chicago, IL
© 1981

Audience: Children
Summary: Lets children know that
it's OK not to be perfect. Suggests
that no one is perfect, and that everyone is good at something.

Moving

My Friend William Moved Away
Martha Whitmore Hickman
Abingdon, Nashville, TN
© 1979

Audience: Children
Summary: Helps child understand
that even though friends move away
there will be new friends.

The Lotus Seed
Sherry Garland
Harcourt Brace Jovanovitch
San Diego, CA
© 1993

Audience: Children
Summary: A young Vietnamese girl
saves a lotus seed and carries it with
her everywhere to remember a brave
emperor and the homeland she has
to flee.

Things You Need to Know
Before You Move
Lisa Ann Marsoli
Silver Burdett, Morristown, NY
© 1985

Audience: Children
Summary: Prepares young people for
the anticipated changes that come
with a move.

Parental Relations

Understanding Parents
Joy Berry
Children's Press, Sebastopol, CA
© 1987

Audience: Children
Summary: Suggests that there are
many different types of parents, and
that parents love their children and
want what is best for them.

Something Is Wrong at My House
Diane Davis
Parenting Press, Seattle, WA
© 1984

Audience: Children
Summary: Explores a boy's feelings
about his parents' fighting, and gives
good solutions.

Planning

Every Kid's Guide to Using Time Wisely
Joy Berry
Living Skills Press, Sebastopol, CA
© 1987

Audience: Children
Summary: Gives advice for managing
time effectively.

The Kid's Guide to Social Action
Barbara Lewis
Free Spirit Publishing
Minneapolis, MN
© 1991

Audience: Children
Summary: Encourages the use of surrounding resources to create petitions, surveys, and letters, so as to make an impact on society. Contains stories that promote social awareness and inspiration.

Prejudice and Race Differences

Yo! Yes?
Chris Raschka
Orchard Books, New York, NY
© 1993

Audience: Children
Summary: Two lonely characters, one black, and one white, meet on the street and become friends.

Every Kid's Guide to Overcoming Prejudice and Discrimination
Joy Wilt Berry
Children's Press, Chicago, IL
© 1987

Audience: Children
Summary: Explores opinions, what they are, and how they form.

Living in Two Worlds
George Ancona
Lothrop, Lee & Shepard Books
New York, NY
© 1986

Audience: Adults and Children
Summary: Mixed race children talk about themselves, including feelings and special challenges they face in belonging to two cultures.

Problem Solving

Every Kid's Guide to Decision Making and Problem Solving
Joy Berry
Children's Press, Chicago, IL
© 1987

Audience: Children
Summary: Fosters understanding of what a decision is and why people make decisions. Outlines decision-making steps.

Did I Ever Tell You How Lucky You Are?
Dr. Seuss
Random House, New York, NY
© 1973

Audience: Children of all ages
Summary: Puts problems in perspective by using humor. Shows that one can be happy with what one has.

The Book of Think
Marilyn Burns
Little, Brown, and Co., Boston, MA
© 1976

Audience: Children
Summary: Offers a variety of problem-solving strategies and approaches as well as practice exercises.

Every Kid's Guide to Responding to Danger
Joy Berry
Living Skills Press, Sebastopol, CA
© 1987

Audience: Children
Summary: Presents situations that could harm a child as well as telling how to avoid or handle those dangerous situations.

Self-Acceptance

The King's Equal
Katherine Paterson
Harper Collins, New York, NY
© 1992

Audience: Children ages seven to ten
Summary: To wear the crown of the kingdom, an arrogant young prince must find an equal in his bride. Instead, he finds someone far better than he.

I Wish I Were a Butterfly
James Howe
Harcourt, Brace, Jovanovich,
Orlando, FL
© 1987

Audience: Children
Summary: A cricket who is unhappy with his appearance learns to accept himself. Encourages children to look at, and accept, what they have.

Least of All
Carol Purdy
Aladdin Books, New York, NY
© 1993

Audience: Children
Summary: A little girl in a big farm family teaches herself how to read using the Bible, and shares this knowledge with her brothers, parents, and grandmother during a long, cold Vermont winter.

Separation/Independence

*Good Answers to Tough Questions
About Dependence and Separation*
Joy Berry
Children's Press, in cooperation
with Living Skills Press, Chicago, IL
© 1990

Audience: Children
Summary: Discusses how children can become dependent on their parents and how the transition to independence can be frightening.

All By Myself
Mercer Mayer
Western Publishing, New York, NY
© 1983

Audience: Children
Summary: A little boy critter finds that there are some things he can do by himself, and that it's OK to ask for help with other things.

Shyness

How Come You're So Shy?
Leone Castell Anderson
A Golden Book Western Publishing,
Racine, WI
© 1987

Audience: Children
Summary: Two girls who are both shy learn to talk to the other and become friends.

Very Shy
Barbara Shook Hazen
Human Sciences Press New York, NY
© 1982

Audience: Children
Summary: Nancy asks her dad to help her get over her shyness and then follows his suggestions.

Sibling Relationships

Your Best Friend, Kate
Pat Brisson
Alladin Books, New York, NY
© 1992

Audience: Children
Summary: Kate's letters to her best friend back home about her family's trip through the South reveal her true affection for her brother, with whom she is always fighting.

Staying Alone

All Alone after School
Muriel Stanek
Albert Whitman & Co., Niles, IL
© 1985

Audience: Children
Summary: Describes a boy's transition into staying alone after school. He talks about the things that he does after school while he is home alone.

Stress/Anxiety

Fighting Invisible Tigers
Earl Hipp
Free Spirit Publishing
Minneapolis, MN
© 1985

Audience: Adolescents
Summary: Provides strategies to improve self-esteem, life satisfaction, and stress management.

Growing Up Feeling Good
Ellen Rosenbert
Beaufort Books, New York, NY
© 1987

Audience: Children and Adolescents
Summary: Explores feelings of uncertainty and anxiety about the onset of puberty and presents typical questions and answers.

Stress in Childhood
Gaston E. Blom
Teachers' College Press
New York, NY
© 1986

Audience: Adults
Summary: Offers teachers and child care professionals the information necessary for identification, intervention, and prevention of harmful stressors.

Helping Children Cope with Stress
Avis Brenner
Lexington Books, New York, NY
© 1984

Audience: Adults
Summary: Details the stressors young children ages one through twelve might face as well as intervention strategies.

Suicide

When Living Hurts
Sol Gordon
Union of American Hebrew
Congregations, New York, NY
© 1985

Audience: Teenagers
Summary: Explores suicide by showing how to deal with feelings such as anger, depression, and peer pressure. Also addresses questions about God and purpose of life.

Traumatic Experiences

When Something Terrible Happens:
Children Can Learn to Cope with Grief
Marge Heegaard
Woodland Press, Minneapolis, MN
© 1991

Audience: Children ages six to twelve
Subject: Helps process reactions to
traumatic events with illustrations
that the reader draws.

Good Answers to Tough Questions
About Traumatic Experiences
Joy Berry
Children's Press, Chicago, IL
© 1990

Audience: Children
Summary: Defines traumas that children may encounter and explains the
steps to overcoming the associated
negative feelings. Points out the positive effects of negative experience.

Every Kid's Guide to Coping
With Childhood Traumas
Joy Berry
Children's Press, Chicago, IL
© 1988

Audience: Children
Summary: Gives children specific
terms to help in understanding their
feelings related to various traumas.
Also gives specific suggestions for
dealing with their trauma.

NOTES

Chapter 1: Discovering Hope

1. Kershaw, as translated by Maxwell-Hysop (1990).
2. Although some writers (e.g., Smith 1983) conclude that the myth of Pandora leaves one with the obvious conclusion that hope was to be the antidote for the evils that escaped from the chest, my reading is that the Greek tradition actually viewed hope as something rather sinister (see Averill, Catlin & Chon 1990, for similar conclusion).
3. For the reader interested in a detailed exposition of what philosophers have had to say about the topic of hope, I would recommend James Muyskens's (1979) *The Sufficiency of Hope*.
4. Shakespeare 1912, 12.
5. Coleridge 1912, 447.
6. By tying hope to goals, the realistic base for such thoughts becomes less vague, but the person still has considerable room to modify subjectively the interpretation of the goals and the pursuit thereof. Although the present model and accompanying measures of hope seek to clarify the endpoints (i.e., goals) of hope, some subjective biasing on the part of the person can and must remain. Remember on this latter point that reality is by necessity a perceptual interpretation process. Goals provide guideposts for promoting more realistic hope, and yet they allow for the inevitable operation of individual subjectiveness. My thinking on this latter point owes to discussions with my colleague Beatrice Wright (see Wright [1968] and Wright and Shontz [1968]).
7. Cantril 1964; Erickson, Post & Paige 1975; Farber 1968; Frank 1968; Gottschalk 1974; Melges & Bowlby 1969; Menninger 1959; Schactel 1959; Stotland 1969.
8. Such views find a home in a new field known as health psychology, where the focus is on understanding the role of positive psychological variables in promoting better health. Alternatives to the time-honored pathology model, with its emphasis on human weaknesses, are being offered by health psychologists who emphasize peoples' strengths and potential

coping assets. See Snyder and Forsyth (1991) and Taylor (1991). More generally, the reader is referred to *Health Psychology*, a monthly professional journal publishing articles in this new tradition.

9. For review, see Pervin (1989).

10. I do not mean to imply that such images are necessarily pictures that we see in our minds. Although they may have visual properties, such images are representations of goals; as such, they may involve verbal descriptions (Pylyshyn 1973).

11. Research has demonstrated that other animals besides homo sapiens form goals. Starting with the research of Edward Tolman (1948), a convincing body of evidence shows that animals have goals in their memory (see Mook 1987).

12. Adler 1964, 68.

13. If persons are truly depressed and in a state of despair, it often is difficult to ascertain their goals. In an extreme passive state, such persons obviously do not entertain the usual goals espoused in society pertaining to relationships, work, and recreation. They do have some minimalist goals, however, that they probably attend to in order to perpetuate their inactivity and general malaise (e.g., staying in bed). The issues surrounding the demise of goal-direction in particular, and hope more generally, are discussed in detail in chapter 4 on the death of hope.

14. Obviously, I am describing a linear view of time. This is not meant to deny the fact that there may be cyclical repetitions of events sequences (as is held in Eastern thought). Nor do I mean to imply absolute unidirectionality of movement toward the future. In this later regard, our views of the future may causally impact on present thoughts (e.g., I am getting a tetanus shot because later I will be going on a fishing trip where I will be exposed to rusty fishhooks and other metals). Further, I would endorse the notion of reciprocal temporal thinking in which at times the past influences the future, and vice versa. Lastly, I would embrace the importance of thinking and feeling in a here and now set to fully enjoy and live the moment. Having provided all of these concessions, however, I believe that we typically think in terms of linking our present to our imagined futures (for a discussion of differing time perspectives related to racial/cultural groups, read Carter [1991]). Thus, the notion of time and our sense of journeying through this continuum are useful and necessary parts of human thought.

15. In his classic *The Nature of Explanation*, Craig (1943) argued that the purpose of the brain was to anticipate such A to B sequences.

16. See for more detailed discussions, Snyder (1989), and Snyder, Harris, Anderson, Holleran, Irving, Sigmon, Yoshinobu, Gibb, Langelle & Harney (1991). In other writings, I have used the term *agency* instead of willpower, and *pathways* instead of waypower.

17. When asked what goals warrant hope, people note that hope is reserved for important goals (Averill et al. 1990).

18. Such an assertion must be considered in the context of any given individual, however. For example, the ease of putting one's shoes on may not necessitate hope for the majority of people, but for the person with severe

arthritis of the hands, this task is by no means automatic and taken for granted.

19. Survey research supports this contention in that people report hope is applicable when there is approximately a 50 percent chance of goal attainment (Averill et al. 1990).

20. Fowlie 1981, 32.

21. This notion of hell involving no probability of attaining one's goals poses a theological problem in that any purgatorial function of hell necessitates free will or choice (thereby implying some probability of goal attainment). Indeed, in Dante's dialogue with Virgil about this very issue, he admits having uncertainty about the answer to this conumdrum (Fowlie 1981).

22. For the reader interested in previous writings about constructs related to willpower (agency), I recommend in chronological order Wundt (1894), McDougall (1908), Rank (1936), Lewin (1951), Adler (in Ansbacher & Ansbacher 1956), White (1959), deCharms (1968), Deci (1975), Ajzen and Fishbein (1980), and Bandura (1977, 1989).

23. Hofler 1993, 174.

24. Cuff 1993.

25. My thinking about the role of planning in goal pursuits is influenced strongly by Miller, Galanter, & Pribram's (1960) *Plans and the Structure of Behavior*, Newell & Simon's (1972) *Human Problem Solving*, as well as Anderson's (1983) *The Architecture of Cognition*.

26. See Berger (1993) for review.

27. The notion of barriers has a long history in psychology, where they have been labeled as lack of clear paths, problems, obstacles, and detours (Kohler 1925; Scheerer 1963; Vinacke 1952; Woodworth & Schlosberg 1954)

28. Babyak, Snyder & Yoshinobu 1993; Snyder et al. 1991.

29. See Snyder et al. (1991) for empirical data relevant to this issue. In my interviews and work with high-hope people, it is as if they go into a search mode for alternative strategies when blocked, and invest themselves in those strategies one by one until they sense that a given pathway is working.

30. High-hope people may experience something akin to a psychological state of flow, in which the person is totally absorbed in a particular experience. See Csikszentmihalyi (1990), and Csikszentmihalyi and Csikszentmihalyi (1988).

31. Along with the cognitive revolution in psychology, the importance of the individual's representation and understanding of his world has become the foundation for understanding human behavior. As such, it is not solely the actual physical reality, but rather the person's phenomenological representation of this reality that drives human beings in their goal-directed behaviors. This viewpoint is based on Heider's (1958) distinction between the distal (the actual object or event) and proximal (the interpretation or perception) stimuli. More recently, this distinction has been advocated by Watzlawick (1976), who suggests that the tangible properties of objects and events as captured sensorily is perceptive reality, and the subjective meaning and understanding of these same objects and events is interpretive reality.

32. Two major and influential psychological theories of motivation not discussed in the main text bear some similarity to hope theory. The first is called *achievement motivation*, with the primary work being done by David McClelland, as well as important contributions by John Atkinson (Atkinson 1957, 1958; McClelland 1955, 1961; McClelland, Atkinson, Clark & Lowell 1953). Using the open-ended stories that people generated in response to pictures that they viewed, researchers inferred their need for achievement if the themes of these stories related to (1) a competitive striving toward a standard of excellence (defined in relation to others and self); (2) long-term or relatively large goals; and (3) indications of pleasure if the objectives were met. Implicitly, achievement motivation appears to indicate the willpower and waypower cognitions for important goals that are explicitly measured in hope theory. What achievement motivation infers from stories about others, however, hope theory directly measures through statements about oneself. (For a more recent exposition of a topic that is related to achievement motivation, see Gilbert Brim's [1992] *Ambition*.) The second theory that has spawned a large amount of interest and research is *self-efficacy*, which has been the brainchild of Albert Bandura (1977, 1982, 1986, 1989; see also Maddux 1991). Bandura reasons that goal-directed behavior results after the person has assessed two expectancies: outcome and efficacy. Outcome expectancies reflect the person's belief that a given behavior will generate an outcome, and efficacy expectancy taps the person's belief that she has the capability of producing the necessary behavior. Bandura's views are that these self-efficacy beliefs are situation specific, and as such differ from the more general premise of hope theory that goal-directed cognitions appear across several important goals. Additionally, Bandura suggests that the efficacy expectancies are more critical in driving goal-directed behavior than are outcome expectancies, while hope theory suggests that willpower and waypower cognitions are equally and iteratively operative in determining goal pursuits. Furthermore, the willpower component of hope theory differs somewhat from efficacy expectancies in that willpower goes beyond one's perception of being able to effectively carry out a goal-directed sequence; in this regard, willpower also involves a willingness to direct one's mental energy to actually initiate and sustain movement toward the goal. Likewise, waypower (pathways) cognitions are more than just one linkage involved in the outcome expectancy; rather, they may involve the thoughts that one can generate several routes, if necessary, to one's goals.

33. Porter 1913.

34. Lauzanne & Wylie 1931.

35. For excellent reviews, see Scheier and Carver (1985, 1987, 1993).

36. Although it is not possible to judge which person has contributed most to this perspective, it was Norman Vincent Peale in his 1956 book who emblazoned the power of positive thinking into our American consciousness. A thorough overview of the positive thinkers in the American scene can be obtained in Meyer (1980).

37. For excellent summaries of this learned optimism perspective, see Peterson and Bossio (1991) and Seligman (1991). Additionally, for an overview of the original theory from which learned optimism evolved, I would

recommend Peterson, Maier, and Seligman's (1993) *Learned Helplessness: A Theory for the Age of Personal Control*, and Mikulincer's (1994) *Human Learned Helplessness*.

38. Snyder & Higgins 1990.
39. Snyder & Higgins 1988a, 1991; Snyder, Higgins & Stucky 1983.
40. Snyder 1989.
41. Friedman & Rosenman 1974; Houston & Snyder 1988.
42. Rieger 1993.
43. Snyder, Irving & Anderson 1991; Snyder et al. 1991.
44. Recent psychological theorization and research have posited that the successful pursuit of important and meaningful goals plays a critical role in the development and maintenance of well-being (Diener 1984; Emmons 1986, 1989; Little 1983, 1989; Omodei & Wearing 1990; Palys & Little 1983; Ruehlman & Wolchik 1988). Further, evidence is accruing to suggest that the perceived progress toward one's important goals is the cause of well-being rather than vice versa (see Brunstein 1993; Little 1989).
45. Steinem 1992, 46.
46. *Newsweek* 1992, 51.
47. Ibid., 49
48. Ibid.
49. Snyder et al., 1991.
50. Some recent writers (e.g., Schulman 1991) have equated intelligence with problem-solving capabilities.
51. Snyder et al. 1991.
52. Elliott, Witty, Herrick & Hoffman 1991; Sherwin, Elliott, Rybarczyk, Frank, Hanson & Hoffman 1992; Snyder in press a & b; Snyder et al. 1991.
53. Snyder et al. 1991.

Chapter 2: Measuring Hope

1. Snyder et al. 1991.
2. Rosenberger & Gould 1992.
3. For an explanation of the phenomenon whereby people (more women than men) believe that they are impostors, read Clance's (1985) *The Impostor Phenomenon: Overcoming the Fear That Haunts Your Success*, and Harvey and Katz's (1985) *If I'm So Successful, Why Do I Feel Like a Fake?: The Impostor Phenomenon*.
4. Rowen 1992, 11–12.
5. Snyder et al. 1991.
6. The measures of optimism that we have employed (e.g., studies by Anderson 1988; Harris 1988; Munoz-Dunbar 1993) include the Life Orientation Test by Scheier & Carver (1985), and the Generalized Expectancy for Success Scale by Fibel and Hale (1978).
7. Crouch 1989.
8. Desirability of control was measured by the Burger-Cooper Life Experiences Survey (Burger & Cooper 1979).

9. The Internal-External Locus of Control Scale by Rotter (1966) was employed to identify locus of control.
10. Anderson 1988.
11. The Problem Solving Inventory by Heppner and Petersen (1982) was utilized for this correlational research.
12. Curry 1994. The measures of competitiveness and winning are subscales of the Sport Orientation Questionnaire by Gill and Deeter (1988).
13. We have used the Rosenberg (1965) Self-Esteem Scale as a dispositional (enduring across time and situations) measure of esteem, and the State Self-Esteem Scale by Heatherton and Polivy (1991) as a short-lived or state index of esteem.
14. Barnum 1993; Munoz-Dunbar 1993; Sympson 1993.
15. Barnum 1993. Harter's (1988) Self-Perception Profile was used as the measure of self-esteem. It measures a general sense of whether a person likes himself or herself and whether the person is happy with his or her life.
16. The measure of positive affect that we have used involves the positive affect scale items of the Positive and Negative Affect Scale by Watson, Clark, and Tellegen (1988).
17. Irving 1991; Snyder et al. 1991.
18. We have used the negative affect scale items of the Positive and Negative Affect Scale by Watson et al. (1988).
19. Irving 1991; Snyder et al. 1991.
20. The measures of anxiety employed in our research have included the Taylor (1953) Manifest Anxiety Scale and the trait form of the State-Trait Anxiety Inventory (Spielberger, Gorsuch & Luchene 1970).
21. Snyder et al. 1991.
22. We have used the Beck Depression Inventory (Beck, Ward, Mendelsohn, Mock & Erbaugh 1961) and the depression subscale of the *Minnesota Multiphasic Personality Inventory* 1st. ed. (Hathaway & McKinley 1951).
23. Irving, Crenshaw, Snyder, Francis & Gentry 1990.
24. Langelle 1989.
25. Harris 1988.
26. We have replicated this study and found that hope predicts the selection of a more difficult goal; this effect remains even when the student's reported levels of positive and negative affect are removed through statistical procedures (Snyder et al. 1991).
27. Anderson 1988.
28. Ibid.
29. Ibid.; Harney 1989; Wiklund 1993.
30. Harney 1989.
31. Ibid.
32. Snyder et al. 1991.
33. Irving et al. 1990.
34. Curry 1994.
35. Yoshinobu 1989.
36. Elliott et al. 1991.
37. Barnum 1993.
38. The total problems score of the Child Behavior Checklist by Achenbach (1991) was employed.

39. Laird 1992.

40. Sherwin et al. 1992.

41. Anderson 1992.

42. Anderson 1988; Snyder in press a; Snyder et al. 1991.

43. Snyder et al. 1991.

44. See for review, Pyszczynski, Hamilton, Greenberg & Becker 1991.

45. Snyder et al. 1991.

46. Munoz-Dunbar 1993; Yoshinobu 1989.

47. Rieger 1993. Rieger employed the Revised UCLA Loneliness Scale by Russell, Peplau, and Cutrona (1980).

48. Dalfiume 1993. Dalfiume used the Perspective Taking subscale of the Interpersonal Reactivity Index by Davis (1983).

49. Dalfiume 1993. Dalfiume used the Intimacy subscale of the Inventory of Psychosocial Balance by Domino and Affonso (1990).

50. Sigmon & Snyder 1993.

51. Laird 1992.

52. Harney 1989.

53. Irving 1991.

54. Erikson 1963, 1980, 1982.

55. Dalfiume 1993. Dalfiume used the Generativity subscale of the Inventory of Psychosocial Balance by Domino and Affonso (1990).

56. Dalfiume 1993. Dalfiume used the Ego Integrity subscale of the Inventory of Psychosocial Balance by Domino and Affonso (1990).

57. Dalfiume 1993. Dalfiume used the Neutral Death Acceptance subscale of the Death Attitude Profile by Gesser, Wong & Reker (1987).

58. For a full and insightful analysis of the importance of remaining mentally engaged as one ages, I highly recommend Ellen Langer's *Mindfulness* (1989).

59. Block 1973; Brehm 1992; Rosenkrantz, Vogel, Bee, Broverman & Broverman 1968; Williams 1982.

60. Snyder et al. 1991.

61. Munoz-Dunbar 1993.

62. Snyder et al. 1991.

63. Langelle 1989.

64. Snyder, Sympson, Ybasco & Borders 1994.

65. Sympson 1993.

66. Borders 1993.

67. Ybasco 1994.

68. Snyder et al. 1994.

69. Gibb 1990; see also Snyder, Rapoff, Ware, Hoza, Pelham, Danovsky, Highberger, Rubinstein, & Stahl.

70. Vance 1994.

71. Endler 1990, 49. Although Endler's particular depression was triggered by biochemical factors and was treated with antidepressant drugs, it is my contention that even with such endogenous depressions, the lowered will- and way-related thoughts for goals influence the process of improvement over time.

72. Selzer 1979, 110.

Chapter 3: The Development of Hope

1. Bullock 1991; Sammons 1989; Schulman 1991. For an enjoyable and easily understood description of infant capacities, see *The World of the Newborn* by Maurer and Maurer (1988). For an overview of cognitive development in the first two years, *In the Beginning: Development in the First Two Years* by Rosenblith and Sims-Knight (1985) is informative.

2. Schulman 1991.

3. In this latter regard, the infant perceives the unknown face as strange because she has not had sufficient time to add it to the ever-expanding category of recognizable things. Related research suggests that infants who are only a few weeks old are able to differentiate varying facial expressions (Cohn & Tronik 1983), and they attend to their mothers' faces longer than they do to other faces (Fantz 1963; Gorman, Cogen & Gellis 1959). Similarly, by three months, infants respond to their mothers' facial expressions and can recognize their moms in a photograph (Barrera & Maurer 1981a, 1981b).

4. Penrose (cited in Forward 1980, 40) describes this as, "The world is an illusion created by a conspiracy of senses." Of course, we live each day on the basis of these illusions.

5. Psychologists believe that mental representations of input from all sensory modalities are based in schemas that facilitate perception. Schemas are not exact replicas of the sensation, but they reflect mental composites or categorizations that facilitate one's perception, which is the conscious understanding of the sensation. Thus, the sequence is sensation to schema representation to perception. For further discussion, see Mussen, Conger, Kagan, and Huston (1990, 108).

6. DeCasper & Fifer 1980; Stevenson, Ver Hoeve, Roach & Leavitt 1986.

7. Whatever the mode of the sensory input, it is the discrepancy between the infant's previous experience with the stimulation relative to the present stimulation that promotes cognitive growth. In this regard, infants have been shown to attend to sensations bearing new information. The novel information represents a challenge to the perceptual process of infants, and their minds adapt to form more complex representations of the sensory input. (For further discussion of this discrepancy principle, see Mussen et al. [1990], 108–12.) Some input may be too discrepant for the infant. Just as some noises may help the baby to understand her environment, some sounds are too far beyond the infant's comprehension at a given point in time. For example, loud noises typically startle the infant, and it may be that the novelty of such sounds is so abrupt that the newborn is overwhelmed by such stimulation.

8. In this regard, infants consistently turn their heads to pads containing their mothers' odor in preference to pads with the odors of other mothers (Schaal 1986).

9. With time, the tactual lessons become more sophisticated. Six months after birth, for example, the baby is using her hands, and passing things from one hand to the other (Schulman 1991).

10. Piaget 1954, 1970. The topic of cognitive development owes a debt to Piaget, who has been called "a giant of the nursery" because of his important

contributions (Elkind 1981). Piaget's central thesis was that young children are active and curious explorers constantly attempting to construct order in their worlds. Although it appears that children are capable of mental feats even sooner than Piaget speculated, he opened our intellectual doors to the precociousness of children's minds. For recent analyses of Piaget's ideas regarding cognitive development, see Siegal (1991) and Wellman and Gelman (1992).

11. Watson 1966.

12. In statistical terms, the child is engaging in a correlational analysis in which the interconnectedness of stimuli are noted.

13. In actuality, this drive to recognize the temporal relationships in our environment continues from the cradle to the grave. As adults, when thrust into a new environment (akin to the newborn), we strive to comprehend not only the stimuli in that environment but also which stimuli appear to be temporally linked. This process probably has been necessary for our successful evolution as a species.

14. As an experimental example of the infant's prowess in making connections, consider a study performed with two-month old babies (Watson & Ramey 1969, as cited in Watson 1971). In a learning condition, by moving their heads on a special pillow, infants could activate a mobile attached to the crib; in a control condition, the infants' head movements had no relationship to the movement of the mobile. This connection was evidently noticed and remembered by the learning condition infants, because they moved their heads and exhibited smiling and cooing not shown by the control condition infants in the presence of the gyrating mobile.

15. Again, for a thorough review of the early connectionism feats of children, including evidence that infants discern temporal sequences within hours of birth, I direct the reader to Schulman's (1991) *The Passionate Mind*, especially chapter 5.

16. Kopp 1989.

17. Heckhausen 1984.

18. Although there is some disagreement about the chronological age at which such pointing behavior occurs, with one researcher noting that this skill is in place by three months of age (Stevenson & Newman 1986), there is general agreement that the one year old is capable of this feat (Schulman 1991).

19. Such referencing of objects is called proto-declarative conversation (Bates, Camaioni & Volterra 1975).

20. Deaf children, raised in families where the parents refused to use or did not know sign language, develop an idiosyncratic "home sign" (Fant 1972) that begins with pointing to desired objects (Goldin-Meadows & Mylander 1990).

21. This is called proto-imperative conversation.

22. Lewis & Brooks-Gunn 1979; Stern 1985. Indeed, the infant must resolve the conflict between oneness and separateness in the context of his early surroundings (often the family) (Kaplan 1978). As adults we know that we are each an identifiable living organism in a world filled with a multitude of animate and inanimate objects. (The existential resolution of this adult insight is that each of us is insignificant and therefore humble in the grand sweep of events.) We adults also know that the skin provides a border

between our physical being and the rest of the world; moreover, we know that our name is our label. Of course, we did not always know these things. According to conventional wisdom, insights about self are not salient to us at birth. After conception, each of us was part of our biological mother. Approximately nine months later with the moment of birth, we were physically separated from our mothers; the placenta was severed, but the psychological links were not. Phenomenologically, mom (or primary caretaker) and each of us were still part of one larger unit. Although the newborn does not possess an awareness of self and is not able to differentiate that which is "me" versus "non-me," I believe that the period of unilateral dependence (see Harvey, Hunt & Schroeder 1961) of infants is exaggerated.

23. This is difficult to pinpoint because previous thinkers evidently have relied on the language of the baby as the vehicle for proving the existence of selfhood. Conceptually, however, infants and toddlers certainly know things before they use speech to reflect their understandings (Clark & Clark 1977). Thus, language skills appear long after the child recognizes selfhood. In reality, the evolution of a sense of self should go hand in hand with the development of goals and pathways thinking as the infant increasingly injects himself as an identifiable object into these processes.

24. Kaplan 1978; Lewis & Brooks 1978; Lewis & Brooks-Gunn 1979; Mahler, Pine & Bergman 1975.

25. Lewis & Brooks 1978. This experiment with humans was modeled after an earlier one by Gallup (1970), in which chimpanzees looking at themselves in mirrors touched painted spots on their faces.

26. Kaplan 1978.

27. Bretherton & Beeghly 1982; Bretherton, McNew & Beeghly-Smith 1981.

28. From Hughes (1929) *A High Wind in Jamaica*, 134–35.

29. Corrigan 1978; van der Meulen 1987.

30. van der Meulen 1991, 30.

31. The emergence of self-as-instigator insights is not limited to hearing toddlers, however. In this regard, a longitudinal study of the communication of deaf children with deaf parents is instructive. At about the same two-year period as hearing children, deaf toddlers make signs that refer to self and the capacity to act (Pettito 1983).

32. In fact, it probably has been advantageous to our survival to know what goes with what in our environment. This *goes with what* phrase is used by Schulman 1991.

33. Barker, Dembo & Lewin 1941; Wright 1934, 1943.

34. The motive to desire objects that are assumed to be available to us, but for whatever reason are restricted from our ready access, is known as psychological reactance. There is a fairly large body of research supporting reactance throughout the age range. See Brehm (1966) and Brehm and Brehm (1981) for reviews.

35. Van Lieshout, 1975.

36. Most parents warn their offspring of the problems that lie ahead in life. In moments of love and concern, we privately wish that we could totally shield our children from the pitfalls that befall us. Of course, this cannot happen, despite all our well-meaning efforts. Even if we could fully protect

our children, it would be counterproductive. Bumps and roadblocks are a part of life, and this premise has been the starting point of several efforts to understand the coping skills of children.

37. For related discussions, see Rutter (1981, 1985, 1987a & b). Dienstbier (1989) has developed a physical toughening model analogous to the cognitive model I am positing here. In particular, Dienstbier suggests that a natural toughening ensues after the human increasingly endures physical stressors or demands.

38. The literature suggests that resiliency in children serves a protective function. Hope, as articulated in the present book, is an overarching model that generally encompasses the various definitions proffered for resiliency. For reviews of resiliency in children and its positive sequelae, see Cowen and Work (1988), Garmezy (1991), Rutter (1987b), and Werner (1984).

39. See for reviews Mischel (1983); Mischel and Mischel (1983); and Mischel, Shoda, and Rodriguez (1989).

40. Mischel & Ebbeson 1970, as cited in Mischel 1983.

41. This essential lesson of early childhood is aptly revealed in the words of William Lynch (1974, 61) in *Images of Hope:* "We learn to hold a goal in sight and seek a way. It is a time of endless motility and exploration. The collapse of the venture is meant to create movement, resourcefulness. Rigidity never wins the game. Each failure of hope becomes a source of energy. It is a time of imagination and freedom."

42. Bowlby 1969.

43. Bowlby (1969, 1973, 1980) introduced attachment theory, and more recently Cicchetti (in press) and Sroufe (1983, 1985) have written clarifying analyses on this topic.

44. Furthermore, the more secure the infant-mother relationship, the greater is the propensity of the baby to explore (Ainsworth & Bell 1970, as cited in Ainsworth 1973).

45. For excellent reviews, see Bretherton & Waters (1985) and Rutter (1987b).

46. Erikson, 1950, 1959, 1963, 1964, 1968, 1980, 1982.

47. Erikson, 1963.

48. A study by Hunt (1981) provides support to the contention that interactive, attentive caregivers foster a sense of trust in infants. Moreover, benefits related to advanced vocal development and language use were evident for these infants exposed to attentive caregivers relative to those infants in control comparison groups.

49. As example of this latter point, consider a research project conducted on the responsiveness of mothers to their offsprings' crying during the first year of life. In the first four months of this study, the crying of babies did not appear to be related to the mothers' responsiveness. After four months, on the other hand, the babies of responsive mothers were crying less. Additionally, after nine months, the babies of responsive as compared to nonresponsive mothers had developed more noncrying pathways of communication. One interpretation of these findings is that the caregivers' responsiveness appears to have fostered varying modes of communication (i.e., pathways) for these babies (Ainsworth & Bell 1974).

50. Yet another theory related to attachment is object relations (Mahler 1968; Mahler, Pine & Bergman 1975; Masterton 1976). Object relations is the

process of learning to effectively deal with ourselves in relation to the important things in our lives. In normal development, according to this perspective, the newborn initially experiences a state of fusion with the mother (called the mother/child unit), and this symbiotic state continues until the age of eighteen to thirty-six months. During this period prior to eighteen months of age, any self-representation of the child is thought to reflect a perceived combination of the mother/child unit. From eighteen to thirty-six months, however, the stage of individuation and separation unfolds such that the toddler increasingly develops an image of herself as being an object separate from mother. This, in essence, is a "psychological mitosis" (my analogy) in which the developing baby progressively learns that one unit (mother and infant) are actually two units (objects). Facilitated by genetic and mastery drives, as well as appropriate cueing from the mother, active self-representation emerges in the toddler (Masterton 1981). In turn, such self-representations supposedly yield an autonomous self in which adaptive relationships with other objects (things and people) can be achieved in subsequent years. What object relations theory makes salient is the importance of comprehending objects (ourselves included) for subsequent adaptation. Additionally, however, I would argue that hope theory serves to specify the particular objects of critical importance to this mindset — the self as instigator and goals as the endpoints anchoring our desires. Furthermore, hope theory details the cognitive forces that drive (i.e., agency) and link (i.e., pathways) the self to goals. Therefore, the cognitive processes related to object relations are inherent to the acquisition and maintenance of a hopeful mindset in the developing child.

51. Case 1992; Lowery 1986.
52. Carey 1978; Templin 1957.
53. Brown 1973
54. Gopnik & Meltzoff 1987.
55. For a more detailed analysis of the reciprocity between language and cognition, see Waxman (1987).
56. Similar views are proffered by strict behaviorists such as Skinner (1957) and social learning theorists such as Bandura (1986).
57. In the area of language acquisition, those who advocate an interactionalist position are espousing a similar position to the one I am positing. For further insights into the interactionist viewpoint, see Bates, Bretherton, and Snyder (1988), Byrnes and Gelman (1991), and Meltzoff and Gopnik (1989). Likewise, Vygotsky (1962, 1987) has championed the view that language serves both the private and public audience functions.
58. Rubin, Fein & Vandenberg 1983.
59. Schank & Abelson 1977.
60. For discussions of the definition and implications of scripts, see Nelson (1981, 1986).
61. Hudson 1990.
62. Nelson 1993.
63. Bem 1981.
64. Leinbach & Hort 1989.
65. Paley 1984.

66. Huston 1983.
67. Clark & Clark 1939.
68. Spencer 1988.
69. Annis & Corenblum 1987.
70. Beuf 1977.
71. The thoughts that adults have about understanding people, as well as the dynamics of interactions among people, have taken on sufficient importance in psychology that an entire subarea examining social cognition has developed.
72. Borrowing from Piaget (1959), I would note that egocentrism is not synonymous with selfishness. In the early preschool years, the child is self-centered because of a lack of experiences and cognitive maturation; as such, egocentrism should not have pejorative connotations.
73. The preschooler is said to have attained a "theory of mind" (Frye & Moore 1991.) Some researchers, such as Miller and Aloise (1989), have found evidence for theory of mind insights in children as young as two.
74. Ruffman & Olson 1989.
75. Shatz & Gelman 1973.
76. My insights into the explorations of children during the middle years owe in large part to my colleagues Roger Barker, Paul Gump, and Herbert Wright, who emphasized the ecological approach in which one pays attention to the environment of the developing child. For superb scientific examples of ecological psychology applied to children, as well as a good read about how and where children actually spend their time, see *One Boy's Day* by Barker and Wright (1951) and *Midwest and Its Children* by Barker and Wright (1955), as well as Wright (1956).
77. Chall's ideas about a stage theory of reading have set the scholarly agenda on this perspective. See Chall's (1983) *Stages of Reading Development*, and Chall, Jacobs, and Baldwin's (1990) *The Reading Crisis: Why Poor Children Fall Behind*.
78. Gelman, Meck, and Merkin (1986) propose these three subcategories of mathematical learning.
79. Kail 1990, 1991. Whether these improvements are a function of enhanced capacities in terms of size of memory per se, or of greater efficiency in using these capabilities is a matter of debate among developmental psychologists (Case 1991).
80. In the extent to which goal activities are related to the content of schooling, school becomes an arena for acquiring useful memory strategies (Cole 1990; Wagner 1974). One needs to be careful not to overinterpret such findings, however, because this is tantamount to saying that school teaches what it teaches. That is to say, when it comes to more general memory capacity, based on the present state of research, one cannot conclude that schooling is any more effective than no schooling. Because school imparts the information that the culture values, such teachings naturally are valuable for pursuing the goals of that culture.
81. Tulviste 1991.
82. See Snyder et al. (1983) for review of the self-focus and attributional egotism of adults.

83. From ages seven through twelve, for example, the child becomes more facile at making inferences about the psychological mindsets of other people (Flapan 1968).

84. Piaget (1962) first described this developmental change from assimilation to accommodation thoughts; and this speculation has been supported in research.

85. For a review of goal-directed activities in the context of groups, see chapter 9 of Snyder and Fromkin's (1980) *Uniqueness: The Human Pursuit of Difference*.

86. For an excellent overview of social problem solving, see the work of Dodge (1986; see also, Dodge, Pettit, McClaskey & Brown 1986). Other scholars, such as Rubin and Krasnor (1986) and Spivak and Shure (1974) also provide insights into this process.

87. Gottman 1983; Hartup 1992.

88. Lever 1976.

89. Ruble & Frey 1991.

90. Ruble, Boggiano, Feldman & Loebl 1980.

91. Rieger 1993.

92. Dunphy 1963. First, boys and girls interact with their same sex groups, and the two groups do not interact very much with each other. Second, the separate groups of girls and boys begin to interact, and form what may be called the crowd. Third, the crowd undergoes a transition in which separate groups made up of both sexes begin to appear. Fourth, the groups of boys and girls dissipate, and heterosexual dyads form; moreover, the girl-boy pairs interact with each other. Dunphy actually discusses five stages, but I have collapsed his stages three and four because they appear to be one understandable unit. Although the examples from research describe the evolution of heterosexual relationships, it is likely that homosexual relationships also may progress from the group to dyadic interactions.

93. Gagnon & Simon 1973.

94. Rieger 1993.

95. Harter & Monsour 1992.

96. Marcia 1966, 1980; Waterman 1985.

97. Adolescence is a time for trying on work roles. From a societal perspective, there are established analogues for possible adult roles. For example, through the high school years, students are encouraged to joins clubs and organizations that teach some basic applied lessons about how one interacts in work settings. Whether it is the school newspaper, junior achievement, career days in which the student follows an adult in a given profession, or volunteer activities, the intent is that the adolescent garners insights about possible job-related goals. In advanced technological societies, the avenues for the more attractive and rewarded adult roles require that the student continue in school beyond adolescence. Accordingly, the aforementioned activities are role-playing for many students. For those students who do not plan to go beyond high school, and even for many who do, the opportunities for acquiring actual work experience are few and generally involve minimum wages. Although adolescents probably do garner some semblance of empowerment and autonomy from such work, and there is the widely held perception that such experience is

conducive to more effective output in school, it may be that too much work is counterproductive to school performance (Steinberg & Dornbusch 1991). Likewise, given the marginality of the typical work available to teenagers, it is doubtful that such work facilitates either educational or vocational goals (Greenberger & Steinberg 1986). Therefore, especially for those adolescents who have further school aspirations, actual work experiences may need to be moderated.

98. Donahue & Costar 1977.
99. Abramowitz, Weitz, Schwartz, Amira, Gomes & Abramowitz 1975.
100. Bachman, Johnston & O'Malley 1987.
101. Farmer 1983; Matlin 1993.
102. Rieger 1993.
103. Not surprisingly, this "Hope as a rope" metaphor is evidently operative in our culture according to Averill et al. (1990).
104. Marcel 1962, 53.
105. Related research suggests that children of various ages rate the support received from mother as quite high; father's support is rated as somewhat lower, but increasing with age (Cauce, Reid, Landesman & Gonzales 1990).
106. Baumrind 1968, 1973, 1975.
107. Kazdin, French, Unis, Esveldt-Dawson & Sherick 1983. The results of the Kazdin et al.'s work on hopelessness in children are discussed in detail in chapter 4, "The Death of Hope."
108. All of the subsequent discussion pertaining to the development and validation of the Children's Hope Scale, including several different samples of children, is summarized in Snyder, Rapoff, Ware, Hoza, Pelham, Danovsky, Highberger, Rubinstein, & Stahl (1994).
109. In an even more precise test of this issue, the correlation between age and scores on the Children's Hope Scale is virtually zero.
110. See for reviews of this dyadic interaction perspective, Belsky, Rovine, and Taylor (1984), and Lamb, Thompson, Gardner, Charnov, & Estes (1984).
111. We have used the Childhood Depression Inventory by Kovacs (1985) as the index of depression.
112. We have employed the Self-Perception Profile for Children: Revision of the Perceived Competence Scale for Children by Harter (1985) to tap situation-specific competencies, as well as global self-worth.
113. We used the Child Behavior Checklist by Achenbach & Edelbrook (1983) items for this index.
114. The scale used to measure locus of control in children was the abbreviated version of Nowicki-Strickland (1973) Locus of Control Scale.
115. We used the Child Behavior Checklist by Achenbach & Edelbrook (1983) items for this index.
116. Researchers are beginning to speculate about those coping-related characteristics of newborns that have a heritability component. There is disagreement about which characteristics have a heritability component, but the ones that may relate to goal-directed thinking involve approach/withdrawal responses to new stimuli, persistence/attention, distractability, and sociability (see Carey 1986; Garrison 1992).

Chapter 4: The Death of Hope

1. This portion of the sequence is similar to the frustration-aggression hypothesis introduced by Dollard, Doob, Miller, and Sears (1939). Since the introduction of this theory, a good deal of supportive research has been produced (Berkowitz 1962; Buss 1961; Zillman 1979).

2. Although I have presented the progression regarding the death of hope as moving linearly from hope to anger/rage to despair/apathy, in point of fact the person may iterate between these stages over time, with the eventual movement toward the apathy/despair pole.

3. In the 1970s and 1980s, Martin Seligman and his colleagues advanced the intriguing notion of learned helplessness (see Maier & Seligman 1976; Seligman 1975; and, Peterson, Maier & Seligman 1993, for thorough overviews). The premise of this theory is that organisms exposed to uncontrollable negative outcomes eventually deteriorate into a passive, nonresponsive state that was likened to human depression. One point to be highlighted about this experimental paradigm is that the organisms in actuality were being presented with blockages to their normal responses to the aversive circumstances. Initial responses to such thwarting of the goal-directed escape behaviors included an active, aroused state in which the organism appeared to be attempting activities aimed at lessening the aversiveness of the experience (e.g., escape tactics); moreover, the organism appeared to be agitated and angry at the circumstances (e.g., clawing behaviors paired with aggressive vocalizations). Wortman and Brehm (1975) have highlighted the importance of the attempts of the organism to reestablish the behavior that previously was possible before the goal blockage (this reactance is discussed in chapter 3); furthermore, they posited that if such attempts repeatedly fail, over time the organism will fall into a state of helplessness (see also Ford & Brehm 1987). One of the important sequelae of such learned helplessness is that the organism appears to remain in the passive state and is relatively impervious to new learning. For the reader interested in the earliest physiologically based analysis of how organisms react over time to stressing events (such as profound goal blockage), I would recommend Hans Selye's work on the general adaptation syndrome (Selye 1936, 1952, 1993). According to this theory, the organism confronted with a stressor goes into an aroused state of alarm; if the stressor continues, the organism responds with a state of continued resistance and eventually falls into a state of exhaustion with repeated exposure to the stressor. In this latter regard, Selye (1993, 10) wrote, "just as any inanimate machine gradually wears out, so does the human machine sooner or later become the victim of constant wear and tear." Obviously, Selye is positing a biological model that is analogous to the cognitive models discussed earlier.

4. Arthur Miller's (1950) portrayal of Willie Loman is a powerful, yet quick read. For an even briefer taste of quiet desperation see James Thurber's (1945) story entitled, "The Secret Life of Walter Mitty."

5. For a discussion of despair and hope, see Novotny (1979) and Marcel (1962).

6. Although hope theory uses one's thoughts about goal-related activities as the central mechanism for many depression-related symptoms, I acknowledge the importance of possible physical, metabolic, and biochemical malfunctions of the central nervous system as causal factors. Norman Endler's (1990) *Holiday of Darkness* is a vivid, first-hand description of the beginnings and treatment of such an endogenous depression. In my estimation, the impact of these physiological and biological factors initially is to lower willpower thinking, and over time waypower thinking also is reduced.

7. American Psychiatric Association 1987.

8. If the depression is a short-term result of bereavement, the diagnosis of major depressive episode is not considered.

9. This case is extracted from Roy (1993).

10. Rieger 1993.

11. For an excellent review of the maltreatment of children, see Bonner, Kaufman, Harbeck, and Brassard (1992); also, see Daro (1988).

12. Sedlack 1990. This means that in the United States, approximately 500,000 such cases are reported each year (American Humane Association 1984), and this number probably reflects a substantial underestimate (Finkelor & Hoteling 1984).

13. Daro 1988.

14. American Association for Protecting Children 1986.

15. Crittenden 1981; Egeland, Sroufe & Erickson 1983.

16. Aragona & Eyberg 1981; Kent 1976.

17. Kent 1976.

18. Hoffman-Plotkin & Twentyman 1984.

19. Egeland et al. 1983.

20. National Center on Child Abuse and Neglect 1981.

21. Gil 1970.

22. Gelles 1973.

23. Wahler 1980. Whatever the cause, more than a thousand deaths related to child abuse occur each year (National Committee for Prevention of Child Abuse 1991).

24. Related research supports this contention in that physical abuse is related to insecure attachments (Crittenden & Ainsworth 1989; Schneider-Rosen & Cicchetti 1984).

25. Gaensbauer & Sands 1979.

26. George & Main 1979.

27. Hoffman-Plotkin & Twentyman 1984.

28. Krugman & Jones 1987.

29. Bonner et al. 1992.

30. Conte & Schuerman 1988.

31. For review, see Wyatt and Powell (1988); also, see Berliner (1991).

32. Bowlby's (1973) classic volume entitled *Separation: Anxiety and Anger* is an excellent source about the two-sided nature of attachment.

33. Vida & Grizenko 1989.

34. Cook & Dworkin 1992.

35. Brown & Harris 1978.

36. Brown, Harris & Bifulco 1986.

37. King 1992.

38. Ibid.
39. Camara & Resnick 1989.
40. Kelly & Wallerstein 1976; Wallerstein & Kelly 1975.
41. Mulholland, Watt, Philpott & Sarlin 1991.
42. Kurdek 1988.
43. Wallerstein 1981.
44. Wallerstein (1986), as cited in King (1992).
45. For the first-hand viewpoints of adults who experienced divorce of their parents during their childhoods, see Claire Berman's (1991) *Adult Children of Divorce*.
46. Wallerstein 1983.
47. Clark 1983; Garmezy 1983; Rutter 1979.
48. Rutter 1979; Werner & Smith 1982; Wilson 1974.
49. One of the seductive aspects of gangs is that they provide a clear rule structure and support system, neither of which the adolescent may be getting through family life.
50. Glueck & Glueck 1950, 1968; Hetherington & Martin 1979; Snyder & Patterson 1987.
51. Rieger 1993.
52. Kauffman, Grunebaum, Cohler & Garner 1979; Rutter 1987b.
53. Billings & Moos 1984; Coyne, Burchill & Stiles 1991. For an excellent review of the effects of lack of actual and perceived social support in children, see *Children' Social Networks and Social Supports* by Belle (1989); for an examination of social support as it pertains to children and adults, see *Social Support* by Sarason, Sarason, and Pierce (1990a).
54. Murphy & Moriarty 1976; Pines 1979; Werner & Smith 1982.
55. For reviews, see Richman and Eliason (1992) and Rourke and DelDotto (1992).
56. Cook, Crosby & Hennigan 1977; Pettigrew 1967; Swallow & Kuiper 1988; Tesser 1988.
57. Brown & Harris 1978; Holmes & Rahe 1967.
58. Stroebe & Stroebe 1987.
59. McCrae & Costa 1988.
60. Glick, Weiss & Parkes 1974; Horowitz 1993.
61. Horowitz 1990.
62. Clayton 1975.
63. For balanced reviews about the impact of loss, I would recommend a chapter by Wortman and Silver (1987) and a paper by Wortman and Silver (1989).
64. Levinger & Moles 1979; Weiss 1975. See also Schlenker (1987) for a theoretical overview of how the identity of people is destroyed by events involving interpersonal loss.
65. Bloom, Asher & White 1978; Somers 1981.
66. Dalfiume 1993.
67. Perloff & Farbisz 1985.
68. Perloff 1987.
69. Chiraboga, Catron & Associates 1991.
70. Spanier & Castro 1979.

71. Hill, Rubin & Peplau 1976; Pettit & Bloom 1984; Spanier & Thompson 1983; Woodward, Zabel & Decosta 1980.

72. Brehm 1987; Brown & Harris 1978.

73. Another devastating possibility is that the person retains his or her job, but realizes that the long-desired goal of becoming a truly noteworthy person in the field is not going to materialize (Arieti & Arieti 1978). This loss often occurs sometime during midlife when fame is not forthcoming to the aspiring person.

74. Brenner 1976. See also Catalano, Dooley & Jackson (1985).

75. Peplau & Perlman 1982.

76. Cutrona 1982.

77. Rieger 1993.

78. Shaver & Rubenstein 1980.

79. See Jones and Carver (1991) for review.

80. For excellent discussions on the counterproductive psychological effects of not talking about one's problems and difficulties, I would recommend T. J. Scheff's (1979) *Catharsis in Healing, Ritual, and Drama*, and J. W. Pennebaker's (1990) *Opening Up: The Healing Power of Confiding in Others*.

81. Rieger 1993.

82. For review of social support, see *Social Support: An Interactional View* by Sarason, Sarason, and Pierce (1990a).

83. For a more detailed description of PTSD, see the *Diagnostic and Statistical Manual of Mental Disorders*, 3rd ed. rev., American Psychiatric Association, 1987, 247–51.

84. For a thorough overview of the topic of traumatic stress syndrome in its various forms, see the professional volume *International Handbook of Traumatic Stress* edited by Wilson and Raphael (1993). For an incisive analysis of how trauma assaults the human mind, I would highly recommend Janoff-Bulman's (1992) *Shattered Assumptions: Toward a New Psychology of Trauma*. Another compelling earlier volume on this topic is Kushner's (1981) *When Bad Things Happen to Good People*.

85. Barnum 1993; Elliott et al. 1991.

86. Pines 1993.

87. Maslach 1982, 3. For an overview of this topic, see *Burnout — The Cost of Caring* by Christina Maslach (1982) who has helped to set the scholarly agenda on this phenomenon.

88. Wallace & Brinkerhoff 1991.

89. Pines 1993. See also, Pines and Aronson (1988).

90. Sherwin et al. 1992.

91. Maslach & Jackson 1981.

92. Snyder 1984.

93. See Higgins and Harris (1988).

94. For a thorough review of such anticipatory excuse-making, see *Excuses: Masquerades in Search of Grace*, by Snyder, Higgins, and Stucky (1983).

95. The term *self-handicapping* was coined by Berglas and Jones, and the original articles were Berglas and Jones (1978) and Jones and Berglas (1978). For an overview of the evolution of this intriguing phenomenon, see *Self-Handicapping: The Paradox That Isn't*, by Higgins, Snyder, and Berglas (1990).

96. For discussions of the progression of anticipatory excuses (self-handicaps) into counterproductive labels, see Snyder and Smith (1982) and Snyder and Higgins (1988b). For a discussion of self-defeating behaviors in general, including self-handicapping, a good overview is given in *Your Own Worst Enemy*, by Berglas and Baumeister (1993).
97. Grier & Cobbs 1968.
98. Grier & Cobbs 1968; Jones 1985; Mays 1985.
99. Franklin 1993.
100. White & Parham 1990.
101. Hardy 1993, 52.
102. For incisive reviews of the processes involved in discrimination and gender, I would recommend *The Mismeasure of Women* by Carol Tavris (1992) and a chapter entitled "Women and Men at Home and at Work: Realities and Illusions" by Faye Crosby and Karen Jaskar (1993).
103. Glick, Zion & Nelson 1988.
104. See Matlin (1993) for summary in which this is called *access discrimination*. To label this as discrimination continues the inappropriate equating of discrimination with prejudice; for this reason, I speak of *access prejudice.*
105. I have changed this from *treatment discrimination* to *treatment prejudice* to separate the discrimination and prejudice processes. See previous footnote.
106. Matlin 1993.
107. See Crocker and Major (1989) for review and a discussion of how the defensive strategies of stigmatized groups may protect their self-esteem.
108. For insights into the importance of losing mental activeness in relation to decrements in the body with aging, see Ellen Langer's (1989) *Mindfulness.*
109. Stokols 1972. While density is the actual or perceived number of people per available space, crowding is a subjective evaluation that there isn't enough space (Holahan 1982).
110. Epstein, Woolfolk & Lehrer 1981; Jain 1987; Schopler & Stockdale, 1977.
111. Schopler & Stockdale 1977.
112. Rodin, Solomon & Metcalf 1978. See also, Baron and Rodin (1978).
113. Baron, Mandel, Adams & Griffin 1976.
114. Shakespeare (1980), *Hamlet*, Act 3, Scene 1 (p. 64 in Bantam Books version edited by Bevington, Kastan, Hammersmith & Turner).
115. Although I am developing the argument at the individual level that blockage leads to hopelessness and possible suicide, it can be argued that certain societies in comparison to others should thwart the activities of their citizens and as such should have higher suicide rate. Indeed, correlational data support this hypothesis (Krauss & Krauss 1968).
116. A review of the structure of suicidal thought can be obtained in Neuringer (1976).
117. For example, problem-solving thoughts are depleted in suicidal as compared to nonsuicidal people (Levenson & Neuringer 1971).
118. This is not meant to deny that at times there may be considerable ambivalence in the mindset of the person contemplating suicide. Nevertheless, experiencing a present that is unbearable and lacking plans for an improved future, the not-to-be goal is the emerging thought of the suicidal person.

119. Schneidman 1985, 203.
120. This story is taken from Jean E. Mizer's (1964) award-winning autobiographical article entitled "Cipher in the Snow."
121. Case history taken from Cynthia Pfeffer's (1986) *The Suicidal Child*, p. 8.
122. Ibid., 4.
123. Pfeffer 1986, 14.
124. Asarnow, Carlson & Guthrie 1987; see also Milling and Martin (1992).
125. Pfeffer 1986.
126. Shafii, Carrigan, Whittinghill & Derrick 1985. Other studies have replicated these results (see Pfeffer 1986, 124–43, for review, as well as Milling and Martin 1992).
127. Aalberg & Hamalainen 1976; Haider 1968.
128. McCulloch & Phillip 1967.
129. Kazdin et al. 1983.
130. The following studies have supported the positive relationship between children's hopelessness and suicidal tendencies: Asarnow & Guthrie 1989; Brent, Kolko, Goldstein, Allan & Brown 1989; Cole 1989 (relationship for boys and not girls); and, Spirito, Williams, Stark & Hart 1988. A study by Rotheram-Borus and Trautman (1988) provided partial support in that suicidal and psychiatric comparison group children both evidenced higher hopelessness than did nondisturbed control children; likewise, a positive, although not statistically reliable relationship between hopelessness and suicidal ideation was obtained. Spirito, Overholser, and Hart (1991) found that suicidal and psychiatric comparison children both evidenced elevated hopelessness scores.
131. Subsequent studies have provided mixed support for this conclusion, with two showing that hopelessness provides unique predictive insights into suicidal intent and action in children (Asarnow & Guthrie 1989; Cole 1989 [relationship for boys, but not girls]), and one suggesting that hopelessness and depression both provide predictive information about childhood suicide (Spirito, Overholser & Hart 1991).
132. Case history taken from Klopfer (1957).
133. Case history taken from Oltmanns, Neale, and Davison (1991).
134. Case history taken from Custer and Wassink (1991).
135. Frankl 1992.
136. Ibid., 83.
137. Bryer, Nelson, Miller & Krol 1987; Goodwin 1981; Herman & Hirschman 1981.
138. See Lester 1992, 57–59.
139. Ibid., 60–63.
140. Bonnar & McGee 1977.
141. Fawcett, Leff & Bunney 1969.
142. Black & Reimer 1985.
143. Jacobson & Portuges 1978; Wasserman 1988.
144. Hanigan 1987.
145. Kaprio, Koskenvuo & Rita 1987. See Lester (1992) for a review of the relationship-related issues as they pertain to suicidal tendencies.
146. Leenaars 1987a, 1987b, 1989.
147. Dahl 1989; Ellis, Atkeson & Calhoun 1982.

148. For reviews, see Barraclough (1985) and Lester (1992, 335–45).
149. See Lester (1992, 97–99) and Platt and Dyer (1987).
150. See Lester (1992, 297–305).
151. Beck & Steer 1989; Morris, Kovacs, Beck & Wolfe, 1970.
152. Beck, Weissman, Lester, & Trexler 1974.
153. See original Beck et al. (1974) article, as well as Wetzel, Margulies, Davis & Karam (1980) for reviews of the hopelessness suicidal tendencies relationship.
154. Beck, Brown, Berchick, Stewart & Steer 1990; Beck, Steer, Kovacs & Garrison 1985; Drake & Cotton 1986; Fawcett, Scheftner, Clark, Hedeker, Gibbons & Coryell 1987.
155. For articles showing that hopelessness is more powerful than depression in predicting suicidal tendencies, see Beck, Kovaks & Weissman 1975; Beck, Steer & McElroy 1982; Bedrosian & Beck 1979; Dyer & Kreitman 1984; Kovacs, Beck & Weissman 1975; Minkoff, Bergman, Beck & Beck 1973; Petrie & Chamberlain 1983; Salter & Platt 1990; Wetzel 1976. Simonds, McMahon & Armstrong (1991) found that depression and hopelessness both predicted suicidal tendencies. Rudd (1990) found that both depression and hopelessness related to suicidal ideation, but that depression was the better predictor.
156. Weissman, Beck & Kovacs 1979.
157. For insights into the historical and religious bases of injunctions against suicide, I would refer the reader to *A Psychology of Hope: An Antidote to the Suicidal Pathology of Western Civilization* by Kaplan and Schwartz (1993). For an analysis of the lifting of responsibility for suicide from the mental health professional and placing it on the individual, see the chapter entitled "The Case against Suicide Prevention" by Szasz (1993).
158. Miller 1981.

Chapter 5: Nurturing Hope in Children

1. Schools generally do not touch the topic of parenting (Anastasiow 1988) and rarely teach future parents about fostering hope in their children. In response to this deficiency in parental training, Anastasiow (1988) proposes that parents be required to obtain a license in the same manner that one has to get a license for driving a car.

2. My focus here is more on increasing hope-related thoughts and behaviors in children, rather than only delimiting those thoughts and behaviors that are antithetical to hopeful thinking. This is based on my reading of the literature on parents' reactions to training programs in which they have participated. For example, Calvert and McMahon (1987) report that parents rate techniques aimed at increasing behaviors as easier to implement, more acceptable, and more useful than techniques that decrease behaviors. For the reader interested in a professional overview of parent training, I recommend Scaeffer and Briesmeister's (1989) *The Handbook of Parent Training: Parents as Co-Therapists for Children's Behavior Problems*.

3. Michael Schulman (1991) coined this term in his informative book entitled *The Passionate Mind*. See this book for excellent examples of how to stimulate the thinking processes in children. Another outstanding book for parents interested in teaching their children effective thinking is Edward deBono's (1993) *Teach Your Child How to Think*, and Alicia Lieberman's (1993) *The Emotional Life of the Toddler*. Although it is directed more toward the professional audience, Paul Trad's (1992) *Intervention with Infants and Parents: The Theory and Practice of Previewing* is a helpful resource.

4. Schulman 1991.

5. Research reveals that the level of encouragement for such attention exercises has a positive influence on the young child's exploration of objects (Belsky, Goode & Most 1980), and the language associated with those objects (Tamis-LeMonda & Bornstein 1989).

6. Schulman 1991, 43.

7. Schlenker & Weigold 1989.

8. Bryan & Locke 1967.

9. Locke, Shaw, Saari & Latham 1981.

10. Case taken from Reisman and Ribordy 1993, 49.

11. Lee, Locke & Latham 1989.

12. Goals that are specific and difficult generally lead to better performance (Lee et al. 1989).

13. Snyder 1993.

14. Lee et al. 1989.

15. Anderson 1983; Locke et al. 1981.

16. Epstein 1982; Pervin 1983.

17. Given that children adopt the standards of their parents and society more generally as part of the normal developmental process, even seemingly internal standards have their roots in something we may have acquired from an external source. As such, the issue of internal and external standards becomes intertwined. For a further discussion, see Snyder et al. (1983).

18. Even when it is necessary for a child to be seen in psychotherapy, the therapist negotiates with the child about the goal of the meetings (see Reisman & Ribordy 1993, 45).

19. Rieger 1993.

20. We consistently have found that lower-hope people tend to think in terms of their deficiencies (see Snyder et al. 1991).

21. Clinical child psychologists often employ similar approaches in the form of cognitive behavior therapy (Meichenbaum 1979). A key component of this approach is to develop a positive script for the child. For an impulsive child, for example, Meichenbaum and Goodman (1971, 117) developed the following self-talk instructions for copying line patterns: "Okay, draw the line, down, down, *good*: then to the right, *that's it*: now down, down, *good*: then to the right, *that's it*: now down some more and to the left. *Good, I'm doing fine so far.* Remember, go slowly. Now back up again, No, I was supposed to go down. *That's okay.* Just erase the line carefully ... *Good.*" As you can see by the words I have italicized, the child is learning frequent positive self-comments. Consistent with my reasoning in footnote 2 in this chapter, these cognitive behavioral approaches have been

more successful when teaching positive self-statements than when teaching reframes of the potential negative. For example, kindergartners who were fearful of the dark responded better to positive self-statements such as "I'm a brave little girl" than they did to reframes such as "The dark is a fun place to be" (Kanfer, Karoly & Newman 1975; see also Graziano & Mooney 1980, 1982). This is not to suggest, however, that reframes cannot be useful to children, because they often are.

22. For an example of the use of "I can do it" statements for an eight-year-old girl who had difficulty being separated from her mother, see Peterson (1987). Examples of self-talk related to various other problems include the following: academics (Lloyd, Hallahan, Kauffman & Keller 1991); fear of dentist (Siegal & Peterson 1981); and, preparation for medical procedures (Dolgin & Jay 1989).

23. This example is taken from Young (1983) and Hughes (1990). This is an example of limiting the negative spread (see footnote 24).

24. The notion of *spread* has been applied to the engulfing of an entire person by a particular label. For example, the person with a deformed foot may be called a disabled person. This is an instance of negative spread, which is more pervasive than a positive spread. Indeed, with children the key often is to make sure they do not conclude that they are dumb because they do not do well in one area. My thinking about this topic has been guided by the pioneering ideas of my colleague Beatrice Wright (1983).

25. Snyder et al. 1991

26. Robin, Schneider & Dolnick 1976.

27. Dweck and other researchers have found that children with priorities on learning rather than end products increase their efforts when encountering impedances to their goals (Ames 1984; Ames, Ames & Felker 1977; Diener & Dweck 1978; see also Dweck 1986).

28. Langer 1989.

29. Elliott & Dweck 1988.

30. Curry 1994.

31. Langer 1989.

32. Several books teach problem-solving skills to children. Although these books are aimed primarily at teachers, they should be useful to parents also. See the following books for elementary school children: *Special Kid's Stuff* (Farnett, Forte & Loss 1976); *Odessey: A Curriculum for Thinking-Problem Solving* (Grignetti 1986); *Think Aloud* (Bash & Camp 1985); and, *Willy the Wisher and Other Thinking Stories: An Open Court Thinking Storybook* (Bereiter & Anderson 1983). For late elementary through junior high and high school, I would recommend *Problem Solving and Comprehension* (Whimbey & Lochhead 1986) and, *125 Ways to Be a Better Student: A Program for Study Skill Success* (DeBrueys 1986).

33. This problem solving is also called solution thinking; children who are better adjusted generate more solutions to problems (Shure & Spivak 1974, 1975; Spivak, Platt & Shure 1976). Within the area of psychotherapy with children, the learning of flexible problem solving is judged to be one of the principal mechanisms of change (Freedheim & Russ 1992).

34. These suggestions are guided by Schulman's (1991) insights, as well as my

discussions with child psychologists. Likewise, I have observed these ideas in action with my own children and grandaughter, as well as other infants.

35. My former colleague, Fritz Heider, who is recognized as the founder of attribution theory (i.e., the study of perceived causes of events), once told me that "Why?" is the longest question. To which I asked "What do you mean?" With a wrinkled smile, Fritz answered, "Because you ask it from the time you begin talking as a child, until your adult days of talking are almost done."

36. For example, four year olds who are more facile at recognizing the causal antecedants of a problem also are better at identifying solutions (Shure & Spivak 1975).

37. These are extrapolations from family therapist Michael White's use of the label *Sneaky Poo* in helping the family and the child with encopresis. Read Tomm's (1989) article for a lucid account of White's techniques.

38. Snyder et al. 1991.

39. Curry 1994.

40. Snyder et al. 1994.

41. Marvin, Greenberg, & Mossler (1976) and Urberg & Docherty (1976) present data suggesting that children's interpersonal sensitivity is a key for problem solving.

42. Children who are high in shyness also are rated as being low on social sensitivity (Marceon & Brumagne 1985), which follows given that hope and shyness are inversely related.

43. Clinical child therapists have employed problem-solving training to decrease interpersonal difficulties children are having. For example, Spivak and Shure (1974) taught preschool children to increase their social reasoning through games involving attending to other people and finding alternative solutions to problems. Other therapists have used problem solving and shown effective results with children who exhibit relatively mild to severe interpersonal difficulties (Russell & Thoreson 1976; Stone, Hinds, & Schmidt 1975). What is important in the present context is that these therapeutic problem-solving approaches emphasize attending to the needs of other children.

44. Hirsch & Dubois 1989.

45. Curry 1994.

46. Participation in sports also increases the willpower of children, as I discussed earlier in the "Rechargers" section.

47. I would hasten to note that other activities such as music, dance, theater, and debate should provide similar lessons in planfulness and determination.

48. Harvey & Katz 1985.

49. Rieger 1993.

50. Pyszczynski et al. 1991; Sarason 1975; Wine 1971, 1980.

51. Although it has been suggested that children under eight years of age have limited imaging skills (e.g., Pressley 1977), young children can and do have the basic skills required for mental practicing.

52. See Markus & Ruvolo (1989) for review.

53. Bandura (1989) cites a 1985 dissertation in which Cervone found that thinking about the difficult part of a task weakened the agentic-type

thoughts of people, while concentrating on the doable parts strengthened such thoughts.

54. As taken from Stark (1990), the rewards might include people with whom your children could spend time, places to visit, things they would like to own, favorite foods or drinks, or other enjoyable activities.

55. Stark, Reynolds & Kaslow 1987.

56. Reynolds & Coats 1986.

57. Research reveals that children are quite conservative in giving themselves rewards (e.g., Bandura & Perloff 1967).

58. Rieger 1993.

59. Elliot & Dweck 1988; Peterson & Bossio 1991; Seligman 1991; Snyder & Higgins 1988a.

60. See Langer (1989) for related discussion.

61. In his book *Learned Optimism*, Martin Seligman (1991) presents a similar case for salespeople making "I used the wrong strategy" attributions when they do not make a sale.

62. Snyder et al. 1983.

63. Lopez 1990, 48.

64. Bowlby 1969, 1980; Kobak & Sceery 1988.

65. Rieger 1993.

66. Given the fact that in custody battles often one parent tries to win, this tends to place the noncustodial parent in a position of having to fight for time with the children. As I have discussed earlier in regard to divorce, children suffer when the father is not seen frequently. The child's welfare warrants a stance where divorcing parents try to spend relatively equal time with the child. For a balanced discussion of this custody issue, read Richard Warshak's (1992) *The Custody Revolution: The Father Factor and the Motherhood Mystique.*

67. Survey research of college students shows that the ability to establish a social support network is related to reports of higher amounts of parental care during childhood (Sarason, Sarason & Shearin 1986).

68. Research on parenting highlights the importance of responsiveness and support as contributing to positive child development (Belsky, Lerner & Spanier 1984; Rollins & Thomas 1979).

69. Research shows that parents are effective when working with the school in tutoring (Greenwood, Delquadri & Hall 1984), and in handling most school-related problems (Kramer 1990).

70. McCormack 1993.

71. Defining limits that are developmentally appropriate routinely is described as being an important aspect of parenting (see Baumrind 1975, 1980).

72. Hetherington, Cox, and Cox (1979, 1981) suggest that after divorce, mothers of preschool children become less affectionate and consistent in discipline.

73. Family system theorists consistently assert that a healthy family context is one where the child has a firm attachment or merger with the parents, and yet is encouraged to differentiate himself or herself wherever possible (see Ackerman 1959; Minuchin 1974; Satir 1967). In a recent empirical test of what type of families facilitate success in their children, it was this base of attachment and support, coupled with encouragement for differentiation

activities, that was most beneficial (Csikszentmihalyi, Rathunde & Whalen 1993).

74. These suggestions about parental attachment behaviors are reported about parents by high-hope young adults (Rieger 1993).

75. Parental warmth and praise are related to children's perceptions of control (Crandall & Crandall 1983).

76. Rieger 1993.

77. Albert Bandura (1969, 1971) is known for his pioneering work on modeling, or observational learning as it was called with children. For a recent overview of the therapeutic implications of modeling for children, see Powers and Rickard (1992).

78. Researchers have found that an adult who the child knows and respects, such as a parent or a teacher, is an especially effective model if a same age child is not available (e.g., Perry & Furukawa 1980).

79. By calling the local community mental health center, a parent can get information about various mental health resources in the geographical area. If you decide to undertake psychotherapy for your child, the prognosis often is favorable, especially for mild to moderately severe problems (Reisman & Ribordy 1993). Research reviewing the results of seventy-five separate studies (Casey & Berman 1985) reveals that psychotherapy with children is quite effective (i.e., across different types of therapy, children receiving treatment had better outcomes than did children in control conditions). Likewise, a more recent review of 108 studies shows that children and adolescents both profit from psychotherapy, with the benefits being stronger for children (Weisz, Weiss, Alicke & Klotz 1987). Indeed, the most recent meta-analytic review studies echo the effectiveness of psychotherapy with children (see Kazdin, Bass, Ayers & Rodgers 1990; Weiss & Weisz 1990).

Chapter 6: Kindling Hope in Adults

1. My view here represents a minimalist position in which large changes in an individual are believed to occur because of relatively small interventions (see Coyne 1987). Small but fundamental changes can have large ripple effects in one's thinking and behavior.

2. For an overview of goal setting, see Locke and Latham's (1984) *Goal Setting: A Motivational Technique That Works*, as well Lee et al.'s (1989) chapter entitled, "Goal Setting Theory and Job Performance." Scholarly papers on various aspects of recent goal research and theory can be found in Pervin's (1989) *Goal Concepts in Personality and Social Psychology*.

3. In Nietzsche's (1990) *Twilight of the Idols/The Anti-Christ*, p. 37.

4. The concept of *should's* is part of gestalt therapy, wherein people are taught to become aware of the crucial expectations that they have incorporated from important other people. If the reader is interested in further information about gestalt therapy, I would recommend Fritz Perls' volumes entitled, *In and Out of the Garbage Pail* (1969), and *Gestalt Therapy Verbatim* (1970), as well as Fagan and Shepherd's (1971) *Gestalt Therapy Now*.

5. Erikson 1950; Ryff 1987.

6. Caspi 1987; Veroff 1983.

7. My thinking on this point is guided by the insights of Ellen Langer (1989), who has written eloquently about the advantages of an active mental state she calls mindfulness.

8. In my experiences with high-hope people, the importance of having choices is a common theme. Choice appears to be valuable to such people because it is invigorating mentally; moreover, choice is inherently conducive to pathways-related thinking.

9. Snyder et al. 1991.

10. We are often creatures of habit and only will pursue those goals that closely fit our notion of who we are (see Cantor & Langston 1989, for related discussion). Some goals are sufficiently discrepant from our self-view that we experience a variety of negative emotions when considering them. That is to say, such goals are threatening.

11. Cited in *The Living Pulpit* 1992, 26.

12. Research shows that training in clarifying one's goals, especially in the context of social (interpersonal) issues, results in enhanced problem-solving activities (Nezu & D'Zurilla 1981a, 1981b). The problem-solving training that undergirds this research is D'Zurilla and Goldfried's (1971) five-stage model (see also D'Zurilla 1986).

13. Nezu & D'Zurilla 1981a.

14. Research reveals that certain people prefer to be in situations that are not diagnostic of their ability. Such people are said to desire attribute ambiguity (Snyder & Wicklund 1981; see also Snyder et al. 1983, for review).

15. Snyder & Higgins 1988b.

16. Averill et al. (1990) report that people believe that hopeful thoughts should be reserved for the more important goals in one's life.

17. Support for the reciprocal relationship between goals and feedback about one's progress has been shown by several investigators (see Locke, Cartledge & Koeppel 1968; Locke, Shaw, Saari & Latham 1981; Mento, Steel & Karren 1987).

18. By prioritizing and committing oneself to a goal, there is increased attention to cues pertaining to that goal and decreased thoughts about goal-irrelevant stimuli (Klinger 1975: Klinger, Barta & Maxeiner 1980). Likewise, goals serve to direct attention and action (Locke & Bryan 1969).

19. Quotation taken from Covey's (1990) *The Seven Habits of Highly Effective People*, 146.

20. See deBono (1978) and Covey (1990) for helpful discussions of the distinctions between an urgent and an important matter.

21. Atkinson 1964; Feather 1982.

22. Goal-setting research shows a strong and consistent effect such that people who set difficult and specific goals, as opposed to easy and general ones, perform better (Latham & Lee 1986; Lee et al. 1989; Mento et al. 1987; Tubbs 1986).

23. Snyder et al. 1991.

24. Averill et al. 1990. In Lynch's (1974) *Images of Hope*, he calls this *realistic imagination*.

25. Snyder et al. 1991.

26. For additional useful descriptions of how to increase your willpower thinking, see *Fatigue Free: How to Revitalize Your Life* by William Green (1992), and *Beyond Negative Thinking: Breaking the Cycle of Depressing and Anxious Thoughts* by Joseph Martorano and John Kildahl (1989). The insights provided in these two books helped to clarify and guide my analysis of interventions for willful thinking.

27. Self-monitoring is a fundamental starting point for psychotherapists with differing orientations (see Martorano & Kildahl 1989; Wilson 1989).

28. For detailed discussions of commitment, read Kiesler (1971) and Brehm (1976).

29. In the psychotherapy literature, choice on the part of the client is facilitative of change (Brehm 1976; Brehm & McCallister 1980).

30. Brehm & Brehm 1981. Related theory and research suggests that when people choose a goal, they are energized in direct proportion to their perception of the difficulty of attaining the goal (Brehm, Wright, Solomon, Silka & Greenberg 1983; Ford & Brehm 1987; Kukla 1972).

31. Snyder et al. 1991.

32. This exemplifies what has come to be called cognitive restructuring methods in psychotherapy (Ingram, Kendall & Chen 1991). The two most widely used of these approaches are Beck's (Beck, Rush, Shaw & Emery 1979; Beck & Weishaar 1989) cognitive therapy, and Ellis's (1962, 1989) rational-emotive therapy.

33. For more on scheduling worry time, see Borkovec, Wilkinson, Folensbee & Lerman (1983). This approach, which is sometimes called paradoxical intention, often enables people to gain control over such intrusive thoughts. The original article on paradoxical intention was by Frankl (1960).

34. Research suggests that suppression of thoughts is counterproductive. For a good read and a thorough analysis of this topic, I would recommend Daniel Wegner's (1989) *White Bears and Other Unwanted Thoughts: Suppression, Obsession, and the Psychology of Mental Control.*

35. Snyder et al. 1983; Snyder & Higgins, 1988b; Snyder & Ingram 1983.

36. This is called emotion-focused coping (see Lazarus & Folkman, 1984).

37. In my experience, most people tend to have memories more for the positive than the negative in their lives. Thus, it may be the good old days in our minds. This is advantageous in the sense that calling on the positively remembered past may infuse us with willpower for the present. There is, however, a small percentage of people for whom the memories may predominantly link the person to negative events (Snyder, Irving, Sigmon & Holleran 1993), and as such the memory exercise will not be productive.

38. Sigmon & Snyder 1993.

39. Mikes (1971, 36) describes it this way: "Laughing at oneself does not mean that one is inferior to others; it means that we accept ourselves as erratic, foolish and bungling as all our fellow creatures are . . . to laugh at oneself does not mean to be modest, insecure, unsure. A man who is unsure usually takes himself deadly seriously and is given to watching himself anxiously at all times." Rollo May (1953, 54) writes similarly about humor: "It is an expression of our uniquely human capacity to experience ourselves as subjects who are not swallowed up in the objective situation. It is the healthy way of feeling a 'distance' between oneself and the problem,

a way of standing off and looking at one's problems with perspective. One cannot laugh when in an anxiety panic, for then one is swallowed up."

40. See Lefcourt and Davidson-Katz (1991) for review.
41. Ibid.
42. Cousins 1979.
43. Higgins & Snyder 1989.
44. Snyder 1989.
45. This consensus-raising tactic is an adaptive coping strategy (Snyder & Higgins 1988a; Snyder et al. 1983).
46. High-willpower people have lows in state willpower and negative feelings, however, that are much higher than those of characteristically low-willpower people (Sympson 1993). Thus, the lows of high-willpower people are not as negative as those reported by low willpower persons.
47. The descriptions of high-hope people are similar to what Csikszentmihalyi (1990; Csikszentmihalyi & Csikszentmihalyi 1988) calls the flow experience. Briefly, flow experiences entail a phenomenology in which the person feels in control, stimulated, and fully absorbed in an ongoing activity.
48. Cited in Fairchild 1980, 19.
49. Our research suggests that high-hope people are able to focus strongly on the task at hand (Snyder et al. 1991).
50. Taken from *The Surgeon General's Report on Nutrition and Health* (United States Department of Health and Human Services, 1988b).
51. This 20 percent is Green's (1992) estimate. Others, such as Weltman (1984), conclude it is closer to 40 percent.
52. Brownell's (1990) *The Learn Program for Weight Control* is an excellent source for weight control techniques.
53. A survey of 100 fourth-grade girls revealed that half of them said they were dieting (Zaslow 1986).
54. Green 1992.
55. Centers for Disease Control 1989.
56. Smoking is the major avoidable cause of death according to a U.S. Department of Health and Human Services report in 1989.
57. Green 1992.
58. Taken from *The Health Consequences of Smoking: Nicotine Addiction: A Report of the Surgeon General* (United States Department of Health and Human Services, 1988a). This does not necessarily mean that such people continue to abstain. For tips on how to stop smoking, see *Freedom from Smoking in 20 Days* (American Lung Association 1986).
59. It has been estimated that approximately 13 percent of the American adult population has some form of alcohol abuse or dependence in their lives (American Psychiatric Association 1987).
60. Green 1992.
61. Seeman & Anderson 1983; Seeman, Seeman & Budros 1988.
62. Snyder 1984; Snyder & Higgins 1988b.
63. Harney 1990.
64. For reviews see Blumenthal, Emery, Madden, George, Coleman, Riddle, McKee, Reasoner, and Williams (1989); Simons, McGowan, Epstein, and Kupfer (1985); and Stephens (1989).

65. See McCann and Holmes (1984) and Roth and Holmes (1987). These authors used the Beck Depression Inventory as the dependent variable. This measure of depression correlates strongly and negatively with the agency subscale of the Hope Scale; for this reason, I report the results in terms of "willpower-related thoughts."

66. See Roth and Holmes (1985). These authors used the Beck Depression Inventory as the dependent variable, and I extrapolated these findings to "willpower-related thoughts" for the same reason explained in the previous footnote. For comprehensive overviews regarding the role of physical exercise on hope-related processes, I would recommend Peter Seraganian's (1993) *Exercise Psychology: The Influence of Physical Exercise on Psychological Processes*, especially Holmes' (1993) chapter entitled, "Aerobic Fitness and the Response to Psychological Stress."

67. The American College of Sports Medicine (1978) recommends at least 15 minutes of continuous aerobic activity three to five times a week, at 60 to 90 percent of your maximum heart rate.

68. Rosenthal 1989, 23.

69. Nelson, Badura & Goldman 1990.

70. See Wehr and Rosenthal (1989) for historical overview.

71. Wehr & Rosenthal 1989.

72. This research is reviewed in Wehr and Rosenthal (1989).

73. Rosenthal, Sack, Skwerer, Jaocobsen & Wehr 1988.

74. See Rosenthal's (1989) book entitled *Seasons of the Mind: Why You Get Winter Blues and What You Can Do About It*, where a full discussion is given to the etiology and treatment of SAD.

75. On rare occasions, especially among the profoundly depressed, the person may be sleeping too much. This can result in a mental fatigue and general lowering of willpower similar to those produced by too little sleep.

76. As noted in chapter 2, among religious people, prayer is associated with both will- and way-related thinking (Laird 1992).

77. Related to this point, the poet, farmer Walter Berry has written a lively piece entitled, "Out of Your Car, Off Your Horse" in the February 1991 issue of *Atlantic Monthly*.

78. Endler 1990; McAllister & Price 1990.

79. Green 1992.

80. Endler 1990.

81. Rosenthal 1989.

82. Rybakowski 1990.

83. Overviews of drugs are taken from the *Physicians' Desk Reference*® (1993) and Green (1992).

84. Low-hope people in general, and particularly low-waypower people, have reported to me their bewilderment at the outcomes in their own lives. In fact, low-hope people tend to have an external locus of control, believing that they are strongly influenced by external events (Snyder et al. 1991). The sense that you cannot form plans will by necessity place you in the throes of other forces that determine the outcome of events (Heppner & Krauskopf 1987).

85. Greeno 1978.

352

86. In this process, people who are focusing on the salient goal closest to them may not be aware of the long-term goals (Vallacher & Wegner 1987; Vallacher, Wegner & Somoza 1989).

87. Various problem-solving training approaches have concentrated on the production of alternative pathways to goals (D'Zurilla & Nezu 1980; Nezu & D'Zurilla 1981b), as well as the adaptive selection from those alternatives (Nezu & D'Zurilla 1979, 1981b).

88. D'Zurilla & Nezu 1980.

89. Claerhout, Elder & Janes 1982; Getter & Nowinski 1981.

90. Dorner 1983.

91. Markus & Nurius 1986, 212.

92. Markus & Ruvolo 1989.

93. Studies on the mental rehearsals of athletes have shown the importance of the viewing oneself actually going through the sequence (e.g., Mahoney & Avener 1977; Orlick 1986). I believe that this perspective is equally important in other performance arenas.

94. Markus and Ruvolo (1989) provide a good review of the benefits that result because of mental simulations.

95. People do produce contingencies in their plans to handle the anticipated blockages to goals (Bruce & Newman 1978; Carbonell 1981; Wilensky 1983).

96. Honeycutt, Zagacki, and Edwards (1989) call these "imagined interactions."

97. Rieger 1993.

98. Baumgardner, Heppner & Arkin 1986.

99. Snyder 1989; Snyder & Higgins 1988a. It is also a basic premise of the learned optimism theory that such people are able to distance themselves from their failures. For a good overviews of this learned optimism approach, I would recommend books by Peterson and Bossio (1991) and Seligman (1991).

100. The self-preoccupation of low-hope people, who are also more anxious (see Snyder et al. 1991), relates to a common finding in the anxiety literature. Namely, part of the debilitating effect of anxiety is that it is fueled by doubts about one's ability to respond adequately to given goal pursuits (Sarason 1984; Wine 1971). Relatedly, low-hope people concentrate more on potential failure than success (Snyder et al. 1991), which is similar to the thoughts of highly anxious people (see Covington 1986).

101. For a full discussion of the adaptive distancing statements that one can make about mistakes, see *Excuses: Masquerades in Search of Grace* by Snyder et al. (1983) or Snyder (1984) for a shorter review.

102. For an overview of the research on assertiveness, see Richard Rakos's (1991) *Assertive Behavior: Theory, Research, and Training*. For a more applied discussion of assertion, read Shan Rees and Roderick Graham's (1991) *Assertion Training: How to Be Who You Really Are* (see 134–39 of this book for a good bibliography for references on assertion training).

103. Heppner and his colleagues have come to a similar conclusion in the area of problem solving (Heppner & Hillerbrand 1991; Heppner & Petersen 1982).

104. Rieger 1993.

105. Dalfiume 1993.
106. Cohen and Wills (1985) give a comprehensive overview of the research on social support.
107. Sarason, Sarason & Pierce 1990b.
108. Rubenstein & Shaver 1982.
109. Swann & Brown 1990.
110. Cohen, Mermelstein, Kamarck, and Hoberman (1985) call this informational support.
111. Cohen et al. (1985) call this instrumental support.
112. Christensen & Magoon 1974; Tinsley, de St. Aubin & Brown 1982; Veroff, Kulka & Douvan 1981.
113. See Pennebaker (1990), as well as Swann and Brown (1990), for incisive discussions of this point.
114. Latham & Locke 1975; Locke 1966.
115. Latham & Baldes 1975.
116. More generally, cognitive psychologists suggest that our thoughts become focused and activated by our mental targets or goals (Gagne 1984).

Chapter 7: Hope for Relationships and Vice Versa

1. Heath 1991, 331.
2. A thorough discussion of the beneficial aspects of varying types of relationships can be found in Marc Pilisuk and Susan Hiller Parks's (1986) *The Healing Web: Social Networks and Human Survival.*
3. Berger (1993) reviews the considerable research in support of how the appraisal of another person's goals and plans provides the basis whereby an observer forms an impression of that person. Although Berger concludes that goal-plan inferences are crucial in understanding another person, I believe that analyses of the person's willfulness related to those goal-plans also is an important part of such appraisals.
4. The role of hopeful thinking between parents and children is not addressed in this chapter because it is the focus of chapter 5.
5. Snyder 1988, p. i.
6. Berger 1993.
7. This Cooledge Effect (Dewsbury 1981) is the heightened sexual arousal for a new partner.
8. Honeycutt 1993.
9. There is experimental support suggesting that men prefer women who are not available for most men to date. In particular, there is an attraction toward the selectively hard-to-get female (Walster, Walster, Piliavin & Schmidt 1973).
10. Survey research shows that, among all possible problems, those dealing with relationships are the ones most commonly reported (Veroff et al. 1981).
11. Duck 1990.
12. Filsinger & Thoma 1988.
13. Sillars, Pike, Jones & Murphy 1984.

14. Especially if you are leaving a physically or psychologically abusive relationship, almost any other relationship should prove more satisfactory. Unfortunately, however, there may be a tendency to end up in yet another abusive relationship.
15. Readers interested in the overall characteristics of effective schools should see Kyle's (1985) *Reaching for Excellence: An Effective Schools Sourcebook.*
16. Because of space constraints, I do not discuss the critical role of principals in fostering an effective school environment. Bickel (1990) gives a succinct summary of the research on this point.
17. Pines 1993.
18. Franklin 1993.
19. For a sobering first-hand discussion by teachers of the hostility and violence in schools, read Catherine Collins and Douglas Frantz's (1993) *Teachers: Talking Out of School.*
20. In a study of twenty-eight third-grade teachers, Emmer and Evertson (1981) report that effective teachers "knew what children needed to function in the classroom setting and its activities, and they proceeded to teach these 'survival' skills as part of the content at the beginning of the year" (345).
21. Martin's (1990) *Teaching through Encouragement* provides an excellent overview of focusing on the student's strengths.
22. Curwin 1992.
23. Learning is enhanced when students clearly understand the objectives of what is to be learned and how this relates to previous lessons (Winne 1985).
24. The lack of parental support is cited as one reason that underprivileged children do more poorly in school than their suburbia counterparts (McKee & Witt 1990). For helpful tips about how to involve parents in school, see chapter 9 entitled, "To Fill the Schools with Parents" in *Making Schools Better* by Larry Martz (1992).
25. See Kamphaus, Yarbrough, and Johanson (1990).
26. Brophy 1986.
27. This subgoaling was first described by the Russian writer Vygotsky (1956, as cited by Wertsch and Rogoff 1984), and more recently is discussed by Wood, Brunner, and Ross (1976).
28. Kuykendall 1992.
29. An excellent overview of how to extrapolate educational psychology research into classroom motivation can be found in Cheryl Spaulding's (1992) *Motivation in the Classroom.*
30. From Peterson's (1946, 341) *Great Teachers.*
31. Described in Richard Curwin's (1992, 36) *Rediscovering Hope: Our Greatest Teaching Strategy.*
32. Brophy 1985.
33. The classic experiment in this area was by Robert Rosenthal and Lenore Jacobson (1968); teachers were informed via test results that some students were about to undergo a cognitive-intellectual spurt (students actually were randomly assigned to groups). Results showed that relative to a control group where teachers received no test-based predictions about the students' future performance, the spurters evidenced increased superior school

performance. Although the strength of this phenomenon varies, it appears to be a consistent effect (see Rosenthal 1985). Generally, such improvement appears to be related to the fact that teachers set higher goals for their talented students; they spend more time with them and call on them more frequently (Cooper 1983; Harris & Rosenthal 1985).

34. Soar & Soar 1987.

35. Pate, McClenaghan & Rotella 1984.

36. Pate, McClenaghan & Rotella 1984; Vernacchia, McGuire & Cook 1992.

37. Yambor 1992.

38. For a thorough review of expectations for coaches, athletes, and related persons such as the media, fans, and administrators, a good source is chapter 2 of Fuoss and Troppmann's (1981) *Effective Coaching: A Psychological Approach.*

39. Anshel 1990; Orlick 1986.

40. Michener 1976, 432.

41. Roberts 1986. In addition to the stress accompanying a win orientation, this perspective rather than a performance one is associated with children giving up the sport (Burton & Martens 1986; Whitehead 1986).

42. Botterill 1978, 1980; Gould 1986; McClements & Botterill 1979.

43. Beggs 1990.

44. For a good synopsis of how coaches can keep their athletes focused, I would recommend Simons' (1992) article entitled, "Psychological Barriers of Major Competitions: Basic Issues and Interventions."

45. Anshel 1990; Pate et al. 1984.

46. See Markus and Ruvolo (1989) for a review of the positive effects of mental rehearsal on performance.

47. Reardon 1992.

48. Fuoss and Troppmann 1981, 188.

49. Peter Drucker is credited with coining the term *management by objectives* (Luthan 1985). For the earliest overviews of this approach, see Drucker's (1954) *The Practice of Management,* as well as Odiorne's (1965) *Management by Objectives,* and Reddin's (1970) *Effective Management by Objectives.*

50. For more detailed recent descriptions of MBO, see Carroll and Tosi's (1973) *Management by Objectives,* Griffin's (1987) *Management,* and Halloran's (1981) *Supervision: The Art of Management.*

51. A discussion of issues related to KISS is given by Peters and Waterman (1982, 63–67).

52. Peters & Waterman 1982.

53. For a good overview of the self-fulfilling prophecy, see Russell Jones's (1977) *Self-Fulfilling Prophecies: Social, Psychological and Physiological Effects of Expectancies.*

54. Peters & Waterman 1982, 31.

55. Autonomy of planning and decision-making increases work involvement and decreases burnout (Pines 1982).

56. I have found that high-hope people are action-oriented and move quickly from the goal and planning stages to implementation. In their interviews of managers in well-run businesses, Peters and Waterman (1982) report similar work styles.

57. For thorough reviews of the properties of monetary rewards, see Lawler (1981, 1987) and Pfeffer and Davis-Blake (1987).

58. Peters & Waterman 1982.

59. This strategy focus is discussed in chapter 6. In the psychological literature, the making of wrong strategy attributions for one's failures results in better subsequent performance and positive well-being (Snyder & Higgins 1988a; Snyder et al. 1983).

60. Moorhead & Griffin 1989.

61. Dessler 1991.

62. Gyllenhammar 1977; Roach 1977.

63. Cousins 1985, 1989; Kasteler, Kane, Olsen & Thetford 1976.

64. I believe that most malpractice suits reflect patients' unhappiness over the nature of their relationships with physicians rather than concerns with inadequate medical care.

65. Nourse 1979.

66. Cassell 1976, 1991.

67. Cassell 1976.

68. Cassell 1991.

69. Hilfiker 1985.

70. Physicians do not escape the pain, however, because as a profession they have high rates of burnout, drug addictions, and suicide. For a moving analysis of the pressures experienced by a physician, read David Hilfiker's (1985) *Healing the Wounds: A Physician Looks at His Work*.

71. Throughout medical training and afterwards, the specialists are held up as the criteria of excellence, both in their efficiency and accuracy of diagnoses. This is inherently unfair to the generalists or internal medicine practitioners who must deal with a wide range of patients, many of whom have no demonstrable disease. Furthermore, the general practitioner is expected to be knowledgeable about an ever-widening set of medical and psychological matters (Lipp 1980).

72. This traditional role enactment has, in at least two studies, resulted in greater stress and in poor treatment outcome (Lorber 1975; Taylor 1979). For a compelling analysis of the reasons patients need to become more active in their interactions with physicians, read Lawrence Horowitz's (1988) *Taking Charge of Your Medical Fate*.

73. Columnist Ellen Goodman (1993) observes that physicians have changed from a position of Dr. God to Dr. Partner, who is a collaborator in our health. She further suggests that we may be moving to another relationship-based view of physicians as Dr. Providers, who are "a purveyor, a kind of grocer of the human body." This latter move, should it happen, places a strong emphasis on the consumers and a do-it-yourself medicine where physicians, according to Goodman, would have too little power.

74. Morganthau 1993.

75. Cassell 1991.

76. For a discussion of how spending more time actually can be counterproductive, see Lipp (1980, 132–35).

77. Taken from Norman Cousins's (1989, 313–14) *Head First: The Biology of Hope and the Healing Power of the Human Spirit*. This book is an excellent source of case histories and research findings addressing the importance of

hopeful thoughts and feelings as established through the physician-patient relationship. Another good source of personal histories of dealing with illnesses, as seen from the perspective of patients, is Wendy Williams' (1990) *The Power Within: True Stories of Exceptional Patients Who Fought Back with Hope*. Likewise, psychologist Brian Stabler's (1993) article entitled, "On the Role of Patient" gives an insightful first-hand account of interactions with physicians. Lastly, Hacib Aoun's (1992) article entitled, "From the Eye of the Storm, With the Eyes of a Physician" details how the physician-patient relationship is critical for battling AIDS.

78. Such pain often is not entirely physical in origin. Studies of primary care settings, for example, suggest that at least 50 percent of patients' presenting problems have a substantial psychological component (Marsland, Wood & Mayo 1976).

79. See Cassell (1991) for a discussion of the role of suffering in the phenomenology of the individual.

80. For reviews of placebo effects, I would recommend Cousins's (1989) chapter entitled, "Belief Becomes Biology," Kirsch's (1990) chapter entitled, "The Power of Placebos," as well as Frank & Frank's (1991) chapter entitled, "The Placebo Response and the Role of Expectations in Medical and Psychological Treatment."

81. This placebo effect is not just delimited to physicians, however, and is part of the natural power that people attribute to healers in their cultures.

82. Often the cause of the pain cannot be traced, and the goal becomes linked to specific treatments (pathways) to lessen the pain.

83. Related to this point, Brown (1980) reports that while physicians in general may be rated somewhat negatively, patients rate their physicians as exceptions to the rule and accord them a more positive rating.

84. Baekeland & Lundwall 1975; DiMatteo & DiNicola 1982.

85. McGuire 1969; Zimbardo, Ebbesen & Maslach 1977.

86. See for review, DiMatteo & DiNicola 1982, 211–13.

87. For a helpful description of how to make medical decisions, read Bursztajn, Feinbloom, Hamm, and Brodsky's (1981) *Medical Choices: How Patients, Families, and Physicians Can Cope with Uncertainity*. For an analysis of the ethical issues involved in complex medical decisions, a good source is Ruth Macklin's (1987) *Mortal Choices: Bioethics in Today's World*.

88. Stone (1979) argues that one major advantage of greater participation by patients in their course of treatment is decreased resistance to complying with these regimens.

89. DiMatteo & DiNicola 1982.

90. DiNicola & DiMatteo 1982; Haynes, Taylor & Sackett 1979: Sbarbaro 1990.

91. Related to this point, people oriented toward their futures also are more likely to comply with treatments (Diamond, Weiss & Grynbaum 1968; Suchman 1967).

92. See for review, DiMatteo & DiNicola 1982, 218–20.

93. Such prompts not only increase appointment keeping (Cook, Morch & Noble 1976; Nazarian, Mechaber, Charney & Coulter 1974) but also increase compliance to medication (Lima, Nazarian, Charney & Lahti 1976). These interactions, plus those with the physician, should increase

the patient's general sense of being listened to and cared for. Additionally, when these latter characteristics are perceived by patients, appointment-keeping increases (Linn & Wilson 1980).

94. In research where patients are interviewed right after their doctor visits, as many as 60 percent did not understand the regimens that had just been given to them (Boyd, Covington, Stanaszek & Coussons 1974; Svarstad 1976).

95. Consistent with this assertion, research shows that physician's technical competence and interpersonal skills are positively related (DiMatteo & DiNicola 1981, 1982; Ware, Davies-Avery & Stewart 1978).

96. Cassell 1991, 76–77.

97. See for reviews Cousins (1989); Siegel (1986); Snyder et al. (1991); and Temoshok and Drehler (1992).

98. Buchholz 1988, 69.

99. The other side of this question is not asked, however. That is to say, isn't the physician giving false despair when emphasizing the negative probabilities associated with the diagnosis? In this regard, see Buchholz (1988) for the conclusion of an enlightening interchange between two physicians.

100. In Norman Cousins's (1989) *Head First: The Biology of Hope and the Healing Power of the Human Spirit,* he also notes that critics have assailed his ideas as creating false hope and guilt. He writes: "My own experiences in dealing with patients may or may not be representative; but in the past ten years I have met with many hundreds of patients involved in a life-or-death struggle, and I have not encountered anyone who felt guilty because hope and a strong will to live were not enough to pull him back from the brink. The key question was whether anything was being missed that might have made a difference in the outcome. A sense of defeat is more readily connected to failure to obtain the best in medical care than to feelings of guilt because hopes were not enough to carry one through" (105).

101. For a discussion of doctor/patient communication, as well as the concept of mutuality, read Roter and Hall's (1992) *Doctors Talking with Patients/Patients Talking with Doctors: Improving Communication and Medical Visits.* DiMatteo and DiNicola (1982, 251 ff.) argue that because of the ethical duties related to their role, physicians carry the major responsibility for engendering hope-related thoughts in patients.

102. Freidson 1970, 263.

103. DiMatteo and DiNicola 1982.

104. For discussions of how the relationship is an important commonality over differing therapies, see Gelso and Carter (1985); Lambert, Shapiro, and Bergin (1986); Orlinsky and Howard (1986); and Strupp (1973). For a detailed description of how relationship factors operate in psychoanalytic, humanistic/existential, behavior and cognitive-behavioral, and systems therapy, read Derlaga, Hendrick, Winstead, and Berg's (1991, 7–19) *Psychotherapy as a Personal Relationship.* For a discussion of the therapist-client relationship across twelve differing therapeutic approaches, read Corsini and Wedding's (1989) *Current Psychotherapies.*

105. In Frank and Frank, *Persuasion & Healing: A Comparative Study of Psychotherapy,* 1991, p. xv. Similar to the notion of therapeutic alliance, which has its roots in the psychoanalytic tradition (Greenson 1967; Zetzel

1956), other cognitive therapy writers have spoken of the therapeutic relationship in terms of collaborative empiricism (Bedrosian & Beck 1980;
Golden & Dryden 1986; Liotti 1993; Safran & Segal 1990). For early and
classic books on the interpersonal perspective of psychotherapy, see Harry
Stack Sullivan's *The Interpersonal Theory of Psychiatry* (1953), *The Psychiatric Interview* (1954), and *Clinical Studies in Psychiatry* (1956).

106. In advancing this argument, I am suggesting that there is more to the
beneficial effects of psychotherapy than just the relationship. Early writers such as Fiedler (1950a, 1950b) and Schofield (1964) argued for the
curative effects of the relationship per se, although subsequent empirical
evidence does not support this simplistic perspective (Reisman 1986).

107. Negative events in the lives of people, including those for which they do
not have the resources to achieve their normal goals, are triggers for seeking help (Brown 1978; Goodman, Sewell & Jampol 1984; Lewinsohn,
Hoberman, Teri & Hautzinger 1985; Norcross & Prochaska 1986).
Although such negative experiences definitely serve as a trigger, the
majority of people experiencing such distress do not get professional help.
For example, one study showed that among those people who are distressed by events in their lives, 73 percent did not go for professional psychotherapeutic help (Neugebauer, Dohrenwend & Dohrenwend 1980).

108. Brickman, Rabinowitz, Karuza, Coates, Cohn & Kidder (1982) develop
a similar argument that persons are motivated to seek help if they perceive the causes of their problems as being beyond their control and the
solutions as being within their control.

109. This conclusion obviously does not include those who are coerced into
therapy because of the legal system or friends. Additionally, in the more
advanced stages of the death of hope, because of real or imagined blockages, there is profound hopelessness. Such people often do not get to the
services of mental health professionals.

110. In regard to age, there is a strong trend for older people to be less likely
to seek psychological treatment (Brown 1978; Veroff et al. 1981). Wills
and DePaulo (1991) report that earlier research shows marked effects
such that higher socioeconomic and educated persons are more likely to
seek psychological treatment, but these effects have been moderated with
recent greater access to services.

111. Frank and Frank 1991, 2.

112. Derlaga et al. 1991. Within clinical psychology for the last several years,
there have been more female than male graduates. In the near future,
therefore, clinical psychology will have a majority of female therapists.

113. I do not mean to suggest that effective outcomes for psychological difficulties are limited to those who see professional psychotherapists.
Although it might be assumed that the amount of professional training
should produce therapists who are more effective in their relationships
with clients, research has shown that paraprofessionals and lay helpers are
equally effective. For example, Durlak (1979) reviewed forty-two studies
and found that professionals (psychologists, clinical social workers, and
psychiatrists) produced client outcomes that were similar to those of
paraprofessionals (medical personnel, psychiatric aides, untrained college
students, and lay adults). Although these results have been challenged

(see Nietzel & Fisher 1981), the general finding appears to hold (see Durlak 1981). In my estimation, the underlying reason for the efficacy of therapeutic interactions, whatever the level of training for the therapist, relates to their underlying emphasis on hopeful thinking.

114. The exception to this still occurs with classically trained psychoanalysts, who typically avoid answering questions about themselves.

115. Smith, Glass & Miller 1980. This study collapsed across 475 controlled studies of psychotherapy, using 1,766 outcome measures. A variety of therapeutic approaches were included, and the average therapist had 3.25 years of experience; across the various psychotherapy approaches, the average client received sixteen hours of treatment.

116. A review is given in Lambert et al.'s (1986) chapter entitled, "The Effectiveness of Psychotherapy." Further, a recent thorough overview of the effectiveness of psychotherapy can be obtained in Lipsey and Wilson's (1993) article entitled, "The Efficacy of Psychological, Educational, and Behavioral Treatments: Confirmation from Meta-Analysis."

117. Generally, the type of therapy makes little difference in outcome (Luborsky, Singer & Luborsky 1975; Smith & Glass 1977; Smith et al. 1980). At least one exception to this conclusion has been reported, such that cognitive and behavioral approaches designed specifically for phobias have been superior to more humanistic approaches (Shapiro & Shapiro 1987). Assuming that the therapy approaches share similar treatment foci, however, they are equally efficacious (Frank & Frank 1991).

118. The most noted advocate of this common factors approach has been Jerome Frank, and in this regard I would recommend Frank, Hoehn-Saric, Imber, Liberman, and Stone's (1978) *Effective Ingredients of Successful Psychotherapy*, and the 3rd. edition of Frank and Frank's (1991) *Persuasion & Healing: A Comparative Study of Psychotherapy*.

119. It is instructive to examine psychotherapy outcome studies in the context of hope theory. In this regard, there have been many studies where clients receive a placebo treatment in which they are led to expect improvement, but are not given any specific treatments. In essence, such people receive a boost in their willpower thinking about reaching their various distress-relieving goals (e.g., "You will improve" or "You can get better"), but they do not receive any specific therapeutic treatments (often called techniques) for reaching the goals. Research shows that this increase in willful thinking results in improved outcomes in comparison to people who receive no feedback at all (i.e., people on a waiting list who will be seen later) (Barker, Funk & Houston 1988). Additionally, in studies where people have been given specific psychotherapy treatments (analogous to waypower thinking) along with willpower thinking, the improvements in outcomes are twice those experienced by persons receiving only the boosts in willpower thinking (Barker, Funk & Houston 1988; see also Landman and Dawes 1982; Prioleau, Murdock, and Brody 1983; Shapiro and Shapiro 1982; and, Smith and Glass 1977). Therefore, when it comes to psychological functioning, willful thinking is beneficial, but the addition of waypower thinking doubles this improvement. Remember that these results were derived across many differing psychotherapy approaches. My point is that these varying psy-

chotherapies all "help clients build their sense of personal efficacy (willpower) and arsenal of strategies (waypower) for coping with problems" (Snyder et al. 1991, 299).

120. Wills 1982.

121. For recommendations regarding psychotherapists, call your local health department or look under "Mental Health" in the Yellow Pages. You also can call the American Self-Help Clearinghouse at (201) 625–7101; or for depression the National Institute for Mental Health call (800) 421–4211.

122. For a review of the importance of developing trust in the early stages of therapy, see Strong's (1991) chapter entitled, "Social Influence and Change in Therapeutic Relationships."

123. Strupp, Fox & Lessler 1969.

124. This result holds whether the client is rating the quality of the therapist in establishing such trusting relationships (Gurman 1977; Lambert, DeJulio & Stein 1978), or this rating is made by outside observers (Truax & Mitchell 1971). Likewise, the importance of such liking and trust variables also has been found in behavior therapies, where the relationship is not thought to be the critical factor in comparison to the procedures themselves (Morris & Suckerman 1974a, 1974b; Ryan & Gizynski 1971; Sloane, Staples, Cristol, Yorkston & Whipple 1975).

125. Fehrenbach & O'Leary 1982; Garfield & Affleck 1961; Parsons & Parker 1968; Wallach & Strupp 1960.

126. Baekeland & Lundwall 1975; Rosenzweig & Folman 1974.

127. Ford 1978; Strupp & Hadley 1979.

128. Liotti 1993, 243.

129. Hilfiker 1985; Pines 1982.

130. Snyder, Ingram & Newburg 1982.

131. Three excellent review chapters of the processes involved in psychological diagnosis are Salovey and Turk's (1991) "Clinical Judgment and Decision Making," Kiesler's (1991) "Interpersonal Methods of Assessment and Diagnosis," and Wright's (1991) "Labeling: The Need for Greater Person-Environment Individuation."

132. The behavioral and cognitive-behavior therapeutic approaches to treatment explicitly make goal-setting part of the early stage of treatment, but more dynamic and existential approaches implicitly use goals as guideposts for subsequent treatment.

133. One particularly promising measurement approach to therapist and client perceptions of the alliance is Horvath and Greenberg's (1986) Working Alliance Inventory. This inventory measures agreement in three areas: goals; interventions that are relevant and reasonable; and, the mutual bond (i.e., trust, liking, caring, etc.). All three of these alliance indices have been shown to relate to more positive treatment outcomes (Horvath & Greenberg 1986).

134. For related discussion, see Imber, Pande, Frank, Hoehn-Saric, Stone, and Wargo (1970) and Wilkins (1979).

135. Hans Strupp (1980a, 1980b, 1980c, 1980d) provides several case histories making this point. He also shows how a nonprofessional therapist tends to let the discussion wander and does not keep the client focused on treatment goals (Strupp 1980c).

136. Bandura 1969.
137. Across several different types of therapy, clients' perceptions of their therapists often are captured by a factor that may be termed *good person*. That is to say, therapists are characterized as competent and generally admirable people (LaCrosse 1977; Strupp et al. 1969).
138. For a review of research supporting this conclusion, see Murdock and Altmaier (1991).

REFERENCES

Aalberg, V., and K. Hamalainen. (1976). On the suicide behavior of young adults: A study of 4,965 Finnish conscripts. *Suicide Research Psychiatria Fennica* 7: 169–77.

Abramowitz, S., L. Weitz, J. Schwartz, S. Amira, B. Gomes, and C. Abramowitz. (1975). Comparative counselor inferences toward women with medical school aspirations. *Journal of College Student Personnel 16*: 126–30.

Achenbach, T. M. (1991). *Manual for the Child Behavior Checklist and Revised Child Behavior Profile*. Burlington, Vt.: University Associates in Psychiatry.

Achenbach, T. M., and C. Edelbrook. (1983). *Manual for the Child Behavior Checklist and Revised Child Behavior Profile*. Burlington, VT: University Associates in Psychiatry.

Ackerman, N. W. (1959). *The psychodynamics of family life*. New York: Basic Books.

Adler, A. (1964). Individual psychology, its assumptions and its results. In *Varieties of personality theory*, ed. H. M. Ruitenbeek. New York: Dutton & Co.

Ainsworth, M. D. S. (1973). The development of infant-mother attachment. In *Review of child development: Vol. 3. Child development and social policy*, ed. B. M. Caldwell and H. N. Ricciuti. Chicago: University of Chicago Press.

Ainsworth, M. D. S., and S. M. Bell. (1974). Mother-infant interaction and the development of competence. In *The growth of competence*, ed. K. Connolly and J. Bruner, London: Academic Press.

Ajzen, I., and M. Fishbein. (1980). *Understanding attitudes and predicting social behavior*. Englewood Cliffs, N.J.: Prentice Hall.

American Association for Protecting Children. (1986). *Highlights of official child neglect and abuse reporting 1985*. Denver, Colo.: American Humane Association.

American College of Sports Medicine. (1978). The recommended quantity and quality of exercise for developing and maintaining fitness in healthy adults. *Medicine and Science in Sports 10*: vii–x.

American Humane Association. (1984). *Trends in child abuse and neglect: A national perspective*. Denver, Colo.: American Humane Association.

American Lung Association. (1986). *Freedom from smoking in 20 days*. New York: American Lung Association.

American Psychiatric Association. (1987). *Diagnostic and statistical manual of mental disorders. 3rd. ed.* Washington, D.C.: American Psychiatric Association.

Ames, C. (1984). Achievement attributions and self-instructions under competitive and individualistic goal structures. *Journal of Educational Psychology 76*: 478–87.

Ames, C., R. Ames, and D. W. Felker. (1977). Effects of competitive reward structure and valence of outcome on children's achievement attributions. *Journal of Educational Psychology 69*: 1–8.

Anastasiow, N. J. (1988). Should parenting education be mandatory? *Topics in Early Special Education 8*: 60–72.

Anderson, J. R. (1983). *The architecture of cognition.* Cambridge, Mass.: Harvard University Press.

Anderson, J. R. (1988). The role of hope in appraisal, goal-setting, expectancy, and coping. Ph.D. diss., University of Kansas, Lawrence.

———. (1992, August). Fostering hope: A report from frontline AIDS health care providers. Paper presented at the American Psychological Association, Washington, D.C.

Annis, R. C., and B. Corenblum. (1987). Effect of test language and experimenter race in Canadian Indian children's racial and self-identity. *Journal of Social Psychology 126*: 761–73.

Ansbacher, H. L., and R. R. Ansbacher. (1956). *The individual psychology of Alfred Adler.* New York: Basic Books.

Anshel, M. H. (1990). *Sport psychology: From theory to practice.* Scottsdale, Ariz.: Gorsuch Scarisbrick.

Aoun, H. (1992). From the eye of the storm, with the eyes of a physician. *Annals of Internal Medicine 116*: 335–38.

Aragona, J. A., and S. M. Eyberg. (1981). Neglected children: Mothers' report of child behavior problems and observed verbal behavior. *Child Development 52*: 596–602.

Arieti, S., and J. Arieti, (1978). *Severe and mild depression: The psychotherapeutic approach.* New York: Basic Books.

Asarnow, J. R., G. A. Carlson, and D. Guthrie. (1987). Coping strategies, self-perceptions, hopelessness and perceived family environments in depressed and suicidal children. *Journal of Consulting and Clinical Psychology 55*: 361–66.

Asarnow, J. R., and D. Guthrie. (1989). Suicidal behavior, depression, and hopelessness in child psychiatric inpatients: A replication and extension. *Journal of Clinical Child Psychology 18*: 129–36.

Atkinson, J. W. (1957). Motivational determinants of risk-taking behavior. *Psychological Review 64*: 359–72.

———. (1958). Thematic apperceptive measurement of motives within a context of motivation. In *Motives in fantasy, action, and society,* ed. J. W. Atkinson. Princeton, N.J.: Van Nostrand.

———. (1964). *An introduction to motivation.* Princeton, N.J.: Van Nostrand.

Averill, J. R., G. Catlin, and K. K. Chon. (1990). *Rules of hope.* New York: Springer-Verlag.

Babyak, M. A., C. R. Snyder, and L. Yoshinobu. (1993). Psychometric properties of the Hope Scale: A confirmatory factor analysis. *Journal of Research in Personality 27*: 154–69.

Bachman, J. G., L. D. Johnston, and P. M. O'Malley. (1987). *Monitoring the future: Questionnaire responses from the nation's high school seniors: 1986.* Ann Arbor, Mich.: Institute for Social Research, University of Michigan.

Baekeland, F., and L. Lundwall. (1975). Dropping out of treatment: A critical review. *Psychological Bulletin 82*: 738–83.

Balck, F. B., and C. C. Reimer. (1985). Suicide and partnership. In *Psychiatry: The state of the art, Vol. 1*, ed. P. Pichot, P. Berner, R. Wolf, and K. Thau. New York: Plenum.

Bandura, A. (1969). *Principles of behavior modification.* New York: Holt, Rinehart, and Winston.

——. (1971). Psychotherapy based upon modeling principles. In *Handbook of psychotherapy and behavior change: An empirical analysis*, ed. A. E. Bergin and S. L. Garfield. New York: Wiley.

——. (1977). Self-efficacy: Toward a unifying theory of behavior change. *Psychological Review 84*: 191–215.

——. (1982). Self-efficacy mechanism in human agency. *American Psychologist 37*: 122–47.

——. (1986). *Social foundations of thought and action: A social cognitive theory.* Englewood Cliffs, N.J.: Prentice Hall.

——. (1989). Human agency in social cognitive theory. *American Psychologist 44*: 1175–84.

——. (1989). Self-regulation of motivation and action through internal standards and goal systems. In *Goal concepts in personality and social psychology*, ed. L. A. Pervin. Hillsdale, N.J.: Erlbaum.

Bandura, A., and B. Perloff, (1967). Relative efficacy of self-administered and externally imposed reinforcement systems. *Journal of Personality and Social Psychology 7*: 111–16.

Barker, R., T. Dembo, and K. Lewin. (1941). Frustration and regression: An experiment with young children. *University of Iowa Studies in Child Welfare 18*: No. 1.

Barker, R. G., and H. F. Wright. (1951). *One boy's day: A specimen record of behavior.* New York: Harper.

——. (1955). *Midwest and its children.* New York: Harper & Row.

Barker, S. L., S. C. Funk, and B. K. Houston. (1988). Psychological treatment versus nonspecific factors: A meta-analysis of conditions that engender comparable expectations for improvement. *Clinical Psychology Review 8*: 579–94.

Barnum, D. D. (1993). Long-term psychosocial adjustment of adolescents with childhood burns. Master's thesis, University of Kansas, Lawrence.

Baron, R. M., D. G. Mandel, C. A. Adams, and L. M. Griffen, (1976). Effects of social density in university residential environments. *Journal of Personality and Social Psychology 34*: 434–46.

Baron, R. M., and J. Rodin. (1978). Perceived control and crowding stress: Processes mediating the impact of spatial and social density. In *Human response to crowding*, ed. A. Baum and Y. Epstein. Hillsdale, N.J.: Erlbaum.

Barraclough, B. M. (1985). Physical illness preceding suicide. In *Psychiatry: The state of the art, Vol. 1*, ed. P. Pichet, P. Berner, R. Wolf, and K. Thau. New York: Plenum.

Barrera, M. E., and D. Maurer. (1981a). The perception of facial expressions by the three-month-old. *Child Development 52*: 203–6.

———. (1981b). Discrimination of strangers by the three-month-old. *Child Development 52*: 558–63.

Bash, M. S., and B. Camp. (1985). *Think aloud: Increasing social and cognitive skills — A problem-solving program for children*. Champaign, Ill.: Research Press.

Bates, E., I. Bretherton, and L. Snyder. (1988). *From first words to grammar*. Cambridge: Cambridge University Press.

Bates, E., L. Camaioni, and V. Volterra. (1975). The acquisition of performances prior to speech. *Merrill Palmer Quarterly 21*: 205–26.

Baumgardner, A. H., P. P. Heppner, and R. M. Arkin. (1986). Role of causal attribution in personal problem solving. *Journal of Personality and Social Psychology 50*: 636–43.

Baumrind, D. (1968). Authoritarian versus authoritative control. *Adolescence 3*: 255–72.

———. (1973). The development of instrumental competence through socialization. In *Minnesota symposia on child psychology, Vol. 7*, ed. A. D. Pick. Minneapolis: University of Minnesota Press.

———. (1975a). Early socialization and adolescent competence. In *Adolescence in the life cycle: Psychological change and social context*, ed. S. E. Dragastin and G. H. Elder. New York: Wiley.

———. (1975b). *Early socialization and the discipline controversy*. Morristown, N.J.: General Learning Press.

———. (1980). New directions in socialization research. *American Psychologist 35*: 639–52.

Beck, A. T., G. Brown, R. J. Berchick, B. L. Stewart, and R. A. Steer. (1990). Relationship between hopelessness and ultimate suicide: A replication with psychiatric outpatients. *American Journal of Psychiatry 147*: 190–95.

Beck, A. T., M. Kovacs, and A. Weissman. (1975). Hopelessness and suicidal behavior: An overview. *Journal of the American Medical Association 234*: 1146–49.

Beck, A. T., A. J. Rush, B. F. Shaw, and G. Emery. (1979). *Cognitive therapy of depression*. New York: Guilford.

Beck, A. T., and R. A. Steer. (1989). Clinical predictors of eventual suicide: A five-to ten-year study of suicide attempters. *Journal of Affective Disorders 17*: 203–9.

Beck, A. T., R. A. Steer, M. Kovacs, and B. Garrison. (1985). Hopelessness and eventual suicide: A ten-year prospective study of patients hospitalized with suicidal ideation. *American Journal of Psychiatry 142*: 559–63.

Beck, A. T., R. A. Steer, and M. G. McElroy. (1982). Relationship of hopelessness, depression and previous suicide attempts to suicidal ideation in alcoholics. *Journal of Studies on Alcohol 43*: 1042–46.

Beck, A. T., C. H. Ward, M. Mendelsohn, J. Mock, and J. Erbaugh. (1961). An inventory for measuring depression. *Archives of General Psychiatry 4*: 53–63.

Beck, A. T., and M. E. Weishaar. (1989). Cognitive therapy. In *Current psychotherapies (4th. ed.)*, ed. R. J. Corsini and D. Wedding. Itasca, Ill.: Peacock Publishing.

Beck, A. T., A. Weissman, D. Lester, and L. Trexler. (1974). The measurement of pessimism: The Hopelessness Scale. *Journal of Consulting and Clinical Psychology 42*: 861–65.

Bedrosian, R. C., and A. T. Beck. (1979). Cognitive aspects of suicidal behavior. *Suicide and Life Threatening Behavior 9*: 87–96.

———. (1980). Principles of cognitive therapy. In *Psychotherapy process*, ed. M. J. Mahoney. New York: Plenum.

Beggs, W. D. A. (1990). Goal setting in sport. In *Stress and performance in sport*, ed. J. G. Jones & L. Hardy. Chichester, England: Wiley.

Belle, D., ed. (1989). *Children's social networks and social supports*. New York: Wiley.

Belsky, J., M. K. Goode, and R. K. Most. (1980). Maternal stimulation and infant exploratory competence: Cross-sectional, correlational, and experimental analyses. *Child Development 51*: 1163–78.

Belsky, J., R. M. Lerner, and G. B. Spanier. (1984). *The child in the family*. Reading, Mass.: Addison-Wesley.

Belsky, J., M. Rovine, and D. G. Taylor. (1984). The Pennsylvania Development Project, III: The origins of individual differences in infant-mother attachment: Maternal and infant contributions. *Child Development 55*: 719–28.

Bem, S. L. (1981). Gender schema theory: A cognitive account of sex-typing. *Psychological Review 88*: 354–64.

Bereiter, C., and V. Anderson. (1983). *Willy the wisher and other thinking stories: An Open Court thinking story book*. LaSalle, Ill.: Open Court.

Berger, C.R. (1993). Goals, plans, and mutual understandings in relationships. In *Individual and relationships. Vol. 1*, ed. S. Duck. Newbury Park, Calif.: Sage.

Berglas, S., and R. F. Baumeister. (1993). *Your own worst enemy: Understanding the paradox of self-defeating behavior*. New York: Basic Books.

Berglas, S., and E. E. Jones. (1978). Drug choice as a self-handicapping strategy in response to noncontingent success. *Journal of Personality and Social Psychology 36*: 405–17.

Berkowitz, L. (1962). *Aggression: A social psychological analysis*. New York: McGraw-Hill.

Berliner, L. (1991). Clinical work with sexually abused children. In *Clinical approaches: Sex offenders and their victims*, ed. C. Hollin & K. Howells. New York: Wiley.

Berman, C. (1991). *Adult children of divorce speak out*. New York: Simon & Schuster.

Berry, W. (1991) Out of your car, off you horse. *The Atlantic Monthly*, February, *267*: 61–63.

Beuf, A. H. (1977). *Red children in white America*. Philadelphia: University of Pennsylvania Press.

Bickel, W. E. (1990). The effective schools literature: Implications for research and practice. In *The handbook of school psychology. 2nd. ed.*, ed. T. B. Gutkin and C. R. Reynolds. New York: Wiley.

Billings, A. G., and R. H. Moos. (1984). Coping, stress, and social resources among adults with unipolar depression. *Journal of Personality and Social Psychology 46*: 877–91.

Block, J. H. (1973). Conceptions of sex-role: Some cross-cultural and longitudinal perspectives. *American Psychologist 28*: 512–26,

Bloom, B., S. J. Asher, and S. W. White. (1978). Marital disruption as a stressor: A review and analysis. *Psychological Bulletin 85*: 867–94.

Blumenthal, J. A., C. F. Emery, D. J. Madden, L. K. George, R. E. Coleman, M. W. Riddle, D. C. McKee, J. Reasoner, and R. S. Williams. (1989). Cardiovascular and behavioral effects of aerobic exercise training in healthy older men and women. *Journal of Gerontology 44*: 147–57.

Bonnar, J. W., and R. K. McGee. (1977). Suicidal behavior as a form of communication in married couples. *Suicide and Life-Threatening Behavior 7*: 7–16.

Bonner, B. L., K. L. Kaufman, C. Harbeck, and M. R. Brassard. (1992). Child maltreatment. In *Handbook of clinical child psychology*, ed. C. E. Walker and M. C. Roberts. New York: Wiley.

Borders, T. (1993). Validation of the State Hope Scale. Honors thesis, University of Kansas, Lawrence.

Borkovec, T. D., L. Wilkinson, R. Folensbee, and C. Lerman, (1983). Stimulus control applications to the treatment of worry. *Behavioral Research and Therapy 21*: 247–51.

Botterill, C. (1978). The psychology of coaching. *Coaching Review 1*: 1–8.

———. (1980). Psychology of coaching. In *Psychology in sports: Methods and applications*, ed. R. M. Suinn. Minneapolis: Burgess.

Bowlby, J. (1969). *Attachment and loss, Vol. 1*. New York: Basic Books.

———. (1973). *Attachment and loss, Vol. 2: Separation*. New York: Basic Books.

———. (1980). *Attachment and loss, Vol. 3: Loss, sadness, and depression*. New York: Basic Books.

Boyd, J. R., T. R. Covington, W. F. Stanaszek, and R. T. Coussons. (1974). Drug defaulting. II. Analysis of noncompliance patterns. *American Journal of Hospital Pharmacy 31*: 485–91.

Brehm, J. W. (1966). *A theory of psychological reactance*. New York: Academic Press.

Brehm, J. W., R. A. Wright, S. Solomon, L. Silka, and J. Greenberg. (1983). Perceived difficulty, energization, and the magnitude of goal valence. *Journal of Experimental Social Psychology 19*: 21–48.

Brehm, S. S. (1976). *The application of social psychology to clinical practice*. Washington, D.C.: Hemisphere.

———. (1987). Coping after a relationship ends. In *Coping with negative life events: Clinical and social psychological perspectives*, ed. C. R. Snyder and C. E. Ford. New York: Plenum.

———. (1992). *Intimate relationships*. 2nd. ed. New York: McGraw-Hill.

Brehm, S. S., and J. W. Brehm. (1981). *Psychological reactance: A theory of freedom and control.* New York: Academic Press.

Brehm, S. S., and D. A. McCallister. (1980). A social psychological perspective on the maintenance of therapeutic change. In *Improving the long-term effects of psychotherapy,* ed. P. Karoly and J. J. Steffen. New York: Gardner Press.

Brenner, M. H. (1976). *Estimating the social costs of national economic policy: Implications for mental and physical health, and criminal violence.* Report prepared for the Joint Economic Committee of Congress. Washington, D.C.: U.S. Government Printing Office.

Brent, D., D. Kolko, C. Goldstein, M. Allan, and R. Brown. (1989, October). Cognitive distortion, familial stress, and suicidology in adolescent inpatients. Poster presented at the American Academy of Adolescent Psychiatry Annual Meeting, New York.

Bretherton, I., and M. Beeghly. (1982). Talking about internal states: The acquisition of an explicit theory of mind. *Developmental Psychology 18*: 906–21.

Bretherton, I., S. McNew, and M. Beeghly-Smith. (1981). Early person knowledge as expressed in gestural and verbal communication: When do infants acquire a "theory of mind"? In *Infant social cognition,* ed. M. E. Lamb and L. R. Sherrod. Hillsdale, N.J.: Erlbaum.

Bretherton, I., and E. Waters, eds. (1985). Growing points of attachment theory and research. *Monographs for the Society for Research in Child Development 50*: Serial 209, numbers 1–2.

Brickman, P., V. C. Rabinowitz, J. Karuza, Jr., D. Coates, E. Cohn, and L. Kidder. (1982). Models of helping and coping. *American Psychologist 37*: 368–84.

Brim, G. (1992). *Ambition: How we manage success and failure throughout our lives.* New York: Basic Books.

Brophy, J. (1985). Teacher-student interaction. In *Teacher expectancies,* ed. J. B. Dusek. Hillsdale, N.J.: Erlbaum.

———. (1986). Teacher influences on student achievement. *American Psychologist 41*: 1069–77.

Brown, B. B. (1978). Social and psychological correlates of help-seeking behavior among urban adults. *American Journal of Community Psychology 6*: 425–39.

Brown, G. W., and T. Harris. (1978). *Social origins of depression: A study of psychiatric disorders in women.* New York: Free Press.

Brown, G. W., T. O. Harris, and A. Bifulco. (1986). The long-term effects of early loss of parent. In *Depression in young people,* ed. M. Rutter, C. E. Izard, and P. B. Read. New York: Guilford Press.

Brown, R. (1973). *A first language: The early stages.* Cambridge: Harvard University Press.

Brown, S. W. (1980). Consumer attitudes toward physicians and health care. *Arizona Medicine 37*: 33–36.

Brownell, K. D. (1990). *The learn program for weight control.* Dallas: Brownell & Hager.

Bruce, B., and D. Newman. (1978). Interacting plans. *Cognitive Science 2*: 195–233.

Brunstein, J. C. (1993). Personal goals and subjective well-being: A longitudinal study. *Journal of Personality and Social Psychology 65*: 1061–70.

Bryan, J. F., and E. A. Locke. (1967). Goal-setting as a means of increasing motivation. *Journal of Applied Psychology 51*: 274–77.

Bryer, J. B., B. A. Nelson, J. B. Miller, and P. A. Krol. (1987). Childhood sexual and physical abuse as factors in adult psychiatric illness. *American Journal of Psychiatry 144*: 1426–30.

Buchholz, W. M. (1988). The medical uses of hope. *Western Journal of Medicine 148*: 69.

Bullock, M., ed. (1991). *The development of intentional action: Cognitive, motivational, and interactive processes.* Basel, Switzerland: Krager.

Burger, J. M., and H. M. Cooper. (1979). The desirability of control. *Motivation and Emotion 3*: 381–93.

Bursztajn, H., R. I. Feinbloom, R. M. Hamm, and A. Brodsky. (1981). *Medical choices, medical chances: How patients, families, and physicians can cope with uncertainty.* New York: Delacorte Press/Seymour Lawrence.

Burton, D., and R. Martens. (1986). Pinned by their own goals: An exploratory investigation into why kids drop out of wrestling. *Journal of Sport Psychology 8*: 183–87.

Buss, A. (1961). *The psychology of aggression.* New York: Wiley.

Byrnes, J. P., and S. A. Gelman, eds. (1991). *Perspectives on language and cognition: Interrelations in development.* Cambridge: Cambridge University Press.

Calvert, S. C., and R. J. McMahon. (1987). The treatment acceptability of a behavioral parent training program and its components. *Behavior Therapy 18*: 165–79.

Camara, K. A., and G. Resnick. (1989). Styles of conflict resolution and cooperation between divorced parents: Effects on child behavior and adjustment. *Journal of Orthopsychiatry 59*: 560–75.

Cantor, N., and C. A. Langston. (1989). Ups and downs of life tasks in a life transition. In *Goal concepts in personality and social psychology*, ed. L. A. Pervin. Hillsdale, N.J.: Erlbaum.

Cantril, H. (1964). The human design. *Journal of Individual Psychology 20*: 129–36.

Carbonell, J. (1981). Counterplanning: A strategy-based model of adversary planning in real-world situations. *Artificial Intelligence 16*: 295–329.

Carey, S. (1978). The child as word learner. In *Linguistic theory and psychological reality.* ed. M. Halle, J. Bresman, and G. A. Miller. Cambridge: MIT Press.

Carey, W. B. (1986). The difficult child. *Pediatrics in Review 8*: 39–45.

Carroll, S. J., and H. L. Tosi. (1973). *Management by objectives.* New York: Macmillan.

Carter, R. T. (1991). Cultural values: A review of empirical research and implications for counseling. *Journal of Counseling and Development 70*: 164–73.

Case, R. (1991). *The mind's staircase.* Hillsdale, N.J.: Erlbaum.

———. (1992). The role of the frontal lobes in regulation of cognitive development. *Brain and Cognition 20(1)*: 51–73.

Casey, R. J., and J. S. Berman. (1985). The outcome of psychotherapy with children. *Psychological Bulletin 98*: 388–400.

Caspi, A. (1987). Personality in the life course. *Journal of Personality and Social Psychology 53*: 1203–13.

Cassell, E. J. (1976). *The healer's art: A new approach to the doctor-patient relationship*. Philadelphia: Lippincott.

———. (1991). *The nature of suffering*. New York: Oxford University Press.

Catalano, R. A., D. Dooley, and R. L. Jackson. (1985). Economic antecedents of help-seeking: Reformulation of time-series tests. *Journal of Health and Social Behavior 26*: 141–52.

Cauce, A. M., M. Reid, S. Landesman, and N. Gonzales, (1990). Social support in young children: Measurement, structure, and behavioral impact. In *Social support: An interactional view*, ed. B. R. Sarason, I. G. Sarason, and G. R. Price. New York: Wiley.

Centers for Disease Control. (1989). *Surgeon General's report on smoking: Reducing health consequences of smoking: 25 years of progress, 1964–1989*. Washington, D.C.: U.S. Government Printing Office.

Chall, J. (1983). *Stages of reading development*. New York: McGraw-Hill.

Chall, J., V. A. Jacobs, and L. E. Baldwin. (1990). *The reading crisis: Why poor children fall behind*. Cambridge: Harvard University Press.

Chiriboga, D. A., L. S. Catron, and Associates. (1991). *Divorce: Crisis, challenge, or relief*. New York: New York University Press.

Christensen, K. C., and T. M. Magoon. (1974). Perceived hierarchy of help-giving sources for two categories of student problems. *Journal of Counseling Psychology 21*: 311–24.

Cicchetti, D. (In press). Attachment and developmental psychopathology. In *Rochester Symposium on Developmental Psychopathology, Vol. 2*, ed. D. Cicchetti. Hillsdale, N.J.: Erlbaum.

Claerhout, S., J. Elder, and C. Janes. (1982). Problem-solving skill of rural battered women. *American Journal of Community Psychology 10*: 605–12.

Clance, P. R. (1985). *The impostor phenomenon: Overcoming the fear that haunts your success*. Atlanta: Peachtree.

Clark, H. H., and E. V. Clark. (1977). *Psychology and language*. New York: Harcourt, Brace, Jovanovich.

Clark, K., and M. Clark. (1939). The development of consciousness of self and the emergence of racial identity in Negro pre-school schoolchildren. *Journal of Social Psychology 10*: 591–99.

Clark, R. M. (1983). *Family life and school achievement: Why poor Black children succeed or fail*. Chicago: University of Chicago Press.

Clayton. P. (1975). The effects of living alone on bereavement symptoms. *American Journal of Psychiatry 132*: 133–37.

Cohen, S., R. J. Mermelstein, T. Kamarck, and H. M. Hoberman. (1985). Measuring the functional components of social support. In *Social support: Theory, research, and applications*, ed. I. G. Sarason and B. R. Sarason. Dordrecht, Netherlands: Martinus Nijhoff.

Cohen, S., and T. A. Wills. (1985). Stress, social support, and the buffering hypothesis. *Psychological Bulletin 98*: 310–57.

Cohn, J. F., and E. L. Tronik. (1983). Three-month-old infants' reactions to simulated maternal depression. *Child Development 54*: 185–93.

Cole, D. A. (1989). Psychopathology of adolescent suicide: Hopelessness, coping beliefs, and depression. *Journal of Abnormal Psychology 98*: 248–55.

Cole, M. (1990). Cognitive development and formal schooling. In *Vygotsky and education: Instructional implications and applications of sociohistorical psychology*, ed. L. C. Moll. Cambridge: Cambridge University Press.

Coleridge, E. H., ed. (1912). *The complete works of Samuel Taylor Coleridge. Vol. 1.* Oxford, England: Clarendon.

Collins, C., and D. Frantz. (1993). *Teachers: Talking out of school.* Boston: Little, Brown.

Cook, A. S., and D. S. Dworkin. (1992). *Helping the bereaved: Therapeutic interventions for children, adolescents, and adults.* New York: Basic Books.

Cook, D., J. Morch, and E. Noble. (1976). Improving attendance at follow-up clinics. *Dimensions in Health Services 53*: 46–49.

Cook, T. D., F. Crosby, and K. M. Hennigan. (1977). The construct of relative deprivation. In *Social comparison processes: Theoretical and empirical perspectives*, ed. J. Suls and R. M. Miller. Washington, D.C.: Hemisphere.

Cooper, H. (1983). Teacher expectancy effects. In *Applied social psychology annual, Vol. 4*, ed. L. Bickman. Beverly Hills, Calif.: Sage.

Conte, J. R., and J. R. Schuerman. (1988). The effects of sexual abuse on children: A multidimensional view. In *Lasting effects of child abuse.* ed. G. E. Wyatt and G. J. Powell. Newbury Park, Calif.: Sage.

Corrigan, R. L. (1978). Language development as related to stage 6 object permanence development. *Journal of Child Language 5*: 173–89.

Corsini, R. J., and D. Wedding. (1989). *Current psychotherapies. 4th ed.* Itasca, Ill.: Peacock Publishers.

Cousins, N. (1979). *Anatomy of an illness as perceived by the patient.* New York: Norton.

——. (1985). How patients appraise physicians. *New England Journal of Medicine 313*: 1422–25.

——. (1989). *Head first: The biology of hope and the healing power of human spirit.* New York: Penguin Books.

Covey, S. R. (1990). *The seven habits of highly effective people: Restoring the character ethic.* New York: Simon & Schuster.

Covington, M. V. (1986). Anatomy of failure induced anxiety: The role of cognitive mediators. In *Self-related cognitions in anxiety and motivation*, ed. R. Schwarzer. Hillsdale, N.J.: Erlbaum.

Cowen, E. L., and W. C. Work. (1988). Resilient children, psychological wellness, and primary prevention. *American Journal of Community Psychology 16*: 591–607.

Coyne, J. (1987). The concept of empowerment in strategic therapy. *Psychotherapy 24*: 539–45.

Coyne, J. C., S. A. L. Burchill, and W. B. Stiles. (1991). An interactional perspective on depression. In *Handbook of social and clinical psychology: The health perspective*, ed. C. R. Snyder & D. R. Forsyth. Elmsford, N.Y.: Pergamon.

Craig, K. J. W. (1943). *The nature of explanation.* Cambridge: Cambridge University.

Crandall, V. C., and B. W. Crandall. (1983). Maternal and childhood behaviors as antecedants of internal-external control perceptions in young adulthood.

In *Research with the locus of control construct, Vol. 2*, ed. H. M. Lefcourt. New York: Academic Press.

Crittenden, P. M. (1981). Abusing, neglecting, problematic, and adequate dyads: Differentiating by patterns of interaction. *Merrill-Palmer Quarterly 27*: 201–18.

Crittenden, P. M., and M. D. S. Ainsworth. (1989). Child maltreatment and attachment theory. In *Child maltreatment*, ed. D. Cicchetti and V. Carlson. New York: Cambridge University Press.

Crocker, J., and B. Major. (1989). Social stigma and self-esteem: The self-protective properties of stigma. *Psychological Review 96*: 608–30.

Crosby, F. J., and K. L. Kaskar. (1993). Women and men at home and at work: Realities and illusions. In *Gender issues in contemporary society*, ed. S. Oskamp and M. Costanzo. Newbury Park, Calif.: Sage.

Crouch, J. A. (1989). The Hope Scale and head injury rehabilitation: Staff ratings as a function of client characteristics. Ph.D. diss. University of Kansas, Lawrence.

Csikszentmihalyi, M. (1990). *Flow: The psychology of optimal experience*. New York: Harper & Row.

Csikszentmihalyi, M., and I. S. Csikszentmihalyi, eds. (1988). *Optimal experience: Psychological studies of flow in consciousness*. New York: Cambridge University Press.

Csikszentmihalyi, M., K. Rathunde, and S. Whalen. (1993). *Talented teenagers: The roots of success and failure*. New York: Cambridge University Press.

Cuff, W. T. (1993). The experience of courage and the characteristics of courageous people. Ph.D. diss., University of Minnesota, Minneapolis.

Curry, L. A. (1994). The role of hope in sport-related goal-setting, goal-appraisal, goal-attainment, and as a predictor of sport performance. Ph.D. diss., University of Kansas, Lawrence.

Curwin, R. L. (1992). *Rediscovering hope: Our greatest teaching strategy*. Bloomington, Ind.: National Educational Service.

Custer, V. L., and K. E. Wassink. (1991). Occupational therapy intervention for an adult with depression and suicidal tendencies. *The American Journal of Occupational Therapy 9*: 845–48.

Cutrona, C. E. (1982). Transition to college: Loneliness and the process of social adjustment. In *Loneliness: A sourcebook of current theory, research and therapy*, ed. L. A. Peplau and D. Perlman. New York: Wiley-Interscience.

Dahl, S. (1989). Acute response to rape. *Acta Psychiatriaca Scandinavica*, supplement 355, 56–62.

Dalfiume, L. (1993). Correlates of hope. Fuller Theological Seminary, Pasadena, California.

Daro, D. (1988). *Confronting child abuse: Research for effective program design*. New York: Free Press.

Davis, M. H. (1983). Measuring individual differences in empathy: Evidence for a multidimensional approach. *Journal of Personality and Social Psychology 44*: 113–26.

DeAngelis, T. (1993). Studies explore roots of ageist attitudes. *The APA Monitor 24(10)*: 22.

deBono, E. (1978). *Opportunities: A handbook of business opportunity search*. London: Penguin Books.

———. (1993). *Teach your child how to think*. New York: Viking.

DeBrueys, M. T. (1986). *125 ways to be a better student: A program for study skill success*. Moline, Ill.: LinguiSystems.

DeCasper, A. J., and W. P. Fifer. (1980). Of human bonding: Newborns prefer their mothers' voices. *Science 208* 1174–76.

deCharms, R. (1968). *Personal causation*. New York: Academic Press.

Deci, E. L. (1975). *Intrinsic motivation*. New York: Plenum.

Derlega, V. J., S. S. Hendrick, B. A. Winstead, and J. H. Berg. (1991). *Psychotherapy as a personal relationship*. New York: Guilford.

Dessler, G. (1991). *Personnel/human resource management*. Englewood Cliffs, N.J.: Prentice Hall.

Dewsbury, D. A. (1981). Effects of novelty on copulatory behavior: The Coolidge Effect and related phenomena. *Psychological Bulletin 89*: 464–82.

Diamond, M. D., A. J. Weiss, and B. Grynbaum. (1968). The unmotivated patient. *Archives of Physical Medicine and Rehabilitation 49*: 281–84.

Diener, C. I., and C. S. Dweck. (1978). An analysis of learned helplessness: Continuous changes in performance, strategy, and achievement cognitions following failure. *Journal of Personality and Social Psychology 36*: 451–62.

Diener, E. (1984). Subjective well-being. *Psychological Bulletin 95*: 542–75.

Dienstbier, R. A. (1989). Arousal and physiological toughness: Implications for mental and physical health. *Psychological Review 96*: 84–100.

DiMatteo, M. R., and DiNicola, D. D. (1981). Sources of assessment of physician performance: A study of comparative reliability and patterns of intercorrelation. *Medical Care 19*: 829–42.

———. (1982). *Achieving patient compliance: The psychology of the medical practitioner's role*. Elmsford, N.Y.: Pergamon.

DiNicola, D. D., and M. R. DiMatteo. (1982). Communication, interpersonal influence, and resistance to medical treatment. In *Basic processes in helping relationships*, ed. T. A. Wills. New York: Academic Press.

Dodge, K. A. (1986). A social information processing model of social competence. In *Cognitive perspectives on children's social and behavioral development. Minnesota Symposium on Child Psychology. Vol. 18*, ed. M. Perlmutter. Hillsdale, N.J.: Erlbaum.

Dodge, K. A., G. S. Pettit, C. L. McClaskey, and M. M. Brown. (1986). Social competence in children. *Monographs of the Society for Research in Child Development 51* (2, Serial 213).

Dolgin, M. J., and S. M. Jay. (1989). Pain management in children. In *Treatment of childhood disorders*, ed. C. J. Mash and R. A. Barkley. New York: Guilford.

Dollard, J., L. W. Doob, N. E. Miller, O. Mowrer, and R. Sears. (1939). *Frustration and aggression*. New Haven, Conn.: Yale University Press.

Domino, G., and D. D. Affonso. (1990). A personality measure of Erikson's life stages: The Inventory of Psychological Balance. *Journal of Personality Assessment 54*: 576–88.

Donahue, T., and J. Costar. (1977). Counselor discrimination against young women in career selection. *Journal of Counseling Psychology 24*: 481–86.

Dorner, D. (1983). Heuristics and cognition in complex systems. In *Methods of heuristics*, R. Groner, M. Groner, and W. F. Bischoff. Hillsdale, N.J.: Erlbaum.

Drake, R. E., and P. G. Cotton. (1986). Depression, hopelessness and suicide in schizophrenia. *British Journal of Psychiatry 148*: 554–59.

Drucker, P. (1954). *The practice of management*. New York: Harper & Row.

Duck, S. W. (1990). Relationships as unfinished business: Out of the frying pan and into the 1990s. *Journal of Social and Personal Relationships 7*: 5–28.

Dunphy, D. C. (1963). The social structure of urban adolescent peer groups. *Sociometry 26*: 230–46.

Durlak, J. A. (1979). Comparative effectiveness of paraprofessional and professional helpers. *Psychological Bulletin 86*: 80–92.

———. (1981). Evaluating comparative studies of paraprofessional and professional helpers: A reply to Nietzel and Fisher. *Psychological Bulletin 89*: 566–69.

Dweck, C. S. (1986). Motivational processes affecting learning. *American Psychologist 41*: 1040–48.

Dyer, J. A. T., and N. Kreitman. (1984). Hopelessness, depression and suicidal intent in parasuicide. *British Journal of Psychiatry 144*: 127–33.

D'Zurilla, T. J. (1986). *Problem-solving therapy: A social competence approach to clinical intervention*. New York: Springer.

D'Zurilla, T. J., and M. R. Goldfried. (1971). Problem solving and behavior modification. *Journal of Counseling Psychology 20*: 1976–80.

D'Zurilla, T. J., and A. Nezu. (1980). A study of the generation-of-alternatives process in social problem solving. *Cognitive Therapy and Research 4*: 67–72.

Egeland, B. A., L. A. Sroufe, and M. F. Erickson. (1983). The developmental consequences of different patterns of maltreatment. *Child Abuse and Neglect 7*: 459–69.

Elkind, D. (1981). Giant in the nursery—Jean Piaget. In *Contemporary readings in child psychology. 2nd. ed.*, ed. E. M. Hetherinton and R. D. Parke. New York: McGraw-Hill.

Elliott, E. S., and C. S. Dweck. (1988). Goals: An approach to motivation and achievement. *Journal of Personality and Social Psychology 54*: 5–12.

Elliott, T. R., T. E. Witty, S. Herrick, and J. T. Hoffman. (1991). Negotiating reality after physical loss: Hope, depression, and disability. *Journal of Personality and Social Psychology 61*: 608–13.

Ellis, A. (1962). *Reason and emotion in psychotherapy*. New York: Lyle Stuart.

———. (1989). Rational-emotive therapy. In *Current psychotherapies. 4th ed.* ed. R. J. Corsini and D. Wedding. Itasca, Ill.: Peacock Publishers.

Ellis, E. M., B. M. Atkeson, and K. S. Calhoun. (1982). An examination of differences between multiple and single-incident victims of sexual assault. *Journal of Abnormal Psychology 91*: 221–24.

Emmer, E. T., and C. M. Evertson. (1981). Synthesis of research on classroom management. *Educational Leadership 38*: 342–47.

Emmons, R. A. (1986). Personal strivings: An approach to personality and subjective well-being. *Journal of Personality and Social Psychology 51*: 1058–68.

———. (1989). The personal striving approach to personality. In *Goal concepts in personality and social psychology*, ed. L. A. Pervin. Hillsdale, N.J.: Erlbaum.

Endler, N. S. (1990). *Holiday of darkness*. Toronto: Wall & Thompson.

Epstein, S. (1982). Conflict and stress. In *Handbook of stress*, ed. L. Goldberger and S. Breznitz. New York: Free Press.

Epstein, Y. M., R. L. Woolfolk, and P. M. Lehrer. (1981). Physiological, cognitive, and nonverbal responses to repeated exposure to crowding. *Journal of Applied Social Psychology 11*: 1–13.

Erickson, R. C., R. Post, and A. Paige. (1975). Hope as a psychiatric variable. *Journal of Clinical Psychology 31*: 324–29.

Erikson, E. H. (1950). *Childhood and society*. New York: Norton.

———. (1959). Identity and the life cycle. *Psychological Issues 1: 1*, 1–100.

———. (1963). *Childhood and society. 2nd. ed.* New York: Norton.

———. (1964). *Insight and responsibility*. New York: Norton.

———. (1968). *Identity: Youth and crisis*. New York: Norton.

———. (1980). *Identity and the life cycle*. New York: Norton.

———. (1982). *The life cycle completed: A review*. New York: Norton.

Fagan, J., and I. L. Shepherd, (1971). *Gestalt therapy now*. New York: Harper & Row.

Fairchild, R. W. (1980). *Finding hope again: A guide to counseling the depressed*. San Francisco: Harper & Row.

Fant, L. (1972). *Ameslan*. Silver Springs, Md.: National Association for the Deaf.

Fantz, R. L. (1963). Patterns of vision in newborn infants. *Science 140*: 296–97.

Farber, M. L. (1968). *Theory of suicide*. New York: Funk and Wagnalls.

Farmer, H. S. (1983). Career and homemaking plans for high school youth. *Journal of Counseling Psychology 30*: 40–45.

Farnett, C., I. Forte, B. Loss. (1976). *Special kid's stuff*. Nashville, Tenn.: Incentive Publications.

Fawcett, J., M. Leff, and W. E. Bunney. (1969). Suicide. *Archives of General Psychiatry 21*: 129–37.

Fawcett, J., W. Scheftner, D. Clark, D. Hedeker, R. Gibbons, and W. Coryell. (1987). Clinical predictors of suicide in patients with major affective disorders: A controlled prospective study. *American Journal of Psychiatry 144*: 35–40.

Feather, N. T., ed. (1982). *Expectations and actions: Expectancy-value models in psychology*. Hillsdale, N.J.: Erlbaum.

Fehrenbach, P. A., and M. R. O'Leary. (1982). Interpersonal attraction and treatment decisions in inpatient and outpatient psychiatric settings. In *Basic processes in helping relationships*, ed. T. A. Wills. New York: Academic Press.

Fibel, B., and W. D. Hale, (1978). The Generalized Expectancy for Success Scale — A new measure. *Journal of Consulting and Clinical Psychology 46*: 924–31.

Fiedler, F. A. (1950a). The concept of the ideal therapeutic relationship. *Journal of Consulting Psychology 14*: 239–45.

———. (1950b). A comparison of therapeutic relationships in psychoanalytic, nondirective, and Adlerian therapy. *Journal of Consulting Psychology 14*: 436–45.

Filsinger, E. E., and S. J. Thoma. (1988). Behavioral antecedants of relationship stability and adjustment: A five-year longitudinal study. *Journal of Marriage and the Family 50*: 785–95.

Finkelor, D., and G. T. Hoteling. (1984). Sexual abuse in the National Incidence Study of Child Abuse and Neglect: An appraisal. *Child Abuse and Neglect 8*: 23–33.

Flapan, D. (1968). *Children's understanding of social interaction.* New York: Teachers College Press.

Ford, C. E., and J. W. Brehm, (1987). Effort expenditure following failure. In *Coping with negative life events: Clinical and social psychological perspectives,* ed. C. R. Snyder and C. E. Ford. New York: Plenum.

Ford, J. D. (1978). Therapeutic relationship in behavior therapy: An empirical analysis. *Journal of Consulting and Clinical Psychology 46*: 1302–14.

Forward, R. L. (1980). Spinning new realities: Theorist Roger Penrose gives Einstein's universe new twist. *Science 80*, December, 40–49.

Fowlie, W. (1981). *A reading of Dante's Inferno.* Chicago: University of Chicago Press.

Frank, J. D. (1968). The role of hope in psychotherapy. *International Journal of Psychiatry 5*: 383–95.

Frank, J. D., and J. B. Frank, (1991). *Persuasion and healing: A comparative study of psychotherapy. 3rd. ed.* Baltimore: Johns Hopkins University Press.

Frank, J. D., R. Hoehn-Saric, S. Imber, B. L. Liberman, and A. R. Stone, (1978). *Effective ingredients of successful psychotherapy.* New York: Brunner/Mazel.

Frankl, V. (1960). Paradoxical intention: A logotherapeutic technique. *American Journal of Psychotherapy 14*: 520–25.

Frankl, V. E. (1992). *Man's search for meaning: An introduction to logotherapy. 4th. ed.* Boston: Beacon.

Franklin, A. J. (1993). The invisibility syndrome. *The Family Therapy Networker 17*: 33–39.

Freedheim, D. K., and S. W. Russ. (1992). Psychotherapy with children. In *Handbook of clinical child psychology,* ed. C. E. Walker and M. C. Roberts. New York: Wiley.

Freidson, E. (1970). *Profession of medicine.* New York: Dodd, Mead.

Friedman, M., and R. H. Rosenman. (1974). *Type A behavior and your heart.* New York: Knopf.

Frye, D., and C. Moore, eds. (1991). *Children's theories of mind: Mental states and social understanding.* Hillsdale, N.J.: Erlbaum.

Fuoss, D. E., and R. J. Troppmann. (1981). *Effective coaching: A psychological approach.* New York: Wiley.

Gaensbauer, T. J., and K. Sands, (1979). Distorted affective communication in abused/neglected infants and their potential impact on caregivers. *Journal of the American Academy of Child Psychiatry 18*: 236–50.

Gagne, R. M. (1984). Learning outcomes and their effects: Useful categories of human performance. *American Psychologist 39*: 377–86.

Gagnon, J. H., and W. Simon. (1973). *Sexual conduct: The social sources of human sexuality*. Chicago: Aldine.

Gallup, G. G., Jr. (1970). Chimpanzees: Self-recognition. *Science 167*: 86–87.

Garfield, S. L., and D. C. Affleck. (1961). Therapists' judgments concerning patients considered for psychotherapy. *Journal of Consulting Psychology 25*: 505–9.

Garmezy, N. (1983). Stressors in childhood. In *Stress, coping and development*, ed. N. Garmezy & M. Rutter. New York: McGraw-Hill.

———. (1991). Resiliency and vulnerability to adverse developmental outcomes associated with poverty. *American Behavioral Scientist 34*: 416–30.

Garrison, W. T. (1992). The conceptual utility of the temperament construct in understanding coping with pediatric conditions. In *Stress and coping in child health*, ed. A. M. LaGreca, L. J. Siegel, J. L. Wallander, and C. E. Walker. New York: Guilford.

Gelles, R. J. (1973). Child abuse as psychopathology: A sociological critique and reformulation. *American Journal of Orthopsychiatry 43*: 611–21.

Gelman, R., E. Meck, and S. Merkin. (1986). Young children's mathematical competence. *Cognitive Development 1*: 1–29.

Gelso, C. J., and J. A. Carter. (1985). The relationship in counseling and psychotherapy: Components, consequences, and theoretical antecedents. *The Counseling Psychologist 13*: 155–243.

George, C., and M. Main. (1979). Social interactions of young abused children: Approach, avoidance, and aggression. *Child Development 50*: 306–18.

Gesser, G., P. T. P. Wong, and G. T. Reker. (1987). Death attitudes across the life-span: The development and validation of the Death Attitude Profile (DAP). *Omega 18*: 113–28.

Getter, H., and J. K. Nowinski. (1981). A free response test of interpersonal effectiveness. *Journal of Personality Assessment 45*: 301–308.

Gibb, J. (1990). The Hope Scale revisited: Further validation of a measure of individual differences in the hope motive. Manuscript, University of Kansas, Lawrence.

Gil, D. G. (1970). *Violence against children: Physical child abuse in the United States*. Cambridge: Harvard University Press.

Gill, D. L., and T. E. Deeter. (1988). Development of the Sport Orientation Questionnaire. *Research Quarterly for Exercise and Sport 59*: 191–202.

Glick, I. O., R. Weiss, and C. M. Parkes. (1974). *The first year of bereavement*. New York: Wiley.

Glick, P., C. Zion, and C. Nelson. (1988). What mediates sex discrimination in hiring decisions? *Journal of Personality and Social Psychology 55*: 178–86.

Glueck, S., and E. Glueck. (1950). *Unraveling juvenile delinquency*. New York: Commonwealth Fund.

———. (1968). *Delinquents and nondelinquents in perspective*. Cambridge: Harvard University Press.

Golden, W., and W. Dryden. (1986). Cognitive-behavioral therapies: Communalities, divergences and future developments. In *Cognitive-behavioral approaches to psychotherapy*, ed. W. Dryden and W. Golden. New York: Harper Collins.

Goldin-Meadow, S., and C. Mylander, (1990). The role of parental input in the development of a morphological system. *Journal of Child Language 17*: 527–63.

Goodman, E. (1993). Doctor-patient partnership. *Lawrence Journal World*, October 26, p. 7B.

Goodman, S. H., D. R. Sewell, and R. C. Jampol. (1984). Contributions to life stress and social supports to the decision to seek psychological counseling. *Journal of Counseling Psychology 31*: 306–13.

Goodwin, J. (1981). Suicide attempts in sexual abuse victims and their mothers. *Child Abuse and Neglect 5*: 217–21.

Gopnik, A., and A. N. Meltzoff. (1987). Language and thought in the child: Early semantic developments and their relations to object permanence, mean-ends understanding, and categorization. In *Children's language. Vol. 6.*, ed. K. Nelson and A. Van Kleeck. Hillsdale, N.J.: Erlbaum.

Gorman, J. J., D. G. Cogen, and S. S. Gellis. (1959). A device for testing visual acuity in infants. *Sight-Saving Review 29*: 80–84.

Gottman, J. M. (1983). How children become friends. *Monographs of the Society for Research in Child Development 48:(3)*.

Gottschalk, L. A. (1974). A Hope Scale applicable to verbal samples. *Archives of General Psychiatry 30*: 779–85.

Gould, D. (1986). Goalsetting for peak performance. In *Applied sport psychology: Personal growth to peak performance*, ed. J. M. Williams. Palo Alto, Calif.: Mayfield.

Graziano, A. M., and K. C. Mooney. (1980). Family self-control instruction for children's nighttime fear reduction. *Journal of Consulting and Clinical Psychology 48*: 206–13.

———. (1982). Behavioral treatment of "night fears" in children: Maintenance of improvement at 2 1/2 to 3 years follow-up. *Journal of Consulting and Clinical Psychology 50*: 398–99.

Green, W. J. (1992). *Fatigue free: How to revitalize your life*. New York: Plenum.

Greenberger, E., and L. Steinberg. (1986). *When teenagers work: The psychological and social costs of adolescent employment*. New York: Basic Books.

Greeno, J. G. (1978). Nature of problem-solving abilities. In *Handbook of learning and cognitive processes: Vol. 5. Human information processing*, ed. W. K. Estes. Hillsdale, N.J.: Erlbaum.

Greenson, R. (1967). *The technique and practice of psychoanalysis*. New York: International Universities Press.

Greenwood, C. R., J. C. Delquadri, and R. V. Hall. (1984). Opportunity to respond and student academic achievement. In *Focus on behavior analysis in education*, ed. W. L. Howard, T. E. Heron, D. S. Hill, and J. Porter-Trap. Columbus, Ohio: Merrill.

Grier, W., and P. Cobbs. (1968). *Black rage*. New York: Basic Books.

Griffin, R. W. (1987). *Management. 2nd. ed.* Boston: Houghton Mifflin.

Grignetti, M. C. (1986). *Odessey: A curriculum for thinking—Problem solving.* Watertown, Mass.: Mastery Education Corporation.`

Gurman, A. S. (1977). The patient's perception of the therapeutic relationship. In

Effective psychotherapy: A handbook of research, ed. A. S. Gurman and A. M. Razin. Elmsford, N.Y.: Pergamon.

Gyllenhammar, P. G. (1977). *People at work*. Reading, Mass.: Addison-Wesley.

Haider, I. (1968). Suicidal attempts in children and adolescents. *British Journal of Psychiatry 114*: 1133.

Halloran, J. (1981). *Supervision: The art of management*. Englewood Cliffs, N.J.: Prentice Hall.

Hanigan, D. (1987). Social networks and social support in a group of young adults with serious suicidal thoughts. In *Proceedings of the 20th Annual Conference*, ed. R. Yufit. Denver: American Association of Suicide.

Hardy, K. (1993). War of the worlds. *The Family Therapy Networker 17*: 50–57.

Harney, P. (1990). The Hope Scale: Exploration of construct validity and its influence on health. Master's thesis., University of Kansas, Lawrence.

Harris, C. B. (1988). Hope: Construct definition and the development of an individual differences scale. Ph.D. diss. University of Kansas, Lawrence.

Harris, M. J., and R. Rosenthal. (1985). Mediation of interpersonal expectancy effects: 31 meta-analyses. *Psychological Bulletin 97*: 363–86.

Harter, S. (1985). *Manual for the Self-Perception Profile for Children: Revision of the Perceived Competence Scale for Children*. Denver: University of Denver Press.

———. (1988). *Manual: Self-Perception Profile for Adolescents*. Denver: University of Denver Press.

Harter, S., and A. Monsour. (1992). Developmental analysis of conflict caused by opposing attributes in the adolescent self-portrait. *Developmental Psychology 28*: 251–60.

Hartup, W. W. (1992). Friendships and their developmental significance. In *Childhood social development: Contemporary perspectives*, ed. H. McGurk. London: Methuen.

Harvey, J. C., and C. Katz. (1985). *If I'm so successful, why do I feel like a fake?* New York: St. Martin's.

Harvey, O. J., D. E., Hunt, and H. M. Schroeder. (1961). *Conceptual systems and personality organization*. New York: Wiley.

Hathaway, S. R., and J. C. McKinley. (1951). The *MMPI manual*. New York: Psychological Corporation.

Haynes, R. B., D. W. Taylor, and D. L. Sackett, eds. (1979). *Compliance in health care*. Baltimore: Johns Hopkins University Press.

Heath, D. H. (1991). *Fulfilling lives: Paths to maturity and success*. San Francisco: Jossey-Bass.

Heatherton, T. F., and J. Polivy. (1991). Development and validation of a scale for measuring state self-esteem. *Journal of Personality and Social Psychology 60*: 895–910.

Heckhausen, H. (1984). Emergent achievement behavior: Some early developments. In *Advances in motivation and achievement: Vol. 3*. The development of achievement motivation, ed. M. Maehr. Greenwich, Conn.: JAI.

Heider, F. (1958). *The psychology of interpersonal relations*. New York: Wiley.

Heppner, P. P., and E. T. Hillerbrand. (1991). Problem-solving training implications for remedial and preventive training. In *Handbook of social and clinical psychology: The health perspective*, ed. C. R. Snyder and D. R. Forsyth. Elmsford, N.Y.: Pergamon.

Heppner, P. P., and C. J. Krauskopf. An information-processing approach to personal problem solving. *The Counseling Psychologist 15*: 371–447.

Heppner, P. P., and C. H. Petersen. (1982). The development and implications of a personal problem-solving inventory. *Journal of Counseling Psychology 29*: 66–75.

Herman, J., and L. Hirschman. (1981). Families at risk for father-daughter incest. *American Journal of Psychiatry 138*: 967.

Hetherington, E. M., M. Cox, and R. Cox. (1979). Family interaction and the social, emotional and cognitive development of children following divorce. In *The family: Setting priorities*, ed. V. Vaughn and T. Brazelton. New York: Science and Medicine.

———. (1981). Effects of divorce on parents and children. In *Nontraditional families*, edited by M. Lamb. Hillsdale, N.J.: Erlbaum.

Hetherington, E. M., and B. Martin. (1979). Family interaction. In *Psychopathological disorders of childhood. 2nd ed.*, ed. H. C. Quary and J. S. Werry. New York: Wiley.

Higgins, R. L., and R. N. Harris. (1988). Strategic "alcohol" use: Drinking to self-handicap. *Journal of Social and Clinical Psychology 6*: 191–202.

Higgins, R. L., and C. R. Snyder. (1989). The business of excuses. In *Impression management in the organization*, ed. R. A. Giacolone and P. Rosenfeld. Hillsdale, N.J.: Erlbaum.

Higgins, R. L., C. R. Snyder, and S. Berglas. (1990). *Self-handicapping: The paradox that isn't*. New York: Plenum.

Hilfiker, D. (1985). *Healing the wounds: A physician looks at his work*. New York: Pantheon Books.

Hill, C. T., Z. Rubin, and L. A. Peplau. (1976). Breakups before marriage: The end of 103 affairs. *Journal of Social Issues 32*: 147–68.

Hirsch, B. J., and D. L. Dubois. (1989). The school-nonschool ecology of early adolescent friendships. In *Children's social networks and social supports*, ed. D. Belle. New York: Wiley.

Hoffman-Plotkin, D., and C. T. Twentyman. (1984). A multimodel assessment of behavioral and cognitive deficits in abused and neglected preschoolers. *Child Development 55*: 794–802.

Hofler, R. (1993). Cityscape: Is the golden city losing its luster? *Travel Leisure 23:5*: 171–77.

Holahan, C. J. (1982). Environmental cognition. In *Environmental psychology*. ed. C. J. Holahan. New York: Random House.

Holmes, D. S. (1993). Aerobic fitness and the response to psychological stress. In *Exercise psychology: The influence of physical exercise on psychological processes*, ed. P. Seraganian. New York: Wiley.

Holmes, T. H., and R. H. Rahe. (1967). The social readjustment rating scale. *Journal of Psychosomatic Research 11*: 213–18.

Honeycutt, J. M. (1993). Memory structures for the rise and fall of personal relationships. In *Individual and relationships. Vol. 1*, ed. S. Duck. Newbury Park, Calif.: Sage.

Honeycutt, J. M., K. S. Zugacki, and R. Edwards. (1989). Intrapersonal communication and imagined interactions. In *Readings in intrapersonal communication*, ed. C. Roberts and K. Watson. Scottsdale, Ariz: Gorsuch Scarisbrick.

Horowitz, L. C. (1988). *Taking charge of your medical fate*. New York: Random House.

Horowitz, M. J. (1990). A model of mourning: Change in schemas of self and other. *Journal of American Psychoanalytic Association 38*: 297–324.

———. (1993). Stess-response syndromes: A review of post traumatic stress and adjustment disorders. In *International handbook of traumatic stress syndromes*, ed. J. P. Wilson and B. Raphael. New York: Plenum.

Horvath, A. O., and L. S. Greenberg. (1986). The development of the Working Alliance Inventory. In *The psychotherapeutic process: A research handbook*, ed. L. S. Greenberg and W. M. Pinsof. New York: Guilford.

Houston, B. K., and C. R. Snyder, eds. (1988). *Type A behavior pattern: Research, theory, and intervention*. New York: Wiley.

Hudson, J. A. (1990). The emergence of autobiographical memory in mother-child conversation. In *Knowing and remembering in young children*, ed. R. Fivush and J. A. Hudson. New York: Cambridge University Press.

Hughes, J. N. (1990). Brief psychotherapies. In *The handbook of school psychology*, ed. T. B. Gutkin and C. R. Reynolds. New York: Wiley.

Hughes, R. (1929). *A high wind in Jamaica*. London: Chatto & Windus.

Hunt, J. M. (1981). Experiential roots of intention, initiative and trust. In *Advances in intrinsic motivation and aesthetics*, ed. H. I. Day. New York: Plenum.

Huston, A. (1983). Sex-typing. In *Handbook of child psychology: Vol. 4. Socialization, personality and social development*, ed. P. H. Mussen. New York: Wiley.

Imber, S. D., S. K. Pande, J. D. Frank, R. Hoehn-Saric, A. R. Stone, and D. G. Wargo. (1970). Time-focused role induction: Report of an instructive failure. *Journal of Nervous and Mental Disorders 150*: 27–30.

Ingram, R. E., P. C. Kendall, and A. H. Chen, (1991). Cognitive-behavioral interventions. In *Handbook of social and clinical psychology: The health perspective*, ed. C. R. Snyder and D. R. Forsyth. Elmsford, N.Y.: Pergamon.

Irving, L. M. (1991). Hope and cancer-related health beliefs, knowledge, and behavior: The advantage of the "negotiated" reality principle. Ph.D. diss., University of Kansas, Lawrence.

Irving, L. M., W. Crenshaw, C. R. Snyder, P. Francis, and G. Gentry. (1990, May). Hope and its correlates in a psychiatric inpatient setting. Paper presented at the Midwestern Psychological Association, Chicago.

Jacobson, G. F., and S. H. Portuges. (1978). Relation of marital separation and divorce to suicide. *Suicide and Life Threatening Behavior 8*: 217–24.

Jain, U. (1987). *The psychological consequences of crowding*. Newbury Park, Calif.: Sage.

Janoff-Bulman, R. (1992). *Shattered assumptions: Toward a new psychology of trauma*. New York: Free Press.

Jones, A. C. (1985). Psychological functioning in Black Americans: A conceptual guide for use in psychotherapy. *Psychotherapy 22*: 363–69.

Jones, E. E., and S. Berglas. (1978). Control of attributions about the self through self-handicapping strategies: The appeal of alcohol and the role of under-achievement. *Personality and Social Psychology Bulletin 4*: 200–206.

Jones, R. A. (1977). *Self-fulfilling prophecies: Social, psychological, and physiological effects of expectancies*. Hillsdale, N.J.: Erlbaum.

Jones, W., and M. D. Carver. (1991). Adjustment and coping implications of lone-liness. In *Handbook of social and clinical psychology: The health perspective*, ed. C. R. Snyder and D. R. Forsyth. Elmsford, N.Y.: Pergamon.

Kail, R. (1990). *The development of memory in children. 3rd. ed.* New York: Freeman.

———. (1991). Processing time declines exponentially during childhood and adoles-cence. *Developmental Psychology 27*: 259–66.

Kamphaus, R. W., N. Yarbrough, and R. P. Johanson. (1990). Contributions of in-structional psychology to school psychology. In *The handbook of school psy-chology. 2nd. ed.*, ed. T. B. Gutkin and C. R. Reynolds. New York: Wiley.

Kanfer, F. H., P. Karoly, and A. Newman. (1975). Reduction of children's fear of the dark by competence-related and situational threat-related verbal cues. *Journal of Consulting and Clinical Psychology 43*: 251–58.

Kaplan, K. J., and M. B. Schwartz. (1993). *A psychology of hope: An anidote to the suicidal pathology of western civilization*. Westport, Conn.: Praeger.

Kaplan, L. (1978). *Oneness and separateness*. New York: Simon & Schuster.

Kaprio, J., M. Koskenvuo, and H. Rita. (1987). Mortality after bereavement. *American Journal of Public Health 77*: 283–87.

Kasteler, J., R. L. Kane, D. M. Olsen, and C. Thetford. (1976). Issues underlying prevalence of "doctor-shopping" behavior. *Journal of Health and Social Behavior 17*: 328–39.

Kauffman, C., H. Grunebaum, B. Cohler, and E. Garner. (1979). Superkids: Competent children of psychotic mothers. *American Journal of Psychiatry 36*: 1398–1402.

Kazdin, A. E., D. Bass, W. A. Ayers, and A. Rodgers. (1990). Empirical and clini-cal focus of child and adolescent psychotherapy research. *Journal of Con-sulting and Clinical Psychology 58*: 729–40.

Kazdin, A. E., N. H. French, A. S. Unis, K. Esveldt-Dawson, and R. B. Sherick. (1983). Hopelessness, depression, and suicidal intent among psychiatri-cally disturbed children. *Journal of Consulting and Clinical Psychology 51*: 504–10.

Kelly, J. B., and J. S. Wallerstein. (1976). The effects of parental divorce: I. The experience of the child in early latency. *American Journal of Orthopsychia-try 46*: 20–32.

Kent, J. (1976). A follow-up study of abused children. *Journal of Pediatric Psychology 1*: 24–31.

Kershaw, S., ed. (1990). *A concise dictionary of classical mythology*. A. R. Maxwell-Hysop, translator. Oxford, England: Basil Blackwell.

Kiesler, C. A. (1971). *The psychology of commitment*. New York: Academic Press.

Kiesler, D. J. (1991). Interpersonal methods of assessment and diagnosis. In *Hand-book of social and clinical psychology: The health perspective*, ed. C. R. Snyder and D. R. Forsyth. Elmsford, N.Y.: Pergamon.

King, H. E. (1992). The reactions of children to divorce. In *Handbook of clinical child psychology*, ed. C. E. Walker and M. C. Roberts. New York: Wiley.

The authors cite J. S. Wallerstein (1986). Children of Divorce Work-
shop. Cape Cod, Mass.

Kirsch, I. (1990). *Changing expectations: A key to effective psychotherapy.* Pacific
Grove, Calif.: Brooks/Cole.

Klinger, E. (1975). Consequences of commitment to and disengagement from
incentives. *Psychological Review 82*: 1–25.

Klinger, E., S. G. Barta, and M. E. Maxeiner. (1980). Motivational correlates of
thought content, frequency and commitment. *Journal of Personality and
Social Psychology 39*: 1222–37.

Klopfer, B. (1957). Psychological variables in human cancer. *Journal of Projective
Techniques 21*: 331–40.

Kobak, R. R., and A. Sceery. (1988). Attachment in late adolescence: Working
models, affect regulation, and representations of self and others. *Child
Development 59*: 135–46.

Kohler, W. (1925). *The mentality of apes.* E. Winter, translator. New York: Harcourt, Brace.

Kopp, C. B. (1989). Regulation of distress and negative emotions: A developmental view. *Developmental Psychology 25(3)*: 343–54.

Kovacs, M. (1985). The Children's Depression Inventory (CDI). *Psychopharmacology Bulletin 21*: 995–98.

Kovacs, M., A. T. Beck, and A. Weissman. (1975). Hopelessness: An indicator of
suicidal risk. *Suicide 5*: 98–103.

Kramer, J. J. (1990). Training parents as behavior change agents: Success, failures,
and suggestions for school psychologists. In *The handbook of school psychology*, ed. T. B. Gutkin and C. R. Reynolds. New York: Wiley.

Krauss, H. H., and B. J. Krauss. (1968). Cross-cultural study of the thwarting-dis-
orientation theory of suicide. *Journal of Abnormal Psychology 73*: 352–57.

Krugman, R., and D. P. H. Jones. (1987). Incest and other forms of sexual abuse.
In *The battered child. 4th ed.*, ed. R. E. Helfer and R. S. Kempe. Chicago:
University of Chicago Press.

Kukla, A. (1972). Foundations of an attributional theory of performance. *Psychological Review 79*: 454–70.

Kurdek, L. A. (1988). Cognitive mediators of children's adjustment to divorce. In
Children of divorce, edited by S. A. Wolchik and P. Karoly. New York:
Guilford.

Kushner, H. S. (1981). *When bad things happen to good people.* New York: Schocken
Books.

Kuykendall, C. (1992). *From rage to hope: Strategies for reclaiming Black and Hispanic
students.* Bloomington, Ind.: National Educational Service.

Kyle, R. M. J., ed. (1985). *Reaching for excellence: An effective schools sourcebook.*
Washington, D.C.: White.

LaCrosse, M. B. (1977). Comparative perceptions of counselor behavior: A replication and extension. *Journal of Counseling Psychology 24*: 464–71.

Laird, S. (1992). A preliminary investigation into the role of prayer as a coping
technique for adult patients with arthritis. Ph.D. diss., University of
Kansas, Lawrence.

Lamb, M., R. Thompson, W. Gardner, E. Charnov, and D. Estes. (1984). Security of infantile attachment as assessed in the strange situation: Its study and biological interpretation. *Behavioral and Brain Sciences 7*: 124–47.

Lambert, M. J., S. S. DeJulio, and D. M. Stein. (1978). Therapist interpersonal skills: Process, outcome, methodological considerations, and recommendations for future research. *Psychological Bulletin 85*: 467–89.

Lambert, M. J., D. A. Shapiro, and A. E. Bergin. (1986). The effectiveness of psychotherapy. In *Handbook of psychotherapy and behavior change*. 3rd ed., ed. S. L. Garfield and A. E. Bergin. New York: Wiley.

Landman, J. T., and R. M. Dawes. (1982). Psychotherapy outcome: Smith and Glass' conclusions stand up under scrutiny. *American Psychologist 37*: 504–16.

Langelle, C. (1989). An assessment of hope in a community sample. Master's thesis, University of Kansas, Lawrence.

Langer, E. (1989). *Mindfulness*. Reading, Mass.: Addison-Wesley.

Latham, G. P., and J. J. Baldes. (1975). The practical significance of Locke's theory of goalsetting. *Journal of Applied Psychology 60*: 122–24.

Latham, G. P., and T. W. Lee. Goal setting. In *Generalizing from laboratory to field settings*, ed. E. Locke. Lexington, Mass.: Lexington Books.

Latham, G. P., and E. A. Locke. (1975). Increasing productivity with decreasing time limits: A field replication of Parkinson's law. *Journal of Applied Psychology 60*: 524–26.

Lauzanne, S., and I. Wylie, (1931). American optimism: Pollyanna is dead. *Living Age 340*: 605–6.

Lawler, E. E. (1981). *Pay and organizational development*. Reading, Mass.: Addison-Wesley.

———. (1987). The design of effective reward systems. In *Handbook of organizational behavior*, ed. J. W. Lorsch. Englewood Cliffs, N.J.: Prentice Hall.

Lazarus, R. S., and Folkman, S. (1984). *Stress, appraisal, and coping*. New York: Springer.

Lee, T. W., E. A. Locke, and G. P. Latham. (1989). Goal setting theory and job performance. In *Goal concepts in personality and social psychology*, ed. L. A. Pervin. Hillsdale, N.J.: Erlbaum.

Leenaars, A. A. (1987a). Protocal analysis of Schneidman's formulation regarding suicide. In *Suicide*, ed. J. Morgan. London, Ontario: King's College Press.

———. (1978b). An empirical investigation of Schneidman's formulations regarding suicide. *Suicide and Life Threatening Behavior 17*: 233–50.

———. (1989). Are young adults' suicides psychologically different from those of other adults? *Suicide and Life Threatening Behavior 19*: 249–63.

Lefcourt, H. M., and K. Davidson-Katz. (1991). The role of humor and the self. In *Handbook of social and clinical psychology: The health perspective*, ed. C. R. Snyder and D. R. Forsyth. Elmsford, N.Y.: Pergamon.

Leinbach, M. D., and B. Hort. (1989, April). Bears are for boys: "Metaphorical" associations in the young child's gender schema. Paper presented at the biennial meeting of the Society for Research in Child Development, Kansas City, Missouri.

Lester, D. (1992). *Why people kill themselves. 3rd. ed.: A 1990s summary of research findings on suicidal behavior.* Springfield, Ill.: Thomas.

Levenson, M., and C. Neuringer. (1971). Problem solving behavior in suicidal adolescents. *Journal of Consulting and Clinical Psychology 37*: 433–36.

Lever, J. (1976). Sex differences in the games children play. *Social Problems 23*: 478–87.

Levinger, G., and O. C. Moles. (1979). *Divorce and separation: Context, causes, and consequences.* New York: Basic Books.

Lewin, K. (1951). Intention, will, and need. In *Organization and pathology of thought*, ed. D. Rapaport. New York: Columbia University Press.

Lewinsohn, P. M., H. Hoberman, L. Teri, and M. Hautzinger. (1985). In *Theoretical issues in behavior therapy*, ed. S. Reiss and R. Bootzin. New York: Academic Press.

Lewis, M., and J. Brooks. (1978). Self-knowledge and emotional development. In *The development of affect*, ed. M. Lewis and L. A. Rosenblum. New York: Plenum.

Lewis, M., and J. Brooks-Gunn. (1979). *Social cognition and the acquisition of self.* New York: Plenum.

Lieberman, A. F. (1993). *The emotional life of the toddler.* New York: Free Press.

Lima, J., L. Nazarian, E. Charney, and C. Lahti. (1976). Compliance with short-term antimicrobal therapy. Some techniques that help. *Pediatrics 57*: 383–86.

Linn, L. S., and R. M. Wilson. (1980). Factors related to a communication style among medical house staff. *Medical Care 18*: 1013–19.

Liotti, G. (1993). Disorganized attachment and dissociative experiences: An illustration of the developmental-ethological approach to cognitive therapy. In *Cognitive therapies in action*, ed. K. T. Kuehlwein and H. Rosen. San Francisco: Jossey-Bass.

Lipp, M. R. (1980). *The bitter pill: Doctors, patients, and failed expectations.* New York: Harper & Row.

Lipsey, M. W., and D. B. Wilson. (1993). The efficacy of psychological, educational, and behavioral treatment: Confirmation from meta-analysis. *American Psychologist 48*: 1181–1209.

Little, B. R. (1983). Personal projects: A rationale and method for investigation. *Environment and Behavior 15*: 273–309.

——. (1989). Personal projects analysis: Trivial pursuits, magnificent obsessions, and the search for coherence. In *Personality psychology: Recent trends and emerging directions*, ed. D. M. Buss and N. Cantor. New York: Springer.

Lloyd, J. W., D. P. Hallahan, J. M. Kauffman, and C. E. Keller. (1991). Academic problems. In *The practice of child therapy*, ed. T. R. Kratochwill and R. J. Morris. Elmsford, N.Y.: Pergamon.

Locke, E. A. (1966). The relationship of intentions to level of performance. *Journal of Applied Psychology 50*: 60–66.

Locke, E. A., and J. F. Bryan. (1969). The directing function of goals in task performance. *Organizational Behavior and Human Performance 4*: 35–42.

Locke, E. A., N. Cartledge, and J. Koeppel. (1968). Motivational effects of knowledge of results: A goal setting phenomenon? *Psychological Bulletin 70*: 474–85.

Locke, E. A., and G. P. Latham. (1984). *Goal setting: A motivational technique that works.* Englewood Cliffs, N.J.: Prentice Hall.

Locke, E. A., K. N. Shaw, L. M. Saari, and G. P. Latham. (1981). Goal setting and task performance: 1969–1980. *Psychological Bulletin 90*: 125–52.

Lopez, B. (1990). *Crow and weasel.* San Francisco: North Point Press.

Lorber, J. (1975). Good patients and problem patients: Conformity and deviance in a general hospital. *Journal of Health and Social Behavior 16*: 213–25.

Lowery, G. H. (1986). *Growth and development of children. 8th ed.* Chicago: Year Book Medical Publishers.

Luborsky, L., B. Singer, and L. Luborsky. (1975). Comparative studies of psychotherapies. Is it true that "everyone has won and all must have prizes"? *Archives of General Psychiatry 32*: 995–1008.

Luthan, F. (1985). *Organizational behavior. 4th ed.* New York: McGraw-Hill.

Lynch, W. (1974). *Images of hope.* Notre Dame, Ind.: University of Notre Dame Press.

Macklin, R. (1987). *Mortal choices: Bioethics in today's world.* New York: Pantheon.

Maddux, J. (1991). Self-efficacy. In *Handbook of social and clinical psychology: The health perspective*, ed. C. R. Snyder and D. R. Forsyth. Elmsford, N.Y.: Pergamon.

Mahler, M. (1968). *On human symbiosis and the vicissitudes of individuation.* New York: International Universities Press.

Mahler, M. S., F. Pine, and A. Bergman. (1975). *The psychological birth of the human infant: Symbiosis and individuation.* New York: Basic Books.

Mahoney, M. J., and M. Avener. (1977). Psychology of the elite athlete: An exploratory study. *Cognitive Therapy and Research 1*: 135–41.

Maier, S. F., and M. E. P. Seligman. (1976). Learned helplessness: Theory and evidence. *Journal of Experimental: General 105*: 3–46.

Marcel, G. (1962). *Homo viator.* E. Craufurd, translator. New York: Harper & Row.

Marceon, A., and M. Brumagne. (1985). Loneliness among children and young adolescents. *Developmental Psychology 21*: 1025–31.

Marcia, J. E. (1966). Development and validation of ego identity status. *Journal of Personality and Social Psychology 3*: 551–58.

———. (1980). Identity in adolescence. In *Handbook of adolescent psychology*, ed. J. Adelson. New York: Wiley.

Markus, H., and P. Nurius. (1986). Possible selves. *American Psychologist 41*: 954–69.

Markus, H., and A. Ruvolo, (1989). Possible selves: Personalized representations of goals. In *Goal concepts in personality and social psychology*, ed. L. A. Pervin. Hillsdale, N.J.: Erlbaum.

Marsland, D. W., M. B. Wood, and F. Mayo. (1976). The databank for patient care, curriculum and research in family practice: 526,196 patient problems. *Journal of Family Practice 3*: 25–28.

Martin, R. (1990). *Teaching through encouragement.* Englewood Cliffs, N.J.: Prentice Hall.

Martorano, J. T., and J. P. Kildahl. (1989). *Beyond negative thinking: Breaking the cycle of depressing and anxious thoughts.* New York: Plenum.

Martz, L. (1992). *Making schools better.* New York: Time Books.

Marvin, R. S., M. T. Greenberg, and D. Mossler. (1976). The early development of conceptual perspective taking: Distinguishing among multiple perspectives. *Child Development 47*: 511–14.

Maslach, C. (1982). *Burnout — The cost of caring.* Englewood Cliffs, N.J.: Prentice Hall.

Maslach, C., and S. E. Jackson. (1981). The measurement of experienced burnout. *Journal of Occupational Behavior 2*: 99–113.

Masterson, J. (1976). *Psychotherapy for the borderline adult: A developmental approach.* New York: Brunner/Mazel.

———. (1981). *The narcissistic and borderline disorders: An integrated developmental approach.* New York: Brunner/Mazel.

Matlin, M. W. (1993). *The psychology of women. 2nd ed.* New York: Harcourt Brace Jovanovich.

Maurer, D., and C. Maurer. (1988). *The world of the newborn.* New York: Basic Books.

May, R. (1953). *Man's search for himself.* New York: Random House.

Mays, V. M. (1985). The Black American and psychotherapy: The dilemma. *Psychotherapy 22*: 379–88.

McAllister, T. W., and T. R. P. Price. (1990). Psychopharmacology and depression. In *Depression: New directions in theory, research, and practice,* ed. C. D. McCann and N. S. Endler. Toronto: Wall & Emerson.

McCann, I. L., and D. S. Holmes. (1984). Influence of aerobic exercise on depression. *Journal of Personality and Social Psychology 46*: 1142–47.

McClelland, D. C. (1955). Some social consequences of achievement motivation. In *Nebraska symposium on motivation. Vol. 3,* ed. M. R. Jones. Lincoln: University of Nebraska Press.

———. (1961). *The achieving society.* Princeton, N.J.: Van Nostrand.

McClelland, D. C., J. W. Atkinson, R. W. Clark, and E. L. Lowell. (1953). *The achievement motive.* New York: Appleton-Century-Crofts.

McClements, J. D., and C. B. Botterill. (1979). Goalsetting in shaping the future performance of athletes. In *Coach, athlete and the sports psychologist,* ed. P. Klavora and J. Daniels. Toronto: University of Toronto Press.

McCormack, P. (1993). How kids survive trauma. *Parents 68*: 70–74.

McCrae, R. R., and P. T., Costa, Jr. (1988). Psychological resilience among widowed men and women: A 10-year followup of a national survey. *Journal of Social Issues 44*: 129–42.

McCulloch, J. W., and A. E. Phillip. (1967). Social variables in attempted suicide. *ACTA Psychiatrica Scandinnavica 43*: 341.

McDougall, W. (1908). *An introduction to social psychology.* London: Methuen.

McGuire, W. J. (1969). The nature of attitudes and attitude change. In *Handbook of social psychology. Vol. 3,* edited by G. Lindzey and E. Aronson. Reading, Mass.: Addison-Wesley.

McKee, W. T., and J. C. Witt. (1990). Effective teaching: A review of instructional, and environmental variables. In *The handbook of school psychology. 2nd. ed.*, T. B. Gutkin and C. R. Reynolds. New York: Wiley.

Meichenbaum, D. H. (1979). Teaching children self-control. In *Advances in clinical child psychology. Vol. 2*, ed. B. B. Lahey and A. E. Kazdin. New York: Plenum.

Meichenbaum, D. H., and J. Goodman. (1971). Training impulsive children to talk to themselves: A means of developing self-control. *Journal of Abnormal Psychology 71*: 115–26.

Melges, R., and J. Bowlby. (1969). Types of hopelessness in psychopathological processes. *Archives of General Psychiatry 20*: 690–99.

Meltzoff, A. N., and A. Gopnik. (1989). On linking nonverbal imitation, representation, and language learning in the first two years of life. In *The many faces of imitation in language learning*, ed. G. E. Speidel & K. E. Nelson. New York: Springer Verlag.

Menninger, K. (1959). The academic lecture on hope. *The American Journal of Psychiatry 116*: 481–91.

Mento, A. J., R. P. Steel, and R. J. Karren, (1987). A meta-analytic study of the effects of goal setting on task performance. *Organizational Behavior and Human Decision Processes 39*: 52–83.

Meulen, M. van der (1987). *Self-references in young children: Content, metadimensions, and puzzlement*. Groningen, Netherlands: Stichting Kinderstudies.

———. (1991). Toddler's self-concept in the light of early action theory. In *The development of intentional action: Cognitive, motivational, and interactive processes*, ed. M. Bullock. Basel, Switzerland: Krager.

Meyer, D. (1980). *The positive thinkers*. New York: Pantheon.

Michener, J. (1976). *Sports in America*. New York: Random House.

Mikes, G. (1971). *Laughing matter: Toward a personal philosophy of wit and humor*. New York: Liberty Press.

Mikulincer, M. (1994). *Human learned helplessness*. New York: Plenum.

Miller, A. (1950). *Death of a salesman*. New York: Viking.

Miller, G. A., E. Galanter, and K. H. Pribram. (1960). *Plans and the structure of behavior*. New York: Holt, Rinehart, & Winston.

Miller, M. (1981). Introduction to suicidology. Center for Information on Suicide, San Diego, California.

Miller, P. H., and P. A. Aloise. (1989). Young children's understanding of the psychological causes of behavior: A review. *Child Development 60*: 257–85.

Milling, L., and B. Martin, (1992). Depression and suicidal behavior in preadolescent children. In *Handbook of clinical child psychology*, ed. C. E. Walker and M. C. Roberts. New York: Wiley.

Minkoff, K., E. Bergman, A. T. Beck, and R. Beck. (1973). Hopelessness, depression and attempted suicide. *American Journal of Psychiatry 130*: 455–59.

Minuchin, S. (1974). *Families and family therapy*. Cambridge, Mass. Harvard University Press.

Mischel, H. N., and W. Mischel. (1983). The development of children's knowledge of self-control strategies. *Child Development 54*: 603–9.

Mischel, W. (1983). The role of knowledge and ideation in the development of delay capacity. In *Piaget and the foundations of knowledge*, ed. L. S. Liben. Hillsdale, N.J.: Erlbaum.

Mischel, W., Y. Shoda, and M. L. Rodriguez. (1989). Delay of gratification in children. *Science 244*: 933–38.

Mizer, J. E. (1964). Cipher in the snow. *National Education Association Journal 53(8)*: 8–10.

Mook, D. G. (1987). *Motivation: The organization of action*. New York: Norton.

Moorhead, G., and R. W. Griffin. (1989). *Organizational behavior*. Boston: Houghton Mifflin.

Morganthau, T. (1993). The Clinton solution. *Newsweek*, September 23, pp. 30–35.

Morris, J. B., M. Kovacs, A. T. Beck, and A. Wolfe. (1970). Notes toward an epidemiology of urban suicide. *Comprehensive Psychiatry 127*: 764–70.

Morris, R. J., and K. R. Suckerman. (1974a). The importance of the therapeutic relationship to systematic desensitization. *Journal of Consulting and Clinical Psychology 42*: 147.

———. (1974b). Therapist warmth as a factor in automated systematic desensitization. *Journal of Consulting and Clinical Psychology 42*: 244–50.

Mulholland, D. J., N. F. Watt, A. Philpott, and N. Sarlin. (1991). Academic performance in children of divorce: Psychological resilience and vulnerability. *Psychiatry 54*: 268–80.

Munoz-Dunbar, R. (1993). Hope: A cross-cultural assessment of American college students. Master's thesis, University of Kansas, Lawrence.

Murdock, N. L., and E. M. Altmaier. (1991). Attribution-based treatments. In *Handbook of social and clinical psychology: The health perspective*, ed. C. R. Snyder and D. R. Forsyth. Elmsford, N.Y.: Pergamon.

Murphy, L. B., and A. E. Moriarty. (1976). *Vulnerability, coping, and growth from infancy to adolescence*. New Haven, Conn.: Yale University Press.

Mussen, P. H., J. J. Conger, J. Kagan, and A. C. Huston. (1990). *Child development and personality*. New York: HarperCollins.

Muyskens, J. L. (1979). *The sufficiency of hope*. Philadelphia: Temple University Press.

National Center on Child Abuse and Neglect. (1981). *Study findings: National study of the incidence and severity of child and abuse and neglect*. Washington, D.C.: U.S. Department of Health and Human Services (Publication UHDS 81-30325).

National Committee for Prevention of Child Abuse. (1991). NCPCA releases new child abuse statistics and prevention trends. *NCPCA Memorandum*, April, p. 1. Chicago: Author.

Nazarian, L., J. Mechaber, E., Charney, and M. Coulter. (1974). Effect of a mailed appointment reminder on appointment keeping. *Pediatrics 53*: 349–52.

Nelson, K. (1981). Social cognition in a script framework. In *Social cognitive development*, ed. J. H. Flavell and L. Ross. Cambridge, England: Cambridge University Press.

———. (1986). *Event knowledge: Structure and function in development*. Hillsdale, N.J.: Erlbaum.

———. (1993). The psychological and social origins of autobiographical memory. *Psychological Science 4*: 7–14.

Nelson, R. J., L. L. Badura, and B. D. Goldman. (1990). Mechanisms of seasonal cycles of behavior. *Annual Review of Psychology 41*: 81–108.

Neugebauer, R., B. P. Dohrenwend, and B. S. Dohrenwend. (1980). Formulation of hypotheses about the true prevalence of functional psychiatric disorders among adults. In *Mental illness in the United States*, ed. B. P. Dohrenwend, B. S. Dohrenwend, M. S. Gould, B. Link, R. Neugebauer, and R. Wunsch-Hitzig. New York: Praeger.

Neuringer, C. (1976). Current developments in the study of suicidal thinking. In *Suicidology: Contemporary developments*, ed. E. S. Schneidman. New York: Grune & Stratton.

Newell, A., and H. A. Simon. (1972). *Human problem solving*. Englewood Cliffs, N.J.: Prentice Hall.

Newsweek. (1992). The curse of self-esteem. February 17, pp. 46–51.

Nezu, A., and T. J. D'Zurilla. (1979). An experimental evaluation of the decision-making process in social problem solving. *Cognitive Therapy and Research 3*: 269–77.

———. (1981a). Effects of problem definition and formulation on decision making in the social problem-solving process. *Behavior Therapy 12*: 100–106.

———. (1981b). Effects of problem definition and formulation on generation of alternatives in the social problem-solving process. *Cognitive Therapy and Research 5*: 265–71.

Nietzel, M. T., and S. G. Fisher. (1981). Effectiveness of professional and para-professional helpers: A comment on Durlak. *Psychological Bulletin 89*: 555–65.

Nietzsche, F. (1889). *Twilight of the idols/The anti-Christ*. Reprint. R. J. Hollingdale, translator. London: Penguin Books, 1990.

Norcross, J. C., and J. O. Prochaska. (1986). The psychological distress and self-change of psychologists, counselors, and laypersons. *Psychotherapy 23*: 102–14.

Nourse, A. E. (1979). *Inside the Mayo Clinic*. New York: McGraw-Hill.

Novotny, J. (1979). Despair and hope. In *The sources of hope*, ed. R. Fitzgerald. Rushcutters Bay, Australia: Pergamon.

Nowicki, S., and B. Strickland. (1973). A locus of control scale for children. *Journal of Consulting and Clinical Psychology 40(1)*: 148–54.

Odiorne, G. (1965). *Management by objectives*. New York: Pittman.

Oltmanns, T. F., J. M. Neale, and G. C. Davison. (1991). *Case studies in abnormal psychology*. 3rd. ed. New York: Wiley.

Omodei, M. M., and A. J. Wearing. (1990). Need satisfaction and involvement in personal projects: Toward an integrative model of subjective well being. *Journal of Personality and Social Psychology 59*: 762–69.

Orlick, T. (1986). *Psyching for sport: Mental training for athletes*. Champaign, Ill.: Human Kinetics.

Orlinsky, D. E., and K. I. Howard. (1986). Process and outcome in psychotherapy. In *Handbook of psychotherapy and behavior change*. 3rd. ed., ed. S. L. Garfield and A. E. Bergin. New York: Wiley.

Paley, V. G. (1984). *Boys and girls.* Chicago: University of Chicago Press.

Palys, T. S., and B. R. Little. (1983). Perceived life satisfaction and organization of personal projects systems. *Journal of Personality and Social Psychology 44*: 1221–30.

Parsons, L. B., and G. V. D. Parker, (1986). Personal attitudes, clinical appraisals, and verbal behavior of trained and untrained therapists. *Journal of Consulting and Clinical Psychology 32*: 64–71.

Pate, R. R., B. McClenaghan, and R. Rotella. (1984). *Scientific foundations of coaching.* Philadelphia: Saunders.

Peale, N. V. (1956). *The power of positive thinking.* New York: Fawcett Crest.

Pennebaker, J. W. (1990). *Opening up: The healing power of confiding in others.* New York: Morrow.

Peplau, L. A., and D. Perlman, eds. (1982). *Loneliness: A sourcebook of current theory, research and therapy.* New York: Wiley-Interscience.

Perloff, L. S. (1987). Social comparison and illusions of invulnerability to negative life events. In *Coping with negative life events: Clinical and social psychological perspectives,* ed. C. R. Snyder and C. E. Ford. New York: Plenum.

Perloff, L. S., and R. Farbisz. (1985, May). Perceptions of uniqueness and illusions of invulnerability to divorce. Paper presented at the Midwestern Psychological Association, Chicago, Illinois.

Perls, F. S. (1969). *In and out of the garbage pail.* Lafayette, Calif.: Real People Press.

———. (1970). *Gestalt therapy verbatim.* New York: Bantam Books.

Perry, M. A., and M. J. Furukawa. (1980). Modeling methods. In *Helping people change. 2nd. ed.,* ed. F. H. Kanfer and A. P. Goldstein. Elmsford, N.Y.: Pergamon.

Pervin, L. A. (1983). The stasis and flow of behavior: Toward a theory of goals. In *Nebraska Symposium on Motivation,* ed. M. M. Page. Lincoln: University of Nebraska Press.

Pervin, L. A., ed. (1989). *Goal concepts in personality and social psychology.* Hillsdale, N.J.: Erlbaum.

Peters, T. J., and R. H. Waterman, Jr. (1982). *In search of excellence: Lessons from America's best-run companies.* New York: Harper & Row.

Peterson, C., and L. M. Bossio. (1991). *Health and optimism.* New York: Free Press.

Peterson, C., S. Maier, and M. E. P. Seligman. (1993). *Learned helplessness: A theory for the age of personal control.* New York: Oxford.

Peterson, H., ed. (1946). *Great teachers: Portrayed by those who studied under them.* New York: Vintage Books.

Peterson, L. (1987). Not safe at home: Behavioral treatment of a child's fear of being alone at home. *Journal of Behavior Therapy and Experimental Psychiatry 18*: 381–85.

Petrie, K., and K. Chamberlain. (1983). Hopelessness and social desirability as moderator variables in predicting suicidal behavior. *Journal of Consulting and Clinical Psychology 51*: 485–87.

Pettigrew, T. F. (1967). Social evaluation theory: Convergences and applications. In *Nebraska Symposium on Motivation, Vol. 15,* ed. D. Levine. Lincoln: University of Nebraska Press.

Pettit, E. J., and B. L. Bloom, (1984). Whose decision was it? The effects of initiator status on adjustment to marital disruption. *Journal of Marriage and the Family 46*: 587–96.

Pettito, L. (1983). From gesture to symbol. Ph.D. diss., Harvard University, Cambridge, Massachusetts.

Pfeffer, C. R. (1986). *The suicidal child*. New York: Guilford.

Pfeffer, J., and A. Davis-Blake, (1987). Understanding organizational wage structures. *Academy of Management Journal 30*: 437–55.

Physicians' Desk Reference®. (1993). Oradell, N.J.: Medical Economics.

Piaget, J. (1954). *The construction of reality in children*. New York: Basic Books.

———. (1959). *The language and thought of the child. 3rd ed.* M. Gabian and R. Gabian, translators. London: Routledge and Kegan Paul.

———. (1962). *Play, dreams and imitation*. New York: Norton.

———. (1970). Piaget's theory. In *Carmichael's manual of child psychology. Vol. 1.* ed. P. H. Mussen. New York: Wiley.

Pilisuk, M., and S. H. Parks. (1986). *The healing web: Social networks and human survival*. Hanover, N.H.: University Press of New England.

Pines, A. (1982). Helpers' motivation and the burnout syndrome. In *Basic processes in helping relationships*, ed. T. A. Wills. New York: Academic Press.

———. (1993). Burnout. In *Handbook of stress: Theoretical and clinical aspects. 2nd. ed.*, ed. L. Goldberger & S. Breznetz. New York: Free Press.

Pines, A., and E. Aronson. (1988). *Career burnout: Causes and cures. 2nd. ed.* New York: Free Press.

Pines, M. (1979). Superkids. *Psychology Today*, January, pp. 53–63.

Platt, S. D., and J. A. T. Dyer. (1987). Psychological correlates of unemployment among male parasuicides in Edinburgh. *British Journal of Psychiatry 151*: 27–32.

Porter, E. H. (1913). *Pollyanna*. Boston: Page.

Powers, S. W., and H. C. Rickard. (1992). Behavior therapy with children. In *Handbook of clinical child psychology*, ed. C. E. Walker and M. C. Roberts. New York: Wiley.

Pressley, M. (1977). Imagery and children's learning: Putting the picture in developmental perspective. *Review of Educational Research 47*: 585–622.

Prioleau, L., M. Murdock, and N. Brody. (1983). An analysis of psychotherapy versus placebo studies. *The Behavioral and Brain Sciences 6*: 275–310.

Pylyshyn, Z. W. (1973). What the mind's eye tells the mind's brain: A critique of mental imagery. *Psychological Bulletin 80*: 1–24.

Pyszczynski, T., J. C. Hamilton, J. Greenberg, and S. E. Becker. (1991). Self-awareness and psychological dysfunction. In *Handbook of social and clinical psychology: The health perspective*, ed. C. R. Snyder & D. R. Forsyth. Elmsford, N.Y.: Pergamon.

Rakos, R. F. (1991). *Assertive behavior: Theory, research, and training*. London: Routledge.

Rank, O. (1936). *Will therapy*. J. Taft, translator. New York: Knopf.

Reardon, J. (1992). Positive "self-talk." *Track and Field Quarterly 92*: 26–27.

Reddin, W. J. (1970). *Effective management by objectives*. New York: McGraw-Hill.

Rees, S., and R. S. Graham. (1991). *Assertion training: How to be who you really are*. London: Routledge.

Reisman, J. M. (1986). Psychotherapy as a professional relationship. *Professional Psychology: Research and Practice 17*: 565–69.

Reisman, J. M., and S. Ribordy. (1993). *Principles of psychotherapy with children. (2nd. ed.)*. New York: Lexington Books.

Reynolds, W. M., and K. I. Coats. (1986). A comparison of cognitive-behavioral therapy and relaxation training for the treatment of depression in adolescents. *Journal of Consulting and Clinical Psychology 54*: 643–60.

Richman, L. C., and M. J. Eliason, (1992). Disorders of communications: Developmental language and cleft palate. In *Handbook of clinical child psychology*, ed. C. E. Walker & M. C. Roberts. New York: Wiley.

Rieger, E. (1993). Correlates of adult hope, including high- and low-hope adults' recollections of parents. Honors thesis, University of Kansas, Lawrence.

Roach, J. M. (1977). Why Volvo abolished the assembly line. *Management Review*, September, 48–52.

Roberts, G. C. (1986). The growing child and the perception of competitive stress in sport. In *The growing child in competitive sport*, ed. G. Gleeson. London: Hodder & Stoughton.

Robin, A. L., M. Schneider, and J. Dolnick, (1976). The turtle technique: An extensive case study of self-control in the classroom. *Psychology in the Schools 1*: 449–59.

Rodin, J., S. K. Solomon, and J. Metcalf. (1978). Role of control in mediating perceptions of density. *Journal of Personality and Social Psychology 36*: 988–99.

Rollins, B. C., and D. L. Thomas. (1979). Parental support, power and control techniques in the socialization of children. In *Contemporary theories about the family. Vol. 1*, ed. W. R. Burr, R. Hill, F. I. Nye, and I. L. Reiss. New York: Free Press.

Rosenberg, M. (1965). *Society and adolescent self-image*. Princeton: Princeton University Press.

Rosenberger, J., and E. Gould. (1992). *Case studies in abnormal psychology*. New York: HarperCollins.

Rosenblith, J. F., and J. E. Sims-Knight. (1985). *In the beginning: Development in the first two years*. Monterey, Calif.: Brooks/Cole.

Rosenkrantz, P., S. Vogel, H. Bee, I. Broverman, and D. M. Broverman. (1968). Sex-role stereotypes and self-concepts in college students. *Journal of Consulting and Clinical Psychology 32*: 287–95.

Rosenthal, N. E. (1989). *Seasons of the mind: Why you get the winter blues and what you can do about it*. New York: Bantam Books.

Rosenthal, N. E., D. A. Sack, R. G. Skwerer, F. M. Jacobsen, and T. A. Wehr. (1988). Phototherapy for seasonal affective disorders. *Journal of Biology Rhythms 3*: 101–20.

Rosenthal, R. (1985). From unconscious experimenter bias to teacher expectancy effects. In *Teacher expectancies*, ed. J. B. Dusek, V. C. Hall, and W. J. Meyer. Hillsdale, N.J.: Erlbaum.

Rosenthal, R., and L. Jacobson. (1968). *Pygmalion in the classroom: Teacher expectation and pupils' intellectual development*. New York: Holt, Rinehart, & Winston.

Rosenzweig, S. P., and R. Folman. (1974). Patient and therapist variables affecting premature termination in group psychotherapy. *Psychotherapy: Theory, Research and Practice 11*: 76–79.

Roter, D. D., and J. A. Hall. (1992). *Doctors talking with patients/patients talking with doctors: Improving communication in medical visits.* Westport, Conn.: Auburn House/Greenwood.

Roth, D. L., and D. S. Holmes. (1985). Influence of physical fitness in determining the impact of stressful life events on physical and psychological health. *Psychosomatic Medicine 47*: 164–73.

———. (1987). Influence of aerobic exercise training and relaxation training on physical and psychological health following stressful life events. *Psychosomatic Medicine 49*: 355–65.

Rotheram-Boris, M. J., and P. D. Trautman. (1988). Hopelessness, depression, and suicidal intent among adolescent suicide attempters. *Journal of the American Academy of Child Adolescent Psychiatry 27*: 700–704.

Rotter, J. B. (1966). Generalized expectancies for internal versus external control of reinforcement. *Psychological Monographs: General and Applied 80*: (No. 609).

Rourke, R. P., and J. E. DelDotto. (1992). Learning disabilities. In *Handbook of clinical child psychology*, ed. C. E. Walker and M. C. Roberts. New York: Wiley.

Rowen, H. (1992). A second opinion. *Washington Post National Weekly Edition*, August 3–9, pp. 11–12.

Roy, C. (1993). Children's stories: Case studies form the FACT files. *Newsletter of the Kansas Early Childhood Research Institute 3*: 6.

Rubenstein, C. M., and P. Shaver. (1982). In search of intimacy. New York: Delacorte.

Rubin, K. H., G. G. Fein, and B. Vandenberg. (1983). Play. In *Handbook of child psychology: Vol. 4. Socialization, personality and social development*, ed. P. H. Mussen. New York: Wiley.

Rubin, K. H., and L. R. Krasnor. (1986). Social-cognitive and social behavioral perspectives on problem solving. In *Cognitive perspectives on children's social and behavioral development. Minnesota Symposia on Child Development, Vol. 18*, ed. M. Perlmutter. Hillsdale, N.J.: Erlbaum.

Ruble, D. N., A. K. Boggiano, N. S. Feldman, and J. H. Loebl. (1980). Developmental analysis of the role of social comparison in self evaluation. *Developmental Psychology 16*: 105–15.

Ruble, D. N., and Frey, K. S. (1991). Changing patterns of comparative behavior as skills are acquired: A functional model of self-evaluation. In J. Suls & T. A. Wills (eds.), *Social comparison: Contemporary theory and research*. Hillsdale, N.J.: Erlbaum.

Rudd, M. D. (1990). An integrative model of suicidal ideation. *Suicide and Life-Threatening Behavior 20*: 16–30.

Ruehlman, L. S., and S. A. Wolchik. (1988). Personal goals and interpersonal support and hindrance as factors in psychological distress and well-being. *Journal of Personality and Social Psychology, 55*: 293–301.

Ruffman, T. K., and D. R. Olson. (1989). Children's ascriptions of knowledge of others. *Developmental Psychology 25*: 601–6.

Russell, D., L. A. Peplau, and C. E. Cutrona. (1980). The revised UCLA loneliness scale: Concurrent and discriminate validity evidence. *Journal of Personality and Social Psychology 39*: 472–80.

Russell, M., and C. Thoreson. (1976). Teaching decision-making skills to children. In *Counseling methods*, ed. J. D. Krumboltz and C. E. Thoreson. New York: Holt, Rinehart, & Winston.

Rutter, M. (1979). Protective factors in children's responses to stress and disadvantage. In *Primary prevention of psychopathology: Vol. 3. Social competence in children*, ed. M. W. Kent and J. E. Rolf. Hanover, N.H.: University Press of New England.

——. (1981). Stress, coping, and development: Some issues and some questions. *Journal of Child Psychology and Psychiatry 22*: 323–56.

——. (1985). Resilience in the face of adversity: Protective factors and resistance to psychiatric disorder. *British Journal of Psychiatry 147*: 598–611.

——. (1987a). Continuities and discontinuities from infancy. In *Handbook of infant development. 2nd. ed.*, J. Osofsky. New York: Wiley.

——. (1987b). Psychosocial resilience and protective mechanisms. *American Journal of Orthopsychiatry 57(3)*: 316–31.

Ryan, V. L, and M. N. Gizynski. (1971). Behavior therapy in retrospect: Patients' feelings about their behavior therapists. *Journal of Consulting and Clinical Psychology 37*: 1–9.

Rybakowski, J. K. (1990). The role of lithium in the treatment of depression. In *Depression: New directions in theory, research, and practice*, ed. C. D. McCann and N. S. Endler. Toronto: Wall & Emerson.

Ryff, C. D. (1987). The place of personality and social structure in social psychology. *Journal of Personality and Social Psychology 53*: 1192–202.

Safran, J. D., and Z. V. Segal. (1990). *Interpersonal process in cognitive therapy*. New York: Basic Books.

Salovey, P., and D. C. Turk. (1991). Clinical judgment and decision-making. In *Handbook of social and clinical psychology: The health perspective*, ed. C. R. Snyder and D. R. Forsyth. Elmsford, N.Y.: Pergamon.

Salter, D., and S. Platt. (1990). Suicidal intent, hopelessness and depression in a parasuicidal population: The influence of social desirability and elapsed time. *British Journal of Clinical Psychology 29*: 361–71.

Sammons, W. (1989). *The self-calmed baby*. Boston: Little, Brown.

Sarason, B. R., I. G. Sarason, and G. R. Pierce. (1990a). *Social support: An interactional view*. New York: Wiley.

——. (1990b). Traditional views of social support and their impact on assessment. In *Social support: An interactional view*, ed. B. R. Sarason, I. G. Sarason, and G. R. Pierce. New York: Wiley.

Sarason, I. G. (1975). Test anxiety and the self-disclosing coping model. *Journal of Consulting and Clinical Psychology 43*: 148–53.

——. (1984). Stress, anxiety, and cognitive interference: Reactions to tests. *Journal of Personality and Social Psychology 46*: 929–38.

Sarason, I. G., B. R. Sarason, and E. N. Shearin. (1986). Social support as an individual difference variable: Its stability, origins, and relational aspects. *Journal of Personality and Social Psychology 50*: 845–55.

Satir, V. (1967). *Conjoint family therapy: A guide to theory and technique. rev. ed.* Palo Alto, Calif.: Science and Behavior Books.

Sbarbaro, J. A. (1990). The patient-physician relationship: Compliance revisited. *Annals of Allergy 64*: 325–31.

Schaal, B. (1986). Presumed olfactory exchanges between mother and neonate in humans. In *Ethology and psychology*, ed. E. Camus and J. Cosnier. Toulouse, France: Private.

Schachtel, E. (1959). *Metamorphosis.* New York: Basic Books.

Schaefer, C. E., and J. M. Briesmeister, eds. (1989). *Handbook of parent training: Parents as co-therapists for children's problems.* New York: Wiley.

Schank, R. C., and R. P. Abelson. (1977). *Scripts, plans, goals, and understanding.* Hillsdale, N.J.: Erlbaum.

Scheerer, M. (1963). Problem solving. *Scientific American 208*: 118–28.

Scheff, T. J. (1979). *Catharsis in healing, ritual, and drama.* Berkeley: University of California Press.

Scheier, M. F., and C. S. Carver. (1985). Optimism, coping, and health: Assessment and implications of generalized outcome expectancies. *Health Psychology 4(3)*: 219–47.

———. (1987). Dispositional optimism and physical well-being: The influence of generalized outcome expectancies on health. *Journal of Personality 55*: 169–210.

———. (1993). On the power of positive thinking: The benefits of being optimistic. *Current Directions in Psychological Science 2*: 26–30.

Schlenker, B. R. (1987). Threats to identify: Self-identification and social stress. In *Coping with negative life events: Clinical and social psychological perspectives*, ed. C. R. Snyder and C. E. Ford. New York: Plenum.

Schlenker, B. R., and M. F. Weigold. (1989). Goals and the self-identification process: Construing desired outcomes. In *Goal concepts in personality and social psychology*, ed. L. A. Pervin. Hillsdale, N.J.: Erlbaum.

Schneider-Rosen, K., and D. Cicchetti. (1984). The relationship between affect and cognition in maltreated infants: Quality of attachment and the development of visual self-recognition. *Child Development 55*: 648–58.

Schneidman, E. (1985). *Definition of suicide.* New York: Wiley.

Schofield, W. (1964). *Psychotherapy: The purchase of friendship.* New York: Prentice Hall.

Schopler, J., and J. E. Stockdale. (1977). An interference analysis of crowding. *Journal of Environmental Psychology 1*: 81–88.

Schulman, M. (1991). *The passionate mind.* New York: Free Press.

Sedlak, A. J. (1990). *Technical amendment to the study findings — National incidence and prevalence of child abuse and neglect: 1988.* Rockville, Md.: Westat.

Seeman, M., and C. S. Anderson. (1983). Alienation and alcohol: The role of work, mastery, and community in drinking behavior. *American Sociological Review 48*: 60–77.

Seeman, M., A. Z., Seeman, and A. Budros. (1988). Powerlessness, work, and community: A longitudinal study of alienation and alcohol use. *Journal of Health and Social Behavior 29*: 185–98.

Seligman, M. E. P. (1975). *Helplessness: On depression, development, and death*. San Francisco: Freeman.

———. (1991). *Learned optimism*. New York: Knopf.

Selye, H. (1936). A syndrome produced by noxious agents. *Nature 138*: 32.

———. (1952). *The story of the adaptation syndrome*. Montreal: Acta.

———. (1993). History of the stress concept. In *Handbook of stress*, ed. L. Goldberger and S. Breznitz. New York: Free Press.

Selzer, R. (1979). *Confessions of a knife*. New York: Simon & Schuster.

Seraganian, P., ed. (1993). *Exercise psychology: The influence of physical exercise on psychological processes*. New York: Wiley.

Shafii, M., S. Carrigan, J. R. Whittinghill, and A. Derrick. (1985). Psychological autopsy of completed suicide in children and adolescents. *American Journal of Psychiatry 142*: 1061–64.

Shakespeare, W. (1912). *The rape of Lucrece*, ed. with notes by C. Porter. New York: Crowell.

———. (1980). *Hamlet*, ed. D. Bevington, D. S. Scott, R. K. Turner & Associates. New York: Bantam Books.

Shapiro, D., and D. Shapiro. (1982). Meta-analysis of comparative therapy outcome studies: A replication and refinement. *Psychological Bulletin 92*: 581–604.

Shapiro, D., and D. A. Shapiro. (1987). Change processes in psychotherapy. *British Journal of Addictions 82*: 431–44.

Shatz, M., and R. Gelman. (1973). The development of communication skills: Modification in the speech of children as a function of listener. *Monographs of the Society for Research in Child Development 38* (5, Serial 152).

Shaver, P., and C. Rubenstein. (1980). Childhood attachment experience and adult loneliness. In *Review of Personality and Social Psychology, Vol. 1*. ed. L. Wheeler. Beverly Hills, Calif.: Sage.

Sherwin, E. D., T. R. Elliott, B. D. Rybarczyk, R. G. Frank, S. Hanson, and J. Hoffman. (1992). Negotiating the reality of care giving: Hope, burnout, and nursing. *Journal of Social and Clinical Psychology 11*: 129–39.

Shure, M. B., and G. Spivak. (1974). *Preschool interpersonal problem-solving (PIPS) test: Manual*. Philadelphia: Hahnemann Medical College.

———. (1975). *A mental health program for preschool and kindergarten children: An interpersonal problem-solving approach toward social adjustment (A comparative report of research and training, No. MH-20372)*. Washington, D.C.: National Institute of Mental Health.

Siegal, L. J., and L. Peterson. (1981). Maintenance effects of coping skills and sensory information on young children's response to repeated dental procedures. *Behavior Therapy 12*: 530–35.

Siegal, M. (1991). *Knowing children: Experiments in conversation and cognition*. Hillsdale, N.J.: Erlbaum.

Siegel, B. S. (1986). *Love, medicine, and miracles: Lessons learned about self-healing from a surgeon's experience with exceptional patients*. New York: Harper & Row.

Sigmon, S. T., and C. R. Snyder. (1993). Hope and coping relationships. University of Maine, Orono, Maine.

Sillers, A. L., G. R. Pike, T. S. Jones, and M. A. Murphy. (1984). Communication and understanding in marriage. *Human Communication Research 10*: 317–50.

Simonds, J. F., T. McMahon, and D. Armstrong. (1991). Young suicide attempters compared with a control group: Psychological, affective, and attitudinal variables. *Suicide and Life-Threatening Behavior 21*: 134–51.

Simons, A. D., C. R. McGowan, L. H. Epstein, and D. J. Kupfer. (1985). Exercise as a treatment for depression: An update. *Clinical Psychology Review 5*: 553–68.

Simons, J. (1992). Psychological barriers of major competitions: Basic issues and coaching interventions. *Track and Field Quarterly 92*: 28–31.

Skinner, B. F. (1957). *Verbal behavior*. New York: Appleton-Century-Crofts.

Sloane, R. B., F. R. Staples, A. H. Cristol, N. J. Yorkston, and K. Whipple. (1975). *Psychotherapy versus behavior therapy*. Cambridge, Mass.: Harvard University Press.

Smith, M. B. (1983). Hope and despair: Keys to the socio-psychodynamics of youth. *American Journal of Orthopsychiatry 53*: 388–99.

Smith, M. L., and G. V. Glass. (1977). Meta-analysis of psychotherapy outcome studies. *American Psychologist 32*: 752–60.

Smith, M. L., G. V. Glass, and T. I. Miller. (1980). *The benefits of psychotherapy*. Baltimore: Johns Hopkins University Press.

Snyder, C. R. (1984). Excuses, excuses. *Psychology Today 18*: 50–55.

———. (1988). The psychology of friends and lovers: Relationships. *Journal of Social and Clinical Psychology 7*: i–ii.

———. (1989). Reality negotiation: From excuses to hope and beyond. *Journal of Social and Clinical Psychology 8*: 130–57.

———. (1993). Hope for the journey. In *Cognitive coping, families, and disability: Participatory research in action*, ed. A. P. Turnbull, J. M. Patterson, S. K. Behr, D. L. Murphy, J. G. Marquis, and M. J. Blue-Banning. Baltimore, Md.: Brookes.

———. (in press a). Hope and optimism. In *Encyclopedia of human behavior*. ed. V. S. Ramachandran. Orlando, Fla.: Academic Press.

———. (in press b). Hope: Theory, measurement, and interventions. *Journal of Counseling and Development*.

Snyder, C. R., and D. R. Forsyth, eds. (1991). *Handbook of social and clinical psychology: The health perspective*. Elmsford, N.Y.: Pergamon.

Snyder, C. R. & H. Fromkin. (1980). *Uniqueness: The human pursuit of difference*. New York: Plenum.

Snyder, C. R., C. Harris, J. R. Anderson, S. A. Holleran, L. M. Irving, S. T. Sigmon, L. R. Yoshinobu, J. Gibb, C. Langelle, and P. Harney. (1991). The will and the ways: Development and validation of an individual-differences measure of hope. *Journal of Personality and Social Psychology 60*: 570–85.

Snyder, C. R., and R. L. Higgins. (1988a). Excuses: Their effective role in the negotiation of reality. *Psychological Bulletin 104*: 23–35.

———. (1988b). From making to being the excuse: An analysis of deception and verbal/nonverbal issues. *Journal of Nonverbal Behavior 12*: 237–52.

———. (1990). Reality negotiation and excuse-making: President Reagan's 4 March 1987 Iran arms scandal speech and other literature. In *Psychology of tactical communication*, ed. M. J. Cody and M. L. McLaughlin. Cleve-don, England: Multilingual Matters.

——. (1991). Reality negotiation and excuse-making. In *Handbook of social and clinical psychology: The health perspective*, ed. C. R. Snyder and D. R. Forsyth. Elmsford, N.Y.: Pergamon.

Snyder, C. R., R. L. Higgins, and R. J. Stucky. (1983). *Excuses: Masquerades in search of grace*. New York: Wiley.

Snyder, C. R., and R. E. Ingram. (1983). "Company motivates the miserable": The impact of consensus information on help-seeking for psychological prob-lems. *Journal of Personality and Social Psychology 45*: 1118–26.

Snyder, C. R., R. E. Ingram, and C. Newburg. (1982). The role of feedback in helpseeking and the therapeutic relationship. In T. A. Wills (ed.), *Basic processes in helping relationships*. New York: Academic Press.

Snyder, C. R., L. M. Irving, and J. R. Anderson. (1991). Hope and health. In *Handbook of social and clinical psychology: The health perspective*, ed. C. R. Snyder and D. R. Forsyth. Elmsford, N.Y.: Pergamon.

Snyder, C. R., L. M. Irving, S. Sigmon, and S. Holleran. (1993). Reality negotia-tion and valence/linkage self theories: Psychic shootout at the "I'm OK" corral. In *Crises and loses in the adult years*, ed. L. Montrada, S. H. Filipp, and M. Lerner. Hillsdale, N.J.: Erlbaum.

Snyder, C. R., and T. W. Smith, (1982). Symptoms as self-handicapping strate-gies: The virtues of old wine in a new bottle. In *Integrations of clinical and social psychology*, ed. G. Weary and H. L. Mirels. New York: Oxford Uni-versity Press.

Snyder, C. R., S. Sympson, F. Ybasco, and T. Borders. (1994, August). Develop-ment and validation of a state measure of hope. Paper presented at the American Psychological Association Convention, Los Angeles, California.

Snyder, C. R., M. Rapoff, L. Ware, B. Hoza, W. E. Pelham, M. Danovosky, L. Highberger, H. Rubinstein, and K. Stahl. (1994). Development and vali-dation of the Children's Hope Scale. University of Kansas, Lawrence.

Snyder, J., and G. R. Patterson. (1987). Family interaction and delinquent behavior. In *Handbook of juvenile delinquency*, ed. H. C. Quay. New York: Wiley.

Snyder, M., and R. A. Wicklund. (1981). Attribute ambiguity. In *New directions in attribution research. Vol. 3*, ed. J. A. Harvey, W. J. Ickes, and R. F. Kidd. Hillsdale, N.J.: Erlbaum.

Soar, R. S., and R. M. Soar. (1987). Classroom management and affect expression. *Professional School Psychology 2*: 3–14.

Somers, A. R. (1981). Marital status, health, and the use of health services: An old relationship revisited. In *Single life: Unmarried adults in social context*, ed. P. J. Stein. New York: St. Martin's.

Spanier, G. B., and R. F. Castro. (1979). Adjustment to separation and divorce: A qualitative analysis. In *Divorce and separation*, ed. G. Levinger and O. C. Moles. New York: Basic Books.

Spanier, G. B., and L. Thompson. (1983). Relief and distress after marital separa-tion. *Journal of Divorce 5*: 33–48.

Spaulding, C. L. (1992). *Motivation in the classroom*. New York: McGraw-Hill.

Spencer, M. B. (1988). Self-concept development. In *Perspectives on black child* development: New directions for child development, ed. D. T. Slaughter. San Francisco: Jossey-Bass.

Spielberger, C. D., R. L. Gorsuch, and R. E. Luchene. (1970). *The State-Trait Anxiety Inventory.* Palo Alto, Calif.: Consulting Psychologists.

Spirito, A., J. Overholser, and K. Hart. (1991). Cognitive characteristics of adolescent suicide attempters. *Journal of the American Academy of Child Adolescent Psychiatry 30*: 604–8.

Spirito, A., C. Williams, L. J. Stark, and K. Hart. (1988). The Hopelessness Scale for Children: Psychometric properties and clinical utility with normal and emotionally disturbed adolescents. *Journal of Abnormal Child Psychology 17*: 213–21.

Spivak, G., J. J. Platt, and M. B. Shure. (1976). *The problem-solving approach to adjustment.* San Francisco: Jossey-Bass.

Spivak, G., and M. B. Shure. (1974). *Social adjustment of young children: A cognitive approach to solving real life problems.* San Francisco: Jossey-Bass.

Sroufe, L. A. (1983). Infant-caregiver attachment and patterns of adaptation in preschool: The roots of maladaption and competence. In *Minnesota Symposium in Child Psychology, Vol. 16*, ed. M. Perlmutter. Hillsdale, N.J.: Erlbaum.

———. (1985). Attachment classification from the perspective of infant-caregiver relationships and infant temperament. *Child Development 56*: 1–14.

Stabler, B. (1993). On the role of patient. *Journal of Pediatric Psychology 18*: 310–12.

Stark, K. (1990). *Childhood depression: School-based intervention.* New York: Guilford.

Stark, K. D., W. M. Reynolds, and N. J. Kaslow. (1987). A comparison of the relative efficacy of self-control therapy and a behavioral problem-solving therapy for depression in children. *Journal of Abnormal Child Psychology 15*: 91–113.

Steinberg, L., and S. M. Dornbusch. (1991). Negative correlates of part-time employment during adolescence: Replication and elaboration. *Developmental Psychology 27*: 304–13.

Steinem, G. (1992). *Revolution from within: A book of self-esteem.* Boston: Little, Brown.

Stephens, T. (1989). Physical activity and mental health in the United States and Canada: Evidence from four population surveys. *Preventive Medicine 17*: 35–47.

Stern, D. N. (1985). *The interpersonal world of the infant.* New York: Basic Books.

Stern, P. C. (1978). When do people act to maintain common resources? A reformulated psychological question for our times. *International Journal of Psychology 13*: 149–58.

Stevenson, H. W., and R. S. Newman. (1986). Long-term prediction of achievement and attitudes in mathematics and reading. *Child Development 57*: 646–59.

Stevenson, M. B., J. N. Ver Hoeve, M. A. Roach, and L. A. Leavitt. (1986). The beginning of conversation: Early patterns of mother-infant vocal responsiveness. *Infant Behavior and Development 9*: 423–40.

Stokols, D. (1972). On the distinction between density and crowding: Some implications for future research. *Psychological Review 79*: 275–78.

Stone, G., W. Hinds, and G. Schmidt, (1975). Teaching mental health behaviors to elementary school children. *Professional Psychology 6*: 34–40.

Stone, G. C. (1979). Patient compliance and the role of the expert. *Journal of Social Issues 35*: 34–59.

Stotland, E. (1969). *The psychology of hope*. San Francisco: Jossey-Bass.

Stroebe, W., and R. G. Stroebe. (1987). *Bereavement and health*. New York: Cambridge University Press.

Strong, S. R. (1991). Social influence and change in therapeutic relationships. In *Handbook of social and clinical psychology: The health perspective*, ed. C. R. Snyder and D. R. Forsyth. Elmsford, N.Y.: Pergamon.

Strupp, H. H. (1973). On the basic ingredients of psychotherapy. *Journal of Consulting and Clinical Psychology 41*: 1–8.

———. (1980a). Success and failure in time-limited psychotherapy. A systematic comparison of two cases: Comparison 1. *Archives of General Psychiatry 37*: 595–603.

———. (1980b). Success and failure in time-limited psychotherapy. A systematic comparison of two cases: Comparison 2. *Archives of General Psychiatry 37*: 708–16.

———. (1980c). Success and failure in time-limited psychotherapy: With special reference to the performance of a lay counselor. *Archives of General Psychiatry 37*: 831–41.

———. (1980d). Success and failure in time-limited psychotherapy. Further evidence: Comparison 4. *Archives of General Psychiatry 37*: 947–54.

Strupp, H. H., R. E. Fox, and K. Lessler. (1969). *Patients view their psychotherapy*. Baltimore: Johns Hopkins University Press.

Strupp, H. H., and S. W. Hadley. (1979). Specific versus nonspecific factors in psychotherapy: A controlled study of outcome. *Archives of General Psychiatry 36*: 1125–36.

Suchman, E. A. (1967). Preventive health behavior: A model for research on community health campaigns. *Journal of Health and Social Behavior 8*: 197–209.

Sullivan, H. S. (1953). *The interpersonal theory of psychiatry*. New York: Norton.

———. (1954). *The psychiatric interview*. New York: Norton.

———. (1956). Clinical studies in psychiatry. New York: Norton.

Svarstad, B. (1976). Physician-patient communication and patient conformity with medical advice. In *The growth of bureaucratic medicine*, ed. D Mechanic. New York: Wiley.

Swallow, S. R., and N. A. Kuiper. (1988). Social comparison and negative self-evaluations: An application to depression. *Clinical Psychology Review 8*: 55–76.

Swann, W. B., and J. D. Brown. (1990). From self to health: Self-verification and identity disruption. In *Social support: An interactional view*, ed. B. R. Sarason, I. G. Sarason, and G. R. Pierce. New York: Wiley.

Sympson, S. (1993). Construction and validation of a state hope measure: A month in the lives of college students. Master's thesis, University of Kansas, Lawrence.

Szasz, T. (1993). *A lexicon of lunacy: Metaphoric malady, moral responsibility, and psychiatry*. New Brunswick, N.J.: Transaction.

Tamis-LeMonda, C. S., and M. H. Bornstein. (1989). Habituation and maternal encouragement of attention in infancy as predictors of toddler language, play, and representational competence. *Child Development 60*: 738–51.

Tavris, C. (1992). *The mismeasure of woman.* New York: Simon & Schuster.

Taylor, J. A. (1953). A personality scale of manifest anxiety. *Journal of Abnormal and Social Psychology 48*: 285–90.

Taylor, S. E. (1979). Hospital patient behavior: Reactance, helplessness or control? *Journal of Social Issues 35*: 156–84.

——. (1991). *Health psychology. 2nd. ed.* New York: McGraw-Hill.

Temoshok, L., and H. Dreher. (1992). *The Type C connection: The behavioral links to cancer and your health.* New York: Random House.

Templin, M. C. (1957). *Certain language skills in children.* Minneapolis: University of Minnesota Press.

Tesser, A. (1988). Toward a self-evaluation maintenance model of social behavior. In *Advances in experimental social psychology. Vol. 21*, ed. L. Berkowitz. New York: Academic Press.

The Living Pulpit. (1992) Quotations on the many views of hope: Leaders, politicians, and statesmen. January-March, p. 26.

Thurber, J. (1945). The secret life of Walter Mitty. In *The Thurber carnival.* New York: Harper & Row.

Tinsley, H. E. A., T. M. de St. Aubin, and M. T. Brown. (1982). College students' help-seeking preferences. *Journal of Counseling Psychology 29*: 529–33.

Tolman, E. C. (1948). Cognitive maps in rats and men. *Psychological Review 55*: 189–208.

Tomm, K. (1989). Externalizing the problem and internalizing personal agency. *Journal of Strategic and Systemic Therapies 8*: 54–59.

Trad, P. V. (1992). *Interventions with infants and parents: The theory and practice of previewing.* New York: Wiley.

Triandis, H. C., C. McCusker, and C. H. Hui. (1990). Multimethod probes of individualism and collectivism. *Journal of Personality and Social Psychology 59:* 1006–20.

Truax, C. B., and K. M. Mitchell. (1971). Research on certain therapist interpersonal skills in relation to process and outcome. In *Handbook of psychotherapy and behavior change: An empirical analysis*, ed. A. E. Bergin and S. L. Garfield. New York: Wiley.

Tubbs, M. E. (1986). Goal setting: A meta-analytic examination of the empirical evidence. *Journal of Applied Psychology 71*: 474–83.

Tulviste, P. (1991). *The cultural-historical development of verbal thinking.* Commack, N.Y.: Nova.

United States Department of Health and Human Services. (1988a). *The consequences of smoking: Nicotine addiction: A report of the Surgeon General.* (DHHS Publication No. 88-8406). Washington, D.C.: U.S. Government Printing Office.

——. (1988b). *The Surgeon General's report on nutrition and health.* (DHHS Publication No. 88-50210). Washington, D.C.: U.S. Government Printing Office.

———. (1989). *Reducing the health consequences of smoking: 25 years of progress: A report of the Surgeon General.* (DHHS Publication No. 89–8411). Rockville, Md.: United States Department of Health and Human Services.

Urberg, K. A., and E. M. Docherty. (1976). Development of role-taking skills in young children. *Developmental Psychology 12*: 198–203.

Vallacher, R. R., and D. M. Wegner. (1987). What do people think they're doing? Action identification and human behavior. *Psychological Review 94*: 3–15.

Vallacher, R. R., D. M. Wegner, and M. Somoza. (1989). That's easy for you to say: Action identification and speech fluency. *Journal of Personality and Social Psychology 56*: 199–208.

Vance, M. (1994). The development and validation of a scale to measure hope in narrative. Ph.D. diss., University of Kansas, Lawrence.

Van Lieshout, C. F. M. (1975). Young children's reactions to barriers placed by their mothers. *Child Development 46:* 879–86.

Vernacchia, R., R. McGuire, and D. Cook. (1992). *Coaching mental excellence.* Dubuque, Iowa: Brown.

Veroff, J. (1983). Contextual determinants of personality. *Personality and Social Psychology Bulletin 9*: 331–44.

Veroff, J. B., R. A. Kulka, and E. Douvan. (1981). *Mental health in America: Patterns of help-seeking 1957–1976.* New York: Basic Books.

Vida, S., and N. Grizenko. (1989). DSM-III-R and the phenomenology of childhood bereavement. *Canadian Journal of Psychiatry 34*: 148–55.

Vinacke, W. E. (1952). *The psychology of thinking.* New York: McGraw-Hill.

Vygotsky, L. S. (1962). *Thought and language.* New York: Wiley.

———. (1987). *Thinking and speech.* N. Minick, translator. New York: Plenum.

Wagner, D. A. (1974). The development of short-term and incidental memory: A cross-cultural study. *Child Development 48*: 389–96.

Wahler, R. G. (1980). The insular mother: Her problems in parent-child treatment. *Journal of Applied Behavior Analysis 13*: 207–19.

Wallace, J. E., and M. B. Brinkerhoff. (1991). The measurement of burnout revisited. *Journal of Social Service Research 14*: 85–111.

Wallach, M. S., and H. H. Strupp. (1960). Psychotherapists' clinical judgments and attitudes toward patients. *Journal of Consulting Psychology 24*: 316–23.

Wallerstein, J. S. (1981). Children of divorce: The long-term impact. *Human Sexuality 15*: 36–47.

———. (1983). Children of divorce: The psychological tasks of the child. *American Journal of Orthopsychiatry 53*: 230–43.

Wallerstein, J. S., and J. B. Kelly. (1975). The effects of parental divorce: Experiences of the preschool child. *Journal of American Academy of Child Psychiatry 14*: 600–616.

Walster, E., G. W. Walster, J. Piliavin, and L. Schmidt. (1973). "Playing hard to get": Understanding an elusive phenomenon. *Journal of Personality and Social Psychology 26*: 13–121.

Ware, J. E., A. Davies-Avery, and A. L. Stewart. (1978). The measurement and meaning of patient satisfaction. *Health and Medical Care Services Review 1*: 1–14.

Warshak, R. A. (1992). *The custody revolution: The father factor and the motherhood mystique.* New York: Poseidon.

Wasserman, D. (1988). Separations. *Crisis 9*: 49–63.

Waterman, A. S., ed. (1985). *Identity in adolescence: Progress and contents.* San Francisco: Jossey-Bass.

Watson, D., L. A. Clark, and A. Tellegen. (1988). Development and validation of brief measures of positive and negative affect: The PANAS scales. *Journal of Personality and Social Psychology 54*: 1063–70.

Watson, J. S. (1966). The development and generalization of contingency awareness in early infancy: Some hypotheses. *Merrill-Palmer Quarterly 12*: 123–35.

———. (1971). Cognitive-perceptual development in infancy: Setting for the seventies. *Merrill-Palmer Quarterly 17*: 139–52.

Watzlawick, P. (1976). *How real is real?* New York: Random House.

Waxman, S. (1987, April). Linguistic and conceptual organization in 30-month-old children. Paper presented at the meeting of the Society for Research in Child Development, Baltimore.

Wegner, D. M. (1989). *White bears and other unwanted thoughts: Suppression, obsession, and the psychology of mental control.* New York: Viking.

Wehr, T. A., and N. E. Rosenthal. (1989). Seasonality and affective illness. *American Journal of Psychiatry 146*: 829–39.

Weiss, B., and Z. Weisz. (1990). The impact of methodological factors on child psychotherapy outcome research: A meta-analysis for researchers. *Journal of Abnormal Child Psychology 18*: 639–70.

Weiss, R. S. (1975). *Marital separation.* New York: Basic Books.

Weissman, A., A. T. Beck, and M. Kovacs. (1979). Drug abuse, hopelessness and suicidal behavior. *International Journal of Addictions 14*: 451–64.

Weisz, J. R., B. Weiss, M. D. Alicke, and M. L. Klotz. (1987). Effectiveness of psychotherapy with children and adolescents: A meta-analysis for clinicians. *Clinical Psychology 55*: 542–49.

Wellman, H. M., and S. A. Gelman. (1992). Cognitive development: Foundational theories and core domains. *Annual Review of Psychology 43*: 337–76.

Weltman, A. (1984). Exercise and diet to optimize body composition. In *Behavioral health: A handbook of health enhancement and disease prevention,* ed. J. Matarazzo, S. Weiss, J. Herd, N. Miller, and S. M. Weiss. New York: Wiley.

Werner, E. E. (1984). Resilient children. *Young Children,* November, 68–72.

Werner, E. E., and R. S. Smith. (1982). *Vulnerable but invincible: A study of resilient children.* New York: McGraw-Hill.

Wertsch, J. V., and B. Rogoff. (1984). Editor's notes. In *Children's learning in the zone of proximal development,* ed. B. Rogoff and J. V. Wertsch. San Francisco: Jossey-Bass.

Wetzel, R. D. (1976). Hopelessness, depression and suicide intent. *Archives of General Psychiatry 33*: 1069–73.

Wetzel, R. D., T. Margulies, R. Davis, and E. Karam. (1980). Hopelessness, depression and suicide intent. *Journal of Clinical Psychiatry 41*: 159–60.

Whimbey, A., and J. Lochhead. (1986). *Problem solving and comprehension.* Hillsdale, N.J.: Erlbaum.

White, J. L., and T. A. Parham. (1990). *The psychology of Blacks.* Englewood Cliffs, N.J.: Prentice Hall.

White, R. W. (1959). Motivation reconsidered: The concept of competence. *Psychological Review 66*: 297–333.

Whitehead, J. (1986). Achievement goals and drop out in youth sports. In *The growing child in competitive sport*, ed. G. Gleeson. London: Hodder & Stoughton.

Wiklund, C. A. (1993). Dispositional and trained hope and the academic progress of first-semester college students. Honors thesis, University of Kansas, Lawrence.

Wilensky, R. (1983). *Planning and understanding: A computational approach to human reasoning.* Reading, Mass.: Addison-Wesley.

Wilken, P. H. (1971). Size of organization and member participation in church congregations. *Administrative Sciences Quarterly 16*: 173–80.

Wilkins, W. (1979). Expectancies in therapy research: Discriminating among heterogeneous nonspecifics. *Journal of Consulting and Clinical Psychology 47*: 837–45.

Williams, J. E. (1982). An overview of findings from adult sex stereotype studies in 25 countries. In *Diversity and unity in cross-cultural psychology*, ed. R. Rath, H. S. Asthana, D. Sinha, and J. B. Sinha. Lisse, Netherlands: Swets and Zeitlinger.

Williams, W. (1990). *The power within: True stories of exceptional patients who fought back with hope.* New York: Harper & Row.

Wills, T. A. (1982). Nonspecific factors in helping relationships. In *Basic processes in helping relationships*, ed. T. A. Wills. New York: Academic Press.

Wills, T. A., and B. M. DePaulo. (1991). Interpersonal analysis of the help-seeking process. In *The handbook of social and clinical psychology: The health perspective*, ed. C. R. Snyder and D. R. Forsyth. Elmsford, N.Y.: Pergamon.

Wilson, G. T. (1989). Behavior therapy. In *Current psychotherapies. 4th. ed.*, ed. R. J. Corsini and D. Wedding. Itasca, Ill.: Peacock Publishers.

Wilson, H. (1974). Parenting in poverty. *British Journal of Social Work 4*: 241–54.

Wilson, J. P., and B. Raphael, eds. (1993). *International handbook of traumatic stress syndromes.* New York: Plenum.

Wine, J. D. (1971). Test anxiety and direction of attention. *Psychological Bulletin 76*: 92–104.

———. (1980). Cognitive-attentional theory of test anxiety. In *Test anxiety: Theory, research, and applications*, ed. I. G. Sarason. Hillsdale, N.J.: Erlbaum.

Winne, P. H. (1985). Steps toward promoting cognitive achievements. *Elementary School Journal 85*: 673–93.

Wood, D. J., J. S. Bruner, and G. Ross. (1976). The role of tutoring in problem solving. *Journal of Child Psychology and Psychiatry 17*: 89–100.

Woodward, J. C., J. Zabel, and C. Decosta. (1980). Loneliness and divorce. *Journal of Divorce 4*: 73–82.

Woodworth, R. S., and H. Schlosberg. (1954). *Experimental psychology.* New York: Holt, Rinehart, & Winston.

Wortman, C. B., and J. W. Brehm. (1975). Response to uncontrollable outcomes: An integration of reactance theory and the learned helplessness model. In *Advances in experimental social psychology. Vol. 8*, ed. L. Berkowitz. New York: Academic Press.

Wortman, C. B., and R. C. Silver. (1987). Coping with irrevocable loss. In *Cataclysms, crises, and catastrophes: Psychology in action*, ed. G. R. VandenBos and B. K. Bryant. Washington, D.C.: American Psychological Association.

———. (1989). The myths of coping with loss. *Journal of Consulting and Clinical Psychology 57*: 349–57.

Wright, B. A. (1968). The question stands: Should a person be realistic? *Rehabilitation Counseling Bulletin 11*: 291–96.

———. (1983). *Physical disability: A psychosocial approach. 2nd. ed.* New York: Harper & Row.

———. (1991). Labeling: The need for greater person-environment individuation. In *Handbook of social and clinical psychology: The health perspective*, ed. C. R. Snyder and D. R. Forsyth. Elmsford, N.Y.: Pergamon.

Wright, B. A., and F. C. Shontz. (1968). Process and tasks in hoping. *Rehabilitation Literature 29*: 322–31.

Wright, H. F. (1934). The influence of barriers upon strength of motivation. Ph.D. diss., Duke University, Durham, North Carolina.

———. (1943). The effect of barriers upon strength of motivation. In *Child behavior and development*, ed. R. G. Barker, J. S. Kounin, and H. F. Wright. New York: McGraw-Hill.

———. (1956). Psychological development in the Midwest. *Child Development 27*: 265–86.

Wundt, W. M. (1894). *Lectures on human and animal psychology*. J. E. Creighton and E. B. Titchener, translators. New York: Macmillan.

Wyatt, G. E., and G. J. Powell, eds. (1988). *Lasting effects of child sexual abuse*. Newbury Park, Calif.: Sage.

Yambor, J. (1992). Improving communication skills and building cohesiveness. *Track and Field Quarterly 92*: 32–34.

Ybasco, F. C. (1994). Further validation of the State Hope Scale: Remembrances of things past. Master's thesis, University of Kansas, Lawrence.

Yoshinobu, L. R. (1989). Construct validation of the Hope Scale: Agency and pathways components. Master's thesis, University of Kansas, Lawrence.

Young, H. S. (1983). Principles of assessment and methods of treatment with adolescents: Special considerations. In *Rational-emotive approaches to the problems of childhood*, ed. A. Ellis and M. E. Bernard. New York: Plenum.

Zaslow, J. (1986). Fourth-grade girls these days ponder weighty matters. *Wall Street Journal*, February 11, pp. 1, 29.

Zetzel, E. (1956). Current concepts of transference. *International Journal of Psychoanalysis 37*: 369–76.

Zillman, D. (1979). *Hostility and aggression*. Hillsdale, N.J.: Erlbaum.

Zimbardo, P. G., E. B., Ebbesen, and C. Maslach. (1977). *Influencing attitudes and changing behavior. 2nd. ed.* Reading, Mass.: Addison-Wesley.

INDEX